MATISSE

MATISSE

A RETROSPECTIVE

Edited by Jack Flam

PARK LANE
New York

Copyright © 1988, Hugh Lauter Levin Associates, Inc., New York
Introduction and annotations copyright © 1988, Jack Flam
All Matisse works, copyright © 1988, ARS, N.Y./SPADEM.
All rights reserved.
This 1990 edition is published by Park Lane,
distributed by Outlet Book Company, Inc., a Random House Company,
225 Park Avenue South, New York, New York 10003, by arrangement
with Hugh Lauter Levin Associates, Inc.
Printed and bound in Hong Kong
Library of Congress Cataloging-in-Publication Data

Matisse : a retrospective / edited by Jack Flam.
        p.   cm.
        Includes bibliographical references and index.

        1. Matisse, Henri, 1869-1954—Criticism and interpretation.
        I. Matisse, Henri, 1869-1954.   II. Flam, Jack D.
N6853.M33M37   1990
709'.2—dc20   90-7297
                                                 CIP

ISBN 0-517-03292-9
8 7 6 5 4 3 2 1

Matisse on Art, edited by Jack D. Flam, E.P. Dutton, New York, 1978. © ARS, N.Y./SPADEM.

Roger Marx, "Le Salon du Champ-de-Mars," *Revue Encyclopédique*, April 25, 1896.

Paul Flat, "Les Salons de 1896," *Revue bleue politique et littéraire*, June 6, 1896.

Edouard Michel, ed., "Gustave Moreau et ses élèves, lettres d'Henri Evenepoel à son pere," *Mercure de France*, January 15, 1923.

Henri Matisse, letter to Lancelle, April 25, 1896, *Arts*, August 1952. © ARS, N.Y./SPADEM.

Raymond Escholier, *Henri Matisse*, Librairie Floury, Paris, 1937.

Jack Flam, *Matisse, The Man and His Art, 1869–1918*, Cornell University Press. © 1986, Jack Flam.

Louis Vauxcelles, "Le Salon d'Automne," October 14, 1904; October 17, 1905; October 5, 1906; September 30, 1907; September 30, 1908; "Le Salon des Indépendants," March 23, 1905; March 20, 1906; March 20, 1907; *Gil Blas*.

Maurice Denis, "La Peinture," *L'Ermitage*, November 15, 1905.

André Gide, "Promenade au Salon d'Automne." © 1905 by and reprinted with permission of *Gazette des Beaux Arts*, Paris.

Léon Rosenthal, "Petites Expositions," *La Chronique des arts et de la curiosité*. © 1906 by and reprinted with permission of *Gazette des Beaux-Arts*, Paris.

Leo Stein, "More Adventures," *Appreciation: Painting, Poetry and Prose*. © 1947, Leo Stein. Used by permission of Crown Publishers, New York.

Gertrude Stein, *The Autobiography of Alice B. Toklas*. © 1933, renewed 1961, Alice B. Toklas. Reprinted by permission of Random House, Inc., New York.

William Carlos Williams, "A Matisse," *The William Carlos Williams Reader*. Copyright 1932 by William Carlos Williams. Reprinted by permission of New Directions Publishing Corp.

Guillaume Apollinaire, *Apollinaire on Art, Essays and Reviews, 1902–1918*, edited by LeRoy C. Breunig. © 1960, Librairie Gallimard. English translation © 1972, The Viking Press, Inc. All rights reserved. Reprinted by permission of Viking Penguin, Inc., New York.

Louis Rouart, "Reflexions sur le Salon d'Automne," *L'Occident*, November 1907.

Michael Puy, "Les Fauves," *La Phalange*, November 15, 1907.

Guillaume Apollinaire, "Henri Matisse," translated in Alfred H. Barr, Jr., *Matisse, His Art and His Public*. © 1951, The Museum of Modern Art, New York.

Mérodack Josephin Péladan, "Le Salon d'Automne et ses retrospectives Greco et Monticelli," *La Revue Hébdomadaire*, October 17, 1908.

Bernard Berenson, letter to the editor, "De Gustibus," *The Nation*, November 12, 1908. © 1908, The Nation Company, Inc. Reprinted by permission of *The Nation*.

Georges Desvallières, preface to "Notes d'un peintre," *La Grande Revue*, December 25, 1908.

Max Weber, transcript of a lecture at The Museum of Modern Art, New York, October 22, 1951.

Sergei Shchukin, letter to Matisse, March 31, 1909, translated in Alfred H. Barr, Jr., *Matisse, His Art and His Public*. © 1951, The Museum of Modern Art, New York.

Matthew Stewart Prichard, letters to Isabella Stewart Gardner, January 2, 1909; Easter Day, 1909; July 7, 1909. By permission of the Isabella Stewart Gardner Archives.

Gelett Burgess, "The Wild Men of Paris." © *Architectural Record*, May 1910.

Jacques Rivière, "Une exposition de Henri-Matisse," *Etudes*, Paris, 1911.

Michel Puy, "Le dernier état de la peinture," *Mercure de France*, July 16, 1910.

Roland Dorgelès, "Le Prince des Fauves," *Fantasio*, December 1, 1910.

P. Skrotsky, "From Paris: The Autumn Salon," *Odessky Listok*, translated by A. Kostenevich, "*La Danse* and *La Musique* by Henri Matisse: A New Interpretation," *Apollo*, December 1917. Reproduced courtesy of *Apollo* magazine.

Kenneth C. Lindsay and Peter Vergo, eds., *Kandinsky: Complete Writings on Art*. © 1982 by and reprinted with the permission of G.K. Hall & Co., Boston.

Matthew Stewart Prichard, letter to Isabella Stewart Gardner, November 22, 1910. By permission of the Isabella Stewart Gardner Archives.

Ilya Ostroukhov, letter to Alexandra Botkina, October 16, 1911, in Y.A. Rusakov, "Matisse in Russia in the Autumn of 1911," May 1975. © 1975, *The Burlington Magazine*.

Ernst Goldschmidt, "Strejtog I Kunsten: Henri Matisse," *Politiken*, December 24, 1911.

André Salmon, "Les Fauves," *La jeune peinture française*, Paris, 1912.

Ludwig Coellen, *Die Romantik der neuen Malerei*. © 1912, E. W. Bonsells and Co., Munich.

Clara T. MacChesney, "A Talk with Matisse, Leader of Post-Impressionism," *The New York Times Magazine*, March 9, 1913. © 1913, The New York Times Company. Reprinted with permission.

Marcel Sembat, "Henri Matisse," *Cahiers d'aujourd'hui*, April 1913.

André Verdet, "A Propos du dessin et des odalisques," *Entretiens notes et écrits sur la peinture*. © 1978, Editions Galilée, Paris.

Walter Pach, "Why Matisse?" *Century*, February 1915.

Willard Huntington Wright, "Henri-Matisse," *Modern Painting: Its Tendency and Meaning*. © Dodd, Mead & Co.

Louis Aragon, *Henri Matisse, roman*. © 1971, Editions Gallimard, Paris.

Georges Besson, "L'Arrivée de Matisse à Nice: Matisse et quelques personnages," July 1939. © *Le Point*.

Henri Matisse, excerpts from letters to Charles Camoin, May 2, 1918; May 23, 1918. © ARS, N.Y./SPADEM.

Ragnar Hoppe, "Pa Visit Hos Matisse," *Städer och Konstnärer Resebrev och Essäer om Konst*, 1931. Reprinted with permission of Albert Bonniers Förlag, Stockholm.

Jean Cocteau, "Deformation professionelle," *Le Rappel à l'ordre*, May 12, 1919. © 1926, Librairie Stock, Paris.

André Lhote, "Exposition Matisse," *La Nouvelle Revue Française*, Paris, 1919.

Marcel Sembat, "Matisse et son oeuvre," *Henri Matisse*, Paris, 1920.

Elie Faure, Jules Romains, Charles Vildrac, Léon Werth, "Opinions," *Henri Matisse*, Georges Cres & Cie, 1920.

René Schwob, "Henri-Matisse," *L'amour de l'art*, 1920.

Clive Bell, "Matisse and Picasso: the Two Apparent Heirs to Cézanne," *Arts and Decoration*, November 1920.

André Gide, "Feuillets d'Automne," *Nouvelle Revue Française*. © Mercure de France.

Charles Vildrac, *Cinquante Dessins par Henri Matisse*. © 1920, Maeght Editeurs, Paris.

Charles Vildrac, "Henri-Matisse," *Exposition Henri Matisse*, November 15, 1920. Courtesy of Bernheim-Jeune.

Otto Grautoff, *Französische Malerei seit 1914*. © 1921, Mauritius Verlag, Berlin.

Elie Faure, *L'art moderne*, Paris. © 1924, B. W. Huebsch, Inc.

Roger Fry, "Henri-Matisse in the Luxembourg," May 1922. © 1922, *The Burlington Magazine*.

Charles Vildrac, *Nice 1921: Seize reproductions d'après les tableaux de Henri-Matisse*, Paris, 1922. Courtesy of Bernheim-Jeune.

Roland Schacht, *Henri Matisse*. © 1922, Rudolf Kaemmerer Verlag, Dresden.

André Lhote, "Notes," *Nouvelle Revue Française*, 1923. © Mercure de France.

Julius Meier-Graefe, "Matisse, das Ende das Impressionismus," *Faust*, 1923/24. © Erich Reiss Verlag, Berlin.

Adolphe Basler, *Henri Matisse*, Reihe "Junge Kunst," Band 46, Leipzig, 1924. Courtesy of Klinkhardt & Biermann Verlagsbuchhandlung GmbH, Munich.

Waldemar George, "Dessins de Henri-Matisse," *Henri-Matisse Dessins*, Editions des Quatre Chemins, 1925.

Forbes Watson, "Henri Matisse," *The Arts*, 1927.

Florent Fels, *Henri-Matisse*, Editions des Chroniques du Jours, Paris, 1929.

André Verdet, "A propos du dessin et des odalisques," *Entretiens notes et écrits sur la peinture.* © 1978, Editions Galilée, Paris.

André Levinson, "Les soixante ans de Henri Matisse," *L'Art vivant*, January 1930.

Fritz Neugass, "Henri Matisse, pour son soixantième anniversaire," *Cahiers de Belgique*, March 1930.

Roger Fry, "Henri-Matisse," Paris © 1931, *Cahiers d'Art*.

Roger Fry, *Henri-Matisse*, Editions des Chroniques du Jour, Paris, 1930.

René Huyghe, "Matisse and Color," *Formes*, January 1930.

George L. K. Morris, "A Brief Encounter with Matisse," *Life Magazine*, August 28, 1970. © Time, Inc. Reprinted with permission.

Henry McBride, "Matisse in America." © 1931, *Cahiers d'Art*.

Christian Zervos, "Notes sur la formation et le développement de l'oeuvre de Henri-Matisse." © 1931, *Cahiers d'Art*.

Curt Glaser, "Henri-Matisse." © 1931, *Cahiers d'Art*.

André Lhote, "Pour ou contre Henri-Matisse," *Chroniques du jour*, April 1931.

Waldemar George, "Psychanalyse de Matisse," *Chroniques du jour*, April 1931.

Paul Fierens, "Evocations," *Chroniques du jour*, April 1931.

Waldemar George, "Dualité de Matisse," *Formes*, June 1931.

Alfred H. Barr, Jr., *Henri-Matisse*. © The Museum of Modern Art, 1931.

Meyer Schapiro, "Matisse and Impressionism," *Androcles*, February 1932. © Meyer Schapiro.

Riichiro Kawashima, *Matisse*. © 1936, Atelier-Sha, Editeur, Tokyo.

Clive Bell, "Matisse and Picasso," *Europa*, May–June, 1933. © 1933.

"Challenging Matisse," *Art Digest*, March 15, 1933. © *Art Digest*.

Fernande Olivier, "Henri Matisse," *Picasso et ses Amis*, Paris, 1933. © 1933. Reprinted with permission of William Heinemann Limited.

Henry Miller, *Tropic of Cancer*. © 1964, Grove Press, Inc. Reprinted with permission of Grove Press.

Pierre Courthion, *Henri-Matisse*. © 1934, Les Editions Rieder, Paris.

Dorothy Bussy, "A Great Man," February 1986. © 1986, *The Burlington Magazine*.

Jean Cassou, *Paintings and Drawings of Matisse*. © 1939, Les Editions Braun & Cie, Paris and New York.

Henri Matisse, letter to Pierre Bonnard, January 13, 1940, *Nouvelle Revue Française*, Paris. © ARS, N.Y./SPADEM.

Alfred H. Barr, Jr., *Matisse, His Art and His Public*, translation © 1951, The Museum of Modern Art, New York. © ARS, N.Y./SPADEM.

Louis Aragon, *Matisse, A Novel*, translation © 1971, Harcourt, Brace Jovanovich. Originally published as *Henri Matisse, roman*. © Gallimard 1971.

Jean Cassou, "La pensée de Matisse," *Art present*. © 1947.

Henri Matisse, letter to Henry Clifford, February 14, 1948, *Henri Matisse: Retrospective Exhibition of Paintings, Drawings, and Sculpture Organized in Collaboration with the Artist*, Philadelphia Museum of Art, 1948. Translation © Jack Flam. © ARS, N.Y./SPADEM.

Alfred M. Frankfurter, "Is He the Greatest?" © ARTnews Associates, April 1948.

Alfred H. Barr, Jr., *Matisse, His Art and His Public*. © 1951, The Museum of Modern Art, New York.

Georges Duthuit, *The Fauvist Painters*. © 1950, Wittenborn Art Books, Inc.

Janet Flanner, "King of the Wild Beasts." © 1951, *The New Yorker*. Reprinted in *Men and Monuments*, Harper & Row, New York, 1957. © Natalia Danesi Murray, literary executor.

Hugo Munsterberg, "Henri Matisse," *Twentieth Century Painting*. © 1931, The Philosophical Library, Inc.

Françoise Gilot and Carlton Lake, *Life with Picasso*. © 1964, McGraw-Hill.

Bernard Berenson, "Encounters with Matisse," *Essays in Appreciation*. Chapman and Hall, London. © 1958, Bernard Berenson.

André Verdet, "La chapelle de Vence," *Entretiens notes et écrits sur la peinture*, 1978. © 1978, Editions Galilée, Paris.

Gotthard Jedlicka, "Begegnung mit Henri Matisse," *Die Matisse Kapelle in Vence*. © 1955, Suhrkamp Verlag Frankfurt am Main. All rights reserved.

Marie Raymond, "Matisse contra de Abstracten," *Kroniek van Kunst en Kultuur*. © 1953.

John Berger, "Henri Matisse, 1869–1954," *The New Statesman and Nation*, November 13, 1954. © 1954.

Madame Ulrich, *Paris-Match*, December 4, 1954. © 1954.

To Robert Motherwell

ACKNOWLEDGMENTS

First of all, I would like to thank Hugh Levin, who proposed this book to me, for having been so supportive while I was working on it. It has been a pleasure to work with him and his able assistant Ellin Yassky; they have been consistently helpful and encouraging.

I also thank the editors and translators of Harkavy Publishing Service. For his excellent work I single out editor Dale Ramsey. The translators all deserve hearty thanks: Todd Bludeau, Nancy Connors, Alexandra Bonfante-Warren, Ecegül Elterman, Yasuhide Fujio, Hallberg Hallmundsson, Japan Editorial Track, Jeffrey High, Thomas Spear, and Charles M. Stern. For his fine review of the translations, I thank Jon Rothschild.

John Schultz, who did the picture research, was a pleasure to work with. Philip Grushkin designed the volume and A&S Graphics of Wantagh, New York, did the typography, and I am grateful to them for the handsome results.

I also thank the authors who have so kindly agreed to have their works reprinted here, and the various scholars, museum curators, and friends who helped with various aspects of this project—particularly Lawrence Gowing, Francis Naumann, Susan Ginsburg, Rose-Carol Washton Long, Roger Benjamin, Margy Betz, and Charlotte Douglas. Thanks also to Helga Feder of the Graduate Center Library of the City University of New York, Jean Vallier of the French Institute/Alliance Française library, New York, and Agnes de Bretagne and Servane Zanotti of the Musée National d'Art Moderne, Paris. My special thanks go to John Elderfield for reading the typescript of the Introduction and Chronology and making a number of helpful suggestions.

I am very grateful to Mr. and Mrs. Pierre Matisse, Claude Duthuit, and Wanda de Guébriant for their particular helpfulness and generosity in making pictures available.

Special thanks are due to Rosemary O'Neill, who helped enormously with the research for this book, always with enthusiasm and good cheer.

Finally, my thanks to Bonnie and Laura, for their patience, as usual.

JACK FLAM

CONTENTS

THE EMBATTLED ARTIST, 1909–1917

THE EARLY YEARS IN NICE, 1918–1930

THE INTERNATIONAL MASTER, 1930–1939

THE FINAL FLOWERING, 1940–1954

CHRONOLOGY

1869

31 DECEMBER. Birth of Henri-Emile-Benoit Matisse at the home of his maternal grandparents in Le Cateau-Cambrésis, in Picardy (Nord). His father, Emile-Hippolyte-Henri Matisse, is a grain merchant at nearby Bohain-en-Vermandois, where Henri is raised. His mother, Anna Héloise Gérard, described as "artistically inclined," paints china and makes hats.

1872

Birth of his brother, Emile-Auguste.

1882–87

Attends Lycée de Saint-Quentin.

1887

OCTOBER. Goes to Paris to study law.

1888

AUGUST. Passes law examinations with "4 boules rouges." Shortly afterward, he returns to Picardy, where he practices law as an *avoué* (solicitor or attorney, as opposed to an *avocat*, or barrister or lawyer).

1890

Does his first paintings while recovering from an attack of appendicitis. His first original painting is a still life, signed "Essatim, H. Juin 90."

1891

OCTOBER. Returns to Paris to study art. Works at the Académie Julian with Gabriel Ferrier and Adolphe William Bouguereau.

1892

Moves to 19, Quai Saint-Michel.

FEBRUARY. Fails entrance examination to the Ecole des Beaux-Arts.

Becomes deeply impressed by Goya's *Youth* and *Old Age* at Lille.

OCTOBER. Registers for three courses at the Ecole des Arts Décoratifs. Meets Albert Marquet.

Accepted as a student by Gustave Moreau. Meets Georges Rouault and Simon Bussy.

1893–94

Does copies at the Louvre.

1894

SEPTEMBER. Birth of his daughter Marguerite Emilienne.

1895

MARCH. Passes his entrance examination and is admitted as a regular student at the Ecole des Beaux-Arts.

SUMMER. Paints in Brittany with Emile Wéry.

Sees an important Cézanne exhibition at Ambroise Vollard's gallery.

1896

APRIL. First public exhibition of his works at the Salon des Cent of the Symbolist journal *La Plume*. Later that month, he exhibits five paintings at the Salon of the Société Nationale des Beaux-Arts (Champs-de-Mars), of which he is elected associate member.

SUMMER. Visits Brittany and Belle-Ile.

1897

Paints *The Dinner Table* at the suggestion of Moreau. Meets Camille Pissarro.

Exhibits *The Dinner Table* at the Salon de la Nationale.

SUMMER. Goes to Brittany and Belle-Ile.

1898

JANUARY. Weds Amélie Noémie Alexandrine Parayre (b. 1872).

Honeymoons in London, where he studies the works of J. M. W. Turner.

FEBRUARY–AUGUST. Goes to Ajaccio in Corsica. Paints landscapes and reads Paul Signac's "From Eugène Delacroix to Neo-Impressionism" as serialized in *La Revue Blanche*.

APRIL. Death of Moreau.

AUGUST. Visits Beauzelle and Fenouillet, near Toulouse.

1899

JANUARY. Birth of his son Jean at Fenouillet.

Buys Cézanne's *Three Bathers*, Gauguin's *Head of a Boy*, and Rodin's plaster bust of Henri de Rochefort.

FEBRUARY. Returns to Paris and lives at 19, Quai Saint-Michel. Works briefly with Fernand Cormon and Eugène Carrière. Meets André Derain and Jean Puy. Begins a copy of Antoine Barye's *Jaguar Devouring a Hare*.

Exhibits for the last time at the Salon de la Nationale.

1900

Works on decorations for the Exposition Universelle. Mme. Matisse opens a millinery shop on the rue de Châteaudun.

JUNE. Birth of his son Pierre.

Shows his drawings to Rodin.

1901

Visits Vallors-sur-Ollon, Switzerland, with his father, to recover from severe bronchitis.

Exhibits for the first time at the Salon des Indépendants.

Father discontinues his allowance. Introduced to Maurice de Vlaminck by Derain.

1902

Participates in group show at Berthe Weill Gallery.

WINTER. Short of money, stays with his parents in Bohain.

1903

Exhibits at the first Salon d'Automne. Works on etchings and drypoints.

Sees an exhibition of Persian miniatures at the Pavillon Marsan of the Louvre.

1904

Becomes friendly with Signac.

JUNE. First one-man show at Galerie Vollard; catalogue includes a preface by Roger Marx.

SUMMER. Visits Saint-Tropez with Signac and Henri-Edmond Cross.

Begins *Luxe, calme et volupté*.

Sends thirteen canvases to the Salon d'Automne. Begins to hyphenate his name to distinguish himself from the painter Auguste Matisse.

Matisse with his students, c. 1910.
© Succession H. Matisse/1988. Archives Matisse.

1905

Exhibits *Luxe, calme et volupté* at the Salon des Indépendants.

SUMMER. Goes to Collioure with Derain. Paints first "Fauve" canvases.

Exhibits *Woman with the Hat* at the Salon d'Automne.

Meets Gertrude, Leo, Sarah, and Michael Stein.

Rents a studio at the Couvent des Oiseaux at 56, rue de Sèvres.

Begins *Le Bonheur de vivre*.

1906

Does his first lithographs.

Exhibits *Le Bonheur de vivre* at the Salon des Indépendants.

MARCH. One-man show at Galerie Druet. Goes to Biskra in Algeria.

APRIL. Meets Picasso.

SUMMER. Goes to Collioure.

Meets the Russian collector Sergei Shchukin.

Buys his first piece of African sculpture.

NOVEMBER. Returns to Collioure.

1907

JANUARY. Does *Reclining Nude I* and *Blue Nude* in Collioure.

Exhibits *Blue Nude* at the Salon des Indépendants.

EARLY SUMMER. Goes to Italy with his wife. Visits the Steins in Florence and goes to Arezzo, Siena, Padua, and Venice.

LATE SUMMER. Goes to Collioure.

1908

JANUARY. Opens his school at 56, rue de Sèvres.

Moves to the Hôtel Biron (the former Couvent des Oiseaux) at 33, Boulevard des Invalides.

Visits Germany with Hans Purrmann. Visits Munich, Nuremberg, and Heidelberg.

APRIL. First American exhibition at 291 Gallery, New York. Has major retrospective at the Salon d'Automne, including eleven paintings, thirteen sculptures, and six drawings.

Publishes "Notes of a Painter."

Goes with Purrmann to Berlin, where he exhibits at Paul Cassirer's gallery; Cassirer refuses to hang all of Matisse's paintings. "Notes of a Painter" is translated into German by Greta Moll.

1909

Shchukin commissions *Dance* and *Music*.

"Notes of a Painter" is published in Russian.

SUMMER. Goes to Cavalière.

AUTUMN. Moves to a house in Issy-les-Moulineaux, a suburb of Paris.

Signs a contract with Bernheim-Jeune Gallery, Paris. Does first *Back* sculpture.

1910

FEBRUARY. Retrospective at Bernheim-Jeune Gallery, and second exhibition at 291 Gallery.

LATE SUMMER. Goes to Munich with Purrmann to see an exhibition of Islamic art.

Exhibits *Dance* and *Music* at the Salon d'Automne.

OCTOBER. Death of his father. Leaves for Spain; travels to Sevilla, Granada, and Cordoba.

1911

JANUARY. Returns to France.

SPRING. Closes his school. Begins large decorative interiors.

SUMMER. Goes to Collioure.

AUTUMN. Visits Moscow at the invitation of Shchukin.

1912

JANUARY. Leaves for Morocco.

APRIL. Returns to Issy.

Studies the exhibition of Persian miniatures at the Musée des Arts Décoratifs, Paris.

AUTUMN. Returns to Morocco.

1913

FEBRUARY. Returns from Morocco via Corsica. Exhibits his Moroccan paintings at Bernheim-Jeune Gallery.

Exhibits in the Armory Show and at the Berlin Sezession; *Blue Nude* is burned in effigy in Chicago.

SUMMER. Goes to Issy.

Finishes *Portrait of Amélie Matisse.*

Rents a studio again at 19, Quai Saint-Michel.

1914

Takes up etching. Works on lithographs.

Paints *Portrait of Mlle. Yvonne Landsberg.*

SUMMER. Goes to Issy.

JULY. Exhibition at Gurlitt Gallery, Berlin.

AUGUST. World War I begins. His mother and brother are behind enemy lines in Le Cateau.

SEPTEMBER. Goes to Collioure, where he becomes friendly with Juan Gris.

OCTOBER. Returns to Paris. Visits Raymond Duchamp-Villon with Walter Pach.

1915

Exhibit at Montross Gallery, New York.

WINTER. Stays at Quai Saint-Michel.

SUMMER. Visits Arcachon, near Bordeaux.

NOVEMBER. Goes to Marseille with Marquet.

1916

Works in Paris and Issy. Paints *Piano Lesson.* Finishes *The Moroccans* and *Bathers by a Stream* (begun in 1909). Begins to work from the model Laurette.

1917

Meets Claude Monet.

SUMMER. Paints *Music Lesson* at Issy.

DECEMBER. Goes to Marseille, then stays in Nice at the Hôtel Beau-Rivage.

Visits Renoir in Cagnes.

1918

MARCH. Rents an apartment at 105, Quai du Midi, near the Hôtel Beau-Rivage.

MAY. Moves to the Villa des Alliés (138, Boulevard du Mont Boron).

SUMMER. Goes to Issy, then to Cherbourg.

AUTUMN. Visits Pierre Bonnard in Antibes, Renoir in Cagnes. Returns to Nice and takes a room at the Hôtel de la Mediterranée et de la Côte d'Azur, at 25, Promenade des Anglais.

1919

Does the *White Plumes* series from the model Antoinette.

Exhibits at Bernheim-Jeune Gallery and at Leicester Gallery, London.

SUMMER. Paints *Tea* in Issy.

AUTUMN. Visits London, where he does the decor and costumes for Igor Stravinsky's *Le Chant du Rossignol,* produced by Sergei Diaghilev's Ballets Russes de Monte Carlo.

1920

Exhibits at Bernheim-Jeune Gallery.

JUNE. Goes to London to see *Le Chant du Rossignol.*

JULY. Goes to Etretat on the English Channel coast.

Begins to work from the model Henriette, who will serve as his main model for the next seven years.

1921

Exhibits at Bernheim-Jeune Gallery.

SUMMER. Goes to Etretat.

AUTUMN. Returns to Nice and rents an apartment at 1, Place Charles-Félix.

The Musée du Luxembourg purchases *Odalisque with Red Trousers*—the first French museum purchase of a Matisse.

1922

Divides the year between Nice and Paris. Exhibits at Bernheim-Jeune Gallery. Begins an extended series of lithographs.

1923

DECEMBER. Marriage of his daughter Marguerite to Georges Duthuit, a scholar of Byzantine art.

1924

Retrospective at Bernheim-Jeune Gallery. Exhibits at Joseph Brummer Galleries, New York. Largest retrospective to date at the Ny Carlsberg Glyptotek, Copenhagen.

1925

Travels to Italy with his wife, daughter, and son-in-law.

Finishes *Large Seated Nude,* his first sculpture in several years.

1927

Exhibits at Valentine Dudensing Gallery, New York.

Wins first prize at the Carnegie International Exhibition, Pittsburgh.

1928–29

Does little painting. Devotes himself largely to drawings, prints, and sculpture.

1930

SPRING. Travels to Tahiti, stopping off in New York and San Francisco on the way. Spends three months in Tahiti, returning directly to Marseille via Suez.

AUTUMN. Returns to the United States to serve on the Carnegie International Exhibition jury (first prize given to Pi-

Music. 1939. Canvas. 45⅜ × 45⅜"
(115.3 × 115.3 cm). Albright Knox Art
Gallery, Buffalo, New York. Room of
Contemporary Art Fund, 1940.

The Dream. 1940. Canvas. 31⅞ × 25½″
(81 × 65 cm). © Succession H. Matisse
1988. Photograph courtesy Archives
Matisse, Collection Claude Duthuit.

casso). Visits the Barnes Foundation, Merion, Pennsylvania, and Etta Cone in Baltimore, Maryland. Albert Barnes proposes a mural commission.

Albert Skira commissions illustrations for Mallarmé's *Poésies.* Retrospective at Galerien Thannhauser, Berlin.

1931
Accepts Barnes's commission.
Retrospective at Galeries Georges Petit, Paris.
Exhibits at the Kunsthalle, Basel, and the Museum of Modern Art, New York. Works on the Barnes and Mallarmé commissions.

1932
Finishes the Barnes mural, but finds that the measurements are wrong. He decides to begin again.
Poésies de Stéphane Mallarmé is published.

1933
Finishes the second Barnes mural, goes to Merion for its installation. Takes a cure at Abano Bagni, near Venice. Studies Giotto's frescoes in Padua.

1934
Works on illustrations for James Joyce's *Ulysses.*

1935
Begins to do paintings of Lydia Delectorskaya, who will be his main model and secretary for the rest of his life. Paints *Pink Nude, Blue Eyes, The Dream.*

1936
Exhibits recent paintings at Paul Rosenberg Gallery, Paris.
Gives his Cézanne, *Three Bathers,* to the Musée d'Art Moderne de la Ville de Paris.
Publishes his drawings in a special issue of *Cahiers d'Art.* Begins to do small works in cut-and-pasted paper.

1937
The Ballets Russes de Monte Carlo commissions decor and costumes for *Rouge et Noir,* Léonide Massine's ballet to the music of Dmitri Shostakovich.
A room is devoted to his work at the Maitres de l'Art Indépendant exhibition, Paris.

1938
Moves to the Hôtel Regina in Cimiez, a suburb of Nice.

1939
MAY. First performance of *Rouge et Noir.*
SUMMER. Stays at Hôtel Lutetia, Paris. Travels to Geneva to see an exhibition of paintings from the Prado, but declaration of war forces him to return to France the same day.
OCTOBER. Returns to Nice.

1940
SPRING. Resides at 132, Boulevard Montparnasse, Paris. Obtains a Brazilian visa but decides to remain in France.

Matisse at Le Rêve, Vence, c. 1944. Henri
Cartier-Bresson/Magnum Photos, Inc.

The interior of Matisse's studio with *The Negress* in progress, 1953/4. Photograph by Hélène Adant/Rapho.

MAY. Visits Bordeaux, then Ciboure. Returns to Nice via Carcasonne and Marseille.

1941
Exhibits recent drawings at Galerie Louis Carré, Paris.
JANUARY. Goes to Lyon for surgery for an intestinal occlusion; nearly dies of complications following surgery.
MAY. Returns to Nice.
Works in bed on illustrations for *Florilège des Amours de Ronsard* and on Henri de Montherlant's *Pasiphaé*. Begins drawings for *Thèmes et variations*.

1942
Works on illustrations for *Poèmes* of Charles d'Orléans.
Exchanges paintings with Picasso.

1943
SPRING. Following an air raid on Cimiez, moves to the villa "Le Rêve" in Vence. Works on cut-outs for what will eventually become the book *Jazz*. *Thèmes et variations* is published.

1944
Works on illustrations for Baudelaire's *Fleurs du Mal*.
Mme. Matisse and Marguerite are arrested for resistance activities.

1945
Exhibits at the Victoria and Albert Museum, London, with Picasso.
Retrospective at the Salon d'Automne.

1946
Illustrates *Lettres d'une réligieuse portugaise* and Pierre Reverdy's *Visages*. Does cut-paper cartoons for the *Oceania* tapestry.

1947
Jazz is published by Tériade. Works increasingly in cut-and-pasted paper.

1948
Does a Saint Dominic for the church of Notre-Dame-de-Toute-Grace in Assy. Begins to work on the Chapelle du Rosaire for the Dominican sisters at Vence. Retrospective at the Philadelphia Museum of Art. *Florilège des Amours de Ronsard* is published.

1949
Returns to the Hôtel Regina in Cimiez. Exhibits recent paintings and cut-outs (this is the first substantial showing) at Pierre Matisse Gallery, New York. Retrospective exhibitions in Lucerne and at the Musée National d'Art Moderne, Paris.

1950
Exhibits his Vence chapel maquettes and numerous sculptures at the Maison de la Pensée Française, Paris.
Wins grand prize at the twenty-fifth Venice Biennale; asks to share the prize with his friend, the sculptor Henri Laurens.
Poèmes de Charles d'Orléans is published.

1951
JUNE. Consecration of the chapel at Vence.
Retrospective at the Museum of Modern Art, New York.

1952
Matisse museum at Le Cateau-Cambrésis is inaugurated. Does *Blue Nude* cut-outs, *The Sorrow of the King, The Swimming Pool, The Parakeet and the Mermaid,* and *The Snail.*
Finishes *Memory of Oceania* and *The Negress.*

1953
First exhibition concerned only with cut-outs, at Berggruen et Cie., Paris.

1954
3 NOVEMBER. Dies in Nice.

Matisse with a cat, in Paris, 1948.
Photograph by Hélène Adant/Rapho.

INTRODUCTION

"It was Matisse who took the first step into the undiscovered land of the ugly," the American author and illustrator Gelett Burgess wrote in 1910. Burgess was not alone in being skeptical toward Henri Matisse, who since 1905 had been considered a leader of the avant-garde. Even though many critics had by that time come to accept the art of Van Gogh, Gauguin, and Cézanne, Matisse still aroused a good deal of antagonism. That same year, for example, the French writer Roland Dorgelès accused Matisse of "mistreating square meters of canvas" and mocked his whole career as a kind of sham. Matisse himself remained somewhat puzzled by the controversy. He had not set out to be provocative; he simply wanted to paint in accordance with his own vision of reality. But since he was a man of great courage (and stubbornness), he was willing to risk public censure for his art, and he remained uncompromising. It is an irony of modern art history that this man who wanted to make no waves turned out to be one of the most controversial artists of his age. One of the fascinations of Matisse is that his art attracted so much critical attention in which—as this volume will show—so many contradictory judgments abound.

The beginning of the century was a time when artistic values—indeed, values of all sorts—were being called into question. When Gelett Burgess was confronted by "the new era of art," he proved relatively open-minded, admitting that his "views on art needed a radical reconstruction." He was excited by his new insights, but also troubled: "Was nothing sacred," he asked, "not even beauty?" The question of beauty was an important one, for it also implied the presence—or absence—of agreed-upon social norms. In being judged so harshly, Matisse's art was also being associated with a broad range of social and political ills, with a breakdown of social values and a weakening of European culture. Matisse's interest in the arts of non-European peoples—which were considered ugly almost by definition—caused him to be suspected of being a political radical as well as an artistic one. When he opened a school in which most of the students were foreigners, he became not only the butt of satire but also seemed, on the eve of the First World War, to be something of a traitor to France.

The specific association of Matisse with ugliness was especially persistent in the United States. "There is a good deal of the ugly in the work of Matisse," Arthur Jerome Eddy wrote in 1914, characterizing the artist as "a good man to study, but a bad man to imitate."[1] Like Burgess, Eddy showed some mixed feelings about the new artistic values that were becoming current. On the one hand, he realized that the slick and sentimental art of such academics as William Bouguereau was essentially false, and that "after Bouguereau, Matisse was inevitable." But on the other hand he was troubled by Matisse's lack of "refinement" and concluded that "a very little of the ugly goes a long ways, a very little of Matisse at his worst is all that is needed as an antidote to Bouguereau."[2]

The irony in this situation—for this label of "worst" was applied by Eddy to radical and innovative work that eventually came to be regarded as Matisse's best—is an irony discernible in the critical fortunes of many modern artists. But it is especially so in the case of Matisse. Indeed, it is hard to think of another modern artist who has had so many different aspects of his work at one time or another characterized as his

---

[1] This essay draws quotations from the selections in this volume, except as noted. Arthur Jerome Eddy's observations are taken from *Cubists and Post-Impressionism*, Chicago, 1914, p. 157.

[2] Ibid., pp. 157–158.

worst. In the popular press, Matisse was branded a madman, a revolutionist, an epileptic, a wild beast. But serious critics, too, in a flood of contradictions, charged him with virtually every excess and shortcoming that an artist might possess. Between the turn of the century and the beginning of the First World War, for example, various writers accused him of being both overly emotional and devoid of feeling, too theoretical and too undisciplined, too intellectual and too instinctive, too methodical and too sloppy.

The contrast between the radicalism of the artist and the apparent conservatism of the man was widely remarked on. Whatever reservations Gelett Burgess had about Matisse's art, he found the man surprisingly "serious" and "conscientious." This was the opinion held by most people who personally knew Matisse, even those who disliked his art. Writing in 1908, though, Joseph Péladan seized on the discrepancy between Matisse's art and his personal manner as evidence of his opportunism and hypocrisy. And Roland Dorgelès was only one of the numerous writers who remarked on Matisse's resemblance to a stuffy "German *Herr Professor*."

Matisse himself, wary and guarded, did not much mind the lackluster image; in fact, he cultivated it. A desire for outward, bourgeois normalcy, as against the controversy that his work elicited, was a constant one for Matisse. "Do tell the American people I am a normal man," he urged Clara MacChesney in 1912; "that I am a devoted husband and father, that I have three fine children, that I go to the theater, ride horseback, have a comfortable home, a fine garden that I love, flowers, etc., just like any man." And MacChesney, though unconvinced by the art, was more or less willing to take the man at his word, noting that he said goodbye to her and invited her to call again "like a perfectly normal gentleman."

Temperamentally, no man was less suited for the role of *enfant terrible*, to be the *bête noir* of the bourgeoisie, than Henri Matisse. It was enough that he could be unsettling to himself. "When I found my true path, I took fright," he confessed in 1952, "realizing that I could not turn back. So I charged ahead into my work with my head down, following the principle that all my life I had understood by the words 'Hurry up!' Like my parents, I hurried along with my work, pushed on by I don't know what, a force that today I see as quite alien to my normal life as a man."[3]

Abuse of Matisse the artist, then, was sometimes qualified by approval of Matisse the man, and vice versa, but more often the paintings alone were the subject of favorable or unfavorable criticism, much of it intelligent. Why did critics direct so much attention to Matisse's work, and why were their responses so contradictory?

First of all, in the early part of his career Matisse was consistently in the public eye. Unlike Picasso and Braque, he showed regularly at the Salon des Indépendants in the spring and at the Salon d'Automne in the fall. He also showed in private galleries and in group shows, in France and abroad.

Second, Paris was a city that took its art seriously. Most of what was written about Matisse before the First World War was occasional—short articles written as exhibition reviews for newspapers and literary magazines. As a result of this kind of press coverage, prompted by a keen public following, the art of this period is documented in criticism of a fascinating continuity, written by men who followed the development of an artist's career as only that of a novelist is followed nowadays. Thus as a matter of course Matisse's art was the subject of frequent discussion.

The critics, interested specifically in the ways that artists developed, more or less independently of the marketplace, sometimes saw them-

---

[3] Raymond Escholier, *Matisse ce vivant*, Paris, 1956, p. 18.

selves as playing an active role in that development. Their criticism was sometimes addressed as much to the artist personally as to the general reader of the reviews. With certain critics, such as Louis Vauxcelles, something like a public dialogue occurred. A case in point: Matisse would exhibit, and Vauxcelles would damn or praise, sometimes admonishing, sometimes congratulating his subject. Guillaume Apollinaire also had a kind of dialogue with Matisse and seemed especially interested in the question of Matisse's relationship to the rest of the European avant-garde.

It was a problematical relationship in the view of a number of critics. Matisse's art in the early years of this century was remarkably diverse and hard to define or categorize. He avoided ideological programs, remained outside specific schools, and resisted easy stylistic classification. Because he was so difficult to categorize using the various *isms* with which modern art was being conveniently labeled, Matisse irked people. Writing in 1912, André Salmon accused him of being the "most incoherent of modern artists" and severely criticized the contradictory nature of his art. Suffice it to say that this "contradictory nature" was less Matisse's failing than a generalized expression of critical annoyance about his hard-to-define creativity—for which his admirers could work at cross-purposes just as his detractors could muddy the stream with their diametrical opinions.

For the so-called contradictory nature of Matisse's art was essential to it. Convinced that there was no single, true way of seeing or imaging reality, Matisse insisted that he painted what he saw, even though the paintings did not conform to established norms of depiction. He dismissed the possibility, moreover, of arriving at a single, true style. Unified in its open-endedness, his career culminated in the novelty (for example) of the late cut-outs, which have resisted the term "collage" much as the paintings of 1911–17 have resisted the appellation "cubist." In the long run, the prodigious variety of his art has turned out to be one of its enduring strengths, though it has continued to give critics and historians difficulty and has drawn—and still draws—a good deal of adverse criticism.

The various attempts to shoehorn Matisse's art into convenient categories resulted in a number of myths and misconceptions that have proved difficult to overcome. Matisse's association with Fauvism is indicative of the way his art has been forced into molds that do not particularly apply to it. Fauvism itself was a short-lived phenomenon, and Matisse worked in a Fauve manner for less than two years. In fact, much of his subsequent painting was something like the opposite of fauvist. And the name itself was one that he disliked. "The epithet 'Fauve' was never accepted by the Fauve painters," he said. "It was always considered just a tag issued by the critics."[4] Nonetheless, Matisse was identified with Fauvism most of his life; even as he drew his last breath, he remained for many people "the king of the Fauves."

Another tag attached to Matisse was that of the hedonist—the painter of "the good armchair." The armchair phrase, so often applied to him in later years, was Matisse's own. In his "Notes of a Painter" of 1908, he had written: "What I dream of is an art of balance, of purity and serenity, devoid of troubling or depressing subject matter . . . a soothing, calming influence on the mind, something like a good armchair that provides relaxation from physical fatigue." The phrase was reprinted only a few months later, in an article by Charles Estienne,[5] and was fre-

[4] E. Tériade, "Matisse Speaks," 1951; reprinted in Jack D. Flam, *Matisse on Art*, London, 1973, p. 132.

[5] Charles Estienne, "Des tendances de la peinture moderne: Entretien avec M. Henri-Matisse," 1909; translated in Flam, *Matisse on Art*, p. 49.

quently referred to over the years as proof of the pleasant, simple-minded optimism that Matisse's painting was supposed to embody. It is interesting to note how in later years, this "soothing" effect was no longer characterized as an *ideal* ("what I *dream* of") that Matisse was working toward in 1908—a time when his work was generally thought to be disturbing and ugly—but as a kind of "sedative" effect that his art was actually supposed to have. "One critic maintains that his works act like a sedative to a tired brain"—Clara MacChesney wrote in 1913, getting the details wrong, but reflecting a widely held attitude toward Matisse—"or as an easy chair to a weary toiler home from his day's work. But I am positive that I should not dare when weary, to sit for long in front of his 'Cathedrals at Rouen'."[6]

As we have seen, most of the adverse criticism up to the First World War took Matisse to task for creating ugly or disturbing art. After the war, the situation changed. Matisse's painting was now decidedly more naturalistic, and he was being attacked by modernists for being too conservative. In 1919 Jean Cocteau compared him to one of the famous creatures in Apollinaire's *Bestiary* ("As do the crayfish, Backing up, backing up") and in 1920 René Schwob remarked on the "excessive docility" of his art. In the face of this second phase of criticism, Matisse enlisted a circle of defenders, led in the early 1920s by Charles Vildrac and Waldemar George, who not only wrote *apologias* for Matisse's art but seem to have done so with arguments provided by Matisse himself. It was at this time that Matisse became known as the painter of French bourgeois luxury and that unfavorable comparisons between him and Picasso became common. As a further irony, Matisse did indeed become more acceptable to the bourgeoisie, whose values he now seemed to affirm rather than attack. As André Lhote observed in 1919, the public thought it saw in Matisse's new "nonchalance" the reflection "of its reluctance to think and judge." It is no mere coincidence that the first Matisse painting purchased by the Musée du Luxembourg (later the Musée National d'Art Moderne) was a sensuous work whose admirers could easily include the self-indulgent—an odalisque of 1921.

By the early 1930s, Matisse was suffering almost as much from the praise of his defenders as from the attacks of his adversaries—as may be seen in André Levinson's fascinating review of Florent Fels's 1929 monograph. In at least one instance, Matisse felt called upon to respond directly to what he felt were misguided statements made by a supporter. In a 1938 essay that insisted upon the formalism of Matisse's drawing, the critic Claude Roger-Marx asserted that Matisse used his models merely as "objects" and that he cared nothing for their "souls." Not so, Matisse countered in his "Notes of a Painter on His Drawing" of 1939, one of his most straightforward statements about his art.

Matisse's international stature grew. In 1930 and 1931 he had a number of important exhibitions, in Berlin, Paris, Basel, and New York. Around the same time, there appeared a number of important publications about him. The most notable of these were three monographs published by Editions des Chroniques du Jour—in English, French, and German, with texts by Roger Fry, Florent Fels, and Gotthard Jedlicka. In 1931 there appeared both a special Matisse issue of *Cahiers d'Art*, the most extensive single publication on Matisse up to that time, and a "For or Against Henri Matisse" installment of the periodical *Chroniques du Jour* in which several of the issues raised by Matisse's art were discussed.

As his fame spread, Matisse drew both praise and blame from all over the world. In 1933, Albert Barnes, who had commissioned a Matisse mural for the Barnes Foundation in Merion, Pennsylvania, co-authored a major monograph, *The Art of Henri-Matisse*. This was roundly attacked

---

[6] In the reference to "Cathedrals at Rouen," MacChesney seems to confuse Matisse with Monet.

by the American critic Thomas Craven, who scornfully suggested that Matisse, whose favorite subject was "the odalisque in the hotel bedroom," looked like "a Polish Jew who had prospered in America."[7] Around the same time, following Hitler's rise to power, Matisse's paintings were being removed from the walls of German museums, along with the works of other modern artists classified as communistic and "degenerate." Nor was his art faring well in the Soviet Union, where he was found guilty of bourgeois estheticism and an unacceptably "hedonistic outlook."[8]

After the Second World War, the abstract pictorial qualities of Matisse's art—especially his fine sense of touch, surface, and color—came to be increasingly appreciated by other artists. In America especially he became an important inspiration to a number of abstract painters, even though he himself remained unconvinced by abstract painting. Gradually he had an influence on contemporary painting which rivalled and eventually surpassed that of Picasso.

But in one form or another, the image of Matisse as a hedonist and a decorator persisted to the end of his life, and persists even today. The characteristically flat and bright paintings of the 1930s and the flat, bright forms of his late cut-outs reinforced this image, and I suspect that when one says "Matisse" today, that is the image that is evoked for most people: "Brightly colored, festive, optimistic; shapes which are soothing, harmonious and restful; a sense of protection from whatever is discordant," as one commentator recently wrote. On that basis, the same writer adds that "in terms of the description, Matisse is already deposed and minor."[9]

Throughout his career, Matisse inspired and provoked and angered people, and he also made them think. From the vast amount of material available on Matisse—some texts remarkable for their acute insights, others for their apparent opacity—I have selected a body of writings that I think will provide a balanced overview of Matisse's career and critical fortunes. The general arrangement of the book is chronological, although the reader will note that not all of the texts are in strict chronological order in terms of the dates when they were written. Occasionally a later text that deals with an earlier period is included among texts from the earlier period, in order to provide a fuller picture of the events under discussion. Thus Max Weber's 1951 recollections of Matisse's school follow the notes that Sarah Stein took as a student there around 1908, and Georges Besson's 1939 account of Matisse's arrival in Nice in 1918 is included with texts written in 1918. Similarly, some of Matisse's own later reminiscences are included among contemporary accounts of events in his career, so as to give continuity to the overall chronological narrative. Though the main body of the text comprises critical writings about Matisse, I have also included a few of Matisse's letters and some of his own particularly important writings on art, such as "Notes of a Painter" (1908) and "Notes of a Painter on His Drawing" (1939). But since a fairly broad selection of Matisse's own writings is readily available in English, the emphasis here has been on writings about him rather than by him.[10]

The texts are arranged so as to constitute a kind of running commentary on Matisse's career. And as the reader will see, they are sometimes grouped around specific works or events in Matisse's life. The

[7] Thomas Craven, *Modern Art*, New York, 1934, pp. 168, 160.

[8] See Alexander Romm, *Henri Matisse*, Moscow, 1937, p. 70. A selection from a different passage in Romm's book appears in this volume.

[9] Norman Bryson, "Signs of the Good Life," *Times Literary Supplement*, 27 March 1987, p. 328.

[10] See Flam, *Matisse on Art*. An overview of the Matisse literature may be found in my *Matisse: The Man and His Art, 1869–1918*, Ithaca, N.Y., and London, 1986, pp. 509–512.

opening selections show Matisse as a young artist struggling to make his way in the world. These are followed by texts that discuss him when he is beginning to attract notice, followed by texts that show him at the center of controversy. Along the way, there are clusters of writings that discuss Matisse as a teacher, give critical reactions to some of his major works, and center around his travels or the places in which he lived. Other texts are grouped in relation to his art at particular times, such as the issues surrounding his increased naturalism in the 1920s, the retrospective exhibitions of the early 1930s, his use of paper cut-outs, and his work on the Dominican Chapel at Vence during his last years.

All the texts I have selected originated during the years Matisse was alive (1869–1954). Many are published here in English for the first time, and a number are reprinted for the first time in any language. As the reader will see, the selection includes negative along with positive appraisals of Matisse. Although I have tried to give the shorter texts in their entirety, I have in some cases excerpted from such texts and deleted passages that repeated biographical information, were generally redundant, or addressed issues peripheral to Matisse. I have also included excerpts from some longer texts on Matisse, in order to convey the flavor of some of the more important monographs and exhibition catalogues. These excerpts from book-length texts had by necessity to be severely limited, and readers familiar with the Matisse literature will notice some glaring absences. Among these are Raymond Escholier's *Henri-Matisse* (Paris, 1937), for many years the more or less standard biograpnical work; Jean Puy's "Souvenirs," published in *Le Point* in July 1939; and Gaston Diehl's *Matisse* (Paris, 1954). While all of these—and others similarly not included in the following selection—make interesting reading and contain much valuable information, they tended to repeat a good deal of biographical material to be found elsewhere in this book and were in other ways repetitive. Since space was limited, I felt that other material would be both more useful and more interesting within the present context.

In some cases, the work of condensing was more or less done for me by other authors. For example, Julius Meier-Graefe's discussion of Léon Werth's ironical 1920 essay made it unnecessary to reprint that essay. A 1933 *Art Digest* article about Thomas Craven's review of Barnes and De Mazia's *The Art of Henri-Matisse* serves as a nice summation of the radically different positions of both reviewer and reviewed; and since Craven's position is summed up so well there, I did not feel it necessary to reprint the long essay on Matisse in his *Modern Art* (New York, 1934). Alfred Barr's evaluation of Matisse's critical position since World War II provides an excellent account of the radically different positions taken at the time by George L.K. Morris and Clement Greenberg, and obviates the necessity of reprinting the essays by Morris and Greenberg.

The pictures in the book are meant to complement the writings rather than to illustrate them, although an effort has been made to illustrate works that are discussed in the various texts. My goal has been to provide the reader with an overview of Matisse's strongest and best work along with an overview of many of the most interesting things that have been written about him, pro and con. This, as Georges Desvallières remarked in his introduction to Matisse's own "Notes of a Painter," will allow the reader to compare what has been said about Matisse with what he did, and to draw his or her own conclusions accordingly.

JACK FLAM
New York and Paris
April 1988

Henri Matisse, Interviewed by E. Tériade
ART NEWS
"Matisse Speaks"
November 1951

BEGINNINGS, 1890–92

I was an attorney's clerk, studying to be a lawyer, at Saint-Quentin. Convalescing after an illness, I met somebody who copied chromos—sort of Swiss landscapes which in those days were sold in albums of reproductions. I bought a box of colors and began to copy them, too. Afterwards, every morning from seven to eight, before going to my studies, I used to go to the Ecole Quentin Latour where I worked under draftsmen who designed textiles. Once bitten by the demon of painting, I never wanted to give up. I begged my parents for, and finally got, permission to go to Paris to study painting seriously.

The only painter in Saint-Quentin was a man named Paul Louis Couturier [sic], a painter of hens and poultry-yards. He had studied with Picot—one of Bouguereau's disciples—which he mentioned, and with Gustave Moreau, which he never mentioned. So I came to Paris with recommendations from Couturier to Bouguereau.

I showed some of my first pictures to Bouguereau who told me that I didn't know perspective. He was in his studio, re-doing for the third time his successful Salon picture, *The Wasp's Nest* (it was a young woman pursued by lovers). The original Salon picture was nearby; next to it was a finished copy, and on the easel was a bare canvas on which he was drawing a copy of the copy. Two friends were with him: Truphème, one of the prize-winners of the Artistes Français group and director of the Municipal School of Drawing on the Boulevard Montparnasse, and a man named Guignon, another of the Artistes Français painters—he only painted olive trees at Menton. Bouguereau was literally re-making his picture for the third time. And his friends exclaimed: "Oh, Monsieur Bouguereau! What a conscientious man you are; what a worker!" "Ah, yes!" responded Bouguereau, "I am a worker, but art is hard."

I saw the unconsciousness (unconscious because they were sincere) of these men who were stamped by official art and the Institute, and soon understood that I could get nothing from them.

I went to the Académie Julian and signed up for the Prix de Rome competition at the Ecole des Beaux-Arts. One of my friends persuaded me that there was nothing to learn at the Ecole de Rome and I began to work from my own experiences. I was enormously helped in this by meeting Gustave Moreau, in whose studio I entered and where I met Dufy and Rouault. Moreau took an interest in my work. He was a cultivated man who stimulated his pupils to see all kinds of painting, while the other teachers were preoccupied with one period only, one style—of contemporary academicism—that is to say their own, the leftovers of all conventions.

COPIES AT THE LOUVRE, 1894–96

We used to make copies at the Louvre, somewhat to study the masters and live with them, somewhat because the government bought copies. But they had to be executed with minute exactitude, according to the letter and not the spirit of the work. Thus the works most successful with the purchasing commission were those done by the mothers, wives and daughters of the museum guards. Our copies were only accepted out of

E. Tériade (pseudonym of Efstratios Eleftheriades, b. 1897), Greek-born writer and publisher involved in several reviews that published works by and about Matisse, such as Cahiers d'Art, L'Intransigeant, Minotaure, *and* Verve. *He published some of Matisse's own illustrated books, most notably* Jazz *(1947), and in 1951 compiled some of his interviews with Matisse as* Matisse Speaks, *which combines biographical detail, reminiscences, and reflections on art and life.*

Philbert-Léon Couturier (1823–1901), a student of the history and genre painter François Picot (1786–1868).

Gustave Moreau (1826–1898), painter and professor at the Ecole des Beaux-Arts, in whose studio Matisse studied between 1892 and 1897.

Adolphe William Bouguereau (1825–1905), French painter and professor at the Ecole des Beaux-Arts, whose highly finished surfaces and sentimental subjects were anathema to the impressionists.

Raoul Dufy (1877–1953), French painter and textile designer, allied first with Fauvism, then with Cubism, at the beginning of the century.

Georges Rouault (1871–1958), French painter and Matisse's fellow pupil in Gustave Moreau's studio.

charity, or sometimes when Roger Marx pleaded our cause. I would have liked to be literal, like the mothers, wives and daughters of the guards, but couldn't.

What is believed to be boldness was only awkwardness. So liberty is really the impossibility of following the path which everyone usually takes and following the one which your talents make you take.

Among the pictures I copied at that time, I remember the *Portrait of Baldassare Castiglione* by Raphael, Poussin's *Narcissus,* Annibale Carracci's *The Hunt,* the *Dead Christ* of Philippe de Champagne. As for the *Still Life* by David de Heem, I began it again, some years later, with the methods of modern construction.

Around 1896 I was at the Ecole des Beaux-Arts and roomed on the Quai Saint-Michel. Next door was the painter Wéry who was influenced by the impressionists, especially Sisley. One summer we went to Brittany together, to Belle-Ile-en-Mer. Working next to him I noticed that he could get more luminosity from his primary colors than I could with my old-master palette. This was the first stage in my evolution, and I came back to Paris free of the Louvre's influence and heading towards color.

The search for color did not come to me from studying paintings, but from the outside—that is from the revelation of light in nature.

Roger Marx (1859–1913), French art critic, art historian, and arts administrator, who helped the Moreau students sell their copies to the state.

Matisse's copy of Raphael's Portrait of Baldassare Castiglione *was actually done in 1904.*

Emile Wéry (1868–1935), French painter with whom Matisse worked in Brittany.

Roger Marx
REVUE ENCYCLOPEDIQUE
"The Salon du Champ-de-Mars"
25 April 1896

Roger Marx was one of Matisse's earliest public supporters. This is one of the first published notices about Matisse's work.

In the very heart of the Ecole des Beaux-Arts, a "hotbed of revolution" has been ignited; all the insurgents against routine, all those who intend to develop in the direction of their individuality, have gathered under the aegis of M. Gustave Moreau; can one hope to evaluate the freedom of the instruction provided and their temperamental diversity from a few works, however attractive they may be, from some studies by M. Matisse, from M. Milcendeau's very distinguished drawings, from that remarkable *Sortie des Ouvriers* by M. Evenepoel. . . ?

Rocks at Belle-Ile. 1896. Canvas. 25½ × 32″ (65 × 81 cm). Photograph: Bernheim-Jeune, Paris.

Paul Flat
REVUE BLEUE POLITIQUE ET LITTÉRAIRE
"The Salons of 1896"
6 June 1896

Here again, by M. Matisse, two little still lifes that are among the best things at the Salon. These two artists are students of Gustave Moreau and the influence of this master's teaching shows most clearly in the use of rich surfaces and harmonious tones.

Letter from Henri Evenepoel
to His Father
On Matisse and Gustave Moreau
12 March 1896

Yesterday afternoon at one-thirty I was walking along the quais when I encountered Gustave Moreau, who, like me, was on his way to meet a close friend of mine, Henri Matisse, a subtle painter, a master of the art of grays. Moreau suffers from terrible neuralgia of the arm and can barely walk. One way or another, we made it to the Quai Saint-Michel, where Matisse was pacing up and back waiting for us. A labored climb up the stairway of the old building at number 19. Finally we arrived in the tiny studio, filled with bits of tapestries and knickknacks gray with dust. "We are the jury," Moreau said to me. He sat in an armchair, I took a seat beside him, and we spent an exquisite hour. He told us the whys and wherefores of his loves and dislikes. Matisse showed us what he had sent to the Champ de Mars exhibition (ten or so canvases, delectable in tone, almost all still lifes; and that set him off on a discourse about everything), and he talked about art, including music. He is still surprisingly young, nothing of the professor about him; not a touch of pedantry; he is a friend. He asked me how you were, wanted to know if you were *patient*—that was his word . . . .

Letter from Matisse to His Cousin Lancelle

On Monetary Rewards

9 June 1896

In his enthusiasm to make a good impression, Matisse gives his cousin a somewhat optimistic account of his career.

I was very pleased to receive your kind letter, and in returning you thanks for it I am happy to be able to announce that my exhibition has brought more than Platonic gratification: the day of the opening, I sold a still life (20 × 30 cm.) for 400 francs, and eight days ago the government bought my interior with a woman reading, seen from behind (the one you saw me sketch out this past summer and finish this winter) for the price of 800 francs. I have also been commissioned by the Louvre (again for the government) to copy a painting by Chardin for at least 1000 francs. I believe I mentioned to you that six or seven months ago the government had already bought a copy of an Annibale Carracci from me for 1200 francs. You see, dear friend, that there is such a thing as painting that pays. . . .

Jean-Baptiste-Siméon Chardin (1699-1779), French painter whose still lifes were among his greatest works.

Matisse's copy of The Hunt *by Bolognese painter Annibale Carracci (1560-1609) in fact brought him only 600 francs.*

Henri Matisse, Interviewed by Jacques Guenne

L'ART VIVANT

"A Conversation with Henri Matisse"

15 September 1925

Then I did a *Desserte*. And already I was not transposing any longer in the transparent tones of the Louvre.
    And what did Gustave Moreau think of that canvas?
    Moreau showed the same indulgence toward me as toward Marquet and Rouault. To the professors who discovered what was already revolutionary in this attempt, he responded: 'Let it be, his decanters are solidly on the table and I could hang my hat on their stoppers. That's what is essential.' I exhibited this work at the Nationale. It was the time when the public was generally terrified of germs. One had never seen so many cases of typhoid. The public found germs at the bottom of my decan-

COLORPLATE 4

La Desserte, *or* The Dinner Table, *done in 1897 at the suggestion of Gustave Moreau, was Matisse's first systematic attempt to incorporate impressionist techniques into his work.*

Albert Marquet (1875-1947), French painter, Matisse's fellow-pupil, neighbor, and lifelong friend.

ters! However, I had been raised to the level of Associate. What a fine civil service career opened before me! I deserve no praise, I assure you, for not having followed it. To tell the truth, it's my modest condition which I have to thank for my success. In effect, painting, even academic, was a poor provider at that time. I was going to be forced to take up another profession. I decided to take a year off, avoid all hindrances, and paint the way I wanted to. I worked only for myself. I was saved. Soon the love of materials for their own sake came to me like a revelation. I felt a passion for color developing within me.

Letter from Henri Evenepoel to His Father

On Matisse's Corsican Paintings

15 June 1898

While he was in Corsica in 1898, Matisse's style underwent a drastic change that some of his former colleagues found shocking.

I also saw my friend Matisse again, back from Corsica for a few days! He brought me back some extraordinary studies, painted as if by an epileptic and crazed impressionist! I told him very frankly what I thought! It is insane, he who had such nice painterly qualities!

COLORPLATE 5

Raymond Escholier (1882–1971), French novelist and critic, was director of the Museum of the City of Paris at the Petit Palais. At the time of this letter, Escholier was writing his book Henri Matisse (published 1937). Matisse had purchased Cézanne's Three Bathers from Ambroise Vollard in 1899.

Letter from Matisse to Raymond Escholier

On Cézanne's Three Bathers

10 November 1936

Yesterday I consigned to your shipper Cézanne's *Bathers*. I saw the picture carefully packed and it was supposed to leave that very evening for the Petit Palais.

Allow me to tell you that this picture is of the first importance in the work of Cézanne because it is a very solid, very complete realization of a composition that he carefully studied in several canvases, which, now in important collections, are only the studies that culminated in the present work.

In the thirty-seven years I have owned this canvas, I have come to know it quite well, I hope, though not entirely; it has sustained me morally in the critical moments of my venture as an artist; I have drawn from it my faith and my perseverance; for this reason, allow me to request that it be placed so that it may be seen to its best advantage. For this it needs both light and perspective. It is rich in color and surface, and seen at a distance it is possible to appreciate the sweep of its lines and the exceptional sobriety of its relationships.

I know that I do not have to tell you this, but nevertheless I think it is my duty to do so; please accept these remarks as the excusable testimony of my admiration for this work which has grown increasingly greater ever since I have owned it.

Allow me to thank you for the care that you will give it, for I hand it over to you with complete confidence. . . .

Matisse at the time of his marriage, 8 January 1898, to Amélie Parayre. Studio Madonnes.

31

Henri Matisse,
Interviewed by Raymond Escholier

HENRI MATISSE

On His Return to Paris in 1899

1937

When Matisse returned to Paris in 1899 after nearly a year's absence, he tried to continue his studies but found his prospects severely limited.

There I found the outlook of the students much changed. The recollections that I raised of our former master were poorly received, and the students told me: "Nowadays, we are taught our trade and how to look out for ourselves in life." I understood what that meant with the first and only critique I saw Cormon give.

When my turn came, after looking at my work and at me, he moved on, without saying a word.

During the model's break, when the students usually showed the teacher the work they were doing outside the studio, I set a painting on the easel in front of the master, a painting of a sunset I'd done from my window on the Quai Saint-Michel, with the buildings of the Louvre as background. Cormon looked at it and didn't say a word. Then he called over his assistant and spoke with him in a low voice.

After the teacher had left, the assistant approached me: "I'm truly sorry to have to tell you this, but the boss asked me your age. I told him: 'Thirty.' 'Is he serious?' he asked. 'Yes, sir,' I answered. 'Then he has to leave.'"

So I had to look elsewhere. At first, I thought of returning to the Académie Julian, thinking that I would not have to receive critiques; but

Fernand-Anne Piestre, called Cormon (1845–1924), a painter whose numerous students had also included Van Gogh and Toulouse-Lautrec.

Paul Cézanne. *Three Bathers.* 1879–82. Canvas. 23¾ × 21½" (60.3 × 54.6 cm). Ville de Paris, Musée du Petit Palais/Art Resource.

COLORPLATE 1. *Interior with a Top Hat.* 1896. Canvas. 31½ × 37⅜″ (80 × 95 cm).
© Succession H. Matisse/1988. Photograph courtesy Archives Matisse, Collection Claude Duthuit.

COLORPLATE 2. *The Sick Woman*. 1899. Canvas. 18⁵/₁₆ × 15⅛″ (46.5 × 38.4 cm).
The Baltimore Museum of Art: The Cone Collection, formed by Dr. Claribel Cone and
Miss Etta Cone of Baltimore, Maryland.

COLORPLATE 3. *Still Life with Oranges, II.* 1899. Canvas. 18⅜ × 21¾" (46.7 × 55.2 cm).
Washington University Gallery of Art, St. Louis, Missouri: Sydney M. Shoenberg, Jr.

COLORPLATE 4. *The Dinner Table (La Desserte)*. 1897. Canvas. 39½ × 51½″ (100 × 131 cm). Private collection.

COLORPLATE 5. *Corsican Landscape: Olive Trees.* 1898. Canvas. 15 × 18⅛″ (38 × 46 cm).
The Pushkin Museum, Moscow.

COLORPLATE 6. *Self-Portrait.* 1900. Canvas. 25³/₁₆ × 17¾″ (64 × 45.1 cm).
© Succession H. Matisse/1988. Photograph courtesy Archives Matisse, Collection Claude Duthuit.

COLORPLATE 7. *Self-Portrait*. 1900. Canvas. 21½ × 18″ (55 × 46 cm). Private collection.

COLORPLATE 8. *Interior with Harmonium*. 1900. Canvas. 28⅞ × 21¾″ (73.3 × 55.3 cm). Musée Matisse, Nice.

I soon had to flee: the students were making fun of my exercises. By chance I learned that in the rue de Rennes—in the courtyard of the Vieux Colombier, I believe—there was a studio that had been set up by an Italian, where Carrière gave weekly critiques. I went there, and I met Jean Puy, Laprade, Biette, Derain, Chabaud; not one of Moreau's students was there.

At last it was possible to work in total peace, since the teacher gave criticism only to his private students, meaning the long-time, obedient ones, and he looked diffidently at the more personal work of the others. Which suited us.

Unfortunately, this studio closed down because of insufficient enrollment. So we banded together to share a model at Biette's, in the rue Dutot.

That whole period, after I left Cormon's, lasted only a year.

Eugène Carrière (1849–1906), French painter.

Jean Puy (1876–1960), Pierre Laprade (1875–1932), André Derain (1880–1954), Auguste-Elisée Chabaud (1882–1955), and Jean Biette became associated with the Fauve group.

Letters from Matisse to Simon Bussy

On Financial Affairs

July 1903

15 JULY 1903

My work more or less satisfies me. I'm aware of continual real progress, more suppleness of execution than in the earlier studies, and a return to the soft harmonies and close values that will certainly be better received by collectors, and even by the Salon officials at the rue de Valois, who were pleased by such works even when they were not supported by solid or discerning drawing. I don't disown my most recent studies, though, for what I'm doing now is the logical follow-up on my past efforts. I don't see the future as rosy, though. My health is good, but my wife's upsets me a bit. When we left Paris three months ago she was anemic after several uninterrupted years of Paris and the fatigue and cares of a business that didn't always go well, a business that she sold a few months ago. Our intention was to return to Paris in October, where my wife could have done tapestry restoration, but the doctor opposes her return just now and we're quite upset. The various cares, small and large, more small than large, which life, though I'm not that old, has already given me a good share of, and the responsibility that I've decided courageously to accept, combined with the pittance that our calling brings in, had almost made me decide to quit painting altogether and do something insipid but lucrative enough to permit me to live. Fortunately, perhaps, I'm once again confident about my artistic calling, whose joys have often made it possible to put up with a life that has already held great bitterness for me.

31 JULY 1903

I know how arduous and difficult life is for a painter and I've already come to understand what a man who was familiar with the bad sides of an artist's life told me about ten years ago: in order to paint, one must be unable to do anything else. All the same, it seems to me I could do something else, though I'm not sure about that. I've already done everything for it (Painting). Now I've completely exhausted my family, which is frankly and purely bourgeois, and I can no longer count on them. Along the way I've created a family of my own, which must count on me absolutely. Perhaps it won't take much to save me. For I'm not

In 1902 and 1903 Matisse was under severe financial stress and wrote about this to his friend Simon Bussy (1870–1954), whom he had met in Moreau's studio.

stupid enough to think that I'm indispensable to the progress of painting, and all I'm thinking of right now is earning my bread. Several years ago, as you know, I did some things that pleased people a lot, things done from instinct. If only this facility would come back to me, I'd get started again; and some painting always sells—Henner, Roylet, Juana, Romani, Caracollas, and Co. are constantly making the shippers sweat. I forgot Bouguereau! Unintentionally. The unfortunate thing is that I can't act like a good bourgeois again (which one has to be a bit, though, since nature inflicts the same obligations on us all) unless I'm pushed into a corner and am no longer myself. What consoles me, I repeat, is to think that my intimate things pleased people and that I did them by instinct. That a good purge could rid me of the good or bad browsings, foreign to my nature, that I've picked up along the way these past six years, and that I could then appear with a calm and smiling face to the crowd of collectors who don't like uneasy or tormented people—this hope isn't ill founded, for it seems to me that it's the direction I've taken for some time now quite steadily, even effortlessly, just by the nature of things—and I strongly feel that one year would be enough to set me right.

Balzac says that necessity is the midwife of genius. The unfortunate thing is that I have no genius. And even if I did have genius, from the pecuniary point of view, it would probably be the same. . . .

A Glimpse of Notre-Dame in the Late Afternoon. 1902. Oil on paper mounted on canvas. 28½ × 21½". (72.4 × 54.6 cm). Albright-Knox Art Gallery, Buffalo, New York. Gift of Seymour H. Knox, 1927.

A view from the artist's studio near Quai Saint-Michel, Paris. Photograph by Hélène Adant/Rapho.

Roger Marx

EXHIBITION OF WORKS BY THE PAINTER HENRI MATISSE

"Preface"

1904

As the spring and autumn Salons take place and the expressions of separatism, individual or collective, succeed one another, experience refutes earlier judgment; it appears unmistakable that, far from offering a haven for plagiarism, the studio of Gustave Moreau has remained for six years a shelter wide open to militant originality. To eliminate this groundless accusation, it has required the flight of years and repeated assertion of undeniable proofs: such as the diversity of talents, the independence and contrast of aims; such as the preference for genres or subjects inspired directly by nature and by life. As long as the tutelage of Gustave Moreau lasted, the inclinations of his pupils joined those of innovators considered to be the most dangerous. Once the instigator had disappeared, the vanishing of his personal influence followed, among certain of his disciples, according to the free law of instinct; others, seeking to complete their education, came to look for advice and for models among the leaders of Impressionism, especially to Manet and Paul Cézanne. Is it therefore so surprising that Gustave Moreau and Paul Cézanne, in reclaiming Poussin, show the same fervor and that they agree in endorsing the principles of sumptuous tone and rich surfaces?

The art of Henri Matisse, who discovered the harmonious synthesis that was to result from the combined teachings of the two masters, has the wherewithal to win over students of history and clear-sighted art-lovers alike. Moreover, the artist's discipline is such that both will find reasons for comfort and esteem. Henri Matisse held his first exhibition in 1896—at the age of twenty-seven—in the Champ-de-Mars Salon. It was a debut of uncommon brilliance. He was raised to the rank of associate with no opposition. His paintings won immediate acceptance in galleries public and private. Had the painter cautiously followed the path that had guaranteed his initial success, he would have had nothing to fear from the future. But this time it so happened that the promise of an easy

After repeated disappointments, Matisse was finally given a one-man show by Vollard, 1–19 June 1904; this is the preface to the catalogue of that show. Its author, Roger Marx, generally supported Gustave Moreau's students.

The 1896 exhibition had been in the spring salon of the Société Nationale des Beaux-Arts, often referred to as the "Salon de la Nationale."

43

Henri Matisse Etching. 1900–03. Etching and drypoint. 5⁵⁄₁₆ × 7⁷⁄₈″ (13.5 × 20 cm). Collection, The Museum of Modern Art, New York. Gift of Mrs. Bertram Smith.

life seemed an unenviable fate. Henri Matisse spurned fashionable success for the trials of struggle and the bitter honor of remaining true to himself. The more one thinks about it, the more evident it is that the continued development of his talent was ensured by the surge of incessantly renewed aspirations and by the stimulus of the noble demands he has made on himself.

Ever on the alert, Henri Matisse delights in capturing anything that pleases his profound and lucid sight. He welcomes the sunbeam that kindles the brilliance of chrysanthemums and tulips in the half-shadows, or the bright reflections on the shimmering surface of a ceramic or of golden tableware. His sense of intimacy—comparable to Francis Jammes's or Edouard Vuillard's—is manifest in the most felicitous ways in his depictions of the family hearth, sometimes deserted, always serene, even when the thread is being spun there. Out of doors, we find a Matisse smitten by the solemnity of mountains whose snowy peaks rip the sky. Or more simply, who paints the wave-battered Belle-Ile coast, the quais of the Seine buried in snow, or Corsica with its blooming almond trees and its olive trees with their gray-green leaves, edging the blue sea. Other festivals of light and color will beckon him in days to come, and always he will strive to capture them with the same all-encompassing effort, ever determined to make the means of expression equal the sensitivity of his vision, and to express the harmonies between the external world and his own character, at once so passionate and tender.

Francis Jammes (1868–1938), French poet and novelist; Edouard Vuillard (1868–1940), French painter and printmaker known for his domestic interiors.

Charles Morice
MERCURE DE FRANCE
"Modern Art"
August 1904

Charles Morice (1869–1919), Symbolist writer, dramatist, critic, and a staunch supporter of Paul Gauguin. He was one of the few critics to review Matisse's show at the Vollard gallery, even though he had been critical of Matisse's contribution to the 1903 Salon des Indépendants.

HENRI MATISSE EXHIBITION. *Vollard Gallery.* I must admit that I was slow to understand the talent, vision, and methods of M. Henri Matisse. Is this entirely my fault? Last year I accused him of unnecessary distortion, for neither beauty nor expression gained anything from that violence—or seemed to me to gain anything. Since then, however, I have registered my esteem for this artist whom I had not understood, or by any means accepted. Today, in view of his latest exhibit, of such importance, I have no hesitation in declaring the growing affinity I feel for him. Is his talent developing, or is it my understanding? Probably both. I believe I have entered more deeply than before into the secrets of a limited but exquisite and sincere vision. Studies such as his *Chezières Road to Villars*, his *Snow Effect (View of Pont Saint-Michel, in Paris)*, his *Woman Reading in a Violet Dress*, his many still lifes, and, perhaps most of all, the composition entitled *Interior, Light*, testify to both a fine instinct and a rare skill. Yet, shall I say that in them I see the signs of a powerful, creative individuality? I shall not. For it is quite clear that Gustave Moreau's pupil has turned toward the ceaselessly broadened and, daily, more crowded path laid by Cézanne, that benevolent despot of young painters. But that choice, while it records resolute preferences, cannot be considered incontrovertible proof of originality. And I see, too, that M. Henri Matisse is eminently a painter, but that is all he is. The artist slips away in the technician's special forays. In other words, M. H. Matisse's painting bears witness to the pleasure he finds in colors, in tones, in their relationships; but those relationships stand for themselves alone. This artist unquestionably has the taste, the passion, for the *techniques* of his art, but he perhaps has not grasped the full meaning *of his art.*

Louis Vauxcelles
GIL BLAS
"The Salon d'Automne"
14 October 1904

The fourth, and incontestably the strongest of the four, is M. Matisse, whose sketches, with their pure singing reds and blues, once recalled the watercolors of Signac. Today he too is quite close to Cézanne. To Moreau and Cézanne, with a stop at Signac. This suggestion is evident in his *Dinner Table*, where velvety and perfumed fruits lie on a white tablecloth. Matisse offers an ensemble of supple diversity: views of the Bois, flowers and fruits, actors in artificial poses, all aspects of nature have attracted his deep and clear gaze. Along with his canvases, Matisse is exhibiting two statues, one of a nude man, vigorously accentuated, the other of a young girl, quite amusingly curved.

Louis Vauxcelles
GIL BLAS
"The Salon des Indépendants"
23 March 1905

And here we are in front of the paintings of Henri Matisse. This young painter—yet another dissident from the Moreau studio who has risen freely toward the summits of Cézanne—is assuming, willingly or not, the

Louis Vauxcelles (pseudonym of Louis Mayer, b. 1870), French writer and art critic who coined the terms "Fauvism" and "Cubism," was one of Matisse's most attentive, supportive, yet demanding critics prior to World War I. On this occasion, Matisse was showing with Charles Camoin (1879–1965), Henri Manguin (1874–1949), and Marquet. The preceding summer, he had worked in Saint-Tropez, near Paul Signac (1863–1935), leading exponent of Pointillism, or Neo-Impressionism.

COLORPLATE 4
COLORPLATE 11

This painting was Path in the Bois de Boulogne, 1902; the sculptures were probably The Serf and Madeleine I.

At the 1905 Salon des Indépendants, Matisse created a stir with Luxe, calme et volupté, his most ambitious painting to date, and his first to be done from imagination rather than directly from nature.

position of leader of a school. His friends, Manguin, Camoin, Paviot, Puy, impressed by his robustness, sometimes transform their elder's direct energy into crudeness. M. Matisse is exhibiting primarily still lifes, fruits and glassware, which are the equal of his *Desserte,* shown at the Salon d'Automne. A small, synthetically constructed southern landscape, *The Terrace of Paul Signac at Saint-Tropez,* is one of the strongest canvases at the Salon, along with Dufrenoy's *Crysanthemums* and Marquet's *Quais*; then he turns back and suddenly becomes a neo-impressionist with *Ordre, Luxe et volupté* [sic]. No! I can't see the happy shades of an Orphic ballet wandering in the chaotic luminosity of this landscape, where everything dances, and the clouds, figures, earth, and hills are never in their proper place and plane. Why this incursion into the realm of the theoreticians of the "dot"? Remember, my dear Matisse, the touching experience of old Pissarro; he too believed one day, toward the end of his career, that he had found his road to Damascus in the path dear to Maximilian Luce. He soon left it, took hold of himself, and once again became himself. Your gifts are too magnificent, mixing and balancing intuitive sensations and will, for you to lose your way in experiments which, though admittedly sincere, run counter to your true nature.

Louis Claude Paviot, genre painter.

COLORPLATE 4

COLORPLATE 14

COLORPLATE 13

Georges-Léon Dufrenoy (1870–1942), landscape painter.

Camille Pissarro (1830–1903) worked in a neo-impressionist manner for a few years beginning in the late 1880s, but became disillusioned with the "method of the dot." Maximilien Luce (1858–1941) developed his own neo-impressionist style.

Henri Matisse, Interviewed by E. Tériade

ART NEWS

"Matisse Speaks"

November 1951

DIVISIONISM, 1904

At Saint-Tropez I met Signac and Cross, theoreticians of Divisionism. In their company I worked on my picture *The Terrace at Saint-Tropez*—really the boathouse at Signac's house, which was called La Hune. I also painted the big composition, *Luxe, calme et volupté*—it is still in the Signac collection—a picture made of pure rainbow colors. All the paintings of this school had the same effect: a little pink, a little blue, a little green; a very limited palette with which I didn't feel very comfortable. Cross told me that I wouldn't stick to this theory, but without telling me why. Later I understood. My dominant colors, which were supposed to be supported by contrasts, were eaten away by these contrasts, which I made as important as the dominants. This led me to painting with flat tones: it was Fauvism.

FAUVISM, 1905–10

Fauvism at first was a brief time when we thought it was necessary to exalt all colors together, sacrificing none of them. Later we went back to nuances, which gave us more supple elements than the flat, even tones.

The impressionists' aesthetic seemed just as insufficient to us as the technique of the Louvre, and we wanted to go directly to our needs for expression. The artist, encumbered with all the techniques of the past and present, asked himself: "What do I want?" This was the dominating anxiety of Fauvism. If he starts from within himself, and makes just three spots of color, he finds the beginning of a release from such constraints.

This period lasted for some time, even some years. Once you have reached the point where you take cognizance of the quality of your desire, you begin to consider the object which you are making, and you need to modify your methods in order to become more intelligible to

Matisse himself soon became impatient with the neo-impressionist method, as predicted by the neo-impressionist Henri-Edmond Cross (pseudonym of Henri-Edmond Delacroix, 1856–1910), who arrived in Saint-Tropez in August.

Matisse in his studio with *The Serf* before the arms were removed. Photograph courtesy The Museum of Modern Art, New York.

others, and to organize all the possibilities that you have recognized within yourself.

The man who has meditated on himself for a certain length of time comes back to life sensing the position he can occupy. Then he can act effectively.

My master, Gustave Moreau, used to say that the mannerisms of a style turn against it after a while, and then the picture's qualities must be strong enough to prevent failure. This alerted me against all apparently extraordinary techniques.

The epithet "Fauve" was never accepted by the Fauve painters; it was always considered just a tag issued by the critics. Vauxcelles invented the word. We were showing at the Salon d'Automne; Derain, Manguin, Marquet, Puy and some of the others were exhibiting together in one of the big galleries. The sculptor Marque showed an Italianate bust of a child in the center of this hall. Vauxcelles came in the room and said: "Well, Donatello among the wild beasts!" ["*Tiens, Donatello au milieu des fauves.*"]

A whole group worked along these lines: Vlaminck, Derain, Dufy, Friesz, Braque. Later, each member denied that part of Fauvism he felt to be excessive, each according to his personality, in order to find his own path.

The sculptor Albert Marque (1872–1947)—not to be confused with the painter Albert Marquet. Vauxcelles published this remark; see the review that follows.

Maurice de Vlaminck (1876–1958), Othon Friesz (1879–1949), Georges Braque (1882–1963).

Louis Vauxcelles
GIL BLAS
"The Salon d'Automne"
17 October 1905

Let's deal straightaway with M. Matisse. He has courage, for his entry—as he well knows—will fare about as well as a Christian virgin fed to wild beasts [*fauves*] in the arena. M. Matisse is one of the most robustly gifted of today's painters. He could have obtained easy bravos: he prefers to drive himself, to undertake passionate experiments, to demand of Pointillism more vibration of luminosity. But his concern for form suffers.

Matisse exhibited some of his most radical canvases at the 1905 Salon d'Automne, including The Woman with the Hat *and some colorful landscapes done at Collioure that summer. Here, Vauxcelles first used the term* fauves *("wild beasts"). Later in the same review, he implicitly referred to the paintings of Matisse and his colleagues by calling a sculpture by Marque "A Donatello among the fauves!" See also Vauxcelles' 1907 review of the Salon des Indépendants.*

Maurice Denis
L'ERMITAGE
"Painting"
15 November 1905

But our age is not really bringing forth more exceptional individuals than any other. There are few true originals. Imitators are numerous. They are divided into various groups: there is the school of Cézanne, the school of Guérin, the school of Matisse . . . , etc. It is the school of Matisse that seems the liveliest, the newest, and the most discussed.

Upon entering the gallery devoted to him, at the sight of landscapes, figure studies, or mere sketches, all violently colored, one prepares to scrutinize intentions, ascertain theories; one feels oneself to be entirely

Maurice Denis (1870–1943), French painter and writer on art theory, had been a Nabi and a foremost exponent of Symbolist theory. In 1890 he wrote that "a picture . . . is essentially a flat surface covered with colors arranged in a certain order," but by 1905 he had become more conservative and deeply involved with questions of subject matter and the revival of religious art.

The painter Charles Guérin (1875–1939) had also been a student of Moreau and a friend of Matisse.

in the domain of abstraction. To be sure, as in Van Gogh's most ardent ravings, something remains of initial natural impetus. But what one chiefly finds in Matisse is the artificial; neither the literary artificial, as a quest for idealist expression would be; nor the decorative artificial, like that which the Turkish and Persian rugmakers devised; no, it is something still more abstract, it is painting relieved of everything accidental, painting in itself, the pure act of painting. All of a painting's qualities, other than those of contrasting tones and lines, anything not arrived at by the painter's reason, everything that comes from our instinct and from nature, in short, all the qualities of representation and sensibility are excluded from the work of art. It is, in fact, the quest for the absolute. And yet—strange contradiction—this absolute is limited by the most relative thing there is: personal emotion.

May Matisse forgive me if I do not understand. I am aware of the keenness of his eye, the gifts of his sensibility, and I do believe that I am not mistaken when I seek, at the source of each of his studies, however summarily set down, an impetus from nature.

Now, what you are doing, Matisse, is called *dialectic*: you start from the individual and the multiple, and by means of *definition,* as the neo-Platonists used to say, that is, by means of abstraction and generaliza-

The Serf. 1900–c. 1906. Bronze. 37⅜″ (94.9 cm). Collection, The Museum of Modern Art, New York. Mr. and Mrs. Sam Salz Fund.

Portrait of André Derain. 1905. Canvas. 15½ × 11⅜″ (39 × 29 cm). The Tate Gallery, London.

Woman at the Window. 1905. Canvas.
12½ × 11¾″ (31.8 × 29.9 cm).
Private collection, Switzerland.

tion, you arrive at ideas, at noumena of paintings. You are not satisfied unless all the elements of your work are intelligible to you. Nothing conditional or accidental must remain in your universe: you strip it of everything that does not coincide with the expressive possibilities that reason supplies you with. As if you could, in the domain of your art, escape all the necessities that limit our experience on every hand! We understand, Taine used to say, millions of facts, but by means of a hundred facts that we do not understand. One must be resigned: not everything is intelligible. The idea of reconstructing a wholly new art through reason alone must be abandoned. Still more must sensibility, instinct, be trusted, and without too many qualms must much of the experience of the past be accepted. Recourse to tradition is our best safeguard against the giddiness of reasoning, against theoretical excess.

As original as Matisse's attempts may be, they derive from a systematic spirit that is not new. In Van Gogh's time, many efforts of the same kind ended with identical results. If, going further back, I compare a painting by Puvis de Chavannes and a painting by Poussin, I already notice, beyond fairly similar qualities, this profound difference: that the latter conceals, beneath ornaments borrowed from the rhetoric of his time and beneath the charms of his sensibility, his rigid awareness of his means; whereas the modern master lays bare all that is artificial and intentional in his work. We debate whether Poussin was directly inspired by nature or whether he was obeying his poetics; but we see clearly that Chavannes was applying a system, that he was deliberately idealizing nature. In Poussin's time, the painter's genius had the duty of sifting from the chaotic appearance of things both truth (or rather, verisimilitude) and beauty.

The painter's duty was, so to speak, to ignore nature as we under-

Hippolyte Adolphe Taine (1828–1893), French aesthetician, critic, and historian whose deterministic theories served as the basis for the naturalistic school.

Pierre Puvis de Chavannes (1824–1898), leading French mural painter. Nicolas Poussin (1594–1665), Classical French painter.

stand it, prosaically and photographically: one did not pit style against nature; in the painter's mind, they were supposed to merge; it was understood that nature, ordinarily imperfect in its particular objects, was perfect in its design and in its works *in general*. It is from that generality, Félibien added, that the ancient sculptors drew the perfection of their works. It had not yet been discovered that it is enough to *stylize*—like that, after the fact—any study *from* nature. Isn't the style of Poussin's drawings and his few painted studies equal to that of his paintings? The same is true of Delacroix and all the great masters. All the classic masterpieces are at once ideally beautiful and full of *the natural*. Ah! Matisse! Let us curse the pedants who taught us to make a distinction between prose and poetry in our pictorial language! Let us curse the academics, the landscape painters, and all the dogmatists who imposed on us, under the guise of an ideal, servility towards nature, towards their photographic nature. It is the materialism of our professors that has led us, in reaction, to seek beauty outside of nature, nature through science, and art in theories. Ah! even so, Matisse, let us be objective!

André Félibien des Avaux et de Jouercy (1619–1695), French historian, architect, and theoretician of French Classicism.

André Gide

GAZETTE DES BEAUX-ARTS

"Strolling Through the Salon d'Automne"

December 1905

André Gide (1869–1951), French novelist and critic, who had traveled in Italy with Denis the previous year and seems to have been influenced by Denis's theories. The notion that Matisse's approach to painting was too theoretical persisted over the years.

For the sake of convenience, I am prepared to admit that M. Henri Matisse has the finest natural gifts. The fact is, he has previously given us works full of life and the most felicitous vigor. The canvases he is now exhibiting look like expositions of theorems. I spent a long time in that room. I listened to people as they passed, and when I heard someone exclaim before a Matisse, "This is madness!" I felt like replying: "Not at all, sir. On the contrary, it is a product of theories." Everything in it can be deduced, explained; intuition plays no part. When M. Matisse paints a woman's brow the color of an apple and a tree trunk pure red, he can doubtless tell us, "It's because. . . . " Oh yes, it is reasonable enough, this painting, even rather argumentative. How far from the lyrical extravagance of a Van Gogh! In the wings I can almost hear: "All the tones *must* be extravagant"; "Gray is the enemy of all painting"; "Let the artist never fear to go too far." M. Matisse, that is what you were told.

And I understand only too well how, when you see "the others" don a semblance of style through the use of connections and dead terms; when you see them, in their timidity, find in transitions the excuses and support for their feigned boldness; when you see the way they refuse to release the line, the contour, and likewise cling to a color, shore it up, and darken it in order to express it in shadow—then yes, I can understand how you drove yourself to extremities. "To write well," said Montesquieu, "one must do away with the intermediate ideas." But finally dispensing with *syntax* is not art. On the contrary, long live he who is able to glorify even the most modest usage, to reveal the value of the slightest conjunction! Art dwells not in extremes; it is a *temperate* thing. Tempered by what? By reason, of course! But not argumentative reason. Let us seek other teachings.

These are phrases from Delacroix's Journal *cited by Signac in* D'Eugène Delacroix au néo-impressionnisme *(Paris, 1899), as Gide says in a footnote.*

Letter from Paul Signac to Charles Angrand
On *Le Bonheur de vivre*
14 January 1906

Matisse, whose work I have liked until now, seems to have gone to the dogs. Upon a canvas of two and a half meters he has surrounded some strange characters with a line as thick as your thumb. Then he has covered the whole thing with flat, smooth colors which, however pure, seem disgusting. . . . Ah, those rosy flesh tones! It evokes the worst Ranson (from the Nabi period), the most detestable *cloisonnismes* of the later Anquetin, the multicolored shopfronts of merchants of "colors, varnishes and household goods." Let us work in peace, we old fellows! . . .

Signac—who worked with Matisse in the summer of 1904 and who owned the neo-impressionistic Luxe, calme et volupté—*was bitterly disappointed by* Le Bonheur de vivre. *Here, he severely criticizes it to Charles Angrand (1854–1926), a neo-impressionist colleague.*

Paul Elie Ranson (1862-1909), French painter and craftsman. Louis Anquetin (1861-1932) was the inventor of the post-impressionist style called Cloissonism.

Le Bonheur de vivre. 1906. Canvas. 68½ × 93¾" (174 × 238 cm). Photograph © Copyright 1988, The Barnes Foundation.

Louis Vauxcelles
GIL BLAS
"The Salon des Indépendants"
20 March 1906

A powerful and singular artist like M. Henri Matisse occupies too high a position among the young for one to refrain from telling him what one really thinks.

M. Matisse is unanimously felt to be one of the most gifted artists of the rising generation. He has shown us works of sumptuous iridescence, of Oriental fleeciness. Then, possessed by a noble disquietude, he sought to command the richest lighting effects in mastering the pointillist palette. His picture at the Indépendants of 1905 and his recent submissions to the Salon d'Automne marked a stage on this path. But in them form was sacrificed and it suffered. Today he seems to heed not the sugges-

Matisse had exhibited Luxe, calme et volupté *at the 1905 Salon des Indépendants.*

tion of M. Paul Signac but the perilous constraint of M. Derain. He has abandoned the dot and ended up with coloration through flat planes.

His canvas, which will not be understood, is called *Le Bonheur de vivre.* Creatures in languorous attitudes, with lovely hips, sleep, dream; one, standing, is stretching, hands crossed behind her head; others are playing the panpipe; at right, a slender girl is throwing her arms behind her, enlacing her lover's head in that cool ring. . . . At the center of the composition, a wild round. There are great qualities here: the masses are rhythmically balanced, the green of the trees, the blue of the sea, the pink of the bodies closely enveloped in a halo of complementary violet, harmonize and blend, and a sensation of refreshing joy emanates from this canvas.

But I owe it to myself to tell M. Matisse where I think his error lies. I am well aware that what he seeks is the highest synthesis. But a synthesis should be preceded by long and laborious analyses; simplification must not be confused with schematized and empty insufficiency. Where art is concerned, theories, system, and the abstract must be avoided like the plague. On the other hand, in execution nothing must be left to chance; to enlarge a lovely sketch by squaring it up is an error.

This suggests that Matisse did a full-size cartoon for Le Bonheur de vivre, *as he had for* Luxe, calme et volupté.

Léon Rosenthal
LA CHRONIQUE DES ARTS ET DE LA CURIOSITÉ
A Matisse Exhibition
31 March 1906

This review by art historian Léon Rosenthal (1870–1932) was one of the rare press notices concerning Matisse's second one-man exhibition, Galerie Druet, 19 March–7 April 1906.

M. Henri-Matisse . . . is intent on astonishing and disconcerting the public. He banks on the fear some people have of seeming backward if they fail to be enraptured by the most outrageous ventures. Doubtless every innovator deserves respect, even if he is incompetent and misguided—but only if there is no question about his sincerity. Here, however, whether deliberate or not, we have playacting, and the best favor M. Henri-Matisse's friends could do for him would be to urge him to return in silence to the sort of painting he was doing several years ago and to work only for himself. In giving him that advice, they would also be serving the cause of free art, against which such exhibitions as this provide easy ammunition.

Louis Vauxcelles
GIL BLAS
"In the Grand Palais, the Salon d'Automne"
5 October 1906

M. Matisse. Well, he has gotten a grip on himself, and his trip to the land of the Ilotes seems to have done him no harm. He is returning to the deep and fleecy shimmering of his canvases of four years ago. No more abstraction, no more painting "in itself," in the absolute, or "noumenon pictures." A little red and blue landscape recalls his Saint-Tropez of 1904. The portrait of a girl is very strong. And the large still life, despite certain aspects that are difficult to accept, has a sumptuous harmony. The imprint of objects could be no better seen or rendered. What still shocks me is the disregard for the laws of perspective, the indifference to volume (a lemon is not *flat*, Matisse!). I note for the first time the use of brown—a brown with green earth, or with English green—in M. Matisse's pictures. Only someone with M. Matisse's prodigious qualities could risk that; it would be muddy and sooty in the work of twenty others.

Leo Stein

APPRECIATION: PAINTING, POETRY, AND PROSE

1947

The homes, persons and minds of Picasso and Matisse were extreme contrasts. Matisse—bearded, but with propriety; spectacled neatly; intelligent; freely spoken, but a little shy—in an immaculate room, a place for everything and everything in its place, both within his head and without. Picasso—with nothing to say except an occasional sparkle, his work developing with no plan, but with the immediate outpourings of an intuition which kept on to exhaustion, after which there was nothing till another came. The difference in mental type between Picasso and Matisse came out vividly in a later incident.

At Durand-Ruel's there were at one time two exhibitions on, one of Odilon Redon, and one of Manet. Matisse was at this time specially interested in Redon, because of his own work and because of friendship with the older man, who was then in difficulties. When I happened in he was there, and spoke at length of Redon and Manet, with emphasis on the superior merits of the lesser man. It was quite common for Matisse, whose mind was not rigid, to overflow in some direction because of a temporary interest. He told me he had seen Picasso earlier, and Picasso had agreed with him. This seemed to me improbable. Picasso's appreciations did not have this fluidity, and he had no special interest in Redon. However, there was no reason to say this, so I let it pass.

Later on that same day Picasso came to the house and I told him what Matisse had said about Redon and Manet. Picasso burst out almost angrily, "But that is nonsense. Redon is an interesting painter, certainly, but Manet, Manet is a giant." I answered, "Matisse told me you agreed with him." Picasso, more angrily: "Of course I agreed with him. Matisse talks and talks. I can't talk, so I just said *oui oui oui*. But it's damned nonsense all the same." Picasso, though often influenced by others, was not so openly receptive as Matisse was.

Matisse was a social person rather than a convivial one. Picasso was more convivial than social. Matisse felt himself to be one of many, and Picasso stood apart, alone. He recognized others, of course, but as belonging to another system. There was no fusion. Matisse exhibited everywhere. He always wanted to learn, and believed there was no better way than to see his work alongside the work of everybody else. Picasso never showed with others. It was partly diffidence, partly pride. Once at a salon he said to me, "I don't see how these fellows can exhibit this stuff; of course my work is bad too, but then I know it"; after a mo-

The term "noumenon pictures" had been used by Maurice Denis in his review of the 1905 Salon d'Automne.

Matisse had met the four Steins— Leo (1872–1947), his sister Gertrude (1874–1946), their brother Michael (1865–1938), and his wife, Sarah (1870–1953)—during the 1905 Salon d'Automne, where the Steins purchased The Woman with the Hat. *Matisse and Pablo Picasso (1881–1973) appear to have first met in the spring of 1906.*

Odilon Redon (1840–1916), painter and printmaker greatly admired by Matisse.

Marguerite. 1906. Pen. Photograph: Bibliothèque Nationale, Paris.

ment, "Perhaps they know it too, but they show because it's the best they can do."

Renoir once said, "I want to remain in the ranks"—something Picasso could never have said. He felt himself a man apart—what the story books call a man of genius, though not pretentiously so. But in those days he was not sure. He was not aggressive, but felt the right to be aggressive. Once we were waiting for places in an omnibus, and many went on. After the passengers with lower numbers than ours had mounted, Picasso burst out, "This is not the way it ought to be. The strong should go ahead and take what they want." But he was not very sure. When he had something in his head he could easily put it forth, but when he was fallow there was nothing behind. Matisse often felt uncertain, but he never felt empty. He was eternally revolving the artist's eternal problem: how to realize (to use Cézanne's favorite term). This did not trouble Picasso. He had always been an illustrator, and when he had his theme he could easily develop it.

Fernande Olivier

PICASSO ET SES AMIS
"Henri Matisse"

1933

Fernande Olivier (1881–1956) was Picasso's mistress from 1904 to 1912.

There was something very sympathetic about Matisse. With his regular features and his thick, golden beard, he really looked like a grand old man of art. He seemed to be hiding, though, behind his thick spectacles, and his expression was opaque, gave nothing away, though he always talked for ages as soon as the conversation moved on to painting.

He would argue, assert and endeavor to persuade. He had an astonishing lucidity of mind: precise, concise and intelligent. I think he was a good deal less simple than he liked to appear.

He was already nearly forty-five and very much master of himself. Unlike Picasso, who was usually rather sullen and inhibited at occasions like the Steins' Saturdays, Matisse shone and impressed people.

They were the two painters of whom the most was expected. Was Matisse the founder of Fauvism? I believe that the real father of this school was Derain who, although very young, had shown the first painting to be baptized with this name by Vauxcelles. There is no doubt, though, that Matisse became the leader of the school.

Picasso and Matisse, who were quite friendly with one another, clashed over the birth of Cubism; a subject which managed to startle Matisse out of his normal calm. He lost his temper and talked of getting even with Picasso, of making him beg for mercy. None of this prevented him, some months later, when the new developments in the Spanish painter's work began to bear fruit, from attempting to see some similarity in their artistic ideas.

Great artists need to be backed up by one another.

The painter Manguin was small and dark and looked thoroughly respectable. He was a little younger than Matisse and already the father of a large family. He made the same impression on one as his pictures: banal, correct, calm and not exceptionally talented, but honest and conscientious in his art as in his life.

It would be impossible to mention all the people who used to come to the Steins'. I shall just pick out Pierre Rocher, Max Jacob, Apollinaire, Rouault and Nadelmann the sculptor.

The evenings we spent there were sometimes gay, sometimes not, but they were always stimulating, if only on account of the quantities of works of art which filled the studio.

The Steins had a very important collection of Chinese and Japanese prints, which were extremely beautiful. If one felt bored one could always retire into a corner and sitting comfortably in an armchair forget oneself in contemplation of these masterpieces.

Gertrude Stein
THE AUTOBIOGRAPHY OF ALICE B. TOKLAS

1933

Miss Stein called me and said she wanted to have me meet Matisse. She was talking to a medium sized man with a reddish beard and glasses. He had a very alert although slightly heavy presence and Miss Stein and he seemed to be full of hidden meanings. As I came up I heard her say, Oh yes but it would be more difficult now. We were talking, she said, of a lunch party we had in here last year. We had just hung all the pictures and we asked all the painters. You know how painters are, I wanted to make them happy so I placed each one opposite his own picture, and they were happy so happy that we had to send out twice for more bread, when you know France you will know that that means that they were happy, because they cannot eat and drink without bread and we had to send out twice for bread so they were happy. Nobody noticed my little arrangement except Matisse and he did not until just as he left, and now he says it is a proof that I am very wicked, Matisse laughed and said, yes I know Mademoiselle Gertrude, the world is a theater for you, but there are theaters and theaters, and when you listen so carefully to me and so attentively and do not hear a word I say then I do say that you are very wicked.

*   *   *

The next thing that happened was in the autumn. It was the first year of the autumn salon, the first autumn salon that had ever existed in Paris and they, very eager and excited, went to see it. There they found Matisse's picture afterwards known as *La Femme au Chapeau*. . . .

The show had a great deal of freshness and was not alarming. There were a number of attractive pictures but there was one that was not attractive. It infuriated the public, they tried to scratch off the paint.

Gertrude Stein liked that picture, it was a portrait of a woman with a long face and a fan. It was very strange in its color and in its anatomy. She said she wanted to buy it. Her brother had in the meantime found a white-clothed woman on a green lawn and he wanted to buy it. So as usual they decided to buy two and they went to the office of the secretary of the salon to find out about prices. They had never been in the little room of a secretary of a salon and it was very exciting. The secretary looked up the prices in his catalogue. Gertrude Stein has forgotten how much and even whose it was, the white dress and dog on the green grass, but the Matisse was five hundred francs. The secretary explained that of course one never paid what the artist asked, one suggested a price. They asked what price they should suggest. He asked them what they were willing to pay. They said they did not know. He suggested that they offer four hundred and he would let them know. They agreed and left.

Gertrude Stein's Autobiography of Alice B. Toklas *is full of telling insights into Matisse and the problems he faced between around 1905 and 1910. Unhappy with Stein's interpretations and bothered by some inaccuracies, Matisse wrote a rebuttal in* Testimony Against Gertrude Stein, *a supplement to* Transition, *no. 23 (The Hague, 1934–1935).*

The first Salon d'Automne was held in 1903, not in 1905, as Stein testifies here.

COLORPLATE 71

The next day they received word from the secretary that Monsieur Matisse had refused to accept the offer and what did they want to do. They decided to go over to the salon and look at the picture again. They did. People were roaring with laughter at the picture and scratching at it. Gertrude Stein could not understand why, the picture seemed to her perfectly natural. The Cézanne portrait had not seemed natural, it had taken her some time to feel that it was natural, but this picture by Matisse seemed perfectly natural and she could not understand why it infuriated everybody. Her brother was less attracted but all the same he agreed and they bought it. She then went back to look at it and it upset her to see them all mocking at it. It bothered her and angered her because she did not understand why because to her it was so alright, just as later she did not understand why since the writing was all so clear and natural they mocked at and were enraged by her work.

* * *

Then we went on and saw a Matisse. Ah there we were beginning to feel at home. We knew a Matisse when we saw it, knew at once and enjoyed it and knew that it was great art and beautiful. It was a big figure of a woman lying in among some cactuses. A picture which was after the show to be at the rue de Fleurus. There one day the five year old little boy of the janitor who often used to visit Gertrude Stein who was fond of him, jumped into her arms as she was standing at the open door of the atelier and looking over her shoulder and seeing the picture cried out in rapture, oh là là what a beautiful body of a woman. Miss Stein used always to tell this story when the casual stranger in the aggressive way of the casual stranger said, looking at this picture, and what is that supposed to represent.

COLORPLATE 23

William Carlos Williams
CONTACT
"A Matisse"
1921

William Carlos Williams (1883–1963), American poet and novelist, saw Blue Nude *in December 1920, when it was exhibited at The Modern Gallery, owned by Marius de Zayas.*

On the french grass, in that room on Fifth Ave., lay that woman who had never seen my own poor land. The dust and noise of Paris had fallen from her with the dress and underwear and shoes and stockings which she had just put aside to lie bathing in the sun. So too she lay in the sunlight of the man's easy attention. His eye and the sun had made day over her. She gave herself to them both for there was nothing to be told. Nothing is to be told to the sun at noonday. A violet clump before her belly mentioned that it was spring. A locomotive could be heard whistling beyond the hill. There was nothing to be told. Her body was neither classic nor whatever it might be supposed. There she lay and her curving torso and thighs were close upon the grass and violets.

COLORPLATE 23

So he painted her. The sun had entered his head in the color of sprays of flaming palm leaves. They had been walking for an hour or so after leaving the train. They were hot. She had chosen the place to rest and he had painted her resting, with interest in the place she had chosen.

It had been a lovely day in the air.—What pleasant women are these girls of ours! When they have worn clothes and take them off it is with an effect of having performed a small duty. They return to the sun with a gesture of accomplishment.—Here she lay in this spot today not like

COLORPLATE 9. *Male Model.* 1900. Canvas. 39⅛ × 28⅝″ (99.4 × 72.7).
Collection, The Museum of Modern Art, New York. Kay Sage Tanguy and Abby Aldrich Rockefeller Funds.

COLORPLATE 10. *Luxembourg Gardens.* 1901–02. Canvas. 23⅜ × 32″ (59.5 × 81.5 cm). The Hermitage, Leningrad.

COLORPLATE 11. *Path in the Bois de Boulogne.* 1902. Canvas. 25½ × 32″ (65 × 81.5 cm).
The Pushkin Museum, Moscow. Photo APN, Agence de Presse "Novosti."

COLORPLATE 12. *Carmelina*. 1903. Canvas. 32 × 23¼″ (81.3 × 59 cm).
Tompkins Collection, Courtesy Museum of Fine Arts, Boston.

COLORPLATE 13. *Luxe, calme et volupté.* 1904–05. Canvas. 33⅞ × 45⅝″ (86 × 116 cm).
Photograph: Musée National d'Art Moderne, Centre Georges Pompidou, Paris.

COLORPLATE 14. *The Terrace, Saint-Tropez*. 1904. Canvas. 28¼ × 22¾″ (71.8 × 57.8 cm).
Isabella Stewart Gardner Museum, Boston/Art Resource.

COLORPLATE 15. *The Open Window*. 1905. Canvas. 21¾ × 18⅛″ (55.3 × 46 cm).
From the Collection of Mrs. John Hay Whitney.

COLORPLATE 16. *View of Collioure.* 1905. Canvas. 23⅜ × 28¾″ (59.5 × 73 cm). The Hermitage, Leningrad.

Diana or Aphrodite but with better proof than they of regard for the place she was in. She rested and he painted her.

It was the first of summer. Bare as was his mind of interest in anything save the fullness of his knowledge, into which her simple body entered as into the eye of the sun himself, so he painted her. So she came to America.

No man in my country has seen a woman naked and painted her as if he knew anything except that she was naked. No woman in my country is naked except at night.

In the french sun, on the french grass in a room on Fifth Ave., a french girl lies and smiles at the sun without seeing us.

Louis Vauxcelles

GIL BLAS

"The Salon des Indépendants"

20 March 1907

Vauxcelles had first used the term fauve in his review of the 1905 Salon d'Automne, excerpted in this volume. But it was not until this review that the term came into common usage.

[A] movement I consider dangerous (despite the great sympathy I have for its perpetrators) is taking shape among a small clan of youngsters. A chapel has been established, two haughty priests officiating, Messers Derain and Matisse; a few dozen innocent catechumens have received their baptism. Their dogma amounts to a wavering schematicism that proscribes modeling and volumes in the name of I-don't-know-what pictorial abstraction. This new religion hardly appeals to me. I don't believe in this Renaissance. I wish I could be sure that M. Matisse will again become the solid painter we have known and admired; his panel at the last Salon d'Automne held out hope. But this time he is riding his chimera again. . . . Patience.

* * *

The Fauves!

M. Matisse, chief Fauve; M. Derain, deputy chief Fauve; Messers Othon Friesz and Dufy, Fauve followers; M. Girieud, indecisive Fauve. . . .

Pierre Girieud (1875–1940).

Reclining Nude, I. 1907. Bronze. Length: 20″ (50.8 cm). The Museum of Modern Art, New York.

Let's speak seriously and stop in front of M. Matisse. I admit that I do not understand. An ugly nude woman lying on opaque blue grass under some palm trees. In no event would I wish to offend an artist of whose passion and conviction I am well aware; but the drawing here seems rudimentary to me, the colors cruel; the right arm of the mannish nymph is flat and weighty; the buttocks of the distorted body form an arabesque of foliage that motivates the curve of the woman. The straining of art toward the abstract here is lost on me completely. M. Matisse has also engraved some drawings of distorted and angular nudes on wood. And I remember profound and velvety pictures by Matisse, and delicate and knowing drawings.

Louis Vauxcelles
GIL BLAS
"The Salon d'Automne"
30 September 1907

The Fauves. . . .

Let's enter their lair and try not to let them devour us. We will begin with the unsettling work of Matisse. There is no cause to sneer like a

Blue Nude *was exhibited as* Tableau no. III.

COLORPLATE 23

The Red Madras Hat. 1907. Canvas. 39¼ × 31¾" (99.7 × 80.6 cm). Photograph © Copyright 1988, The Barnes Foundation.

bourgeois snob; I will never laugh at an artist whose efforts are sincere, even if aimed at the false and erroneous. But when I recall the canvases that Matisse and Friesz (his blind follower) once painted, I must warn them once again, even at the risk of causing them pain.

I am, of course, well aware of the decorative merits that Matisse exhibits in his stunning panel of nudes, even in his almost caricatural effigy of a woman. The peacock-blue background of this portrait, considered in itself, is an acceptable thing . . . and the gradations of tones, the transitions that lend them nuance, are seen with an artist's eye. But think of what I am reduced to: praising only the background . . . in a portrait! I also admit that the relations of the yellows and browns with the blue are daring. But what is the meaning of this barbarous drawing? (Compare it, alas—or for the better—to the fine pen drawings by this same Matisse.) What is this bizarre face? Why this hateful contempt for form? You profess that painting, whose goal is to enclose rhythmic volumes in a frame, should resolutely distance itself from the object. No, a thousand times no; all the masters, from El Greco to Manet, from Poussin to Cézanne and Van Gogh—your patron saints—sought to represent the object. To strip painting of its vital elements and reduce it to an abstraction is to act the theoretician, the symbolist, the whatever you will, but it is not painting. When will this true painter find his way out of the impasse he has been treading for the past three years?

Moreover, he is creating a school. . . .

Vauxcelles refers to The Red Madras Hat, *1907, shown on the facing page.*

Guillaume Apollinaire
JE DIS TOUT
"The Salon d'Automne: Matisse"
12 October 1907

Guillaume Apollinaire (pseudonym of Wilhelm Apollinaris de Kostrowitsky, 1880–1918), poët and critic who was an early supporter of Matisse, Picasso, and the avant-garde in general. Here he tells how Matisse was refused by the jury of the 1907 Salon d'Automne.

The *fauve* of *fauves*. No one dared oppose his canvases. The jury had delivered its verdict. The paintings were accepted. The vote had been taken. Then M. Frantz Jourdain remembered the mission entrusted to him by M. Jansen, leader of the Salon d'Automne and a well-known tapestry-maker.

M. Jansen doesn't like Cézanne, or Matisse, or any painting that surpasses M. Abel-Truchet in boldness.

It was to defend his good taste as a tapestry-maker that M. Jansen delegated M. Frantz Jourdain, who handled his assignment rather well.

The works of M. Henri Matisse had been accepted. Then M. Jourdain got up and had *La Coiffeuse*—the largest canvas submitted by Matisse—brought back.

"Gentlemen," said Frantz Jourdain, "in the interests of the Salon d'Automne and those of Matisse himself, I ask that this painting be refused."

Desvallières protested as a spokesman for cultivated taste:

"We are reviewing the work of our friend Matisse as comrades. It is true that it may appear extreme to eyes little familiar with painting. Nevertheless, the vote was taken, and it would be proper to follow the rules."

Rouault, for his part, voiced an objection less gracefully. He too invoked the famous rules. He became enraged and gesticulated in front of the president who, with an iron grip, held him by the neck and shook him like a plum tree.

"I am committed to following the rules," cried Frantz Jourdain, while Rouault, under restraint, began to turn purple. "You understand, I must

Frantz Jourdain (1847–1935); Max Jansen (1871–1912).

Georges-Olivier Desvallières (1861–1950), among other things a painter who became known for religious subjects. See his preface to Matisse's "Notes of a Painter," further in this volume.

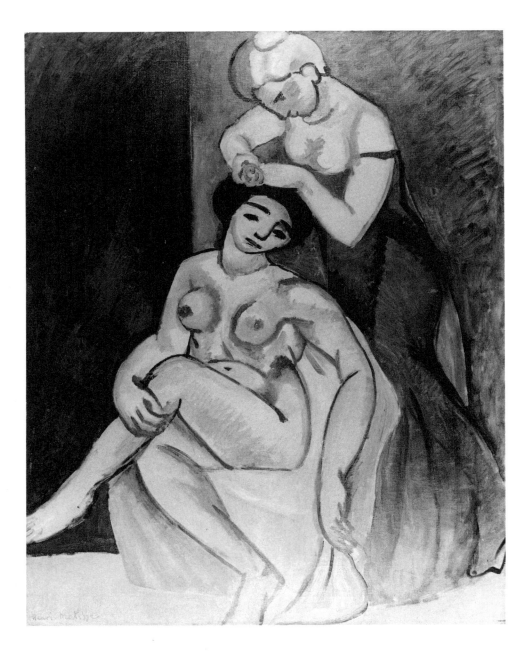

La Coiffure. 1907. Canvas. 45⅝ × 35″
(116 × 89 cm). Staatsgalerie, Stuttgart.

follow the rules. I know very well that I will be devoured by the 'wild beasts,' but I don't give a damn."

And he did not allow anyone to change his mind. While the unhappy Rouault, collapsed on a chair, was regaining his breath, the previous vote was overturned and Matisse's *La Coiffeuse* was refused.

Louis Rouart

L'OCCIDENT

"Reflections on the Salon d'Automne"

November 1907

In this review, Louis Rouart (1833–1912), a friend of Maurice Denis, reflects the anti-Semitism that sometimes got mixed up with aesthetic issues around the time of the Dreyfus case.

What can be said about M. Matisse? In the eyes of some he is a scholar who, to cover his canvases with painting, must rely on mathematics. . . . Others regard him as a narrow-minded fanatic who forces wrong-headed ideas to absurd conclusions. The most clear-sighted view him as nothing but a mediocre, ordinary figure tortured by the desire to be original. He is taken seriously only by two or three Jews from San Francisco and by a few dealers who think that works of art . . . need have no more real value than stocks do.

Michel Puy

LA PHALANGE

"The Fauves"

15 November 1907

The critic Michel Puy (b. 1878), brother of painter Jean Puy, gives here one of the first formulations of the history of Fauvism, exerting much influence on subsequent accounts.

Beginning in 1906, he returned to his earlier tendencies; at the Indépendants' he showed a large decorative canvas, which had the flaw of appearing too schematic. Since then he has continued until the Salon d'Automne of this year, 1907, where he is represented by *Tête d'expression, Le Luxe, Music,* and two landscapes.

Are these five canvases really sketches, as the catalogue would have it? One would prefer that Matisse give up putting into a painting forms that matter only for guidance and for the general understanding that

Tête d'expression is The Red Madras Hat, *1907.* Music, *in this case, is* Music (Sketch), *1907.*

COLORPLATE 24

The Riverbank. 1907. Canvas. 28¾ × 23⅝" (73 × 60 cm). Öffentliche Kunstsammlung Basel.

they impart, but do not at all enter into the conception we have of a definitive work; as for his "expressive head," in which he attempts to suggest relief solely by the way he guides and limits the outline, a certain comical effect was inescapable.

But if this determination to simplify, this disdain of accommodating himself to the spectator's imagination, is disturbing, one cannot, looking at these canvases together, keep from admiring their pictorial beauty. One perceives such confidence in their color distribution—their various tones complement each other so fully—that one feels uplifted by the painterly qualities displayed in them, though they may appear less in conformity with the requirements that our most admired painters—to say nothing of Cézanne and Gauguin—have for interpreting the human form in a finished work. And when one leaves these canvases, having grown fiercely demanding about the paintings one is going to see, one is inclined not to forgive other artists for failing to give us this impression of strength, solidity, and confidence that Matisse has offered.

It may be difficult for the public to explain the disdain for presentation that certain artists flaunt. This disdain is more apparent than real. Matisse is fully aware of the interest a less disturbing rendition would have had for most viewers.

But before thinking of pleasing, and especially pleasing a great many people, one must satisfy one's own need to grasp a truth that is elusive and glimpsed only at a distance. The artist obeys reasoning not so much as the promptings of his own temperament. He is guided by an internal force he knows poorly, one which often leads him astray, but which invariably sets him on his way. Having tended toward rather realistic transcription, Matisse dreamt of freeing himself, of painting boldly, without worrying about detail, of fulfilling his desire for repose, peace, a relaxation almost purely physiological, which constitutes a profound human feeling in an age when mankind, beset by professional cares, grows exhausted and worn out. He might well have recalled the words of the poet Jean Royère: "My poetry is an intense stillness." There is nothing stranger in an impassioned, tortured, fervent artist than this desire to achieve tranquility.

Jean Royère (b. 1871), poet.

Actually, his oeuvre, which has gone from dark to light, through some wide-ranging volleys, continues perfectly intact; when he was at the Ecole des Beaux-Arts, his dark canvases, which had, already with a subtle harmony about them, the patina of old leather, aspired to the same structural stability he would give to his later works. Afterward, his manner became more conscious, stronger; he gave order to his composition by paying closer attention to the broader outlines and reducing the importance of secondary lines and details. Finally, he thought he discovered the futility of laboring to direct each stroke precisely from place to place that because of its heartbreaking minutiae makes the artist a slave to his craft, stunts his efforts and, shackling him to grammatical and syntactical matters alone, keeps him from revealing himself. Since then, he has been grappling with decorative panels, where his gifts as a harmonist, supported by his exceptional skill, are happily put to use.

He pursues his aim so ardently and is so steeped in his subject that incidentals fall away. In his passion for the decorative, he runs the risk of losing himself in one decorative theme. The danger for him is that of lacking restraint and of drawing too-categorical conclusions from his observations.

James Huneker

NEW YORK SUN

On the Photo-Secession Gallery
Exhibition

July 1908

This is a sample of the reviews Matisse received on his first New York exhibition, 6–25 April 1908. The gallery, also known as the 291 Gallery, was co-founded in 1905 by photographers Alfred Stieglitz and Edward Steichen as a showplace for the work of the Photo-Secession Group.

For agility of line, velocity in its notation and an uncompromising attitude in the presence of the human machine, we must go to the exhibition of drawings, lithographs, watercolors, and etchings by Henri Matisse at the Little Galleries of the Photo-Secession, 291 Fifth Avenue. . . . The French painter is clever, diabolically clever. Lured by the neo-impressionists, by Gauguin's South Sea sketches, he has outdone them all by his extravagances. His line, its zigzag simplifications evidently derived from the Japanese, is swirling and strong. With three furious scratches he can

Decorative Figure. 1908. Bronze. 28¾" (73 cm). Hirshhorn Museum and Sculpture Garden, Smithsonian Institution, Gift of Joseph H. Hirshhorn, 1966.

give you a female animal in all her shame and horror. Compared to these memoranda of the gutter and brothel the sketches of Rodin (once exhibited in this gallery) are academic, are meticulous. There is one nude which the fantasy of the artist has turned into a hideous mask. The back of a reclining figure is on the wall opposite, and it is difficult not to applaud, so virile and masterly are its strokes. Then a creature from God knows what Parisian shambles leers at you—the economy of means employed and the results are alike significant—and you flee into another room. The watercolors are Japanese in suggestion, though not in spirit. They are Impressionism run to blotches, mere patches of crude hectic tintings. What Matisse can do in his finished performances we shall see later. His sketches are those of a brilliant, cruel temperament. Nor has he the saving cynicism of a Toulouse-Lautrec. To be cynical argues some interest; your pessimist is often a man of inverted sentiment. But Matisse is only cold, the coldness of the moral vivisector.

Louis Vauxcelles

GIL BLAS

"The Salon d'Automne"

30 September 1908

M. Matisse. For some years his name had been synonymous with "bourgeois amusement." Philistine Parisian snobs would beat a path to the Grand-Palais or the Serres de la Ville to marvel at Matisse's latest efforts. And I must admit that for the past two or three years this greatly talented colorist has been showing disturbing signs of a lack of balance. He has been seeking, groping, losing his way. The Polynesian hematinism of some of his friends has haunted him. But here, at last, he is in full and masterful possession of his talents, despite the portrait of a young boy and the large central decoration, which I fail to appreciate.

His *Desserte* is superb. The warm harmonies of blue and black, combined with the glimmering red and yellow glints of the apples and lemons, are a match for a beautiful Cézanne. The other still life is a sumptuous Turkestan rug. Playfully, perhaps to demonstrate the logic of his efforts and his development, Matisse is also exhibiting a set of two *Nudes:* one, painted ten years ago, is notable for its robust austerity; the other, on a green background, painted a few weeks ago, is a grand synthesis, superb in its bulk. Other works by the same spirited painter—one of the most powerful works of the past, one of the most powerful of today—complete the exhibit: a red carnation in a black jar against a bronze statue, tulip bulbs in those slightly acidic hues that Cézanne often liked. And several handsome drawings. In addition—apart from a plaster statue that seems half-Gothic, half-Hindu—there is a display of sculpture of the same material, the shapes sometimes warped into bizarre contortions, but their character tense and quite lively.

At the 1908 Salon d'Automne, Matisse was given a retrospective similar to those that had been given to major nineteenth-century masters like Renoir, Gauguin, and Cézanne. He sent eleven paintings, six drawings, and thirteen sculptures, effectively classing himself among the modern masters.

COLORPLATE 29

The "large central decoration" is Harmony in Red, *1908; This* Desserte *is also known as* Blue Still Life, *1908.*

Mérodack Josephin Péladan

LA REVUE HEBDOMADAIRE

"The Salon d'Automne and Its El Greco and Monticelli Retrospectives"

17 October 1908

Mérodack Joséphin Péladan (1859–1918), novelist and critic, founder of a Parisian mystical order of Catholic Rosicrucians, the Rose + Croix. Matisse responded to this criticism in "Notes of a Painter," below.

Each year it becomes more difficult to speak of these people who are called *les fauves* in the press. They are curious to see beside their canvases. Correct, rather elegant, they might be taken for department-store floorwalkers. Ignorant and lazy, they try to offer the public colorlessness and formlessness.

The "school art" society has a zealot, M. Georges Moreau, who brought together in a delightful volume highly curious samples of infantile drawing. In it can be seen sketches by urchins between the ages of six and sixteen, none of whom is gifted, except in sincerity: They could become masters and have the calling for an autumn salon and generally be quite a bit better than *les fauves* usually are.

* * *

The public, insensitive to the arduous striving toward beauty, asks only to be entertained. A clown is the leading attraction at the circus, and thousands of artists ape Chocolat. Except that it is the canvas that suffers the blows in color. Truth, most despairing of the Muses, terrible Truth, would say: "Were M. Matisse to paint honestly he would be virtually unknown; he shows off as at the fairground and the public knows him." By "honestly" I mean with respect to the ideal and the rules, without which there is no hope, nor bread, for the artist.

Chocolat was a popular clown.

Charles Morice

MERCURE DE FRANCE

"Modern Art"

1 November 1908

M. Henri-Matisse, whose exhibition is, by all means, very important, continues to worry his enemies without reassuring his friends. One cannot explain the kind of quiet exasperation through which his deformations appear if not by a need to escape false rules, to avoid success in a time where art is on the fringe of life; but there are perhaps other ways out. . . .

I have—like he himself, as I could say, in the choice of his direction—very much hesitated in my appreciation of this artist, whose audacities are surely rational but disconcerting. Science and calculation are more perceptible than instinct in M. Matisse's work. One cannot deny, though, that as a painter he had the gift of a rare colorist, and as a sculptor, a sense of modeling. It is with sympathy that I look for the meaning of the exaggerations of the forms, of the sudden breaking of lines, which is the price we pay for enjoying his powerful and ostentatious color and the charm of certain bits of sculpture—ah! the back of one of these little figurines of women, in the glass case—I am looking for it . . . and, immediately, I cannot be proud of having found it. But if a friend of mine, touching my shoulder while I am studying the *Decorative Panel for a Dining Room*, obliges me to turn around: beyond the friend, I see suddenly the considerable painting of M. Vallotton, *Europe*, and immediately after, I go back to M. Matisse, irresistibly. With what eloquence those two in their dialogue work, these two aesthetics. And in the structure of this room, there is some great art criticism! It is not completely fair to stay with the absolute. Some excesses become clear through their opposites. The possibility of M. Vallotton implies the necessity of M. Matisse. Not that I deny the merits of the first, or his knowledge or sincerity; but they are distorted by their use, which leads to a negative conclusion. On the other hand, I do not want to exaggerate M. Matisse's personality. The method of his mind, although systematic, lacks clarity. The draftsman and the colorist, separated, are very interesting; in their union, one of them succumbs, and it is the draftsman, the constructor: how else can one explain the way the alphabet of tones, in this painter's work, is so harmoniously explicit, while his alphabet of lines is so obscure? I believe I see in M. Henri-Matisse, whose artistic loyalty is beyond question, the expression, acute to the point of being tragic, of the modern torment. Like all his emulators, he felt the need to react against traditions, old or recent, by going back to principles. But as a rational and critical mind, he sought principles not so much in nature as in himself and in the mathematics of his art. He forbids himself all kinds of spontaneity and holds his imagination back firmly. Perhaps this is the source of the dryness and the violence that in his best pieces make us sad.

COLORPLATE 29

Félix Vallotton (1865–1925), Swiss painter and graphic artist.

Two Negresses. 1908. Bronze. 18½″ (47 cm). Hirshhorn Museum and Sculpture Garden, Smithsonian Institution, Gift of Joseph H. Hirshhorn, 1966.

One senses in him a constant tension, a nervous exacerbation that is not, I believe, natural to him, but that reflects the sickly state of a mind over-worked by probing and ambition. There is nothing more noble, and, no doubt, nothing more painful.

Bernard Berenson
THE NATION
"Letter to the Editor"
12 November 1908

Bernard Berenson (1865–1959), art historian, critic, and connoisseur, especially of Italian Renaissance art. His letter was a reply to a review of the 1908 Salon d'Automne in The Nation, *29 October 1908, that characterized Matisse's works as "direct insults to eyes and understanding."*

Will you allow one of the fools whom Matisse has thoroughly taken in to protest against these phrases? They are more hackneyed than the oldest mumblings in the most archaic extant rituals. There is nothing so hoary in the sacrificial Vedas. They have been uttered with head-shakings in Akkadian, in Egyptian, in Babylonian, in Mycenaean, in the language of the Double-Ax, in all the Pelasgic dialects, in proto-Doric, in Hebrew, and in every living and dead tongue of western Europe, wherever an artist has appeared whose work was not as obvious as the "best seller" and "fastest reader." Of what great painter or sculptor or musician of the last centuries has it not been said in the cant phrase of the Boulevards—*"C'est un fumiste. Il cherche à épâter le monde"*?

C'est un fumiste. Il cherche à épâter le monde: *He's a charlatan. He wants to shock everyone.*

Henri Matisse seems to me to think of everything in the world rather than of the need of "doing differently from all other artists." On the contrary, I have the conviction that he has, after twenty years of very earnest searching, at last found the great highroad traveled by all the best masters of the visual arts for the last sixty centuries at least. Indeed, he is singularly like them in every essential respect. He is a magnificent draftsman and a great designer. Of his color I do not venture to speak. Not that it displeases me—far from it. But I can better understand its failing to charm at first; for color is something we Europeans are still singularly uncertain of—we are easily frightened by the slightest divergence from the habitual.

Fifty years ago, Mr. Quincy Shaw and other countrymen of ours were the first to appreciate and patronize Corot, Rousseau, and the stupendous Millet. *Quantum mutatus ab illo!* It is now the Russians and, to a less extent, the Germans, who are buying the work of the worthiest successors of those first mighty ones.

Quantum mutatus ab illo! *How changed from what he once was!*

Georges Desvallières
LA GRANDE REVUE
Preface to "Notes of a Painter"
25 December 1908

Georges-Olivier Desvallières (1861–1950), painter, esteemed figure in Parisian art circles, and chief art critic of La Grande Revue, *who apparently solicited an article from Matisse for the December issue. Desvallière's essay prepared his mainly literary readers for Matisse's pictorial ideas.*

The work of M. Matisse arouses too much disdain, anger, and admiration for the *Grand Revue* to be content with the inevitably hasty evaluations offered thus far by the critics we have sent to cover the various exhibitions in which that work has been available for examination.

It was felt that the best exponent of these works would be their author himself. He was kind enough to offer us the remarks that follow, and we requested that he accompany these notes with a sampling of reproductions of his paintings and drawings so that the public may compare what M. Matisse says, thinks, and actually does.

It must be acknowledged, after reading these notes and examining the drawings, that whatever reservations one may have about this artist, his efforts have aided the development of our techniques of creative expression—not by extravagant innovations, but simply by relying on the instinctive inspiration of medieval artists, Hindus, and Oriental decorators.

Like our ancestors, the Romanesque craftsmen who distorted their figures in accordance with the need for balance between the overall structure and the personalities who had to be depicted within it, Matisse takes full account of the rectangle formed by the paper on which he draws.

The drawing in the picture on page [97], for example, though not an accurate depiction of the idea we may have of a woman in that position, is nevertheless not untrue to that idea, for the size of the head is just what it must be, given the volume of the foot and the slenderness of the torso, these various parts of the body having been carefully designed so that the white spaces between the edge of the paper and the lines of the figure form an expressive decoration. In short, the structure Matisse creates with these disproportionate fragments is a solid one whose proportions are correct, even though the figure depicted gives an impression of nature different from that commonly seen. In his treatment of the colors of objects and people he has also made use of the relationships of color found in Persian carpets, and has achieved this through a method in which the contributions of modern knowledge are not without their influence. Indeed, that influence may even be too great, sometimes causing him to fall into paradox.

Our personal sense of good taste may therefore be occasionally affronted, but even then our artistic intelligence never remains unmoved by this artist's discoveries, for they have freed us from innumerable pedestrian habits of the hand. He has in a sense freed our eye and broadened our understanding of drawing, and no one can produce sound work today without studying the contributions of this school.

Desvallières refers to a nude, Standing Model, *1906–07. See page 97 of this volume.*

Henri Matisse
LA GRANDE REVUE
"Notes of a Painter"
25 December 1908

A painter who addresses the public not just in order to present his works, but to reveal some of his ideas on the art of painting, exposes himself to several dangers.

In the first place, knowing that many people like to think of painting as an appendage of literature and therefore want it to express not general ideas suited to pictorial means, but specifically literary ideas, I fear that one will look with astonishment upon the painter who ventures to invade the domain of the literary man. As a matter of fact, I am fully aware that a painter's best spokesman is his work.

However, such painters as Signac, Desvallières, Denis, Blanche, Guérin and Bernard have written on such matters and been well re-

Matisse's earliest, most important theoretical credo became one of the most influential artistic statements of the twentieth century. He explains some basic tenets of his art and responds to his critics. It was translated into German and Russian soon after its publication in French. For an analysis of this seminal text, see Roger Benjamin, Matisse's "Notes of a Painter": Criticism, Theory, and Context, 1891–1908, *(1987).*

Jacques-Emile Blanche (1861–1942), Emile Bernard (1868–1941).

ceived by various periodicals. Personally, I shall simply try to state my feelings and aspirations as a painter without worrying about the writing.

But now I foresee the danger of appearing to contradict myself. I feel very strongly the tie between my earlier and my recent works, but I do not think exactly the way I thought yesterday. Or rather, my basic idea has not changed, but my thought has evolved, and my modes of expression have followed my thoughts. I do not repudiate any of my paintings but there is not one of them that I would not redo differently, if I had it to redo. My destination is always the same but I work out a different route to get there.

Finally, if I mention the name of this or that artist it will be to point out how our manners differ, and it may seem that I am belittling his work. Thus I risk being accused of injustice towards painters whose aims and results I best understand, or whose accomplishments I most appreciate, whereas I will have used them as examples, not to establish my superiority over them, but to show more clearly, through what they have done, what I am attempting to do.

What I am after, above all, is expression. Sometimes it has been conceded that I have a certain technical ability but that all the same my ambition is limited, and does not go beyond the purely visual satisfaction such as can be obtained from looking at a picture. But the thought of a painter must not be considered as separate from his pictorial means, for the thought is worth no more than its expression by the means, which must be more complete (and by complete I do not mean complicated) the deeper is his thought. I am unable to distinguish between the feeling I have about life and my way of translating it.

Expression, for me, does not reside in passions glowing in a human face or manifested by violent movement. The entire arrangement of my picture is expressive: the place occupied by the figures, the empty spaces around them, the proportions, everything has its share. Composition is the art of arranging in a decorative manner the diverse elements at the painter's command to express his feelings. In a picture every part will be visible and will play its appointed role, whether it be principal or secondary. Everything that is not useful in the picture is, it follows, harmful. A work of art must be harmonious in its entirety: any superfluous detail would replace some other essential detail in the mind of the spectator.

Composition, the aim of which should be expression, is modified according to the surface to be covered. If I take a sheet of paper of a given size, my drawing will have a necessary relationship to its format. I would not repeat this drawing on another sheet of different proportions, for example, rectangular instead of square. Nor should I be satisfied with a mere enlargement, had I to transfer the drawing to a sheet the same shape, but ten times larger. A drawing must have an expansive force which gives life to the things around it. An artist who wants to transpose a composition from one canvas to another larger one must conceive it anew in order to preserve its expression; he must alter its character and not just square it up onto the larger canvas.

Matisse himself had in fact "squared up" a number of his larger works, such as Luxe, calme et volupté *(1904–05),* The Port of Abaill, Collioure *(1905–06),* Le Bonheur de vivre *(1905–06), and* Le Luxe *(1907).*

Both harmonies and dissonances of color can produce agreeable effects. Often when I start to work I record fresh and superficial sensations during the first session. A few years ago I was sometimes satisfied with the result. But today if I were satisfied with this, now that I think I can see further, my picture would have a vagueness in it: I should have recorded the fugitive sensations of a moment which could not completely define my feelings and which I should barely recognize the next day.

I want to reach that state of condensation of sensations which makes a painting. I might be satisfied with a work done at one sitting, but I would soon tire of it; therefore, I prefer to rework it so that later I may

77

recognize it as representative of my state of mind. There was a time when I never left my paintings hanging on the wall because they reminded me of moments of over-excitement and I did not like to see them again when I was calm. Nowadays I try to put serenity into my pictures and re-work them as long as I have not succeeded.

Suppose I want to paint a woman's body: first of all I imbue it with grace and charm, but I know that I must give something more. I will condense the meaning of this body by seeking its essential lines. The charm will be less apparent at first glance, but it must eventually emerge from the new image which will have a broader meaning, one more fully human. The charm will be less striking since it will not be the sole quality of the painting, but it will not exist less for its being contained within the general conception of the figure.

Charm, lightness, freshness—such fleeting sensations. I have a canvas on which the colors are still fresh and I begin to work on it again. The tone will no doubt become duller. I will replace my original tone with one of greater density, an improvement, but less seductive to the eye.

The impressionist painters, especially Monet and Sisley, had delicate sensations, quite close to each other: as a result their canvases all look alike. The word "impressionism" perfectly characterizes their style, for they register fleeting impressions. It is not an appropriate designation for certain more recent painters who avoid the first impression, and consider it almost dishonest. A rapid rendering of a landscape represents only one moment of its existence [durée]. I prefer, by insisting upon its essential character, to risk losing charm in order to obtain greater stability.

Underlying this succession of moments which constitutes the superficial existence of beings and things, and which is continually modifying and transforming them, one can search for a truer, more essential character, which the artist will seize so that he may give to reality a more lasting interpretation. When we go into the seventeenth- and eighteenth-century sculpture rooms in the Louvre and look, for example, at a Puget, we can see that the expression is forced and exaggerated to the point of being disquieting. It is quite a different matter if we go to the Luxembourg; the attitude in which the sculptors catch their models is always the

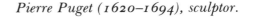

Pierre Puget (1620–1694), sculptor.

Sculpture and Persian Vase. 1908.
Canvas. 23⅝ × 29″ (60 × 73.7 cm).
Nasjonalgalleriet, Oslo.

one in which the development of the members and tensions of the muscles will be shown to greatest advantage. And yet movement thus understood corresponds to nothing in nature: when we capture it by surprise in a snapshot, the resulting image reminds us of nothing that we have seen. Movement seized while it is going on is meaningful to us only if we do not isolate the present sensation either from that which precedes it or that which follows it.

There are two ways of expressing things; one is to show them crudely, the other is to evoke them through art. By removing oneself from the literal *representation* of movement one attains greater beauty and grandeur. Look at an Egyptian statue: it looks rigid to us, yet we sense in it the image of a body capable of movement and which, despite its rigidity, is animated. The Greeks too are calm: a man hurling a discus will be caught at the moment in which he gathers his strength, or at least, if he is shown in the most strained and precarious position implied by his action, the sculptor will have epitomized and condensed it so that equilibrium is re-established, thereby suggesting the idea of duration. Movement is in itself unstable and is not suited to something durable like a statue, unless the artist is aware of the entire action of which he represents only a moment.

I must precisely define the character of the object or of the body that I wish to paint. To do so, I study my method very closely: If I put a black dot on a sheet of white paper, the dot will be visible no matter how far away I hold it: it is a clear notation. But beside this dot I place another one, and then a third, and already there is confusion. In order for the first dot to maintain its value I must enlarge it as I put other marks on the paper.

If upon a white canvas I set down some sensations of blue, of green, of red, each new stroke diminishes the importance of the preceding ones. Suppose I have to paint an interior: I have before me a cupboard; it gives me a sensation of vivid red, and I put down a red which satisfies me. A relation is established between this red and the white of the canvas. Let me put a green near the red, and make the floor yellow; and again there will be relationships between the green or yellow and the white of the canvas which will satisfy me. But these different tones mutually weaken one another. It is necessary that the various marks I use be balanced so that they do not destroy each other. To do this I must organize my ideas; the relationship between the tones must be such that it will sustain and not destroy them. A new combination of colors will succeed the first and render the totality of my representation. I am forced to transpose until finally my picture may seem completely changed when, after successive modifications, the red has succeeded the green as the dominant color. I cannot copy nature in a servile way; I am forced to interpret nature and submit it to the spirit of the picture. From the relationship I have found in all the tones there must result a living harmony of colors, a harmony analogous to that of a musical composition.

For me all is in the conception. I must therefore have a clear vision of the whole from the beginning. I could mention a great sculptor who gives us some admirable pieces: but for him a composition is merely a grouping of fragments, which results in a confusion of expression. Look instead at one of Cézanne's pictures: all is so well arranged that no matter at what distance you stand or how many figures are represented you will always be able to distinguish each figure clearly and to know which limb belongs to which body. If there is order and clarity in the picture, it means that from the outset this same order and clarity existed in the mind of the painter, or that the painter was conscious of their necessity. Limbs may cross and intertwine, but in the eyes of the spectator they will nevertheless remain attached to and help to articulate the right body: all confusion has disappeared.

Matisse appears to provide the rationale for his repainting around that time of Harmony in Red, *which began as a mostly blue–green composition.*

Auguste Rodin (1840–1917).

79

The chief function of color should be to serve expression as well as possible. I put down my tones without a preconceived plan. If at first, and perhaps without my having been conscious of it, one tone has particularly seduced or caught me, more often than not once the picture is finished I will notice that I have respected this tone while I progressively altered and transformed all the others. The expressive aspect of colors imposes itself on me in a purely instinctive way. To paint an autumn landscape I will not try to remember what colors suit this season, I will be inspired only by the sensation that the season arouses in me: the icy purity of the sour blue sky will express the season just as well as the nuances of foliage. My sensation itself may vary, the autumn may be soft and warm like a continuation of summer, or quite cool with a cold sky and lemon-yellow trees that give a chilly impression and already announce winter.

My choice of colors does not rest on any scientific theory; it is based on observation, on sensitivity, on felt experiences. Inspired by certain pages of Delacroix, an artist like Signac is preoccupied with complementary colors, and the theoretical knowledge of them will lead him to use a certain tone in a certain place. But I simply try to put down colors which render my sensation. There is an impelling proportion of tones that may lead me to change the shape of a figure or to transform my composition. Until I have achieved this proportion in all the parts of the composition I strive towards it and keep on working. Then a moment comes when all the parts have found their definite relationships, and from then on it would be impossible for me to add a stroke to my picture without having to repaint it entirely.

In reality, I think that the very theory of complementary colors is not absolute. In studying the paintings of artists whose knowledge of colors depends upon instinct and feeling, and on a constant analogy with their sensations, one could define certain laws of color and so broaden the limits of color theory as it is now defined.

What interests me most is neither still life nor landscape, but the human figure. It is that which best permits me to express my almost religious awe towards life. I do not insist upon all the details of the face, on setting them down one-by-one with anatomical exactitude. If I have an Italian model who at first appearance suggests nothing but a purely animal existence, I nevertheless discover his essential qualities, I penetrate amid the lines of the face those which suggest the deep gravity which persists in every human being. A work of art must carry within itself its complete significance and impose that upon the beholder even before he recognizes the subject matter. When I see the Giotto frescoes at Padua I do not trouble myself to recognize which scene of the life of Christ I have before me, but I immediately understand the sentiment which emerges from it, for it is in the lines, the composition, the color. The title will only serve to confirm my impression.

What I dream of is an art of balance, of purity and serenity, devoid of troubling or depressing subject matter, an art which could be for every mental worker, for the businessman as well as the man of letters, for example, a soothing, calming influence on the mind, something like a good armchair which provides relaxation from physical fatigue.

Often a discussion arises as to the value of different processes, and their relationship to different temperaments. A distinction is made between painters who work directly from nature and those who work purely from imagination. Personally, I think neither of these methods must be preferred to the exclusion of the other. Both may be used in turn by the same individual, either because he needs contact with objects in order to receive sensations that will excite his creative faculty, or because his sensations are already organized. In either case he will be able to arrive at that totality which constitutes a picture. In any event I think

The "autumn landscape" referred to is apparently The Forest at Fontainebleau, *1908.*

COLORPLATE 31

This celebrated passage, for many years used to trivialize Matisse's art, probably refers to his desire to accommodate his patron, Sergei Shchukin, who had suffered a number of personal tragedies and for whom "living in a picture" provided spiritual comfort.

COLORPLATE 17. *Landscape at Collioure*. 1905. Canvas. 15⅜ × 18¼″ (39 × 46.7 cm).
Collection Mrs. Bertram Smith. Photograph courtesy The Museum of Modern Art, New York.

COLORPLATE 18. *Landscape at Collioure: Study for Le Bonheur de vivre.* 1905. Canvas. 18⅛ × 21⅝″ (46 × 55 cm). Statens Museum for Kunst, Copenhagen, J. Rump Collection.

COLORPLATE 19. *Madame Matisse: The Green Line.* 1905. Canvas. 16 × 12¾″ (40.6 × 32.4).
Statens Museum for Kunst, Copenhagen, J. Rump Collection.

COLORPLATE 20. *Pink Onions.* 1906. Canvas. 18⅛ × 21⅝″ (46 × 55 cm).
Statens Museum for Kunst, Copenhagen, J. Rump Collection.

COLORPLATE 21. *Girl Reading (La Lecture)*. 1906. Canvas. 29½ × 24½" (75 × 62.5 cm).
Mr. and Mrs. David Rockefeller, New York.

COLORPLATE 22. *The Young Sailor, II.* 1906. Canvas. 39⅜ × 31⅞″ (100 × 81 cm). Private collection.

COLORPLATE 23. *Blue Nude (Souvenir de Biskra)*. 1907. Canvas. 36¼ × 55¼″ (92.1 × 140.3 cm).
The Baltimore Museum of Art: The Cone Collection, formed by Dr. Claribel Cone and
Miss Etta Cone of Baltimore, Maryland.

COLORPLATE 24. *Le Luxe, I.* 1907. Canvas. 82¾ × 54⅜″ (210 ×aa 138 cm).
Photograph: Musée National d'Art Moderne, Centre Georges Pompidou, Paris.

COLORPLATE 27. *Zorah on the Terrace.* 1912. Canvas. 45⅝ × 39⅜″ (116 × 100 cm).
The Pushkin Museum, Moscow. Photograph: Editions Cercle d'Art.

COLORPLATE 26. *Window at Tangier (Paysage vu d'une fenêtre, Tanger)*. 1912. Canvas. 45⅝ × 31½″ (116 × 80 cm).
The Pushkin Museum, Moscow. Photo APN, Agence de Presse "Novosti."

COLORPLATE 25. *Conversation.* c. 1908–1912?
Canvas. 69¾ × 85½" (177× 217 cm).
The Hermitage, Leningrad.

COLORPLATE 28. *The Casbah Gate*. 1912. Canvas. 45⅝ × 31½″ (116 × 80 cm).
The Pushkin Museum, Moscow. Photo Studio Adrion/Artephot, J. P. Ziolo.

COLORPLATE 29. *The Red Room: Harmony in Red (La Desserte)*. 1908. Canvas. 70⅞ × 86⅝″ (180 × 220 cm).
The Hermitage, Leningrad.

that one can judge the vitality and power of an artist who, after having received impressions directly from the spectacle of nature, is able to organize his sensations to continue his work in the same frame of mind on different days, and to develop these sensations; this power proves he is sufficiently master of himself to subject himself to discipline.

The simplest means are those which best enable an artist to express himself. If he fears the banal he cannot avoid it by appearing strange, or going in for bizarre drawing and eccentric color. His means of expression must derive almost of necessity from his temperament. He must have the humility of mind to believe that he has painted only what he has seen. I like Chardin's way of expressing it: "I apply color until there is a resemblance." Or Cézanne's: "I want to secure a likeness," or Rodin's: "Copy nature!" Leonardo said: "He who can copy can create." Those who work in a preconceived style, deliberately turning their backs on nature, miss the truth. An artist must recognize, when he is reasoning, that his picture is an artifice; but when he is painting, he should feel that he has copied nature. And even when he departs from nature, he must do it with the conviction that it is only to interpret her more fully.

Some may say that other views on painting were expected from a painter, and that I have only come out with platitudes. To this I shall reply that there are no new truths. The role of the artist, like that of the scholar, consists of seizing current truths often repeated to him, but which will take on new meaning for him and which he will make his own when he has grasped their deepest significance. If aviators had to explain to us the research which led to their leaving earth and rising in the air, they would merely confirm very elementary principles of physics neglected by less successful inventors.

An artist always profits from information about himself, and I am glad to have learned what is my weak point. M. Péladan in the *Revue Hébdomadaire* reproaches a certain number of painters, amongst whom I think I should place myself, for calling themselves "Fauves," and yet dressing like everyone else, so that they are no more noticeable than the floor-walkers in a department store. Does genius count for so little? If it were only a question of myself that would set M. Péladan's mind at ease, tomorrow I would call myself Sar and dress like a necromancer.

Matisse replies, as noted earlier, to Péladan, who called himself Sâr Péladan and dressed in a long black cape.

In the same article this excellent writer claims that I do not paint honestly, and I would be justifiably angry if he had not qualified his statement by saying, "I mean honestly with respect to the ideal and the rules." The trouble is that he does not mention where these rules are. I am willing to have them exist, for were it possible to learn them what sublime artists we would have!

Rules have no existence outside of individuals: otherwise a good professor would be as great a genius as Racine. Any one of us is capable of repeating fine maxims, but few can also penetrate their meaning. I am ready to admit that from a study of the works of Raphael or Titian a more complete set of rules can be drawn than from the works of Manet or Renoir, but the rules followed by Manet and Renoir were those which suited their temperaments and I prefer the most minor of their paintings to all the work of those who are content to imitate the *Venus of Urbino* or the *Madonna of the Goldfinch*. These latter are of no value to anyone, for whether we want to or not, we belong to our time and we share in its opinions, its feelings, even its delusions. All artists bear the imprint of their time, but the great artists are those in whom this is most profoundly marked. Our epoch for instance is better represented by Courbet than by Flandrin, by Rodin better than by Frémiet. Whether we like it or not, however insistently we call ourselves exiles, between our period and ourselves an indissoluble bond is established, and M. Péladan himself cannot escape it. The aestheticians of the future may perhaps use his books as evidence if they get it in their heads to prove that no one of our time understood anything about the art of Leonardo da Vinci.

Henri Matisse
On Photography
1908

Photography can provide the most precious documents existing and no one can contest its value from that point of view. If it is practiced by a man of taste, the photograph will have an appearance of art. But I believe that it is not of any importance in what style they have been produced; photographs will always be impressive because they show us nature, and all artists will find in them a world of sensations. The photographer must therefore intervene as little as possible, so as not to cause photography to lose the objective charm which it naturally possesses, notwithstanding its defects. By trying to add to it he may give the result the appearance of an echo of a different process. Photography should register and give us documents.

In 1908 the publication of the New York Photo-Secession Group, Camera Work, *solicited views on photography from a number of painters. Though he does not mention it here, Matisse had been using photographs as an aid in sculpting and painting.*

Henri Matisse, Quoted by Sarah Stein
On Painting: Notes
from Matisse's School
c. 1908

Sarah Stein helped organize Matisse's school in early 1908. Her notes from her studies with him are the most careful and extensive that we have on Matisse's teaching.

When painting, first look long and well at your model or subject, and decide on your general color scheme. This must prevail. In painting a landscape you choose it for certain beauties—spots of color, suggestions

Photograph of an artist's model from the
publication *Mes Modèles*, used by Matisse
as a basis for *Standing Model*, 1906–7.

of composition. Close your eyes and visualize the picture; then go to
work, always keeping these characteristics the important features of the
picture. And you must at once indicate all that you would have in the
complete work. All must be considered in interrelation during the process—nothing can be added.

One must stop from time to time to consider the subject (model,
landscape, etc.) in its ensemble. What you are aiming for, above all, is
unity.

Order above all, in color. Put three or four touches of color that you
have understood, upon the canvas; add another, if you can—if you can't,
set this canvas aside and begin again.

Construct by relations of color, close and distant—equivalents of the
relations that you see upon the model.

You are representing the model, or any other subject, not copying it;
and there can be no color relations between it and your picture; it is the
relation between the colors in your picture which are the equivalent of
the relation between the colors in your model that must be considered.

I have always sought to copy the model; often very important con-

Matisse's sculpture class in the old Couvent du Sacré-Coeur, Boulevard des Invalides, c. 1909. Left to right: Jean Heiberg, unknown woman, Sarah Stein, Hans Purrmann, Matisse, and Patrick Henry Bruce. Photograph courtesy The Museum of Modern Art, New York. Gift of Hans Purrmann and Alfred H. Barr, Jr.

siderations have prevented my doing so. In my studies I decided upon a background color and a general color for the model. Naturally these were tempered by demands of atmosphere, harmony of the background and model, and unity in the sculptural quality of the model.

Nature excites the imagination to representation. But one must add to this the spirit of the landscape in order to help its pictorial quality. Your composition should indicate the more or less entire character of these trees, even though the exact number you have chosen would not accurately express the landscape.

In still life, painting consists in translating the relations of the objects of the subject by an understanding of the different qualities of colors and their interrelations.

When the eyes become tired and the rapports seem all wrong, just look at an object. "But this brass is yellow!" Frankly put a yellow ochre, for instance on a light spot, and start out from there freshly again to reconcile the various parts.

To copy the objects in a still life is nothing; one must render the emotion they awaken in him. The emotion of the ensemble, the interrelation of the objects, the specific character of every object—modified by its relation to the others—all interlaced like a cord or a serpent.

Max Weber
On Matisse's School
22 October 1951

Max Weber (1881–1961), American painter, was arguably the strongest artist to come out of Matisse's school. He recounted his experiences there in this lecture, given at the Museum of Modern Art, New York.

A spirit of great unrest pervaded the private art schools and the antiquated academies. Questful students made pilgrimages to places where Cézanne's work could be studied, and a marked deviation from academic rule and influence was very obvious. A spirit of independence and *recherche* displaced the hackneyed processes and concepts. Cézanne was regarded and revered as the father and liberator, the Bach of Art, to be emulated and worshiped. He was the beacon light in the stormy years of this historic transition and development.

Inspired by Cézanne's archaic gifts and primitivism, a group of young French painters labeled Les Fauves, or wild beasts, with Matisse as their valorous leader, were experimenting and searching for new means of expression in order to free themselves from slavish copying of nature, and the academic tendencies and pitfalls of the young painters from foreign countries were also touched by the fervent spirit of this revival. They, too, realized the futility of academism, and even after they had gained the praise from their academic masters, like Les Fauves before them, preferred the long, rigid road of the free spirit in art, to official recognition and glory.

I left Jean Paul Laurens' class at the Julian Academy in February 1906, and in the two years that followed I painted by myself, visited and copied in the Louvre and the Prado Museum, and exhibited in the Indépendants and the Autumn Salons.

From time to time, during 1907, I painted from the model in a life class of the Colarossi Academy, but I did not take criticism from the visiting professor. In that atelier there was another young painter from Berlin who did likewise. In the course of conversation with Hans Purrmann, who was a very close friend of Matisse, he suggested that we might be able to organize a class of our own, under the tutelage of Matisse. He felt quite certain that he could persuade Matisse to give us criticism. Our dream was realized. Matisse graciously agreed to give us and a few other serious students criticism every Thursday morning. Although he lived in modest circumstances, he would not accept any remuneration for the precious time and energy he gave us—a spirit now almost extinct.

Fortunate as we were, we had two more difficult problems yet to solve—finding an appropriate atelier, and a few more sympathetic and serious students to help pay the rent, hire models, purchase easels, a stove and studio accessories. I went to the American Art Club on the rue Vavin, corner of the rue de la Grande Chaumière, in the hope of finding American art students to join the class, but my mission was in vain. They would not hear of it, and I was even ridiculed for making such efforts. However, we were not discouraged. Leo Stein and his sister-in-law, Sarah, Mike Stein's wife, who were among the first few patrons of Matisse, joined the class. A very close friend and classmate of Matisse in the Gustave Moreau class also joined, as did an American painter, Patrick Bruce, from Virginia, Mr. and Mrs. Moll from Berlin, and Fräulein Von Knierim from Hamburg, and Fräulein Devard from Holland. By now we had a class of about ten students, and we were able to bridge over our economic difficulties. We were even able to purchase a life-sized cast of one of the finest Greek Apollos of the fifth century, which Matisse recommended and strongly advised us to study. There were weeks when the living model was suspended, and our entire time was given up to drawing and even painting from this exquisite plaster cast.

The Matisse class was founded on the first of January 1908, in the Couvent des Oiseaux. The atelier was a large, well-lit room, flooded with light from three large French windows. We also had the use of the beautiful and spacious gardens of this vacated monastery, where we painted from the draped model as soon as spring came.

I shall never forget the first Thursday of the first week of the class. The atmosphere of the first three days before Matisse's first visit was tense with anticipation and fear, but with deep inner joy and pride as well, for we felt that a rising master was coming to bring us light and lead us out of chaos towards the right path of a veritable renaissance. With the passing of the weeks and months, our trials and errors increased, but

Patrick Henry Bruce (1880–1937), American painter; Greta Moll was the translator of "Notes of a Painter" into German.

Matisse's school was started at the Couvent des Oiseux, 56, rue de Sèvres and later moved to the Hôtel Biron on the Boulevard des Invalides.

Portrait of Greta Moll. 1908. Canvas.
36½ × 28¾" (92.7 × 73 cm). Reproduced
by courtesy of the Trustees, National
Gallery, London.

our expectations were more than fulfilled. Our gratitude and enthusiasm were bountiful.

Matisse's criticism was generous and very searching, at times very severe and admonishing, but always constructive, enlightening and sympathetic. His warm interest in our technical problems and difficulties
gave us confidence and courage. He abhorred technical bravura or superficial calligraphic flourish. He encouraged experimentation, but cautioned us of the subtle inroads and dangers of capricious violence,
exaggerations and dubious emphasis. He insisted upon good logical
construction of the figure, and did not disapprove of the study of anatomy or the use of the plumb line. In calling our attention to the salient
points in the human body, its movements, volume, sculpturesque content and equilibrium, he would refer to the African Negro sculpture, the
great archaic Greece of the fourth and fifth centuries B.C., and unfailingly to Cézanne's architectonic, masonic plasticity. His unique vision and
unexcelled meticulous execution, spiritual values, poetic nuance and
significant gesture were sought, no less than the plastic attributes and
values.

Great stress was laid upon the problems of color values and harmonies, color construction and gradation. Matisse cautioned against violent,
discordant pigmentation. "Good color sings," he would say. "It is melo-

dious, aroma-like, never over-baked." And he preferred good *local* color to garish, illogical, chromatic transposition of local color. Scientific theories of color by Chevreul, Helmholtz, and our own Ogden N. Rood were discussed. In this connection, the origin and theory of Pointillism, Impressionism was explained to us, and what influences the basic principles of design and color in the great ancient arabesque of Far Eastern art—Chinese, Persian and Hindu—had upon Western art.

Matisse abstained from demonstrating or making corrections on students' work. He felt that that was too involving and deprived some students of their weekly individual criticism. Now and then, he advised us to take account of ourselves, of our efforts and experiments, so as not to lose time in wrong directions. At the same time, however, he advised us to strive for things we were not yet able to do, rather than to go on repeating our modest "successes." In spite of the iconoclastic spirit and enthusiasm of the class, nevertheless Matisse would call our attention to the wise, ancient dictum, "There's nothing new under the sun." He revered the great art legacies and traditions, and advised us to study the ancients, but cautioned us not to become enslaved by their productive and overpowering influences.

Discussing the principles of composition in the class one day, it occurred to us that we would benefit greatly by bringing in compositions for criticism by Matisse. The first week, I was the only one who brought in a composition, which was discussed and criticized for the benefit of the class and myself. The second week, I was again the only one who brought in a composition, and again my composition was criticized, and I was very embarrassed in the presence of the class. There and then I decided not to serve as a guinea pig for the class. The following week, no one brought in a composition, and that was the end of the composition project. But I kept up the practice by myself. Instead of original compositions, however, we brought in reproductions of great art examples. These were discussed and analyzed during the model's rest periods. Matisse took part in these discussions and warned us repeatedly to guard against being submerged by them.

What might be considered an annex to the Matisse class was a studio, a Friday evening salon, at 27, rue de Fleurus, where Leo and Gertrude Stein graciously received art students, students of philosophy and languages at the Sorbonne, writers, young poets, musicians and scientists who came to study the painting by Cézanne and those of other rising artists. For hours they stood around the large table in the center of the spacious and well-lighted room, examining portfolios full of drawings by Matisse, Picasso, and others, and folios well stocked with superb Japanese prints. This salon was a sort of international clearinghouse of ideas and matters of art for young and aspiring artists from all over the world. Lengthy and involved discussions on the most recent developments and trends in art took place, with Leo Stein as moderator and pontiff, and many cerebral explosions did take place. Another welcome rendezvous for the young artists was the charming residence of Mr. and Mrs. Mike Stein, whose collection was made up almost entirely of paintings by Matisse. Here the soirées were less frequent, more exclusive, but festive and hospitable nevertheless.

As a counterpoint and enhancement of the workaday spirit of the class there were occasional visits to Matisse's studio in another part of the Couvent des Oiseaux. During those veritably festive afternoon hours, he showed us many of his early drawings and paintings, and spoke freely and intimately about them, explaining the various directions and tendencies. Along with his own work, he showed us with great pride and loving care examples of the work of his colleagues. I remember very distinctly the figure drawings in sanguine by Maillol, and black and whites by Rouault, and four large ink drawings by Van Gogh. With great modesty and deep inner pride, he showed us his painting *Bathers* by Cé-

Local color refers to the "natural" color of an object, as seen against white in diffused daylight.

Michel Eugène Chevreul (1786–1889), French chemist who wrote on color contrasts and influenced the neo-impressionists; Hermann Ludwig Ferdinand von Helmholtz (1821–1894), German physician who wrote on physiological optics; Ogden Rood (1831–1902), professor of physics at Columbia University.

Aristide Maillol (1861–1944), French sculptor and decorative painter.

zanne. His silence before it was more evocative and eloquent than words.
A spirit of elation and awe pervaded the studio at such times.

Matisse was very proud of his small but very choice collection of African Negro sculpture, and this was before Negro sculpture overwhelmed, if not conquered, the art of the continent. He would take a
figurine in his hands, and point out to us the authentic and instinctive
sculpturesque qualities, such as the marvelous workmanship, the unique
sense of proportion, the supple palpitating fullness of form and equilibrium in them.

Occasionally we had the pleasure of meeting some of Matisse's distinguished friends. One afternoon Odilon Redon, whom Matisse greatly
admired, came to see him. There was a large canvas on his easel, but it
was hidden from view. In the course of conversation, Matisse turned it
around. It was *La Desserte* (1908), and he explained to us how and why

The La Desserte *referred to here is now
widely known as* Harmony in Red.

COLORPLATE 29

he changed the color of the background to that of the foreground and vice versa. M. Redon seemed pleased and fully in accord with Matisse over the change he had made.

Matisse was a great lover of music. He had a tiny pump organ in his studio, on which he played rolls of classical music. To get some music out of *that* organ required strong lungs, and strenuous pedaling with the feet. At a soirée in his studio he played for us Beethoven's Fifth Symphony. By the time he reached the middle of the symphony, he was exhausted, but he persisted in finishing it, and when he did he was completely out of breath. Then he would rise slowly, straighten out his shoulders, take a few steps, and convey the feeling of great satisfaction. His happy mood and sparkling eyes gave proof that the strenuous effort, the sweating and pumping, was worthwhile. At another soirée in his studio, Mme. de Ward, a young Dutch pianist and a member of the class, played several piano selections, and I sang the first recitative and several arias from Handel's *Messiah* and several lieder by Schubert and Franz, accompanied by her. One Sunday afternoon in the spring of 1908, Purrmann invited Matisse and me to attend a concert at the Chatelet Theater, known as the *Concert Cologne*. The entire program consisted of music by Richard Strauss, and the orchestra was directed by Herr Strauss himself. Matisse, although pleased with the performance, was not strongly impressed. He found the brass instruments too loud and too metallic.

Fortunate were the young aspiring artists who availed themselves of the privileges and opportunities that Paris offered in these early years of the modern art movement. Those who imbibed the spirit of renewal and innovation were able to lay a strong foundation for creative work of the future years.

Hans Purrmann, Albert Weisgerber, and Matisse in the Loewenbräukeller, Munich, summer 1910. Photograph courtesy The Museum of Modern Art, New York.

Henri Matisse,
Interviewed by Jacques Guenne
L'ART VIVANT
"A Conversation with Henri Matisse"
15 September 1925

Jacques Guenne, critic and writer, elicited from Matisse this brief personal account of his school.

Can you tell me what reasons led you to open the school and then to close it?

I thought it would be good for young artists to avoid the road I traveled myself. I thus took the initiative of opening a school in a convent on the rue de Sèvres, which I then moved near the Sacré Coeur, in a building where the Lycée Buffon now stands. Many students appeared. I forced myself to correct each one, taking into account the spirit in which his efforts were conceived. I especially took pains to inculcate in them a sense of tradition. Needless to say, many of my students were disappointed to see that a master with a reputation for being revolutionary could have repeated the words of Courbet to them: "I have simply wished to assert the reasoned and independent feeling of my own individuality within a total knowledge of tradition."

The effort I made to penetrate the thinking of each one tired me out. I reached the point where I thought a student was heading in the wrong direction and he told me (revenge of my masters), "That's the way I think." The saddest part was that they could not conceive that I was depressed to see them "doing Matisse." Then I understood that I had to choose between being a painter and a teacher. I soon closed my school.

Gustave Courbet (1819–1877), French realist painter.

Back, O. 1909. Clay. (No longer extant.)

Henri Matisse,
Interviewed by E. Tériade

ART NEWS

"Matisse Speaks"

November 1951

Among the collectors who were interested in my work from the beginning, I must mention two Russians, Shchukin and Morosov. Shchukin, a Moscow importer of Eastern textiles, was about fifty years old, a vege-

Two Russian collectors, Sergei Shchukin (1854–1936) and Ivan Morosov (1871–1921), played a crucial role in Matisse's career before the First World War. Matisse had especially high regard for Shchukin, stating: "It took sheer nerve to paint in this manner, and it took sheer nerve to buy."

tarian, extremely sober. He spent four months of each year in Europe, traveling just about everywhere. He loved the profound and tranquil pleasures. In Paris his favorite pastime was visiting the Egyptian antiquities in the Louvre, where he discovered parallels to Cézanne's peasants. He thought the lions of Mycenae were the incontestable masterpieces of all art. One day he dropped by at the Quai Saint-Michel to see my pictures. He noticed a still life hanging on the wall and said: "I buy it [sic], but I'll have to keep it at home for several days, and if I can bear it, and keep interested in it, I'll keep it." I was lucky enough that he was able to bear this first ordeal easily, and that my still life didn't fatigue him too much. So he came back and commissioned a series of large paintings to decorate the living room of his Moscow house—the old palace of the Troubetzkoy princes, built during the reign of Catherine II. After this he asked me to do two decorations for the palace staircase, and it was then I painted *Music* and *The Dance*.

Morosov, a Russian colossus, twenty years younger than Shchukin, owned a factory employing three thousand workers and was married to a dancer. He had commissioned decorations for his music room from Maurice Denis, who painted *The Loves of Psyche*. In the same room were six big Maillol sculptures. From me he bought, among other pictures, *Window at Tangier*, *The Moroccans on the Terrace* and *The Gate of the Casbah*. The paintings of both these collectors now belong to the Museum of Western Art in Moscow.

When Morosov went to Ambroise Vollard, he'd say: "I want to see a very beautiful Cézanne." Shchukin, on the other hand, would ask to see all the Cézannes available and make his choice among them.

In March 1909 Shchukin came to Paris and saw the first version of Matisse's Dance, *which served as a kind of prospectus for the commission of one or more large decorative panels. After much hesitation, Shchukin confirmed his order in the letter below.*

COLORPLATE 36
COLORPLATE 35

COLORPLATE 26
COLORPLATE 28

Letter from Sergei Shchukin to Matisse

On the Commission for *Dance* and *Music*

31 March 1909

I find your *Dance* panel so noble that I resolved to brave our bourgeois public opinion and place upon my staircase a subject with THE NUDE. At the same time, I will need a second panel, for which music would do nicely as the subject.

I was very pleased to receive your reply: accept firm order dance panel fifteen thousand and music panel twelve thousand price confidential. Thank you very much, and I hope to have a sketch of the second panel soon. . . .

In my house, we play a great deal of music. Every winter there are ten or so classical concerts (Bach, Beethoven, Mozart). The music panel must suggest the character of the house somewhat. I have every confidence in you, and I am sure that the music will be as successful as the dance.

Please give me news of your work.

All my reservations in the two preceding letters are superceded by my telegram of last Sunday. Now you have my firm order for the two panels. My regards to Mme. Matisse. . . .

Portrait of Sergei Shchukin. 1912. Charcoal. 19½ × 12" (49.5 × 30.5 cm). Private collection.

The "Matisse Room" in the home of
Sergei Shchukin, Moscow, 1912. Top
row, left to right: *Still Life* (1901?); *Nymph
and Satyr*, 1909; *Game of Bowls*, 1908; *The
Luxembourg Gardens*, c. 1902; *View of
Collioure*, 1905. Bottom row: *The Bois de
Boulogne*, 1902; *Still Life—Seville*, 1911;
Coffee Pot, Carafe, and Fruit Dish, 1909;
Still Life, 1900; *Still Life* (c. 1907?).
Photograph courtesy The Museum of
Modern Art, New York.

Alexandre Mercereau

ZOLOTOYE RUNO

"Henri Matisse and Contemporary Art"

1909

The common trend, which first Matisse and then Derain evoked in their
early painting, was first and foremost a reaction against Impressionism,
their initial point of departure. Moreover, this new trend did not negate
previous ones, but was used as already-gathered material for the realization of a new ideal. In fact, isn't it from a formal recognition of reality
that a truly human ideal may be created? Can a pure idea really be created? Is it the deepening of sensation, and can it evoke an aesthetic
emotion if it isn't connected to feeling? Therefore, before one can pro-
ceed to synthetic creation, doesn't it make sense to begin with a careful
analysis? Otherwise, what would be the criterion by which, for the sake
of the perfection of the whole, useless detail would be rejected?—in an

*Alexandre Mercereau (b. 1884), writer,
critic, and early, influential supporter of
the cubists, was editor of the French
section of Zolotoye Runo (Golden
Fleece), which dedicated one issue entirely
to Matisse. This essay preceded a Russian
translation of "Notes of a Painter" and
numerous reproductons of Matisse's works.*

artistic work, everything that is useless is harmful. Thus, Impressionism was the logical basis of a new trend, just as the latest trend will be in its turn the basis for future trends, appearing as the expression of an artistic condition singularly possible in a given era, for art is always the mouthpiece of aristocratic thought, common for all times but constantly developing according to the relentless laws of Nature. All the outstanding features of the contemporary movement clearly appear in the creative work of Matisse, mainly in his work of recent years, precisely those after 1901 when he left the "Salon National" where he had already exhibited for a few years with the rights of a member. During this time the dominating figures in the eyes of the intelligentsia were Maurice Denis and the inseparable trio of Vuillard, Bonnard, and Roussel.

Pierre Bonnard (1867–1947), Edouard Vuillard (1868–1940), and Ker-Xavier Roussel (1867–1944), painters.

Henri Matisse immediately distinguished himself by not being content with refinement, which he considered too transitory. Instead, he strived for solidity of construction and required more than pithiness of impression and sketchiness of character. His use of color, though bright, remained serene and, like Ceźanne, he created relief with precision of tones. But in 1905 Matisse suddenly abandoned his peculiar manner, which had already characterized him in the critics' eyes. Following the neo-impressionists, he traveled the path of Seurat and Signac, although it seemed that the latter had extracted all the possibilities from the principle of decomposition of tones. Naturally, Matisse contributed his own, individual traits to this area, but this only made him less accessible to the public, from whom he demanded the same vision and powers of observation that he possessed. Moreover, beginning with the following year (1906), apparently convinced that he had chosen a false path, he returned to his former course, where he had abandoned it, but with new acquisitions; or, at least, with a new precision called up by his technical investigations. From this time on, he continued logically to develop in the direction that was truly his own and from which he no longer deviated.

Among his characteristic canvases, especially typical is *The Bather, Emerging from the Water* (1906). With a white peignoir in hand, she walks with the movement of one of the Graces. The almost total monotone of this painting signifies a completely exceptional moment in his work. Later we can note the painting *La Coiffure* (1907), where a nude woman is depicted, her hair brushed by another woman in a green peignoir. Here the ever-growing concern for decorativeness vividly appears. Here we see intensity of action and the vital unity of both figures. Another painting portrays a semi-nude woman. The expression is deeply melancholic. The color is black with gold, which in general is rarely encountered in his work. In 1908 Matisse painted a decorative panel for a dining room in a sumptuous and tender red tone, which seems even warmer thanks to the contrast with the strong and bright light blue color of the wallpaper designs and the caustic color of the fruits. Later there follows a red still life with a Turkestan rug. The composition is very simple. The warm tones, red and yellow, are counterbalanced by cold ones: blue and green which change the strength of their corresponding tones. In the painting *Bathers*, three naked boys are playing ball after swimming. The general tonality is cold: the blue of the sea and the green of the grass are softened by the warmer color of the green orbs and the black hair with greenish tints. Two boys have black hair with a blue tint. The whole painting is warmed only by red drapery and black hair, with red shading, of the third player.

In 1909 *The Spanish Woman* was painted in gloomy, somewhat tragic tones. This painting, depicting a nude woman with a white scarf on a bright and luxurious red background, as well as a painting which shows an Algerian woman in the costume of an Almeh, completes a series of paintings in which red tones practically dominate on an equal basis, but acquire a special flavor, owing to the accompanying tones. Finally, we have *The Dance,* a drawing on a panel designed for the decoration of a

He apparently refers here to Standing Model, *1906–07.*

COLORPLATE 29

COLORPLATE 35

Back, I. 1909. Bronze. 74¾ × 46"
(190 × 116.8 cm). The Tate Gallery,
London.

staircase and about which the artist says, "I must decorate a three-story
staircase. I take the standpoint of a visitor, coming in from the outside.
I need to achieve a strength, convey a feeling of relief. My first panel
depicts a dance, a flying round dance atop a hill. On the second flight,
you are well within the house; in its plan and its silence I see a musical
scene with attentive listeners; finally, on the third floor, total serenity
dominates, and I paint a scene of repose: people lying on the grass, con-
versing, or dreaming."

I do not think it superfluous to give a color description of some of
Matisse's latest canvases, in order to show which colors and which subjects especially attracted him. I list the basic features of his work, which

*Matisse's words first appeared in an
article by Charles Estienne, "Some
Tendencies in Modern Painting:
Interview with M. Henri-Matisse," Les
Nouvelles, (12 April 1909).*

draw him to the attention of all who seek in art more than a momentary pastime—which, according to Pelagan's accurate observation, would be the lowest and unworthiest of all human phenomena. His goal has been to impart to his lines a higher degree of expressiveness. He had to simplify and reduce to several basic lines, including among them some broad strokes, sufficient for imparting intensity to the paint and real meaning to volumes and planes. The main task was to construct, distribute, and compose firmly, that is, not on the basis of a chance contact, fleeting impression, or ephemeral flash, but according to the artist's will and total consciousness. Unity and diversity here merge into a powerful harmony. Unity is expressed not by the contradiction of one plane by another, or by the negation of one line by another, but by the blending of each part with the whole, aiding in its completion and calculated to impart great value to the whole painting. The painting's unity is equally expressed by the way form and color find themselves in such a tight corelationship that it is impossible to violate the harmony of one without violating the harmony of the other. Any alteration in one part must absolutely be accompanied by an adequate alteration in another.

Diversity is expressed by the way each part is strictly put in its proper place, that is, is illuminated in conformity with the basic meaning that falls to it. In a painting nothing fastens the viewer's gaze on one detail to the detriment of another; each part, conforming to its shape and magnitude, has a special color and a special manner; the composition is always subordinate to the size of the canvas, and the background is always the resultant force of the subject's color.

It is possible to have a different ideal of form, to prefer other color associations, just as some people prefer noise to silence, night to day, or mountains to the sea, but it is impossible to deny the knowledge which governs Henri Matisse's every gesture—the powerful simplicity of his technical skills, the conformity of all strokes of his brush, the logic of accommodation of works for the better realization of his own ideal, and the complete exteriorization of his artistic ideas, remote from any feeling, alien to Platonic art. It is equally impossible to deny that from the contemplation of his canvases one distinguishes a higher goal of art: clarity and serenity of spirit in the most beneficial and exalted atmosphere—an atmosphere of ideas, conquered by the refinement of feelings.

The Game of Bowls (Les Joueurs aux boules or *Jeu de balles).* 1908. Canvas. 44⅝ × 57" (113.5 × 145 cm). The Hermitage, Leningrad. Artephot, J. P. Ziolo.

Matisse at work on the sculpture
La Serpentine in 1909. Photograph by
Edward Steichen. Courtesy The Museum
of Modern Art, New York.

La Serpentine. 1909. Bronze. Height:
22¼" (56.5 cm). Collection, The Museum
of Modern Art, New York. Gift of Abby
Aldrich Rockefeller.

Letters from Matthew Stewart Prichard
to Isabella Stewart Gardner
On Matisse

1909

2 JANUARY 1909

Potter went to see some of Matisse's paintings before he left and since
then I have seen some also. He is a man working towards a scale, is most

*Matthew Stewart Prichard (1865–1936),
a British Byzantinist, aesthete, and mystic,
went to Paris in 1907, after serving as
assistant director of the Boston Museum of
Fine Arts. In Paris he read philosophy,
tried drawing, followed Henri Bergson's
lectures at the Collège de France, and
made Matisse's acquaintance. In
correspondence with American art collector
Isabella Stewart Gardner (1840–1924),
he frequently gave his impressions and
opinions of Matisse.*

COLORPLATE 30. *Woman with a Carnation.* 1909. Canvas. 25½ × 21¼″ (65 × 54 cm).
The Hermitage, Leningrad. Photograph: Editions Cercle d'Art.

COLORPLATE 31. *The Forest at Fontainebleau.* 1909. Canvas. 23⅝ × 29″ (60 × 73.5 cm). Private collection.

COLORPLATE 32. *Nymph and Satyr*. 1909. Oil on board. 35 × 46″ (89 × 117 cm).
The Hermitage, Leningrad. Photograph: Editions Cercle d'Art.

COLORPLATE 33. *The Dance* (first version). 1909. Canvas. 102¼ × 153½″ (259.7 × 390 cm).
Collection, The Museum of Modern Art, New York. Gift of Nelson A. Rockefeller in honor of Alfred H. Barr, Jr.

COLORPLATE 34. *Fruit, Flowers, and "The Dance" (Nature Morte à la Danse).* 1909. Canvas. 35½ × 41¾″ (90.2 × 106 cm). The Hermitage, Leningrad.

COLORPLATE 35. *The Dance.* 1909–10. Canvas. 102⅜ × 153⅞″ (260 × 391 cm). The Hermitage, Leningrad.

COLORPLATE 36. *Music*. 1910. Canvas. 102⅜ × 153⅛″ (260 × 389 cm). The Hermitage, Leningrad.

COLORPLATE 37. *The Blue Tablecloth*. 1909. Canvas. 34⅝ × 46½″ (88 × 118 cm). The Hermitage, Leningrad.

emotional, a free draftsman, but is coarse, is shortsighted and perhaps has some other optical trouble. . . . Matisse has written an account of his effort which I am more anxious to see even than his paintings and sculpture. He is always designing to be seen at great distances and may make wonderful things for a Panthéon, for instance. . . .

EASTER DAY, 1909

I suppose Matisse will go out of date in turn, but in spite of his horribly untidy technique he seems the greatest of the modern men. Being both painter and sculptor he has a greater foundation than most, and he has founded himself on a tremendous draftsmanship. I have seen a photograph of his last composition, a ring of dancing women, or a ring expressing the rhythm of women dancing, for their existence is only suggested by light female symbols against a blue and darker background. . . .

7 JULY 1909

Claude Phillips told me that Sargent said to him that Matisse's painting was worthless. I replied insolently that if Mr. S. knew the truth he would commit hari-kiri before one of his own portraits, but you will understand that I should deplore genuinely any such catastrophe. . . .

Prichard had read "Notes of a Painter."

COLORPLATE 35

John Singer Sargent (1856–1925), American painter.

Gelett Burgess

ARCHITECTURAL RECORD
"The Wild Men of Paris"

May 1910

Gelett Burgess (1866–1951), American illustrator and humorist (he wrote "The Purple Cow" and Goops and How To Be Them), *went to Paris in 1908 to learn about "the new art." He met first with Matisse, whom he considered the leader of the modern movement, and subsequently with others, including Derain and Picasso, as Matisse recommended.*

I had scarcely entered the Salon des Indépendants when I heard shrieks of laughter coming from an adjoining wing. I hurried along from room to room under the huge canvas roof, crunching the gravel underfoot as I went, until I came upon a party of well-dressed Parisians in a paroxysm of merriment, gazing, through weeping eyes, at a picture. Even in my haste I had noticed other spectators lurching hysterically in and out of the galleries; I had caught sight of paintings that had made me gasp. But here I stopped in amazement. It was a thing to startle even Paris. I realized for the first time that my views on art needed a radical reconstruction. Suddenly I had entered a new world, a universe of ugliness. And, ever since, I have been mentally standing on my head in the endeavor to get a new point of view on beauty so as to understand and appreciate this new movement in art.

* * *

What did it all mean? The drawing was crude past all belief: the color was as atrocious as the subject. Had a new era of art begun? Was ugliness to supersede beauty, technique give way to naiveté, and vibrant, discordant color, a very patchwork of horrid hues, take the place of subtle, studied nuances of tonality? Was nothing sacred, not even beauty?

* * *

It was Matisse who took the first step into the undiscovered land of the ugly.

Matisse at work on *The Dance* in 1909. Photograph courtesy The Museum of Modern Art, New York.

Matisse himself, serious, plaintive, a conscientious experimenter, whose works are but studies in expression, who is concerned at present with but the working out of the theory of simplicity, denies all responsibility for the excesses of his unwelcome disciples. Poor, patient Matisse, breaking his way through this jungle of art, sees his followers go whooping off in vagrom paths to right and left. He hears his own speculative words distorted, misinterpreted, inciting innumerable vagaries. He may say, perhaps: "To my mind, the equilateral triangle is a symbol and manifestation of the absolute. If one could get that absolute quality into a painting, it would be a work of art." Whereat, little madcap Picasso, keen as a whip, spirited as a devil, mad as a hatter, runs to his studio and contrives a huge nude woman composed entirely of triangles, and presents it in triumph. What wonder Matisse shakes his head and does not smile! He chats thoughtfully of the "harmony of volume" and "architectural values," and wild Braque climbs to his attic and builds an architectural monster which he names Woman, with balanced masses and parts, with openings and columnar legs and cornices. Matisse praises the direct appeal to instinct of the African wood images, and even sober Derain, a co-experimenter, loses his head, molds a neolithic man into a solid cube, creates a woman of spheres, stretches a cat out into a cylinder, and paints it red and yellow!

Maitre Matisse, if I understand him, which, with my imperfect facility with French, and my slighter knowledge of art, I am afraid I didn't, quite, stands primarily for the solid existence of things. He paints weight, volume, roundness, color and all the intrinsic physical attributes of the thing itself, and then imbues the whole with sentiment. Oh, yes, his paintings do have life! One can't deny that. They are not merely models posed against a background, like thousands of canvases in the Salons, they are human beings with souls. You turn from his pictures, which have so shockingly defied you, and you demand of other artists at least as much vitality and originality—and you don't find it! He paints with emotion, and inspires you with it. But, alas! when he paints his wife with a broad stripe of green down her nose, though it startlingly suggests her, it is his punishment to have made her appear so to you always. He teaches you to see her in a strange and terrible aspect. He has taught you her body. But, fearful as it is, it is alive—awfully alive!

COLORPLATE 19

Painting so, in a burst of emotion, he usually comes to an end of his enthusiasm before he has attained beauty. You point out the fact to him that his painted woman has but three fingers. "Ah, that is true," he says; "but I couldn't put in the other two without throwing the whole out of drawing—it would destroy the composition and the unity of my ideal. Perhaps, some day, I may be able to get what I want of sentiment, of emotional appeal, and, at the same time, draw all five fingers. But the subjective idea is what I am after now: the rest can wait."

Matisse, however, should not be classed amongst the Wild Beasts of this Parisian menagerie. But of him I learned something of the status of the movement, which is a revolt against the subtleties of Impressionism. It is a revolt against "mere charm," against accidental aspects of illumination; a return to simplicity, directness, pure color and decorative qualities.

Jacques Rivière
ETUDES
"An Exhibition of Henri-Matisse"
1911

Jacques Rivière (1886–1925), French writer associated with La Nouvelle Revue Française. As a review of a Matisse retrospective at the Bernheim-Jeune Gallery, 14 February–5 March 1910, this article may have been first published around then.

The pure torment of seeing too deeply. A fine painter, knowing and sensitive, is paralyzed by his prophetic gift. He sees in a flash exactly what he is going to do and how he will do it: it is as if the work stands complete before his eyes. That is why he never actually paints it: his initial conception is so clear that when he picks up the brush, he feels that he is going to repeat himself, and the picture he is painting tries to diverge from what he imagined. Great artists confront their own work as if it were a stranger; they do not foresee every step from the beginning; covertly they watch it develop; they discover it passionately, little by little. Matisse seeks to imitate this wondrous ignorance, denied him by his excessively clear awareness; he hopes to generate it artificially within himself, turning away from what inner necessity imposes on him, choosing a path quite different from the one first illuminated by the perspicacity of his vision. But this very act of voluntary blindness robs him of his own spontaneity; he is no longer driven by anything, and we are disconcerted not to sense the force of any compulsion in his paintings.

The gratuitousness of this painting results from its *abstract* character. Matisse stands *apart* from things when he paints. He looks at them, but draws a few steps back from them. He takes in the sensation he gets from them, carries it away with him and, having taken his distance, then carefully unfolds it; the sensation is still full, for he can see well enough and the world, for him, is the unrolling of a thick, rich fabric. But the mind worms its way into this sensuality; it unravels his deliberate richness; it clarifies, purifies, and articulates it, distills it until all that is clumsy, murky, and carnal vanishes, along with all that is insufficiently uncommon. Then, slowly, with a protective indulgence, he recombines images now bare and rarefied, abstract, though a shred of primitive sensation may sometimes still quiver within. There are painters who commit their feelings to canvas all at once, without analyzing them, and who immediately seek their plastic equivalent in a spurt of color. Others work completely isolated from things, committing to canvas only the phantoms of their thought. Matisse differs from both; he draws from reality the material for pictorial speculation. The strengths and defects of his painting flow, as a joint consequence, from this sort of abstraction.

Matisse's color shines with an intellectual splendor. It has the mute force of ideas that spring suddenly and dazzlingly to mind. It lacks the density of objects; it is weightless; but it covers the canvas with its matte thinness, spreads its clean and violent richness in a fine layer. It is as immobile as thought, whose rigid brilliance it imitates. It does not palpitate because nothing that breathes is part of it; it is a sparkling and inert extract. The best evidence of its artificial origin is that it is uncommon without being weak; it is ever incomparable, and Matisse prefers to leave white spaces rather than fill them without serendipity. Thus the color unfolds, always perfect and unmoving, never allowing itself to be disturbed by the drab effusion of the real. The still lifes are the best of these paintings, for indeed their subject is already abstract; the objects are chosen and grouped in accordance with their pictorial importance; their arbitrary character is attenuated by this prior adaptation of the model to its future image. Moreover, since Matisse has prepared the still lifes to his taste, he allows his senses a more confident expression; he transcribes them more exactly; he is won over by the sensual pleasure that objects harbor; his color becomes more muted, more weighty, more swollen with matter.

But he is sensual only accidentally, almost despite himself. In drawings he becomes completely abstract again. His drawings are not connected to objects; nor does he distort them to make them more expressive; he is neither realistic nor lyrical; he acts in the manner of an idea. An idea at first is an empty form, its content indiscernible; it is quintessentially indistinct. But little by little it takes shape, in other words, it proliferates internally, the details within it complement its generality. Likewise Matisse, in shaping the frame or sheet of paper he selects, all at once glimpses a hint, of which his drawing will be the development. In effect, the drawing is born little by little under the influence of the frame; it is coiled up in the center, in the position suggested to it by its external dimensions; the lines balance one another, recall one another, and express the general theme in varying degrees of complexity. Their very dissimilarity serves to accentuate the same idea. It is a pleasing variation; the charcoal strokes voluptuously encompass the correspondences and points of balance, lend rhythm to the equilibrium, echo the right angles in related curves. The painting thus imitates itself by proliferating within. But its most special details still derive from the initial schema and they retain its abstract character. This design often attains an austere and exquisite grace, as in *La Coiffeuse* or *Music*. Often, too, it has the absurdity of logic; since it is neither disturbed nor restrained by reality, it exhibits a gratuitous barbarism, as in *Nude with a White Scarf*.

COLORPLATE 36

But even when the design is beautiful, it is not enough to make the painting beautiful; indeed, the qualities of the color never merge with the quality of the work. Matisse seems determined to use color and design separately; he refuses to bring them together in a complete work; never once has he achieved a full work. He wishes to paint conclusions only; he neglects everything a subject has in common with others; he waits to the last minute, the moment of divergence, before acting. Before he sets brush to canvas, the entire past must have been suggested. Here we find the error into which his abstraction leads him. Since he works apart from things, he sees in them no more than invitations to diversity; each sight tends to differ from all others; Matisse embraces this tendency and extends it in himself to the point of actual separation. For him a canvas is not an image of reality, but a plastic speculation. He therefore has to make it as unique as possible, without precedent or analogy. That is why the work will be driven to the limit in one direction; that is why the painter will put only a part of his resources into it. The diversity of these paintings is disconcerting, because it is a diversity of frugality, not of richness.

If Matisse agreed to subject himself to the dictates of objects, if he were willing to draw his originality from submission, perhaps he might attain it at a higher cost. Real things acquire their distinction only after patiently resembling all others. They have to be mingled together for a long time before managing to stand out one from the other. But then their individuality is not merely superficial, and the uniqueness that finally arises in their features reflects their real depth and expresses their entire being.

Michel Puy

MERCURE DE FRANCE

"The Latest in Painting"

16 July 1910

The painters who were called, for a time, the Fauves are reacting fully against the previous group, among whom they link themselves only with Vallotton, who disclaims any connection with them. They dreamed of basing their effort on a thorough command of drawing. Little by little, their drawing became condensed, and to strengthen it they did not scruple to use brilliant colors. They sought to state line precisely and pushed it to the point of sometimes rendering it contorted and elliptical. They went so far as to concern themselves more with line for its own sake than with whatever strength it could bring to their drawing, and they wanted to assure it a predominant place in their composition. Starting from a strict observation of reality, they ended by focusing on the fantastic above all. Decorative speculation replaced their realist impulses; the more advanced among them wanted to create a purely mathematical world, where the forms to which our eyes are accustomed are replaced by polyhedrons or cylinders. Others want to strike the spectators' imagination and, the better to achieve this, do not shrink from an outward extravagance.

All these painters have compelled the public's attention, scandalized many people, and met with numerous defenders. It is very difficult, in a movement such as the one they have created, to make a completely lucid distinction between what corresponds to the action that, as their various temperaments require, must be taken upon the methods offered by the age, and what is merely accident, exaggeration, whim, intoxication, swagger. Yet if one considers the group's overall evolution, one must recognize that they have cultivated, with violent logic, the pictorial craft and the general principles that their elders bequeathed to them.

It would be impossible to speak of these painters without mentioning Matisse first of all. That he commands knowledge no one would deny. He is sensitive to every modulation of form, every variation of color. He is like one of those rare writers for whom every word has meaning, every turn of phrase its weight. He can fill a large canvas with the simplest of elements—a bowl of fruit, a human figure, a drapery. Let him sketch a model in haste and even that drawing will have decorative value. He always goes beyond the sensation of grace and abandon that radiates from a woman's body, the joyful sensuality that emerges from appearances. With a single color, he can fill a wide space, and that color will be chosen so as to highlight all the rest of the painting. Gathered in a room, his canvases sumptuously dress the walls, harmonize with the tonalities of the most beautiful carpets. When Matisse exaggerates distortion—whether in his statues or in his paintings—he is guided by a temperamental necessity that prompts him, once he has glimpsed a truth, to affirm it unceremoniously and to stretch it to the limits of paradox. He loves his craft too passionately not to restore it to its rightful place, and without burdening himself with any concern that is irrelevant to the plastic art, he manages—while shunning psychological trickery, and apart from the characteristics of a work of feeling or imagination—to imbue a statuette of a woman, a landscape, or a decorative composition with an emotion that arouses a profound echo in our minds and hearts.

Roland Dorgelès (1886–1973), French writer and Ecole des Beaux-Arts graduate.

Roland Dorgelès

FANTASIO

"The Prince of the Fauves"

1 December 1910

"House painters, stay away from Matisse! Matisse has done more harm in a year than an epidemic! Matisse causes insanity!"

A few years ago, the street urinals of Montmartre were covered with these rude inscriptions, which M. Matisse and his pious disciples were not numerous enough to erase. It was at the time that the house painters were pasting up leaflets on every wall denouncing the damages done by white lead, and a delightfully fantastic poet had the brilliant idea of replacing the words "white lead" with M. Matisse's name on every handbill. Thus you could no longer enter a public convenience without the warning leaping to your eyes: "Matisse causes insanity!"

That laconic and severe criticism is perhaps the best ever to be formulated about M. Matisse's painting, which is costly, puerile, and stupefying.

One day at the Salon d'Automne a tiny tot asked his father, who was sinking, before a painting by the prince of the Fauves, into a state of dazedness approaching senility:

"Why didn't the man do balloons, too?"

That child was judging the master's work soundly. Indeed, to achieve a masterpiece, M. Matisse would only have to enrich his skies with a linear Eiffel Tower and a few captive balloons. He would then recall to us the innocent drawings we did when we were eight years old, and we would cherish an art that would bring to light in us the erased memories of our dreamy childhood.

On varnishing days, when the gentle gawkers flock before M. Matisse's consignment, which always attracts notice, most of them imagine that this canvas was dashed off on an idle morning by the facetious brush of some playful student.

Serious mistake.

M. Matisse is not a humorist.

M. Matisse has the grave face of a *Herr Professor*, M. Matisse is a beloved master, M. Matisse has disciples, M. Matisse is the head of a school wherein Württembergers, Moravians, Lithuanians, and Slavonians commune in admiration of him.

No, he does not paint as his fancy takes him: he has his method, and his most laughable paintings are the fruit of painstaking efforts and long meditations.

"What I dream of," he has written, "is an art of balance, of purity. . . ." One can convince oneself, by casting a glance at the *Coiffeuse,* that M. Matisse has realized his dream.

The prince of the Fauves did not always have the reprehensible conception of pictorial art that he has today.

But with the perspicacity of an insightful psychologist, he understood that the worst excesses are always beneath the simple-minded admiration of the gawkers, and that one can always find people to proclaim genius when faced with a thing that their neighbors do not understand, in order to crush the latter with their intellectual superiority. So he abandoned his original manner—which was that of a very interesting artist—and quickly made himself famous by mistreating square meters

Severe poisoning produced by the lead in white paint can result in brain damage.

The interior of Matisse's studio at Issy in 1911.

of canvas, which he smeared malignantly according to the elementary precepts of Senegalese aesthetics. Then again, since his orders increased in direct proportion to his eccentricities, one should render homage to his shrewd business sense.

At the last exhibition he held, only ten paintings were still for sale, out of sixty-two that he was exhibiting. No other painter could say the same. M. Matisse's products sell for insane prices, German museums buy his canvases, and the private houses that he has decorated are countless.

The master once told a student of his academy—for he has an academy: "If you were not meant to have genius, I cannot give it to you, but if you attend my courses assiduously, in three years you will be earning ten thousand francs a year." M. Matisse earns ten times that himself.

The prince of the Fauves has an enormous influence over the young foreign painters. He has already undermined the common sense of many unfortunates, and one can say that contemporary painting is in his debt for its worst horrors. In Germany, where he toured triumphantly, M. Matisse was crowned with laurels. Upon his return to Paris, his students beseeched him to give at least one lesson with his wreath on, and the master, having accepted, taught his course with laureled brow, and no one burst out laughing in his face.

Thomas Whittemore (1871–1950), American Byzantinist who later uncovered the mosaics at Hagia Sophia in Constantinople, sent Matisse a laurel crown after his return from Germany in 1908.

M. Henri Matisse receives the most preposterous praise with the gravity of a dervish. Severity is his usual mask, and the strollers who see him every morning, passing on horseback down the drives of the Bois, are persuaded that this young man with the carefully trimmed beard and the severe spectacles is a German military attaché.

Buttoned up tight in his suit jacket, as if in a hussar's coat, M. Henri Matisse, miserly with his greetings, follows the Acacias, skirts the Lakes, and, his long outing at an end, is off to take up his brushes again in his luxurious studio in Issy-les-Moulineaux. Indeed, the young master earns enough money to refuse himself nothing that he desires. After all, it is natural enough that, in a time when the Jean-François Millets and the Monticellis were unable to sell their works, M. Henri Matisse manages to place his painted canvases advantageously.

As long as he was painting with a sincerity equal to his boldness—this was the period of his views of Notre-Dame, the landscapes, and the first portraits—no one thought of proclaiming that this inventive artist had genius. But his first oddities were sufficient to earn him what his best works had not granted him: success. Finally, M. Matisse perpetrated *Le Bonheur de vivre* and exhibited it at the Indépendants instead of giving it to a circus as a present, as sound logic demanded, and from being merely known of, the young painter became famous. It is conceivable, for all that, that one would remember the name of the painter of such a thing. "I paint my dreams," M. Matisse has said. One may ask oneself, with concern, if his nights are not troubled by frequent nightmares.

We feel no rancor toward M. Matisse for painting in the manner of the Malagassian decorators; it's a good livelihood; but one thing that cuts us to the quick is the thought that credulous foreigners may judge French art by his stupefying productions. If there is a Czech or a Rumelian decrepit enough to believe that *Music* and *Dance* are the last word in our art, M. Matisse has a lot to answer for. It is true that some people compare M. Matisse to Puvis de Chavannes without laughing; there may well be others who take the canvases of the prince of the Fauves for so many masterpieces. In this business, one can't be surprised by anything. We mustn't even be surprised when M. Matisse declares that he is interested above all in the figure, "which permits him best to express the almost religious feeling that he has toward life." It's amusing, that's all.

M. Matisse has managed to dress his dumbfounding art in very noble theories and he paints like a nigger, while speaking like a Magus. Some of his published notes attain the sublime.

"I have to paint the body of a woman," he writes. "First, I give it grace, charm. . . ."

Reread this sentence well, then look at M. Matisse's "graceful bodies" impartially. . . .

After that, we can frankly find nothing further to say. M. Matisse is merrier than we are.

Malagassian: a native of Madagascar. Rumelian: a native of Rumelia, a Balkan state now part of Bulgaria.

COLORPLATE 35
COLORPLATE 36

P. Skrotsky

P. Skrotsky, Russian journalist and critic.

ODESSKY LISTOK

"From Paris: The Salon d'Automne"

20 November 1910

Let us go to the Salon d'Automne and stop in front of the two Matisse panels (the property of the merchant Shchukin). Here there are constant bursts of indignation, rage, mockery. Admittedly, the loud, poisonous colors give the idea of a diabolical cacophony, the draftsmanship is simplified almost to vanishing-point, and the shockingly hideous forms express the artist's intention with insolence and arrogance. The world created by Matisse in these naive, cannibalistic panels is, I think, a most unpleasant world. Matisse tries to convey, not one, but a succession of impressions, but the first unpleasant sense of disappointment remains unabated and does not cool as you scrutinize the panels. This, it seems to me, is an unfortunate example of Matisse's art, proving once again that Matisse—one of the most remarkable draftsmen of our times—can turn out work of very unequal quality.

Letter from Matthew Stewart Prichard to Isabella Stewart Gardner

On Reactions to *Dance* and *Music*

22 November 1910

Matisse meanwhile exhibited at the Salon d'Automne two large compositions *La Danse* . . . and *La Musique* with life-size figures and in three saturated colors, green, blue and red, the red not quite pure, perhaps, and brought down upon himself a storm of abuse, not only of the papers, but of his fellow artists as well. I saw them only without their final touches, but my companion in arms wrote and told me they were extraordinarily wonderful, and I expect this is true. Matisse withdrew under the hail of opposition to Munich and now he has lost his father and has gone to Spain, to reflect with El Greco, perhaps. . . .

COLORPLATE 35
COLORPLATE 36

Matisse's father died in mid-October; the artist left for Spain in mid-November and did not return until the following January.

Letter from Ilya Ostroukhov to Aleksandra Botkina

On Matisse's Visit to Russia

16 October 1911

The latest news is Matisse's arrival. His first day in Russia was, for him, a let-down. He had passionate dreams of seeing the Hermitage (they went to St. Petersburg for that purpose). I wrote to Tolstoi asking him to arrange a possible view and, probably, Dmitrii Ivanovich would have done that, but Shchukin, on learning from the doormen that the Hermitage was closed for the whole winter, felt too shy to trouble the Director—and now, it would seem, Matisse won't be able to see the Hermitage at all. He ran from the Autumn Exhibition and the Alexander III Museum in horror. He liked St. Petersburg as a city very much.

The day before yesterday they arrived in Moscow and Matisse stayed with Shchukin. The first day they looked round his collection and Ivan Morozov's collection. Yesterday evening he visited us. And you should have seen his delight at the icons. Literally the whole evening he wouldn't leave them alone, relishing and delighting in each one. And with what finesse! . . . At length he declared that for the icons alone it would have been worth his while coming from a city even further away than Paris, that the icons were now nobler for him than Fra Beato. . . . Today Shchukin phoned me to say that Matisse literally couldn't sleep the whole night because of the acuity of his impression. Tomorrow I'm taking him to the Cathedral, the Vestry and to one of the Old Believer chapels. This evening we're going to *Sadko*. (Yesterday he heard Igumnov play at our place and liked it very much.) Then one of these days I'll arrange a concert of the Synod Choir for him and also a celebration at *The Bat* on 1 November, and so on. I hope he'll like it all. I find Matisse very nice and I'm awfully sorry that you're not here—he's such a refined, cultivated and original man. And everyone who talked to him yesterday carried away the same impression. . . .

Ilya Ostroukhov (1850–1929), collector and artist, was an important personality in Russian artistic circles. Aleksandra Pavlovna Botkina was the daughter of Pavel Tretyakov (founder of the Tretyakov Gallery) and the widow of the collector S. S. Botkin. In the autumn of 1911, Matisse went to Russia at the invitation of Sergei Shchukin.

Count Dmitrii I. Tolstoi was director of The Hermitage.

The Russian State Museum in St. Petersburg (now Leningrad) was then called the Russian Museum of the Emperor Alexander III.

Matisse reached Moscow on 5 November 1911 (23 October 1911, in the Old Style Russian calendar).

Fra Beato, better known as Fra Angelico (Guido di Pietro, 1387–1455), Renaissance painter.

Nikolay Rimsky-Korsakov's opera Sadko (1898). Konstantin Nikolaevich Igumnov (1873–1948), well-known pianist. The Bat was a cabaret-theater founded in 1908 by actors from the Moscow Art Theater.

Ernst Goldschmidt

POLITIKEN

"Henri Matisse"

24 December 1911

Ernst Goldschmidt (1879–1959), Danish painter and art historian who interviewed Matisse in Issy in the autumn of 1911.

"You're looking for the red wall," Matisse said to me as I gazed at the objects depicted in the painting and mentally compared them to what I could see in the studio. "That wall simply doesn't exist. As you can see here, I painted the same furniture against a completely blue-gray studio wall. These are experiments, or studies if you will. I am not happy with them as paintings. Once I had discovered that red color, I put these studies in a corner, and that's where they'll stay. Where I got that red from I couldn't say. But in a little while we'll take a walk in the garden, and maybe then things will seem clearer to you. I find that all these things—flowers, furniture, the commode—become what they are for me only when I view them together with that red. I don't know why that is, and as for the question you're asking me, well, I might as well ask you the same thing.

"Take that landscape with the two female nudes, for example. Fine, you find the figures weak but the landscape beautiful. You may be right, I don't know. But let me tell you how I painted them. You told me that a few months ago you visited Collioure, where I usually spend the winter. I find that that part of France has a beauty perhaps less obvious but ultimately much richer than that of the other coast, the Riviera, whose landscapes everyone loves so much. In Collioure I take walks every day in the hills along the shore, and that's where I saw the landscape you find so beautiful. I found it impossible to paint. I made many attempts, but I found the paintings I produced trivial, they didn't say anything. There were many more paintings in what I was seeing than in what I was painting. This is the only one that came close to satisfying me, and the reason, I think, is precisely the two female figures, imperfect as they are in more than one respect. The color yellow came to me one day when I was trying, in vain, to paint those hills. So I painted the canvas over again, this time painting the whole of the landscape in relation to the yellow color I gave the nude bodies in the middle of the picture, and I think I can say that it is only because of that yellow that the landscape turned out such that you venture to call it a good painting. Here are a few sketches."

*   *   *

"Here is my garden. Apart from Collioure, this is my favorite place. Isn't that flower bed more beautiful than the finest Persian rug? Look at the colors, how different each is from the next, yet how they blend together. Look how that very dark blue shades off into a bold, light color clearer and more luminous than the sky itself and yet so intense and precise in its force. Or that cactus flower. It looks like it's made of silk and velvet—look how it shines like a burning coal against the grayish-green background, like a spider web hanging above thick, dark green silk! Have you ever seen such gigantic violets? In the spring, when all these shoots sprout from the earth and creep down the garden pathways like a lavishly decorated train, I'm going to watch how the seeds, spindly and pale, suck strength and color from the sun day by day. The big horticulture companies sometimes send me illustrated catalogues. If I see something that looks beautiful, I order seeds and plant it, first in

COLORPLATE 42

Matisse refers here to The Red Studio, *1911, in which is visible a landscape with two female nudes.*

my greenhouse and then in my garden. It is instructive to look at the difference between the crude reproductions in the gardening catalogue and the actual flower when it blossoms. In fact, compared to the colors here, my paintings aren't much better than those reproductions. The intensity of these colors, that texture, is unattainable. Sometimes I put flowers right alongside my paintings, and how poor and dull all my colors seem! In the last analysis, it is not at all white, it is not at all, finally, a well-defined color that can be painted. It suggests soft light on white—like the glimmer of sunset on eternal snows. Have you ever seen the peak of Canigou in spring, bathed in the evening's red reflection?"

Canigou, a granite peak of the east Pyrenees, which rise, only 50 kilometers from the sea, to an altitude of some 10,000 feet.

André Salmon

LA JEUNE PEINTURE FRANÇAISE
"The Fauves"
1912

André Salmon (1881–1969), French poet, writer, and art critic. Salmon was close to Apollinaire and Max Jacob and was especially supportive of the cubists.

In the Symbolist period there were literary cases quite similar to the case of Henri-Matisse. Leaders surfaced, authorizing some remarkable audacities. Others had the strength for and the joy of carrying on.

From 1895 to 1899, Henri-Matisse paints wisely and not without vigor. He is a studious pupil of Gustave Moreau, who consulted the realists. At the dawn of the twentieth century, he seems troubled, and while bursting the academic screen, he makes a refreshing appeal to light; not as a continuator of the impressionists, who were only interested in one luminous instant.

It is a considerable revolution, and so violent that all of a sudden, Fauvism is invented. Others will search with Henri-Matisse, breaking with the old laws; others—who were already searching—feel comforted by his audacities and follow him.

Henri-Matisse, who wanted the greatest light, by rejecting lighting arrives at color, and that is what enslaves him. However, from this period date his best still lifes and some very nice flower paintings.

And then come the landscapes of Collioure, the famous *Girl with Green Eyes,* and these nudes, deliberately executed, still arbitrary, but which give the evidence in his work of a logical striving toward style. From one stage to the next, Henri-Matisse contradicts himself: he is the most incoherent of modern artists.

His real gifts are gifts of skill, flexibility, prompt assimilation, of an exact science, but one quickly acquired—feminine gifts. The more facility he acquires, the more color has the upper hand over drawing, which, finally, he does not consider anymore. His drawing is summary, reduced to the last discoveries absorbing the essential; moreover, the figures consist in the multiplication of three or four characters, among which is *The Man with the Violin* tirelessly repeated.

Henri-Matisse's taste has been very much praised. Though undeniable, it is second rate. It is a modiste's taste, whose love of color equals the love of *chiffon*.

So, this master who presided over an academy was not a leader, but, to be frank, only a schoolmaster. Henri-Matisse's teaching will be sought only by minor artists sent from abroad to Paris and if, in Germany, a few painters still translate Matisse, like the vaudevillians of Berlin translate

The Man with the Violin *apparently refers to the standing violinists in* Music (Sketch), *1907, and* Music, *1910.*

Matisse had been repeatedly criticized for having mostly foreign students.

our playwrights, French salons are less and less encumbered by Muscovite or Scandinavian "Matisseries."

What was pleasing and deserving—coming from Odilon Redon—in the work of the first Fauve, was absorbed by the most different painters and the most unacquainted with his immediate concerns.

So it was with almost all of Henri-Matisse's attempts. With Picasso and Derain, he studied barbarian images, perhaps he may have even discovered them before Picasso. The Polynesians, Dahomeans, and Sudanese artists' lesson was followed, and Henri-Matisse got left out, as a result of his impatience to do virtuoso paintings one right after the other.

This painter who is, despite all, something quite similar to a great painter (so, too, great poets are by no means pure poets) is henceforth an isolated man.

Othon Friesz, who followed him most closely, was the first one to break loose of him. Everything is nihilism in Henri-Matisse's work; it comes to nothing, it is sterile, yet one cannot ignore it.

We must pay attention to it, not only for the temporary enthusiasm it has aroused, but also for the definitive date it marks in the history of painting.

Henri-Matisse and Picasso, whose career cannot be forecast further, will have the destiny of giving the signal for an outpouring of talents, the remembrance of which will prove more enduring than that of the romantic revolution.

Wassily Kandinsky

ON THE SPIRITUAL IN ART

1912

Wassily Kandinsky (1868–1944), Russian artist and theorist best known for his role in the Munich expressionist movement The Blue Rider, was an admirer of Matisse from as early as 1906.

Cézanne, the seeker after new laws of form, . . . treats these objects just as he does people, for he had the gift of seeing inner life everywhere. He expresses them in terms of color, thus creating an inner, painterly note, and molds them into a form that can be raised to the level of abstract-sounding, harmonious, often mathematical formulas. It is not a man, nor an apple, nor a tree that is represented; they are all used by Cézanne to create an object with an internal, painterly quality: a picture. This is what Henri Matisse, one of the greatest of the modern French painters, also calls his works. He paints "pictures," and in these "pictures" he seeks to reproduce the "divine." [See his article in *Kunst und Künstler* (1909).] To achieve this, the only resources he uses are the object (a person or whatever it may be), which he uses as a point of departure, and those means that belong to painting and painting alone—color and form.

Guided by his purely personal qualities, with his particularly French chromatic gift, Matisse stresses and exaggerates color. Like Debussy, he is unable to free himself for long from conventional beauty: Impressionism is in his blood. And so with Matisse, among pictures possessing great inner life, one finds other pictures that, owing their origin principally to external causes, to external stimuli (how often this makes one think of Manet!), possess principally or exclusively a merely external life. In these pictures, the specifically French, refined, gourmandizing, purely melodic beauty of painting is raised up to cool heights above the clouds.

Ludwig Coellen

Ludwig Coellen (b. 1875), German art historian.

DIE ROMANTIK DER NEUEN MALEREI

1912

It was Matisse who first developed the previously patchy manner of representation to its full purity. He was the first, in his better paintings, to make color a finely tuned instrument, from which he summoned a romantic mood-music. He was the first, again only in his better paintings, to refute claims of objectivity so judiciously that style, in the most pronounced manner, became form, in the objective simplicity that is the prerequisite for success. The flat style, in which one color spreads broadly onto another, appears here as a law for the first time.

Pure lyricism, which Matisse came to by way of Gauguin, is the first and most immediate manner of perception that, with its connection to nature, was able to fulfill the new striving for spiritualization: the spiritual essence of things had to be discovered in the appearances of things, in their outward being and in the value of that being—that is, as a sphere in which things consist of feeling. The modern artist must find this essence as a metahuman, objective sphere of feeling which acquires the diversity of its worth through the diversity of things. That sphere could best be revealed artistically in painting, in the creation of an outward appearance. But this was merely the visible surface of the spiritual in the world, and the romantic presses to its deepest core. He wants more than merely to penetrate the object. He wants to lay bare the law, the primeval law of the object's spirituality, of its inner being, just as Van Gogh drove to its primeval power. He wants to penetrate and reconstruct the vital force in which that sphere of feeling is created.

It is out of this artistic intent, which naturally operates only as a particular manner of perception, that the work of Pablo Picasso arises. And it arises in astonishing consistency as a style that has been called Cubism. Nowhere in this entire development of a painting style is the true function of Romanticism as work and conquest as clearly apparent as in the case of Picasso, in contrast to the classical arrangement of an acquired richness.

This striving for the vital force of the law in which the spiritual sphere of appearances is born could be achieved for the painter only through the purest means possible—that is, universal–spiritual conception of space. Whereas it was color that afforded Matisse the means to express pure feeling, Picasso turned to pure space and its differentiation. For it is from space that arise the colors that enable feeling to be expressed. It is in the spatial formation that the law of the origin of the subject becomes manifest. Whereas Van Gogh undertook a dynamic atomization of the color spectrum, for Picasso it was necessary to advance to pure space perception as the human–spiritual function. However, the law of pure space perception in this sense is the geometric formation as such, and therewith the geometric differentiation of the painting's space became the fundamental procedure of Cubism.

Clara T. MacChesney

THE NEW YORK TIMES MAGAZINE

"A Talk with Matisse"

9 March 1913

Clara Taggart MacChesney (1860–1928), American painter and writer, studied at the San Francisco School of Design and the Colarossi Academy, Paris. MacChesney interviewed Matisse in Issy in June 1912; the article was published just before the Armory show closed in New York.

In speaking of the different post-impressionists, it is always Matisse's name which heads the list. At first it was a name which to many suggested the most violent extremes in art; it was spoken of with bated breath, and even horror, or with the most uproarious ridicule. But time has converted many, even of our most conservative critics and art lovers, to his point of view. One says: "He is a recluse in revolt, a red radical, whose aim is not to overturn pomps, but to escape from them. He discards traditions, and seeks the elemental," and "he paints as a child might have painted in the dawn of art, seeing only the essentials in form and color."

Five of his canvases were placed before me by a Paris dealer last summer, and arranged in chronological order. The first was an ordinary still life, painted in an ordinary manner. The next two were landscapes, broader and looser in treatment, higher in key, showing decidedly the influence of the impressionists. The last two I studied long and seriously, but I failed absolutely to discover what they expressed—still life, landscapes, or portraits.

Thus it was with keen interest that I sought this much-ridiculed man, whose work is the common topic of many heated arguments today. After an hour's train ride and walk on a hot June day, I found M. Matisse in a suburb southwest of Paris. His home, the ordinary French villa, or country house, two-storied, set in a large and simple garden and inclosed [*sic*] by the usual high wall. A ring at the gate brought the gardener, who led me to the studio, built at one side, among trees, leading up to which were beds of flaming flowers. The studio, a good-sized square structure, was painted white, within and without, and had immense windows (both in the roof and at the side), thus giving a sense of out-of-doors and great heat.

A large and simple workroom it was, its walls and easels covered with his large, brilliant, and extraordinary canvases. M. Matisse himself was a great surprise, for I found not a long-haired, slovenly dressed, eccentric man, as I had imagined, but a fresh, healthy, robust blond gentleman, who looked even more German than French, and whose simple and unaffected cordiality put me directly at my ease. Two dogs lay at our feet, and, as I recall that hour, my main recollection is of a glare of light, stifling heat, principally caused by the immense glass windows, open doors, showing glimpses of flowers beyond, as brilliant and bright-hued as the walls within; and a white-bloused man chasing away the flies which buzzed around us as I questioned him.

"I began at the Ecole des Beaux-Arts. When I opened my studio, years after, for some time I painted just like anyone else. But things didn't go at all, and I was very unhappy. Then, little by little, I began to paint as I felt. One cannot do successful work which has much feeling unless one sees the subject very simply, and one must do this in order to express one's self as clearly as possible."

Striving to understand, and failing to admire, a huge, gaudy-hued canvas facing me, I asked: "Do you recognize harmony of color?"

A show of Matisse's work at the Bernheim-Jeune Gallery in 1913. Photograph courtesy Galerie Bernheim-Jeune.

Almost with indignation he replied: "I certainly do think of harmony of color, and of composition, too. Drawing is for me the art of being able to express myself with line. When an artist or student draws a nude figure with painstaking care, the result is drawing, and not emotion. A true artist cannot see color which is not harmonious. Otherwise it is a *moyen*, or recipe. An artist should express his feeling with the harmony or idea of color which he possesses naturally. He should not copy the walls, or objects on a table, but he should, above all, express a vision of color, the harmony of which corresponds to his feeling. And, above all, one must be honest with one's self."

"But just what is your theory on art?" I persisted.

"Well, take that table, for example," pointing to one nearby, on which stood a jar of nasturtiums. "I do not literally paint that table, but the emotion it produces upon me."

After a pause full of intense thought on my part, I asked: "But if one hasn't always emotion. What then?"

"Do not paint," he quickly answered. "When I came in here to work this morning I had no emotion, so I took a horseback ride. When I returned I felt like painting, and had all the emotion I wanted."

"What was your art training?" I asked.

"I studied in the schools mornings, and I copied at the Louvre in the afternoons. This for ten years."

"What did you copy?" I asked curiously.

"I made a careful copy of *La Chasse* ("The Hunt") by Carraccio [*sic*], which was bought by the government for the Hotel de Ville, at Grenoble; and *Narcisse*, by Poussin, which was also bought for the provinces. Chardin's large still life of fish I worked at for six years and a half, and then left it unfinished. In some cases I gave my emotional impressions, or personal translations, of the pictures, and these," he said sadly, "the French government did not care to buy. It only wants a photographic copy.

"No, I never use pastels or watercolors, and I only make studies from models, not to use in a picture—*mais pour me nourrir*—to strengthen my knowledge; and I never work from a previous sketch or study, but from memory. I now draw with feeling, and not anatomically. I know how to draw correctly, having studied form for so long.

"I always use a preliminary canvas the same size for a sketch as for a finished picture, and I always begin with color. With large canvases this is more fatiguing, but more logical. I may have the same sentiment I obtained in the first, but this lacks solidity, and decorative sense. I never retouch a sketch: I take a new canvas the same size, as I may change the composition somewhat. But I always strive to give the same feeling, while

COLORPLATE 47

carrying it on further. A picture should, for me, always be decorative. While working I never try to think, only to feel."

As he talked he pointed to two canvases of equal size. The sketch hung on the wall at my left, and the finished canvas was on an easel before me. They represented nude figures in action, boldly, flatly, and simply laid in in broad sweeps of vivid local color, and I saw very little difference between the two.

"Do you teach?" I asked.

"Yes, I have a class of sixty pupils, and I make them draw accurately, as a student always should do at the beginning. I do not encourage them to work as I do now."

Yet I had heard he was not always successful in this respect.

"I like to model as much as to paint—I have no preference. If the search is the same when I tire of some medium, then I turn to the other—and I often make *pour me nourrir;* a copy of an anatomical figure in clay."

"Tell me," I said, pointing to an extraordinary lumpy clay study of a nude woman with limbs of fearful length, "why—?"

He picked up a small Javanese statue with a head all out of proportion to the body.

"Is not that beautiful?"

"No," I said boldly. "I see no beauty when there is lack of propor-

The similar canvases are the two versions of Nasturtiums with the Dance, *1912.*

Portrait of Pierre Matisse. 1909. Canvas. 16 × 13″ (40.6 × 33 cm). Private collection.

134

COLORPLATE 38. *Fruit and Bronze (Nature Morte au tapis d'Orient)*. 1910. Canvas. 35 × 45⅞″ (89 × 116. 5 cm).
Photo APN, Agence de Presse "Novosti."

COLORPLATE 39. *Goldfish and Sculpture*. 1912. Canvas. 46 × 39⅝″ (116.8 × 100.6 cm).
Collection, The Museum of Modern Art, New York. Gift of Mr. and Mrs. John Hay Whitney.

COLORPLATE 40. *Interior with Eggplants.* 1911. Distemper on canvas. 82⅔ × 96″ (210 × 244 cm).
Musée de Peinture et de Sculpture, Grenoble.

COLORPLATE 41. *The Painter's Family.* 1911. Canvas. 56¼ × 76⅜" (143 × 194 cm). The Hermitage, Leningrad.

COLORPLATE 42. *The Red Studio*. 1911. Canvas. 71¼ × 86¼″ (181 × 219.1 cm).
Collection, The Museum of Modern Art, New York. Mrs. Simon Guggenheim Fund.

COLORPLATE 43. *Moroccan Landscape.* 1912. Canvas. 46½ × 31½″ (118.1 × 80 cm).
Moderna Museet, Stockholm. Photograph: Statens Konstmuseer.

COLORPLATE 44. *The Pink Studio*. 1911. Canvas. 70¹¹/₁₆ × 87″ (179.5 × 221 cm). The Pushkin Museum, Moscow.

COLORPLATE 45. *Goldfish.* 1912. Canvas. 57⅞ × 38⅝″ (147 × 98 cm). The Pushkin Museum, Moscow.

tion. To my mind no sculpture has ever equaled that of the Greeks, unless it be Michael Angelo's."

"But there you are, back to the classic, the formal," he said triumphantly. "We of today are trying to express ourselves today—now—the twentieth century—and not to copy what the Greeks saw and felt in art over two thousand years ago. The Greek sculptors always followed a set, fixed form, and never showed any sentiment. The very early Greeks and the *primitifs* only worked from the basis of emotion, but this grew cold, and disappeared in the following centuries. It makes no difference what are the proportions, if there is feeling. And if the sculptor who modeled this makes me think only of a dwarf, then he has failed to express the beauty which should overpower all lack of proportion, and this is only done through or by means of his emotions."

Yet I gazed unconvinced at the little figure of a dwarf from Java, for I failed to see anything of beauty.

"Above all," he said, struggling with the fly problem, "the great thing is to express one's self."

I thought of a celebrated canvas Matisse once produced of blue tomatoes. "Why blue?" he was asked. "Because I see them that way, and I cannot help it if no one else does," he replied.

"Besnard's work? It is full of feeling, but *sans naiveté*. Monet is very big. Cézanne seeks more the classic. Raffaelli I do not like at all. Goya, A. Dürer, Rembrandt, Corot, Manet are my favorite masters.

"Yes, I often go to the Louvre," he replied, in answer to my question, asked rather perfunctorily.

"Whose work do I study the most? Chardin's," he answered, to my great surprise.

"Why?" I asked curiously, for there is not a trace of that great man's manner in Matisse's work.

"I go there to study his technique."

Audible silence.

His palette, lying near by, was a large one, and so chaotic and dis-

Paul Albert Besnard (1849–1934) and Jean-François Raffaelli (1850–1924), popular painters in a generally acceptable, watered-down "modern" style.

orderly were the vivid colors on it, that a close resemblance could be traced to some of his pictures.

"I never mix much," he said. "I use small brushes and never more than twelve colors."

"Black?"

"Yes, I use it to cool the blue."

I pondered on this statement a few moments before asking him if he had traveled much.

"No, I've only made a trip or two to Germany, and lately to Tangier in Morocco, and I've never been to America.

"No; I seldom paint portraits, and if I do only in a decorative manner. I can see them in no other way."

The few hanging on the wall were forceful, boldly, simply executed, and evidently done in stress of great emotion. An eye, in one canvas, was placed on the right cheek, and in another one-half of the face was drawn so unpleasantly to one side as to suggest a paralytic stroke.

One's ideas of the man and of his work are entirely opposed to each other: the latter abnormal to the last degree, and the man an ordinary, healthy individual, such as one meets by the dozen every day. On this point Matisse showed some emotion.

"Oh, do tell the American people that I am a normal man; that I am a devoted husband and father, that I have three fine children, that I go to the theatre, ride horseback, have a comfortable home, a fine garden that I love, flowers, etc., just like any man."

As if to bear out this description of himself, he showed me the salon in his perfectly normal house, to see a normal copy which he had made at the Louvre, and he bade me good-bye and invited me to call again like a perfectly normal gentleman.

As I walked down to the station in the blazing sun in the throes of a brain-storm from all I had seen and heard, Augustus John's opinion of Matisse stood out clear in my mind: "He has a big idea, but he cannot yet express it."

The English painter Augustus John (1878–1961), rebellious and independent early in his career, subsided into painting fashionable portraits in a bravura manner.

M. Matisse sells his canvases as fast as he can paint them, but, if the report is true, speculators buy the majority. He certainly has the courage of his convictions; his work is constructive, and not destructive; he has many followers, who, unlike him, are not expressing themselves, but are imitating him. One critic maintains that his work acts like a sedative to a tired brain, or as an easy chair to a weary toiler home from his day's work. But I am positive that I should not dare when weary, to sit for long in front of his *Cathedrals at Rouen*.

A facetious American asked: "Are these ruins?" for none of the pillars were perpendicular, but standing or falling at all angles to the horizon. She asked the reason of this apparent intemperance of the pillars and walls and was told: "Oh, we do not see as you do; we are perfectly free, and are bound by no rules, and we see as we please!"

MacChesney is confusing Matisse with Claude Monet, who painted his famous series of the Rouen cathedral facade from 1892 to 1894.

Marcel Sembat

CAHIERS D'AUJOURD'HUI

"Henri Matisse"

April 1913

Marcel Sembat (1862–1922), socialist politician and art collector. This article was the most extended essay on Matisse's work published up to that time.

He is forty-three years old and already shrouded in legend. Paleographers think you have to scour antiquity to find mythic beings. But not at all! Here we have a fabulous being in our own time.

He arouses scandal, fear, pity, envy, wrath. "The man's a clown!" "No he's not; he's just crazy, that's all. Crazy as a loon. But quite serious, I assure you." "Oh come on! All he's interested in is shock value. He's a phony, he's buggering us!" "I'm telling you the man is sick." "Sick? No way. If he's crazy, it's crazy like a fox. He's taking us for a ride, us and the public too." "Well, if so, that's not all he's taking. He gets as much as he wants—sells whatever he wants and at the price he wants. His paintings go like hotcakes. A hundred thousand francs a year." "You must be joking!" "No, word of honor, didn't you know? There are Russians who swear by Matisse—and Germans, and Americans. Anything he wants!" "It's disgusting! Revolting!" "He's got a mansion of his own in the suburbs, and he goes horseback-riding every morning in the Acacias. Quite the life!"

Oh, Matisse's income, his hundred thousand francs, his customers! People fume with rage. Once there was a rumor that one of his major foreign buyers had died. The good news traveled fast. So much for human feeling these days!

Stripped of the legend, the real Henri Matisse, the man who comes to the gate in gardener's gear when you ring the bell in Clamart, the flesh-and-blood Matisse, is no monster or raving madman, no hoodlum or phony, and no skilled manipulator of snobs and scandals either. Just the opposite. A fair-haired gentleman of slow, deliberate speech, he has a serious and reflective air. Academic people sometimes thought he looked like a German professor with those horn-rimmed glasses he liked to wear.

His greatest desire is to explain himself, to prove himself, to make himself understood—and understood by everyone, by any passerby, no matter whom. Say you go with him to the opening of some salon. The bores in the crowd will stop you every time. They all want to meet Matisse, and you can see they're going to plunge right in. You shoot him a warning glance: why bother with such people? But Matisse doesn't notice your signals. He goes ahead, and soon he is engaged in a frank and straightforward effort to enlighten some well-meaning simpleton who would be perfectly content with Dagnan-Bouveret.

Taine spoke somewhere of those well-meaning types who would buttonhole a philosopher on a street corner and ask him to explain metaphysics and the nature of the human soul. Many lovers of paintings—or perhaps I should say people who like to look at paintings—are like that. But Matisse is the kindly philosopher who is only too happy to answer their questions. Anyone who has ever heard him speak that way, his voice sincere and conscientious, pausing to search for the right word, hesitating and then continuing confidently, will simply laugh when he hears anyone question Matisse's good faith. Matisse's good faith: to think that I've actually heard people doubt it! Can't you see that his art is his whole life? That his efforts absorb him entirely, that he clings to them with all his soul, all his being, like a Bernard Palissy or a Christopher Columbus? If he wanted, he could easily have applied his talent and powers to well-trod paths.

Virgil tells us in the *Georgics* that a threatening swarm of bees will scatter at a mere handful of dust. I wouldn't know. I have never tried it and have no desire to test that theory. But I do know—and this I have tried—that a seething swarm of spiteful people can be reduced to silence with a single question: Does he have talent or not?

Ah! Silence all around. Some mumble softly, some grumble, others look away, still others simply shrug. Never—and I mean never—will anyone, will any painter, honestly respond with a brisk "Matisse? No talent!"

Never. Not a soul. "No talent? I didn't say that! Talent, yes, but he's wasted it, ruined it. Talent? Sure he has talent! *That's exactly why he's unforgivable!*"

Bernard Palissy (c. 1510–1589), French ceramist and scientist known for his idealism and dedication to his work.

That is no small admission; it is of some importance, is it not? Henri Matisse at least has the power to compel everyone, even his most determined enemies, to admit that he has talent, that he is a painter, and that if he wanted. . . .

Indeed, if he wanted. His very first exhibitions at the Salon of the Société Nationale des Beaux-Arts proved it well enough: if he wanted, he could have taken an honored place in the front ranks of recognized painters. Even now, every time he exhibits a painting from which it is erroneously deduced that his intransigence is on the wane, what a rush of gratitude we hear! He is congratulated as though thanks were being offered. I still remember those exquisite flowers of his at the Salon d'Automne. People who normally tear him apart were praising him with tears in their eyes. At last he's becoming human!

Is it necessary to add that if Matisse exasperates so many people, his enthusiasts are equally numerous? The two go hand in hand. An artist must be hated by some to be fervently loved by others.

But what do friends and enemies matter? The paintings are there, the work exists. Look at it! Friend or foe, you recognize a Matisse painting from the very first glance. It resembles nothing else, it bears his personal stamp. It is his and his alone! It is original.

But there are innumerable ways to ape originality. You can hit upon it by chance or achieve it by artifice, give an appearance of it through tricks, facile quirks, or eccentricity. But that is a superficial originality, wholly external and forced. Matisse is profoundly original. The least of his canvases has that gift of authority and mastery; and it is a gift he seems to have been born with: go to the Bernheim gallery and ask Fénéon to show you one of his very early paintings, a studio exercise or a still life reminiscent of Chardin, and even then you can sense a master's touch.

Of what does this mastery consist? Ah! That gift—the most important one of all, the secret that goes to the essence of art—cannot be analyzed. If we were standing in front of a painting, I might say to you, "Look at that big, bold red sprawling there so placidly, unaware of its own insolence! Look at those contrasts of strong and simple colors. Savor the clarity and inevitability of the relation between them, and the overall harmony born of those contrasts, drawn together into such a well-balanced system. Aren't you gripped, too, by the powerful composition? Every stroke has such magnificent certitude, such independent force. The uniform impression of mastery comes through everywhere: in the bold, contrasting colors, the imposing composition, the overall balance of the work, the perfect proportions of its arrangement." Even then I would not be saying anything illuminating, but at least you would be looking at the painting all the time I was talking!

One day an old painter friend of mine was chatting with me, leaning against the mantelpiece in my office in the rue Cauchois. As he talked, he stared at a photograph on the opposite wall, a reproduction of a drawing of a woman seated on a bench, her torso bent slightly. Suddenly he broke off in mid-sentence and, walking over to the work, said, "But what have you here, good friend? Why, this is superb! Who did it?" He leaned closer to read the signature, straightened up, turned on his heels, and, clearing his throat, went back to the fireplace.

"Well," he went on, "as I was saying, we have to follow up on that project for outdoor art schools. We have to get organized for the Beaux-Arts students." Then all of a sudden he exclaimed, "Look, I have no quarrel with that Matisse of yours. My God, I can see that it's a superb drawing. But there are other things of his that. . . ."

I didn't say a word, simply sat back and enjoyed the spectacle of an established painter swallowing the bait of a Matisse and thrashing at the end of the line.

Matisse is original without trying to be. I know no one more insistent

Félix Fénéon (1861–1944), French art and literary critic who directed La Revue Blanche *from 1895 to 1903 and later was associated with the Bernheim-Jeune Gallery.*

Five Heads of Jeannette. Bronze. The Los Angeles County Museum of Art. Presented by the Art Museum Council in memory of Penelope Rigby.

From right to left:

Jeannette, I: 1910. 12⅞″ (32.7 cm).
Jeannette, II: 1910. 10½″ (26.7 cm).
Jeannette, III: 1911. 23½″ (59.7 cm).
Jeannette, IV: 1913. 24″ (61 cm).
Jeannette, V: 1916. 22⅞″ (58.1 cm).

about the necessity of influences and the folly of seeking to evade or deny them. He feels strong enough to assimilate, digest, and incorporate everything from outside. Let weaker artists copy! They will find no escape, try as they might. He, for his part, has examined everything, and with passion: Cézanne, Van Gogh, Gauguin, the impressionists, Odilon Redon. He has learned all the lessons and has used whatever techniques served his character and suited his genius.

I take great pleasure, for example, in tracing in his work signs of the efforts and discoveries of the great Odilon Redon in those marriages of contrasting colors that I mentioned earlier. I recall one of Odilon Redon's screens whose expert effects intrigued me. It had a wonderful bud with a purplish shimmer: if you came closer and stood with your nose to the canvas you saw a yellow patch thrown into relief by a black patch right next to it; if you stepped back a bit, those two sharp, crude colors merged again into a velvety unity. Such exquisite magic will often catch you by surprise in Matisse's paintings. There is no need to belabor what he owes to Cézanne. But what of it? Borrowings? On the contrary! Lessons, if you will, sustenance, everything a great artist absorbs from his predecessors, what Wagner took from Beethoven, Victor Hugo from Shakespeare, Zola from Balzac, Anatole France from Le Sage, the early Paul Bourget from Stendhal, Taine, and Lamartine.

But from whom, I ask you, could Matisse have taken what is, in my view, his real secret, of which even he is unaware, the very essence of his worth? I would sum it up this way: each of his paintings, from the earliest works to the most recent, has always offered the viewer a *harmony of feeling*. Whether it be a still life, a landscape, or a studio model, the artist has always—instinctively at first, then ever more consciously—gone beyond nature, controlled it, extracted its essential features, its *tendencies*, selecting and emphasizing those features whose tendencies harmonized, rejecting and ignoring the others. Hence the profound unity, the captivating understanding, the emotional tone of each painting and of his work as a whole. Who could have told him that secret? What modern artist could have taught him that?

He sensed it before knowing it at all. His character, his soul, revealed it to him ever more clearly as he worked. He found it by looking for it.

Matisse unburdened himself five years ago in the *Grande Revue* (the 25 December 1908 issue). Of course, I have no intention of paraphrasing those sober and judicious pages here. But he has developed further since then, and the truth I have spoken has become more evident.

Sembat refers to Matisse's article "Notes of a Painter," reprinted in this volume.

One day Matisse was coming back from the south after a summer in Cavalière. My wife and I had gone to see him, and after lunch, with the connivance of Madame Matisse, we went rummaging through his boxes. All at once we gasped. We had come across a strange little painting, a thrilling thing, unprecedented, startlingly new, almost startling even to the man who painted it.

Matisse spent the summer of 1909 at Cavalière; the "strange little painting" referred to is Seated Nude, *1909.*

On a harsh pink ground that blazed among the shadows of a deep blue redolent of Chinese or Japanese colors sat a purplish-blue female figure. All four of us stood there looking at it, stunned, dazzled, the master seeming no more familiar with it than we were. Little by little its real character became clearer: it was impossible to look at any individual piece of that painting—the figure, for example, or the shadows, or the light greenery of the top; you had to take in the total shock of the whole all at once, with your eyes and with your soul. This work was, in the highest sense, indivisible and *synthetic*. "I didn't want to paint a woman," Matisse said. "I wanted to convey my total impression of the south."

Of all Matisse's works it is this little painting that I cherish most, because, if I may be permitted a word I have often used when talking to Matisse himself, it is like an egg, and in that egg lay the germ of a brood of new works, in particular his great decorative efforts, *The Dance* and *Music*.

COLORPLATE 35
COLORPLATE 36

There is not enough time to speak of this today. In any event, almost anything I could say about it will be suggested by the splendid exhibition of paintings he has brought back from Morocco, which are now on view at the Bernheim gallery.

Do you recall the large painting of the *Moorish Café*? If not, go see it. All of Matisse is in it! Take a good look at it and you will see everything in it. But you have to look closely, as Ruskin looked at the Spanish Chapel.

COLORPLATE 49

The exhibition of Matisse's Moroccan paintings, scheduled for 14 to 22 February at the Bernheim-Jeune Gallery, was actually on view 14 February to 5 March 1913.

Bear in mind that those reclining figures, all of the same shade of gray, a gray so serene, their faces rendered by yellow-ochre ovals, were not always painted that way. Look at the gentleman at the top left: he was once red. Another, at his side, was blue; yet another was yellow. Their faces had features, eyes, mouths. The one on top was smoking a pipe. Examining the bottom of the painting we find traces of a row of Oriental slippers that had been eloquently placed outside the café.

Why did he eliminate the slippers, the pipe, the features on the faces, the varied colors of the burnooses?

Because for Matisse, to perfect is to simplify. Because consciously or not, deliberately or despite himself, whenever he has strived hardest he has moved toward simplicity. A psychologist would see it immediately: by instinct Matisse goes from the concrete to the abstract, the general.

I have told him this. "The thing is," he answered, "I move the way my feelings point, *toward ecstasy*." And my heart leapt with joy, for the phrase reminded me of a famous passage in which Th. Ribot deftly analyzed the *Castillo Interior* of Saint Teresa.

Augustin Théodule Ribot (1823–1891), French painter and engraver. Saint Teresa of Avila (1515–1582), Roman Catholic mystic whose writings on the soul's union with God include The Interior Castle *(1588).*

"Then too," Matisse continued, "it's how I find peace of mind."

Peace of mind! How many times, and for how many years, has he told me that! Peace of mind is what he craves! What he needs! What he wants to bestow! He wrote as much in the 1908 article I mentioned earlier. He said it to me again in front of *The Dance* and *Music,* those great works that aroused so much commotion! *"What I dream of is an art of balance, of purity and serenity, devoid of troubling or depressing subject matter, an art which could be for every mental worker, for the businessman as well as the man of letters, for example, a soothing, calming influence on the mind. . . ."*

In this striving toward the higher realm of great peace, however, the craft retains its prerogatives. Let us savor it before his painting of the *Moorish Café:* ". . . I have my goldfish bowl and my pink flower. That's what struck me most, those devils who spend hours contemplating a flower and some red fish. Well, if I paint them red, this vermilion would turn my flower violet. So what can I do? I want my flower pink, otherwise it's not my flower anymore. Unlike the fish, which could be yellow, I don't care about that, so yellow is what they'll be!"

But, you may ask, what about reality? Remember that the painter is compelled, by his materials themselves, to transform the real so as to express its essence. Do you think you can imitate a storm with zinc thunder and magnesium lightning?

Note also how highly decorative this painting of the Moorish café is. That is because Matisse does not tunnel into the wall, for its two dimensions—height and width—are enough for him. Seurat used to say: "A painting is a surface you excavate," but Manet said, "The flatter it is, the more it's art." And: "Let's make playing-cards!" Let the masters of intimate, agonizing art excavate! Let Rembrandt excavate! Matisse keeps his sorrows to himself! He does not wish to broadcast them. He wants to offer others only peace of mind.

And it is true that, the more you look at it, that painting of the Moorish café peacefully imbues you with a tranquil feeling of dreamy contemplation. A host of birds sang sweetly in cages hanging from the ceiling; Matisse declined to paint the cages, but a touch of the sweetness of the song passed into his painting.

I mentioned before that from his earliest works Matisse achieved a *harmony of feeling* in every painting. As you can see, he has remained faithful to himself; but you can also see that as he has developed and be-

According to Daumier, in creating areas of flat color in his pictures, Manet initiated a "return to the playing card." The phrase, distorted by Sembat, reappears in Levinson, "Henri Matisse at Sixty," further in this volume.

Henri and Amélie Matisse in Tangier, 1912. © Succession H. Matisse/1988. Archives Matisse.

come more possessed of himself, the essential features he wrests from nature have become increasingly abstract.

Now do you realize the grandeur of his undertaking? To express the *Emotional Abstract*, to paint the eternal, to extract the quintessence of feeling! Look! *The Dance*, whose magnificent boldness of design caused such a stir, was universally compelling for the frenzied, soaring movement that infused it. After *Music*, Matisse was sorry that *The Dance* had not been more refined, more tranquil, more nobly calm! And I have seen a charcoal sketch of *The Dance* as he sees it now, in which the movement has a solemn sweep.

He strives toward the eternal, the sublime, and he means for you to rise with him. If you do not, there will have been a misunderstanding between you. Tear your hair out or revile him because his faces have no nose, no eyes. It's just that you have remained on the ground, pedestrian level, too cleaved to the earth.

"What you're saying is nonsense!" my painter friends cry out. "Your Matisse is mad! He's not the first lunatic, the first mystic, to try to paint the soul! It's beating your head against the wall! The painting he wants is impossible!"

You think so?

That's what they told Columbus the day before he landed on the island of San Salvador. So what? I give up, you're right, there's no such thing as America. But is he any less a hero, he who gives his life to have a pure heart and to try the noble adventure?

Open your eyes, children, and look! You are painters, are you not? Then you know well enough that he who dares ascend to the heavens, even when he stays near earth, is more of a painter than you who protest so loudly.

The *Moorish Café* is not the only thing on exhibit. I lingered there because it reveals so much, but your eyes might well have alighted on that little marvel, the *View of Tangier*, with its flowers, its masses of blue, the green roof of the English church, and the pink run of the surrounding wall. And what do you think of the woman seated on a blue rug, in the corner of a terrace?

And the man from the Rif! How handsome he is, that great Rif devil, with his angular face and his savage build.

Can you look upon this splendid barbarian without dreaming of the warriors of yesteryear? The Moors of the *Chanson de Roland* had that same wild air.

In this Riffian, moreover, as in the woman seated on the terrace and the woman standing with a hand on her waist, you will recognize that same effort to extract the dominant features, the essential feelings, the great emotional traits, and to express them harmoniously, subordinating all else to them, sacrificing whatever would conflict with them.

I spoke of effort? Yes, the spontaneous effort of the artist seeking to satisfy himself, following his own path, the path to which the secret and irresistible call of his genius beckons him. Effort, but not procedure. The product of an instinct that has finally raised itself to self-consciousness, but whose drive remains instinctual, for conscious analysis comes only later!

"You know, *afterwards* I explain why I do something, but *at first*, when I do it, I feel the necessity as a whole!"

A maladroit sentence, clumsy and obscure, and it would be easy to straighten it out. But I find it enlightening as is, and would add nothing to it.

COLORPLATE 26

The Riffian, *1913, depicts a villager, in colorful native costume, of the Rif mountains in Morocco.*

Guillaume Apollinaire

L'INTRANSIGEANT

"M. Bérard Inaugurates the Salon d'Automne"

14 November 1913

By 1913, Matisse had lost his position as leader of the avant-garde to the cubists. But his Portrait of Amélie Matisse created such a strong impression at the 1913 Salon d'Automne that Guillaume Apollinaire wrote two reviews of it— excerpted here and below—and published them on consecutive days.

The painting by Bonnard, who pleasantly imitates Vuillard, has attracted much admiration, but I far prefer the Henri-Matisse painting on exhibit in the same hall. This portrait of a woman is the most voluptuous work that painting has produced in a very long time. The color sensitivity is superb, and the outward qualities of this internal painting are so intense and unusual that we can well understand why the artist now occupies a unique position outside the art of his era and why he cannot found a school. If there is a masterpiece on view at the Salon d'Automne, it is this and nothing else.

COLORPLATE 48

Guillaume Apollinaire

LES SOIRÉES DE PARIS

"Salon d'Automne: Henri-Matisse"

15 November 1913

Henri-Matisse's portrait of a woman is the best thing at this year's otherwise meager Salon d'Automne exhibition. To my mind, this portrait, along with the *The Woman with the Hat* of the Stein collection, is the artist's masterpiece. Never, I believe, has color been given so much life. Today's art, inward-looking as it is, having affected an austerity unprecedented in the arts since the reforms of David, no longer condescends to appear pleasant, and the Orphism of some painters is a devout and admirable intoxication with color. Henri-Matisse has always had a hedonistic concept of art, but he has also raised Gauguin's teaching to new heights. He has not remained a slave to verisimilitude and has understood, as no one else, the necessity proclaimed by the South Seas recluse for a double distortion, objective and subjective alike. His great merit, the characteristic feature of his personality, is that his work contains no trace of mysticism beyond the symbolism of color. He matches this moral soundness with a marvelous instinct that he has been careful to respect. His art is all sensitivity. This painter has always been a sensualist. Nevertheless, what was most striking in his older works was the eloquence of the colors, and the discriminating choice of forms. The figure being exhibited here, laden with charm and sensual delight, would seem to inaugurate a new stage in Matisse's art, and perhaps in contemporary art itself, from which sensual delight had almost entirely disappeared, nowhere to be found except in the magnificent and carnal paintings of the aged Renoir.

151

Henri Matisse,
Interviewed by André Verdet
ENTRETIENS NOTES ET ECRITS SUR LA PEINTURE
On Cubism
c. 1978

André Verdet (b. 1913), French poet and critic who, as an interviewer of a number of French artists, elicited one of Matisse's most detailed discussions of Cubism around 1952.

H.M. A difficult watershed for me was the period of Cubism's triumph. At my age, one can own up to one's past anguish, all the more because death does not cause me as much anguish as the physical suffering that sometimes leads to it. I was virtually alone in not participating in the others' experiment—Cubism—in not joining the direction that was acquiring more and more followers and whose prestige was becoming increasingly widespread.

A.V. You continued your work separately.

H.M. I was entrenched in my pursuits: experimentation, liberalization, color, problems of color-as-energy, of color-as-light. Of course, Cubism interested me, but it did not speak to my deeply sensory nature, to the great lover that I am of line, of the arabesque, those bearers of life.... For me to turn toward Cubism would have been to go counter to my artistic ideas.

A.V. Nevertheless, Cubism brushed against you.

H.M. Brushed against me, exactly. It was written about some of my compositions of the period that they were para-cubist. At the time, Picasso and I frequently exchanged ideas. We used to go for walks together.

A.V. When was this?

H.M. Shortly before the war, in '12 or '13. Our differences were amicable. Sometimes, strangely, our points of view met. Picasso and I were in one another's confidence. We mutually gave one another a great deal in those exchanges. We cared passionately about our respective technical problems. There is no question that we each benefited from the other. I think that, ultimately, there was a reciprocal interpenetration between our different paths. This was, it must be emphasized, this was at a time when one or another's discoveries were offered generously to all, a time of artistic fraternity. Look, when I think of Cubism, it is the coupled faces of Braque and Picasso that appear, along with their joint works.

A.V. Your relations with Picasso must have taken place in a rather extraordinary environment.

H.M. I liked Picasso very much those times when, seemingly playing devil's advocate, he insistently tried to counter something in me that, in reality, he cared about deep within himself, that roused his curiosity.... Then he would suddenly burst out laughing at the trap he had so mischievously set for me!

Ultimately, you know, I was very close to the cubists, since one of the strictest of them, Juan Gris, had also become a great friend of mine. We spent a summer holiday together at Collioure.

A.V. A few days ago, Picasso spoke of you to me, following a visit to you here in Cimiez in your studio.

Juan Gris (1887–1927), Spanish cubist painter who met Matisse at Collioure late in the summer of 1914; there, the two talked at length about painting.

H.M. Ah! and what did he tell you?

A.V. He said something very original and very beautiful. That if all the great colorist painters of this century could have composed a banner that comprised each one's favorite colors, the result would certainly have been a Matisse!

H.M. No, Picasso said that?

A.V. It was his way of paying homage to the great liberator, the limpid wise man of color that you were and that you continue to be with the recent paper cut-outs.

H.M. Come now, don't put my modesty to the test. I'm a bit tired. I'll get a scolding from Lydia. We have to stop. . . .

Lydia Delectorskaya (b. 1910), Matisse's secretary and model.

Head, White and Rose. 1914. Canvas. 29½ × 18⅛″ (75 × 46 cm). Photograph: Musée National d'Art Moderne, Centre Georges Pompidou, Paris.

Kenyon Cox
ARTIST AND PUBLIC
1914

Kenyon Cox (1856–1919), American painter, sculptor, illustrator, and writer who studied with Jean-Léon Gérôme (1824–1904) and Charles Carolus-Duran (1838–1917) in Paris.

With Henri Matisse we have not to deplore the deliquescence of a great talent, for we have no reason to suppose he ever had any. It is true that his admirers will assure you he could once draw and paint as everybody does; what he could *not* do was to paint enough better than everybody does to make his mark in the world; and he was a quite undistinguished person until he found a way to produce some effect upon his grandmother the public by shocking her into attention. His method is to choose the ugliest models to be found; to put them into the most grotesque and indecent postures imaginable; to draw them in the manner of a savage, or a depraved child, or a worse manner if that be possible; to surround his figures with blue outlines half an inch wide; and to paint them in crude and staring colors, brutally laid on in flat masses. Then, when his grandmother begins to "sit up," she is told with a grave face that this is a reaction from naturalism, a revival of abstract line and color, a subjective art which is not the representation of nature but the expression of the artist's soul. No wonder she gasps and stares!

Walter Pach
THE CENTURY MAGAZINE
"Why Matisse?"
February 1915

Walter Pach (1883–1938), American etcher, painter, and critic who considered studying with Matisse after meeting him, through the Steins, in 1907. An author of books on French art, he also translated Delacroix's Journal.

In art we cannot speak of progress as we understand the word in other relations; but there is such a thing as the insistence by a given generation on some quality which has been neglected for a time, and so we have at least the illusion of progress. The phase of art which developed through Corot and Renoir, and which finds its purest expression today in Matisse, is that of sensibility. Notice any pair of colors as they come together in his work, and you will feel that they could have been so related only by one who is deeply sensitive to color. Notice, too, how each line in his drawing moves according to the working of his thought, not from the accident of an appearance in the external world. So the volumes and masses of his composition are adjusted always under the control of a mind which is increasingly in contact with nature. What differentiates the sensibility of Matisse from that of others is its intensity. Where the layman feels the beauty of color and design for a moment and then lets his attention turn to something else, where the mediocre artist gives up the struggle after a short time and contents himself (and his public) with the copy of an object, Matisse keeps up the search for a month, perhaps for a year, and will not let the work go from his studio until the particular expression he needed has been reached. And if it is there, each detail will be found well in its place, and the useless ones, even if agreeable in themselves, will have disappeared. Sensibility is of course no new thing in art, but it is a quality specially emphasized in our time. And the fact that Matisse's work is thus modern in the best sense is reason enough for showing it in New York again.

The pursuit of the image that is our own and that is of interest, beyond all, to convey to others, the really creative act of producing something that did not exist before, develops quite different faculties from those which come from skill in reproducing—either the appearances of nature or the pictures of the past. The time comes when an artist working in such a manner gives each thing he sees a new existence, and he has the right to use those lines and colors which seem fitting to him to express it. As long as he is sure that his inspiration is genuine, original, not the result of the minds outside of his own or the things which are equally apart from him, he can add to his subject or subtract from it just what he likes, things seen or things imagined. And men are fundamentally so much alike that when one of them has satisfied himself in such a matter, his fellows will find that he has answered a need of theirs in doing so. There can be no other explanation of the fact that thousands of people who were at first baffled by the difference in exterior between Matisse's art and that of his predecessors have come to admire profoundly the painter whom they thought at first a wanton breaker with all that was best in the past.

At the present exhibition there will surely be many more who will see that the work before them is rich in the classic qualities, re-incorporated by one alive to the spirit of the world he lives in. It is the lesson of such an art that our people, artists and laymen, need more than any other. On the one hand we are constantly being asked to intensify our study of the past; on the other we are told that in our new country, where tradition has loosened its hold, we must strive to make something new. Matisse shows how the two things go together.

No effort could be more futile than that of the student who took it into his head to "paint just like Matisse." It has been tried by clever men, and all of them have failed. The stimulus and inspiration he affords are for everyone; his means of procuring for us these experiences are personal and indivisible. For those who want to produce art once more, the message of this painter reads clearly, that there is the great world current, with its ceaseless changes, and there are the masters and nature which must be consulted. What have we in ourselves?

Portrait of Walter Pach. 1914.
Etching and drypoint. 6⅜ × 2⅜"
(16.2 × 6 cm). Collection,
The Museum of Modern Art,
New York. Purchase.

*Willard Huntington Wright (1888–1939),
American journalist, writer, and critic
who, under the pseudonym S. S. Van
Dine, created the fictional detective Philo
Vance. His brother was synchronist artist
Stanton MacDonald-Wright
(1890–1973).*

Willard Huntington Wright

MODERN PAINTING:
ITS TENDENCY AND MEANING

"Henri-Matisse"

1915

It is this same desire to do away with the hackneyed forms of art that has driven the modern poets away from classic meters and caused them to seek a more plastic and adaptable medium in *vers libre*. Rondeaux, ballades, quatrains, octaves and the like are today as intrinsically perfect forms as they ever were, but the significance of their beauty has been lost through overuse, through too great familiarity. Our minds pass over them as over well-learned lessons committed to memory.

It is thus Matisse felt about the classic forms of his predecessors. These forms had once been beautiful: intrinsically they were still beautiful; but they had been habitualized by constant repetition, and new ones were needed. In order to find them Matisse says that, when before a model, he tried to forget that he had even seen a nude before and to look upon it with the eyes of one who had never seen a picture. By this he does not mean that his vision was naive, but that it was innocent of set rules and preconceived ideas of how form should be obtained. As a theory this attitude proved fruitful because, while he did not succeed in setting aside memory, he was nevertheless led to a conscious thrusting aside of his first impulses to depict form as he saw it. All painters, even the greater artists of the past, had copied form as it presents itself to the eye, but Matisse forced himself, through painstaking analysis, to express form in a totally novel manner; and to a certain extent he succeeded. One might well ask why, in modifying the human body, he did not, for instance, omit a leg or a head, thus making his expression at once purer and more abstract. The answer is that he realized that the spectator, after the first shock at seeing the unexpected form and the consequent men-

Portrait of Greta Prozor. 1916. Canvas. 57⅞ × 37¾″ (147 × 64 cm). Musée National d'Art Moderne, Centre Georges Pompidou. Photo Flammarion.

Portrait of Madame Matisse. 1915. Crayon.
24⅞ × 18⅞" (63 × 48 cm). Musée
Matisse, Nice.

tal readjustment to the new vision, would nevertheless recognize the picture as a depiction of the human figure. Therefore a complete recognizability must be maintained. If the artist omitted an eye or a mouth, for example, the spectator would experience physically the incompleteness of the vision. He would feel, through personal association, the blindness or the suffocation as suggested in the picture; and these shocks, being secondary physiological sensations, would detract from the *aesthetic* pleasure provoked by the work. The point is an important one, for it demonstrates the impossibility of appreciating art purely as abstract form so long as recognizable objects are presented. As modern painting progressed the illustrative gradually became relegated.

Much impetus for his abbreviations and accentuations of form came to him with his personal discovery of the wood carvings of the African negroes, the sculpture of natives of Polynesia and Java and of the Peruvian and Mexican Indians.

* * *

His modern means were the outgrowth of his understanding of color in its capacity to incite emotion. His first essays in this field were grayish. Later, through divisionistic methods, they grew brighter; and finally his color became pure and was applied in large planes. His works of this period shine as a source of light, and with his development of exaggerated forms his color interpretations also became exaggerated. Where he saw a green in a shadow he painted it a pure green; where he saw a yellow in light he made it a pure yellow; and so on with the other colors. But in these interpretations there is more than a mere desire to record hastily an optical vision. Each color is pondered at length in its relation to the others. It is changed a score of times, modified and adjusted; and when it is finally posed it is artistically "right." In other words, it fills harmoniously an important part in a picture where understanding and taste are the creators. In the work of Matisse *sensibilité* plays the all-important role, and while his results are satisfying as far as they go, there are times when we could wish for a greater rhythmic sense, a more conscious knowledge of the profundities of composition, and a less dominating desire to free each form and line from classic dictates.

With his color we can find no such fault. Though here his knowledge, like that of all other artists before him, is limited, the perfect harmony between tints, which in him reaches a more advanced stage than in any preceding artist, is the result of a highly sensitive eye and an impeccable taste. The beauty of his color alone makes him of paramount importance. Every one of his canvases is a complete color gamut created by taste and authenticated by science not only as to pure color but also as to grays and tone. In his still lifes he chooses objects alone for their color and form, and his sense of proportion is so developed and his reduction of line is carried to so final an economy that, as flat as these objects are, they seem to have a rich consistency and to extend themselves into visual depth. As in the case of all men who deviate from the narrow and well-worn path of monotonous tonality, Matisse is accused of dealing in raucous and blatant colors which set the head aching and the eyes smarting. But the accusation is true only of his followers who display little sensitivity and even less artistry, and who, in imitating the superficial aspects of his work, see only grotesque distortions and pure color. Matisse once had a school where he endeavored to develop the native talent of the Americans, Poles, Russians and Germans; but when a Bohemian woman, in reply to his question as to what she wished to do, answered, "*Je veux faire le 'neuf,'*" he abandoned the enterprise and retired to Clamart. She unwittingly summed up the desire of those meagre painters who, on seeing something novel, immediately throw themselves into imitating it. Matisse's followers approach his color gamut, but they never bridge that lacuna which separates a precise art from one which is *à peu près*. It is the last delicate refinement of perfect harmony which Matisse possesses and which his imitators cannot attain to, which places him in the rank of greatness.

Je veux faire le 'neuf': I want to do what is new.

A peu près: approximately.

Henri Matisse, Interviewed by Louis Aragon

On Nice

1943

Louis Aragon (1897–1982), French poet, novelist, and journalist who became a militant Communist in the 1930s and edited the Communist newspaper Le Soir *until 1953. He became a close friend of Matisse's in the 1940s.*

Nice, why Nice? In my work, I have tried to create a translucent setting for the mind. I have found the necessary limpidity in several places around the world: New York, the South Pacific, and Nice. If I had painted in the north, as I did thirty years ago, my painting would have been different. There would have been browns, grays, shadings of color through perspective. The painters over in New York say, How can any-

In December 1917, Matisse went to Nice, where he spent the better part of each year for most of the rest of his life.

COLORPLATE 46. *The Blue Window.* 1913. Canvas. 51½ × 35⅝″ (130.8 × 90.5 cm).
Collection, The Museum of Modern Art, New York. Abby Aldrich Rockefeller Fund.

COLORPLATE 47. *Nasturtiums and "The Dance"* (first version). 1912.
Canvas. 75⅝ × 44⅞″ (190.5 × 114 cm). The Pushkin Museum, Moscow.

COLORPLATE 48. *Portrait of Madame Matisse.* 1913. Canvas. 57 × 38⅛″ (145 × 97 cm).
The Hermitage, Leningrad.

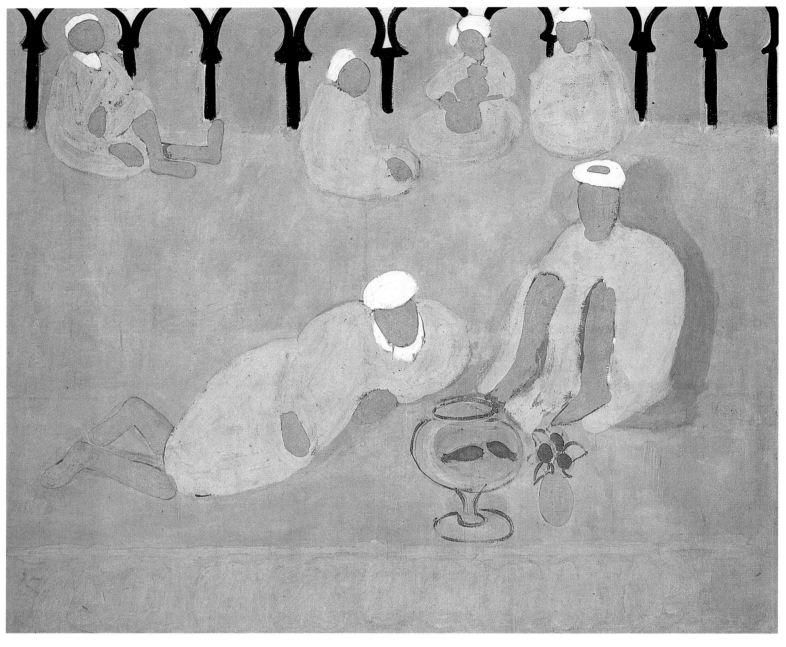

COLORPLATE 49. *The Moorish Café*. 1913. Canvas. 69¼ × 82¾″ (176 × 210 cm). The Hermitage, Leningrad.

COLORPLATE 50. *The Open Window, Collioure.* 1914. Canvas. 45⅞ × 34⅝″ (116.5 × 88 cm).
Photograph: Musée National d'Art Moderne, Centre Georges Pompidou, Paris.

COLORPLATE 51. *View of Notre-Dame*. 1914. Canvas. 58 × 37⅛″ (147.3 × 94.3 cm).
Collection, The Museum of Modern Art, New York. Acquired through the Lillie P. Bliss Bequest and the
Henry Ittleson, A. Conger Goodyear, Mr. and Mrs. Robert Sinclair Funds, and the
Anna Erickson Levene Bequest given in memory of her husband, Dr. Phoebus Aaron Teodor Levene.

COLORPLATE 52. *The Yellow Curtain*. 1914–15. Canvas. 59 × 38⅝″ (150 × 98 cm).
Collection Stephen Hahn, New York.

COLORPLATE 53. *Artist and Goldfish*. 1914. Canvas. 57¾ × 44¼″ (146.5 × 112.4 cm).
Collection, The Museum of Modern Art, New York. Gift of Florene M. Schoenborn and Samuel A. Marx.

one paint here, with this zinc-colored sky? But in fact it's wonderful! Everything becomes clear, translucent, exact, limpid. Nice, in this sense, has helped me. What I paint, you see, are objects conceived with plastic means. When I close my eyes, I see the objects better than I do with my eyes open, stripped of accidental detail, and that is what I paint.

Georges Besson
LE POINT
"Matisse's Arrival in Nice"
July 1939

It was around 20 December 1917 that Matisse moved into the Hôtel Beau-Rivage in Nice; a little later to the Hôtel de la Méditerranée on the Promenade des Anglais; then, for two months in the summer, with his son Pierre to a small villa, "des Alliés," located in luxuriant Harris Park, beneath Mont-Boron, amid the eucalyptus, olive trees, cypresses, the hedges of roses, and the field of wild anemones; and finally to Place Charles-Félix, in the quarter of the old commercial streets, the church of Sainte-Réparate, the steps up to the château and the market saturated with the hearty scents of lemons, fresh fish, and carnations. In these successive homes, Nice procured for Matisse the serenity so favorable to his work: portraits, landscapes, the first tricolor interiors of his hotel room: the reds of the rug, the white of the large net drapes, the blue of the sea or of a half-open violin case. And Nice would procure for Matisse the company of Renoir.

* * *

I am fairly certain that Matisse paid his first visit to Renoir on 31 December 1917. Relations between the two painters quickly became frequent and cordial. Of the "wild beast" and his work Renoir knew only what the occasional companions and the dealers disclosed about him, some reproductions chosen from among the most displeasing.

Matisse became, at the end of the day, the regular interlocutor of the old man, who had a horror of evening and sought relief from his apprehension about his nightly sufferings.

Renoir loved to chat, and he reminisced about his pals and readily answered the questions of his visitor, who, methodical in the practice of his art, discreetly warned the master against certain overbold mixtures of colors. Infirm and mummified in his armchair, his hands wrapped in linen bandages except for the hooked thumb that gripped the brush every day for hours, his eyes piercing beneath the gray cap, Renoir listened. Then he returned to his anxieties, the dangers faced by his sons called to war, badly wounded, and several times operated upon. He recounted domestic worries that, coming from that emotional old man, took on exaggerated proportions.

* * *

Matisse took his first works to Cagnes in early 1918. These were the landscape with pines near the château, showing the Baie des Anges, his just-completed self-portrait, an *Open Window* that must have excited Renoir with its stability, the overall harmony without superfluous details, the "state of condensation of the sensations" that makes the painting: "What willful energy, what an exact and profound expression of the

Georges Besson (1882–1971), critic, journalist, publisher, and friend to many of the artists whose work he collected and wrote about, notably Albert Marquet (1875–1947) and Albert André (1869-1954). In mid-December 1917, Matisse went to Marseille with Marquet; there he did a small portrait of Besson; he did a second later in Nice. Besson arranged Matisse's meeting with Renoir and photographed Matisse painting his 1918 self-portrait. Despite Besson's precise recollection, Matisse was long thought to have first settled in Nice in late 1916. We now know Besson's account to be accurate.

The visit to Renoir was in effect a gift for Matisse for his forty-eighth birthday. His renewed interest in the impressionists had caused him to seek out Claude Monet not long before.

The Painter and His Model. 1916–17.
Canvas. 57⅝ × 38³/₁₆″ (146. 5 × 97 cm).
Photograph: Musée National d'Art
Moderne, Centre Georges Pompidou,
Paris.

COLORPLATE 62

Matisse later illustrated Repli *and*
Apollinaire, *by poet and writer André
Rouveyre (1879–1962). His friendship
with Pierre Bonnard (1867–1947) lasted
until that painter's death. Jules Romains
(pseudonym of Louis Farigoule,
1885–1972), poet, writer, and the
founder of "Unanimism."*

hotel room in Nice! The blue of your sea should jump forward but it
stays where it should be! Same with the black curtain rod . . . that makes
me angry as hell!" Then Renoir would say, laughing and trying to pass
an imaginary brush under his leg: "I thought Matisse worked like
this. . . . It's not true. This boy takes a lot of trouble. . . ."

The day after moving into the Hôtel Beau-Rivage, Matisse must have
already put his austere and hard-working life in order: the frugal
breakfast, his violin exercises at a remove in a bathroom so as not to disturb his neighbors on the floor, the sessions of painting and drawing,
afternoon and morning, the diversion of an hour's sculpting at the Ecole
des Arts Décoratifs before a cast of Michelangelo's *Night*, the time devoted to his friends in Nice, the visits from friends from the coast and
from Parisians passing through: the painter Simon Bussy, roosting up in
Cabbé-Roquebrune, and his friend André Gide; Rouveyre, living in
Vence; Bonnard, at the Hôtel de l'Ilette in Antibes, etc., and Jules Romains.

Guillaume Apollinaire

CATALOGUE DES OEUVRES DE MATISSE ET PICASSO

"Henri Matisse"

1918

This text is from the preface to the catalogue for a Matisse and Picasso exhibition at the Galerie Paul Guillaume, 23 January to 15 February 1918. The remainder of the preface dealt with Picasso, whose art Apollinaire compared to a "beautiful pearl." This was Apollinaire's last text on Matisse; the poet, severely wounded in the war, died of influenza in November 1918.

Every painting, every drawing by Henri Matisse possesses a certain virtue that one cannot always define but that always strikes one as an authentic force. It is the artist's strength that he does not attempt to oppose this force but allows it to act as it will.

If one were to compare Henri Matisse's work to something, it would have to be an orange. Like the orange, Matisse's work is a fruit bursting with light.

Inspired by a total good faith and by a genuine desire to know and to realize himself, this painter has never ceased following his instinct. He allows his instinct to choose among his emotions, to judge and delimit his fantasy, and to look searchingly into the depths of light, nothing but light.

With the years, his art has perceptibly stripped itself of everything that was nonessential; yet its ever-increasing simplicity has not prevented it from becoming more and more sumptuous.

It is not mere skill that has made this art simpler and this work more intelligible. Rather, as the beauty of light has gradually become merged with the power of the artist's instinct—an instinct in which he trusts implicitly—all the obstacles to this union have disappeared, the way memories sometimes melt into the mists of the past.

Letters from Matisse to Charles Camoin

On Style and Work Habits

May 1918

The painter Charles Camoin had met Matisse through Marquet in 1899, soon after Matisse returned to Paris from the south; in 1904, after Camoin's first military service, they became good friends. (Camoin had worked briefly in Moreau's studio, when Matisse had already left.) The two kept up a lively correspondence from 1905 through the Second World War. This selection dates from Camoin's French army service in the First World War.

2–9 MAY 1918

Outline produces grand style (though half-tones bring you closer to the truth but less grand).

Don't you think that this is a slightly one-sided view of the matter, and that you can do outlines in a mere semblance of the grand style or half-tones in a genuine grand style? Who had the greater style, Gauguin or Corot? I believe that style comes from the order and nobility of the artist's mind, whether the order is acquired and developed or entirely intuitive, which is perhaps the consequence of order. But it results from a particular slant, it yields no more than half-tones. This is said without pretensions. . . .

23 MAY 1918

Yes, I will still be in Nice early next month, and it will be hot.

I expect to stay until 15 June, maybe longer, but it's so hot that I'm a little afraid. I've been working in the sun all this time, from 10 to noon, and I'm exhausted for the rest of the day. I'm going to change my schedule—as of tomorrow I start at 6:30 or 7 in the morning. That should give me a good hour or two of work. The olive trees are so beautiful then—high noon is superb, but oppressive. I think Cézanne captured its tonal harmonies very well, but not, fortunately, its glare, which is unbearable. A little while ago I took a nap under an olive tree, and the color harmonies I saw were so touching. It's like a paradise you have no right to analyze, but you are a painter, for God's sake! Nice is so beautiful! A light so soft and tender, despite its brilliance. I don't know why it often reminds me of the Touraine (should that have two *r*'s?). The Touraine light is a little more golden; here it is silvery. Even though the objects it touches have rich colors—the greens, for example, I often break my back trying to paint them. Having written that, I let my eyes wander the room where some of my old daubings are hanging, and it occurs to me that I may have hit the mark once in a while after all, though I can't be sure.

I am proud that you've been made a sergeant. I can already see myself taking walks with you here. I hope to show you some spots you don't already know. Unfortunately, I won't be able to put you up. I say that mainly because I probably won't be able to show you what I see every day: the 5 o'clock sunrise that colors Nice and its mountains (actually the other way around). My place overlooks Nice; I'm on the Villefranche ridge, and the sun comes up behind me. First I see the mountains near Cagnes light up, then the Nice château, and finally the city itself, every day at 5 (you can see I'm serious). Perhaps I could take you on a walk at 7, it would be worth all the trouble and might stand you in good stead

This letter contains a sketch of Matisse napping.

The Music Lesson. 1917. Canvas.
96 × 82½″ (243.8 × 209.5 cm). Photograph
© 1988, The Barnes Foundation.

later on, when you're a civilian again. Which you will be some day. I'll show you how to get to my villa soon, so you won't have trouble finding me. Write to me again before that.

I clasp your hand. . . .

Ragnar Hoppe
STÄDER OCH KONSTNÄRER
"My Visit with Matisse"
1920

Knut Ragnar Johan Hoppe (b. 1885), Scandinavian critic, interviewed Matisse at 19, Quai Saint-Michel in June 1919 after Matisse's first large post-war exhibition, "Oeuvres recentes de Henri-Matisse," at the Bernheim-Jeune Gallery, 2 to 16 May 1919.

COLORPLATE 51

I rang. The master himself opened the door. We went through a couple of rooms with blinds drawn—the family was in the country—and finally came to his studio, a room of intermediate size with a low ceiling and rather bourgeois furnishings but a wonderful view of the quay, Notre-Dame, and the Saint-Michel bridge, with its swarms of pedestrians, cars, and buses. I recognized the view at once; Matisse had painted it many times. And I told him so. Yes, he answered, I never tire of it; for me, it is always new, and just now it is more dear to me than ever before. The fact is, you see, that I was down by the Mediterranean for a couple of months, and that enables me to look again with fresh eyes at Paris, which is always Paris, that is, something indescribably glorious. To be sure, this little apartment here is inconvenient, but I have lived here for many years, I've grown attached to it, and I can't be without the view.

On the walls all around hung unframed studies held up by thumb-tacks, most of them by Matisse himself, but also a couple of paintings by Courbet and Cézanne. A few chairs of old-fashioned design, a pair of tables with a painter's paraphernalia, books, magazines, and heaps of drawings filled the rest of the room, which gave the impression of joy in work more than in order. Matisse offered me a cigarette, and we sat down in two comfortable armchairs. I had not previously had the opportunity to study his features closely, since I had met him only fleetingly once before, but now I could observe him in peace and quiet. Matisse is now fifty years old, but he continues to be extremely lively and voluble, and he talked almost nonstop all the time, so I only once in a while had to ask him a question or briefly answer one of his. He most resembles one of those French professors who commonly give lectures to society audiences, and this impression of scholarliness is perhaps, for the most part, attributable to the spectacles that adorn his face, which also is framed by a dark beard. Like almost all Frenchmen, he gesticulated a great deal, and while talking, he invariably illustrated his sentences with expressive hand movements. He is of average height but fairly sturdy and square of build. As elegantly dressed as an English gentleman, he was wearing a light-gray suit of the latest cut, and I noticed that the color of his neckerchief and his soft silk shirt had been chosen with great care and taste.

"Well, did you see my show at Bernheim's?"

"No," I answered. "Unfortunately, it had closed by the time I arrived here in Paris, so I could only see the paintings that had not been sold. But I did notice that you have now pretty much abandoned strong, very intense colors and that even your form seems softer and more impressionistic. May I ask you if there is a definite idea or intent behind this style, which to me seems almost a return to an earlier stage?"

"Yes, you see, when you have achieved what you want in a certain sphere, when you have exploited the possibilities that lie in one direction, you must, when the time comes, change course, search for something new. For the time being, I am working predominantly in black and gray, with neutral, subdued tones, because I felt that this was necessary for me right now. It was quite simply a question of hygiene. If I had continued down the other road, which I knew so well, I could have ended up as a mannerist. One must always keep one's eye, one's feeling, fresh; one must follow one's instincts. For the rest of it, I am seeking a new synthesis, and if you go down to the Triennale exhibition, you will find a composition there, a canvas from last summer, in which I have combined all that I've gained recently with what I knew and could do before. My friends say it is my best painting, but in that respect I do not share their opinion. I'm sure I have done better things, and I will do still better in the future; you may rely on it. But you must promise me, anyway, to go and look at that painting because I set great store by it. Yes, I'm the happiest man in the world; I've always known the way I should go, I have never for a moment strayed from it, and I see now that it leads to the goal, my goal. I have not made any blunders, and I am proud and glad of that. I worked as an impressionist, directly from nature; I later sought concentration and more intense expression both in line and color, and then, of course, I had to sacrifice to a certain degree other values,

Matisse exhibited three paintings at "La Triennale, exposition d'art français" at the Ecole des Beaux-Arts, Paris, 5 May to 30 June 1919.

COLORPLATE 60

The Plumed Hat. 1919. Pencil. 19⁵/₁₆ × 14⁹/₁₆" (49 × 37 cm). The Cone Collection, formed by Dr. Claribel Cone and Miss Etta Cone of Baltimore, Maryland.

The Plumed Hat. 1919. Pencil.
13¾ × 11½″ (34.9 × 29.2 cm). Mr.
and Mrs. William R. Acquavella.

body and spatial depth, the richness of detail. Now I want to combine it all, and I believe I will be able to, in time. Look at that portrait over there, for example, the young lady with the ostrich feather in her hat. The feather is put there as an ornament, decorative, but it also has body; you sort of feel its lightness, the soft, airy fluff that you really can blow on. The material of the blouse is a fabric of a quite particular kind, the pattern of it has its own distinct character. I want to depict the typical and the individual at the same time, a distillation of all I see and feel in a motif. Now, you may think, like so many others, that my paintings appear improvised, haphazardly and hurriedly composed. If you don't mind, I'll show you some drawings and studies so you may better understand how I work."

Matisse took out a huge portfolio, with close to fifty drawings, all for the same lady's portrait. On the wall hung a couple of oil studies for the same canvas; the completed one was in a sales gallery. "You see here," Matisse continued, "a whole series of drawings that I did for one single detail, the Vandyke collar around the young lady's neck. The very first ones are worked out minutely, each mesh, yes, almost each thread; then I could simplify more and more, and in this last one, when I sort of knew the lace by heart, I was able to translate it with a couple of quickly drawn lines into an ornament, an arabesque, without losing the character of

COLORPLATE 66

Because his account refers to the White Plumes *series, Hoppe makes it possible to date these pictures to the first half of 1919.*

lace, and of that particular lace. And at the same time, it is a whole Matisse, isn't it? I worked the same way on the face, the hands, and all the other details, and of course I did a lot of movement and composition studies. There is a great deal of work but also a great deal of joy behind a painting like that. You can see for yourself how nicely and securely the hands rest in her lap. The problem wasn't solved quite as easily as all that, believe me. But it is just that way that the hands should rest for their position to be in harmony with the bearing of the body and the expression of the face. It was only little by little that I realized this, but when I became fully aware of it, then I could also fix my impression with lightning speed.

"Yes, that drawing is bad, but I keep it all the same, because I may be able to learn from it some day, just because I failed. One learns something every day; how could it be otherwise? For example, I have never been as conscious as now, at this time, of the beauty of the color black, all that it can do, both as a contrast and by itself. When you see my interior from Nice, you'll understand some of that. If I had had the painting here, I should have liked to show it to you, but it will have to wait until another time."

"But M. Matisse," I said, "you don't have any real compositions here. All I see on the walls are just studies for portraits or sketches made outdoors. Aren't you working on any larger things?"

"Yes, but I can't paint them in this small room here. I need space around me, large dimensions, distance, and that's why I have built myself a studio out in my villa at Issy-les-Moulineaux, where I work on all my decorative projects. There, too, I have a glorious garden with lots of flowers, which for me are by far the best lessons in color composition. The flowers often give me impressions of color that are indelibly burnt onto my retina. Then, one day when I stand, palette in hand, before a composition and know only approximately which color I should apply, a memory like that may appear in my mind's eye and come to my aid, give me a start. In that way, I, too, become a naturalist, if you can call it naturalist to listen to one's memories and to the selective instinct that is so closely related to all creative talent.

"You are welcome to come out there some day, and you can just call me up here some afternoon; then we could keep each other company on the way. You see, I had a telephone installed in this little apartment just today." We chatted awhile about the Parisian telephone service, which is well below the level of the Swedish one, and parted with a handshake and an *au revoir*.

Jean Cocteau
LE RAPPEL À L'ORDRE
"Professional Distortion"
12 May 1919

Jean Cocteau (1889–1963), French author, painter, and filmmaker, was a leading avant-gardist. This response to Matisse's 1919 Bernheim-Jeune Gallery show was one of the first critiques of the more "relaxed," naturalistic style of the early Nice paintings.

The exhibition of Henri Matisse's recent paintings at the Bernheim gallery is quite intriguing. The sun-soaked *fauve* has become a Bonnard kitten. The atmosphere of Bonnard, Vuillard, and Marquet prevails in the room. The window of a Vuillard room opens onto a Marquet sea. You look for Matisse and what you find, dare I say it, is a case of professional distortion.

The impressionists were blinking in the sunlight. Along came Matisse. He braved the sun, which deceives our eyes, filling them with green after we've looked at red. Freely, joyously, and bravely, he painted works that gave the flavor of life.

What's going on?

Matisse is working without underlying discipline, without the hidden geometrics of Cézanne and the old masters, whose traces young painters seek and which, unfortunately, too often take the place of painting in their canvases. Matisse doubts, gropes, and hesitates instead of deepening his discovery. Does he realize the true value of this discovery and how it enchants us? These latest works hint of an artist of the Ecole des Beaux-Arts who holds that "painting is a wretched occupation," and "if I had a son . . . ," and so on and so forth, just the opposite of the delightful genius that produced his earlier paintings.

On the way out of the exhibition I found myself humming "The Crayfish" from Guillaume Apollinaire's *Bestiary*, recently set to music by Francis Poulenc and Louis Durey.

> *Uncertainty, o my delights,*
> *You and I we go about*
> *As do the crayfish*
> *Backing up, backing up.*

André Lhote

LA NOUVELLE REVUE FRANÇAISE
"Matisse Exhibition"

1919

André Lhote (1885–1962), painter, critic, and illustrator whose work, though generally associated with Cubism, represented a somewhat drier, more academic cubist style.

M. Matisse's exhibition, coming after M. Braque's, gives us occasion to observe a struggle between the two most violently opposed aesthetics of our time. While M. Braque is smitten with the esoteric, cultivating mystery even more than technique, to the same extent M. Matisse confines the meaning of his works to the precise appeal of the colorful surface. While M. Braque is captivated by intellectual speculation, M. Matisse, scorning the *a priori,* claims that his sensory responses alone suffice as a motivation for working. His activity is purely receptive. This painter excels in theorizing about sensory impact; in fact, he pronounces himself unable to paint without some immediate stimulus. Now M. Matisse's mind can be aptly compared to a steel trap. Putting little trust in his imagination, the artist leaves his studio, which no ghost haunts. He goes into the street, the garden, or the fields, and there, attentive to the most unexpected impression, he captures it with unequaled skill the instant it appears. The bird of sensation, stroked and gorged, grows plump; it is at that moment that the painter lavishes his ingenuity on giving the most brilliant luster to his captive's plumage. This method of working, one must admit, produces rare developments in color, of which no painter before M. Matisse would have ever dreamed—I wonder if it would not be more appropriate to say: "ever *dared* to dream."

Indeed, what was M. Matisse's chief preoccupation, if not to take over one major element of pictorial art, that of color, and to give this element, dominated until now by form, a predominating value over form? Being a victim of the fashionable malady that spared no one—but of which some of us have tried very hard to cure ourselves—M. Matisse has found his personality not through enthusiastic or thoughtful adoption of a balanced technique, but rather through disequilibrium, in the overthrow of the values which constitute this technique. The study of the properties of color, replacing drawing, modeling, and chiaroscuro absorbed him completely: an eye astonishingly gifted at picking up the subtlest reflections easily solved those problems which a painter always sets himself in accordance with his personal capacities. This cultivation of a favored talent to the exclusion of all others is very characteristic of a certain contemporary frame of mind; it represents an absolute novelty in the history of art and merits special study.

If M. Matisse has achieved at Bernheim's gallery a complete success hitherto denied him by the public, it is not because the paintings he showed there revealed any greater mastery than his earlier works had. *La Toilette* or *Nude No. 3* were very fine works, much superior to those that triumph today; their unpopularity resulted from their revealing in the artist a certain will to control his first impression, whereas his recent works allow us to see him abandoning himself unreservedly to his perceptions. The public loves this nonchalance, seeing in it the reflection and almost the counterpart of its own laziness in thinking and judging.

COLORPLATE 23

Violinist at the Window. 1917. Canvas. 59 × 38½″ (150 × 98 cm). Photograph: Musée National d'Art Moderne, Centre Georges Pompidou.

Here is the reason why the best of Matisse, those paintings from 1910 which, despite their almost too-pronounced stamp of an era, were humanized by the painter's meditation, were the last to please the public.

But isn't it inopportune to deplore the success of Matisse's most superficial works, and isn't it befitting for him to be proud of his latest adventure? One would be inclined to believe him, recalling the words of this painter brave enough to write of the work of art—summing up as well the aspirations of most artists of his time—that he wished it to have "for the businessman as well as for the man of letters a soothing, calming influence on the mind, something like a good armchair which provides relaxation from physical fatigue."

M. Matisse has exerted considerable influence; it is less important today now that the war has changed the outlook of most artists, inducing them to meditate on deeper problems. We should note that this influence was felt especially by the painters of the north, those less analytic of temperament who would be seduced by the early conclusions of the master. Among the novices and self-taught artists, this influence was equally powerful. The experiments Matisse made exclusively with color revealed to the young painters an element of painting which, lacking education, they were unable to detect through the veil of the chaste French tradition. The harmony of adjacent colors, the balance between warm and cool colors, and the resonances of complementaries are problems easily resolved in all periods by the masters in the museums, but the sole solution to the problem is introduced by them in their works. The result is presented so naturally that one accepts it without perceiving it; the genius of it is recognizable only if one knows the craft. By contrast, a canvas by M. Matisse, stripped of the details which, in reality and in those classic works, *support* color and help to hide its technical importance, offers us a solution not so much complete as *in the process of becoming.* The artist makes us a witness to his *tour de force;* he even goes as far as admitting his anxiety by leaving "blanks," and showing the feverish pace of his work by leaving, as though with reverence, pencil marks, smudges, and spots on the canvas.

One might object that Cézanne, too, left "blanks." But in his eyes they were only temporary: to fill them in he was waiting to discover that elusive and suitable shade. The master of Aix, a Titan less fortunate than Michelangelo, did not live long enough to finish that great painting *The Bathers* (in the Pellerin collection), which was to be our *Last Judgment*. A crack remains in that work; M. Matisse has slipped through it. (And in his wake how many others!) He has shattered a facade of the edifice, and so has carried painting beyond its classical boundaries. The problem Cézanne solved is thus brought back for consideration. But, to be fair, after the empiricism of Impressionism (which Renoir escaped, being, with less outward severity, as disciplined as Cézanne), we needed, in order to see clearly again, to straighten out our tainted perceptions as we took time to think through the laws of the architecture of painting and drawing. Matisse has helped us resolve various primordial dilemmas, and this is what we must remember. He figures, in the garden of French painting, as an extremely fragile and precious flower, representing the most troubled period in the history of art.

But an artist, even if more specialized than M. Matisse, is never alone. The pursuits of the latter, be they ever so singular, harmonize with those of many recent schools. Orphism and Futurism owe him a great deal.

At a certain point, his influence even won over those painters fated to be the most ungrateful to the tasks of reformulation: the cubists. Following him, they studied the irradiating properties of the colors of objects. Like Matisse, they separated the elements that constituted external reality in order to study each one on its own. Here is an excerpt from an article by M. Severini, signifying what the goals of M. Matisse and the cubists have in common:

Lhote, like a number of commentators, notes the fact that most of Matisse's students between 1908 and 1911 were Scandinavian, German, or American.

One day Matisse showed me a study he had "from life" in a
street of Tangier. In the foreground was a wall painted blue.
This blue affected all the rest, and Matisse gave it the greatest
emphasis possible while still retaining the objective construction
of the landscape. In spite of that, he must have admitted to
himself that he had not rendered the hundredth part of the
"sensory intensity" provoked in him by that blue. He achieved
that degree of intensity in another picture (*The Moroccans*), but
there the real structure of the landscape disappeared, giving
way to a willed yet sensory architecture.

COLORPLATE 57

One discerns how the mechanism by which M. Matisse gives his sense
of color an absolute power over his sense of form connects with the
mechanism by which the cubists seek, primarily through color, to "reconstruct" reality with plasticity. This parallel will let us identify the
mental process of each of these opposing schools: where M. Matisse

moves from sensation to idea, the cubists work from idea to sensation. [For example, M. Matisse needs to see a plate in order to conceive little by little the plastic virtue of a circle. The cubists first conceive of a circle and will condescend to "motivate" it by means of a plate.] They acknowledge the informing power of the latter only after having scientifically mastered it.

The physicist Charles Henry has somewhere written: "Perception of light and perception of forms are considerably affected by the exercise or relaxation of the visual apparatus, while perception of color remains independent of this." This was enough for the cubists to accept M. Matisse's premises, but to conclude also that, in order to save the purity of form, it is necessary not to inflate form by the explosive force of color, as Matisse has done, but to put the "local color" over the "local form." These were prodigal new speculations that plainly show the excesses to which these artists were driven as slaves to a dogma, victims of a theory based on something other than the exercise of a deeply felt understanding of painting.

Charles Henry (1859–1926), physicist known for his study of light and color.

When Lhote reprinted this text in La Peinture *(1933), he changed the last lines to read: "These are prodigious speculations of novelty, which should not arouse laughter but whose resolution should be patiently awaited. That resolution will occur easily and naturally once the cubists allow themselves to breach the fortress of their theories under the gentle prodding of feeling and attain a wider knowledge of the eternal laws of painting."*

Marcel Sembat
HENRI MATISSE
"Matisse and His Work"
1920

How is it that we know that Matisse has mastered himself so fully? Because his power is becoming harmonious and blossoms softly. He produces a totality. The effort is concealed. The hardy underlying structure is no longer visible. The artist offers us the finished masterpiece, fully constructed, without flaunting the means he has used.

There is a time when the artist in search of himself is all too enamored of his own effort. How well we can understand! And how right he is! For is not every invention of a new technique a triumphant discovery? The artist makes us share in that achievement, and what a joy it is for us to be involved. At that stage, we savor in the painter's canvases the robust daring of the various parts, and are swept away by the mighty recklessness of an effort so violent that it outstrips its goal.

Then the artist's ambition matures. He becomes the master of his work, and henceforth it is the goal that fascinates him more than the method, more than the striving. He refuses to display efforts that exceed the results achieved. His friends will say that he is now taking pains not to show his hand just as assiduously as he previously flaunted it.

Do not look for any essential difference between his earliest and his latest paintings. If you do, trivial appearances will mislead you. No, at bottom it is the same painting. But in the latest works you will find a more perfect awareness of the artist's goal and of the skill he commands. He knows himself better; he knows his method; he has self-control.

Sembat's 1913 tribute to Matisse was succeeded by the first volume in the Nouvelle Revue Française series, "Les Peintres français nouveaux," excerpted here. The first true monograph on Matisse, it reproduced works from 1897 to 1919 and affirmed the continuity and high quality of Matisse's recent work, which faced rising criticism.

*   *   *

Those years in Nice marked a supreme moment in Matisse's work. I refer not to this or that painting which may have turned the art world upside down but manifested no more than his known and familiar skills. A deeply shadowed room, for instance—with the thin luminous slit of the window overlooking the sea and the solid props of an armchair and a violin—enchanted everyone who knows what to look for. The new gift, the supreme expertise, is that Matisse's masterpieces are now perfect

COLORPLATE 64

wholes. It is easy enough, of course, to compose a whole by bringing together merely second-rate skills. But Matisse achieves wholeness without sacrificing or losing any of his vigor. His stroke of genius is to have succeeded in disciplining it.

Elie Faure

HENRI MATISSE

"Opinions"

1920

Jacques-Elie-Paul Faure (1873–1937), physician, critic, and art historian whose four-volume Histoire de l'art *(1909–1921) is a classic of its kind. This excerpt is from one of a number of monographs he wrote on modern painters.*

I had been told long ago that what Matisse did was metaphysics. For a few years I believed it. Then one day, looking at one of his paintings, it struck me that this painting was alive. I liked it. I tried to understand why I liked it, and why I liked others of his paintings less. Pursuing this train of thought, I realized that Matisse's metaphysics, which began in his youth with feelings vividly and powerfully expressed, had for a time crossed deserts of pure abstraction, a kind of tension and painful tautness, a need to cry out, against all: "Here is what my senses tell me." Then, just because of that excessively tense energy of investigation and expression, he came to rediscover, within his senses themselves, those lines of force that he had earlier had to tear from them with such intransigence, lines of force that constituted none other than the spiritual framework that is his and his alone. You may say that at bottom this is the history of all great painters, probably the history of all great men and, perhaps, to some extent the history of all men: a period of pure instinct, a period of painful efforts to reconcile the mind's tyrannical discoveries with the needs of that instinct, a period of equilibrium in which the mind, having sought to subdue or destroy instinct, resigns itself to a continual give-and-take between mind and instinct, with mutual inquiry, concession, and encouragement, through which the man at last attains his freedom by creating it. Granted. But I must say that I can think of few bodies of work in which instinct's initial cry was louder, in which the battle between instinct and intelligence so sharply exhibited both intellectual suffering and a clamorous expression of it, in which the slowly acquired equilibrium gives such a stirring impression of its victory. That an artist's work may serve as paradigm for the development of nearly all true artists is a phenomenon so rare as to demand that respectful and special attention be paid to the artist in question.

His choice began with pure emotion, the powerful emotion to which we owe the uneasy early paintings, their subject so splendid that it seems to raise the backgrounds and carry them away, to absorb them, exhaust their resources and toss them back, enriched with the mute iridescence and deep tones it has imparted to them. But a choice it was, assured and decisive, out of which he soon felt the need to extract, if I may put it that way, the spiritual joists that would create a framework that could sustain and shape the entire architecture of his future work. This is painting in the purest sense, from which all incidentals, all embellishment, all dross, are banished. I know of no finer example since Cézanne of a constant and sustained determination to eliminate from artistic emotion anything that diverts or fails to enhance it. One may become metaphysical about Matisse's painting, perhaps one ought to. But never literary. To explain to himself the sensual choice revealed in his early paintings,

Reclining Model. 1919. Pencil. 14⅜ × 21³/₁₆″ (36.5 × 53.9 cm). Yale University Art Gallery, New Haven, Conn. Gift of Edith Malvina K. Wetmore.

which gave expression to his first emotions as a man, Matisse exaggerated angles and curves, striving for a play of lines so bold that he sometimes went beyond his own equilibrium and fell into a kind of caricatural Expressionism, and a play of color so pure that he often came to a kind of hallucinatory vision reminiscent of the techniques of Oriental potters and weavers, though perhaps still forced and representing no more than a chance encounter. As I have said, this dangerous but necessary game was a fruitful transition. From a twofold lode of fiery sensations he extracts prime materials that are tested and tempered and around which he forges a fresh creation unburdened by the slag, mud, ash, and gloom of its primeval chaos.

Here, then, against generally abstract and bare backgrounds, we have a nearly tragic condensation. Not only does the subject stand alone, but the lines, fairly devoid of accidental light, isolate the primary sensation and—after pondering it so deeply that it seems to exist in itself, independent of the setting, independent of the artist—abandon it. It is left, so to speak, suspended in silence. It is like an unmoving pebble beneath a pool of transparent water. Make no mistake: the pebble lives. But with a life of its own, hard and dense, owing little to the caress of light; and when we touch it in the darkness, we feel its shape and texture. Not much else can be said of Matisse's painting, for it is painting, no more and no less.

Jules Romains

HENRI MATISSE

"Opinions"

1920

"Classicism," someone wrote about ten years ago, "is neither a subject nor a technique; it is a structure." If one takes the meaning of the word as such, I think that sooner or later people will be led to realize that, since the beginning of the twentieth century, the different art forms in our country have made a positive effort in rediscovering classic dignity.

Doubtlessly the most vulgar methods never stopped being favored and the public at large did not clearly indicate that it had had enough of them. Besides, numerous desperate attempts to break with the old enchantment of tradition have been known to occur—gestures so constricted and cries so painful that, even with the greatest kindness, it would be difficult to discern any promise of joy and serenity in them. But it is not for statistics to outline the physiognomy of a given period's art forms. And, among the thousands of contradictory sketches, all it takes is for a few great works to be in harmony for a period of humanity's time to find in them its face and its voice.

If our era receives the praise from the future that I risk giving it here, it seems to me that it will partially be owed to a few painters, and particularly to Henri Matisse.

His works, less than all others, bring to mind a prisoner's desperate attempt, in incoherent fits of anger, against walls that are too solid. It is possible that what was first noticed in his compositions was their expression of audacity, that they have been applauded or scorned especially for the nonconformity that they openly declare. But neither admirers nor adversaries of Matisse have the right to stop there. It is essential not to confuse anarchy with autonomy, even if autonomy's constitution may sometimes have the appearance of disorder.

From one work to another, Matisse has better shown to what equilibrium he has brought his forces, to what domination of himself he has risen. For this reason, the maturity found in him now gives a true contentment to the mind. He has not at all "settled down" the pathetic means by which the weakening of creative passion, the renunciation of youth, and the surrender to mediocrity are usually expressed. On the contrary, he has, more than ever, distanced himself from conventional formulas. But he controls and governs himself with a surprising economy of effort.

This is how he will unhastily reunite with the eternal Classicism which is a "structure" and not a collection of subjects or an arsenal of methodology, Classicism which is another name for the style which endows with nobility an ode by Horace, a certain Japanese drawing, a Bach prelude, and a poem by Goethe, Baudelaire, or Mallarmé.

René Schwob

L'AMOUR DE L'ART

"Henri-Matisse"

October 1920

René Schwob (b. 1895), French art historian and critic.

Matisse's painting, without subject and seemingly relieved of the potential for accidental charms, was only an equilibrium of abstractions, until today.

To evoke, with pure colors and curves, bodies moving further and further away from all appearance of materiality, to strip them of superfluity—and not only from their clothing in its transience but from their flesh and from their very skeleton—if that is not what Matisse sought, at least it is what he succeeded in doing.

Reduced by dint of simplicity to a few colored elements that call to, that answer one another, that sing to one another, each canvas shone like a child's dream.

COLORPLATE 54. *Marguerite Matisse with Black Velvet Ribbon.* 1916. Canvas. 7¼ × 6¾″ (18.4 × 17.1 cm).
© Succession H. Matisse/1988. Photograph courtesy Archives Matisse, Collection Claude Duthuit.

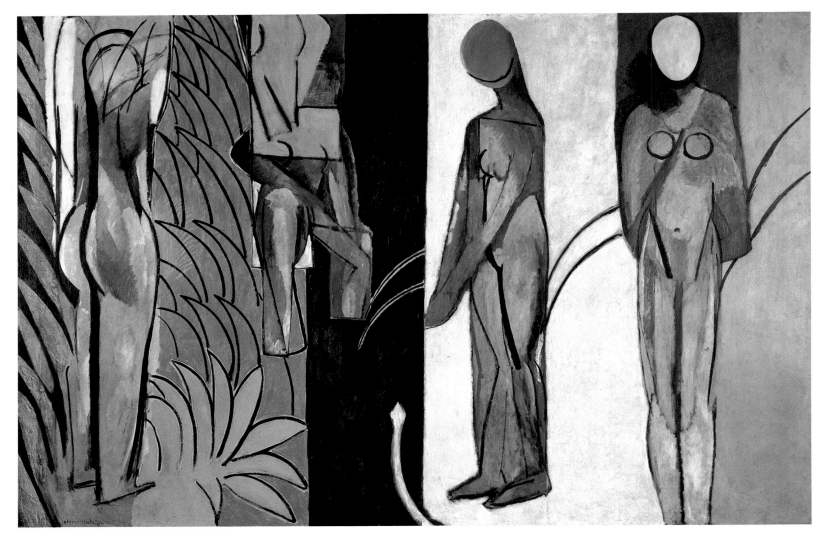

COLORPLATE 55. *Bathers by a Stream*. 1916. Canvas. 102¼ × 153½″ (259.7 × 389.9 cm).
Charles H. and Mary F. S. Worcester Collection. © 1988, The Art Institute of Chicago. All rights reserved.

COLORPLATE 56. *The Piano Lesson*. 1916. Canvas. 96½ × 83¾″ (245.1 × 212.7 cm).
Collection, The Museum of Modern Art, New York. Mrs. Simon Guggenheim Fund.

COLORPLATE 57. *The Moroccans.* 1916. Canvas. 71⅜ × 110″ (181.3 × 279.4 cm).
Collection, The Museum of Modern Art, New York. Gift of Mr. and Mrs. Samuel A. Marx.

COLORPLATE 58. *The Studio, Quai Saint-Michel.* 1916. Canvas. 58¼ × 46″ (147.9 × 116.8 cm).
The Phillips Collection, Washington, D.C.

COLORPLATE 59. *A Path in the Woods of Clamart.* 1917. Canvas. 35⅞ × 29⅛″ (91 × 74 cm).
© Succession H. Matisse/1988. Photograph courtesy Archives Matisse, Collection Claude Duthuit.

COLORPLATE 60. *Interior with a Violin.* 1918. Canvas. 45^{11}/$_{16}$ × 35^{3}/$_{16}$″ (116 × 89).
Statens Museum for Kunst, Copenhagen, J. Rump Collection.

COLORPLATE 61. *Montalban (Paysage Montalban)*. 1918. Canvas. 28¾ × 35¾″ (73 × 90.8 cm).
© Succession H. Matisse/1988. Photograph courtesy Archives Matisse, Collection Claude Duthuit.

Matisse drawing from a model in his apartment on Place Charles-Félix, Nice, c. 1928. Photograph courtesy The Museum of Modern Art, New York.

Above all, Matisse understood that it is less important to let things speak than to use them, and less important to use them than to discern the color relationship that their combination has produced.

In the things of this world he still made note only of the projection of their geometric outlines and the tonality which gave them their place in the symphonic movement that they awoke in him by chance association.

He was the first among modern painters to understand this immense and childish mystery: that a painting, being but a colored surface, must conserve its internal equilibrium, no matter where it is placed. He therefore no longer needed to construct bodies in their normal posture, since bodies no longer interested him except for their, as it were, superspatial equilibrium.

Thus, while others were seeking the key to a fourth dimension, Matisse, through a stroke of genius, was bringing painting back to the study of the two sole dimensions which are the exclusive object of this art.

A stroke of genius and, moreover, the proud invention of the man who, transcending his sensory gifts and representations of reality, imposed the laws of his mind on the image of the world.

Speculations about the fourth dimension were associated with cubist and futurist art.

Proud invention of his sincerity! Because it was for having wanted to reproduce, with utmost exactness, a colorful arabesque inspired in him by an external spectacle that, at the same time, he found certain necessities of his art.

He opened to us the secrets of his thoughts while restoring equilibrium to painting.

Art of relationships and spontaneous composition!

Coming out of Impressionism, where man had stifled himself in an objective state, he had nothing left to do but go in the opposite direction.

Matisse's adventure is a strange one, in that, still cloistered in Impressionism and completely incapable of detaching himself from it, he was able to pull himself up from the very middle of that worm-eaten edifice, which made it collapse around him.

Matisse remained an impressionist through his need of an exterior model (landscape, body, still life) without which Matisse cannot exist.

But, while a Monet dismantles himself in the face of a landscape to the point that it settles on the canvas all by itself while he only lends the aid of his arm like a pantograph, before the same landscape Matisse feels colorful sensations awaken in his mind which he merely strives to reproduce.

In Matisse's work, living things do not live for themselves.

They exist for him only in the combination of the several acid secretions they draw from his intelligence.

Monet is a slave of nature. He is an eye which sees it.

Matisse submits to it only in order to make use of it. This is a motive that requires his excitement but that dissects it only in order to express it.

Would that I were swayed so!

In yet another way is Matisse an impressionist.

What he observes in himself is not, in fact, his essential law. It's a reaction, one that remains subject to external time.

With time his emotions change.

How far we are from the discipline of a Poussin!

All he brought, then, to clear the smoke of Impressionism was a more precise brush, a simpler vision, a sensitive intelligence where pure sensitivity had reigned, and the desire to compose an organism sufficient unto itself instead of fixing upon a fleeting charm. This was a major correction.

It was not yet the total revolution that remained for the cubists to carry out and that, if it were perhaps beyond the scope of art, ought at least to be pursued with an absolute and logical rigor in a severe and beautiful austerity.

He therefore continued to move further and further away from the pursuits of young painters.

But may the meeting of his art—though completely devoid of literature—with the art of today's young poets bring about ardent emotions to those who unveil it.

Temporary union—an unexpected meeting on roads that were thought to be divergent!

Two-dimensional poetry has its origin in this painting.

Scorn of explanations and of developments may not have spread in poets if they had first had the example of the painter.

Strange force of attraction that one art has over another, that one process has over another of a different order.

And, if there is a relation between painting and poetry, does the latter therefore lag behind the other?

Like Matisse, our youngest poets suppress between the several essential polarities of their emotions all the intermediaries that alone could make the logic of knowledge understood.

Beyond this social logic, they seek the internal logic which governs all their laws. Thus Matisse, like them, got further away from the accidental only by yielding to it a bit more.

Because, freeing themselves only from the allure of external experiences, they dove with delight into pure inventions of the imagination, scornful of communicating with the rest of the world.

And, although they could believe in delivering their art from romantic turmoil, still they are prey to it to such an extent that only in yielding to it completely can they be liberated.

But, as the painters deserted him, Matisse already abandons the poets.

The poets run in place.

Painters construct pure abstractions or merely fret over geometric volumes.

Matisse returns to nature.

Did he fear the total emaciation to which, more and more, his speculations were leading him, and the solitude into which he felt himself sink?

Here he is, excited to rediscover flesh and the play of shadows that accompanies the accidents of fleeting light.

Here he is, back in the world of forms.

Matisse, who for a year has been going back to his beginnings, becomes a bit more of a realist each day!

Taking a nude study by Courbet from the wall just as we finished talking about Lhote, he said to me, "This is what I call painting.

"Rembrandt and Courbet, those are painters. Whereas this Cézanne (he pointed to an admirable portrait), beautiful though it may be, since it appears to me first as an oval, rather than striking me as a living portrait, this Cézanne has less of an effect on me!"

I could not help being surprised.

Had I not liked in Matisse's art only that which he considered an imperfection?

He confirmed this for me.

But what do I care of what a man thinks of himself?

Is there an inadequacy more beautiful than plenitude?

Matisse taught a great lesson: it matters little to me to know whether he proceeded intentionally or by ineptitude.

But I know that Matisse is resigned to the admirable simplicity of his canvases only because, having all painting to reinvent, he was forced to return to the beginning.

Yet what exhilaration in the canvases that, until now, poured from him in abundance!

What light, that no shadow spoiled! Joy, brilliance, equilibrium—he reproduced infinite combinations from these three cardinal virtues.

He cast a pure light, issuing from no source, image of his joy, upon an equilibrium of pretexts.

That is no longer enough for him.

What he wants now is no longer to conceive of this equilibrium of pretexts, but to penetrate into the rich harmony of the universe.

He wants his canvases—until now colorful surfaces—henceforth to be skies, seas, boats, riggings . . . with a sense of shadows and the rotation of volumes.

His *cerebral Impressionism* is tending more and more towards a realism that his total love of life suggests to him and makes him desire.

There at least he succeeds, not by paltriness but enriched with so many analyses that the beings of flesh and earth that he aspires to paint will maintain that internal logic to which it will be subject. And, in his future syntheses, perhaps after a period of excessive docility, he will know anew how to impose onto the things of this world the lone sovereignty which matters: that of the mind.

From around 1918 Matisse's art had become increasingly naturalistic.

Matisse owned Sleeping Blonde Woman *(1849) by Gustave Courbet.*

Clive Bell

ARTS AND DECORATION

"Matisse and Picasso"

November 1920

Clive Bell (1881–1964), English critic and writer who formulated the theory of "significant form" and, with Roger Fry, helped to foster appreciation of Cézanne and the post-impressionists. Beginning around 1920, critics tended increasingly to single out and compare the work of Matisse and Picasso. See also Bell's 1933 article in this volume.

The names go together, as do those of Shelley and Keats or Fortnum and Mason. Even to people who seldom or never look seriously at a picture they have stood, these ten years, as symbols of modernity. They are pre-eminent; and for this there is reason. Matisse and Picasso are the two immediate heirs to Cézanne. They are in the direct line; and through one of them a great part of the younger generation comes at its share of the patrimony. To their contemporaries they owe nothing: they came into the legacy and had to make what they could of it. They are the elder brothers of the movement, a fact which the movement occasionally resents by treating them as though they were its elder sisters.

Even to each other they owe nothing. Matisse, to be sure, swept for one moment out of his course by the overwhelming significance of Picasso's early abstract work, himself made a move in that direction. But this adventure he quickly, and wisely, abandoned; the problems of Cubism could have helped him nothing to materialize his peculiar sensibility. And this sensibility—this peculiar emotional reaction to what he sees—is his great gift. No one ever felt for the visible universe just what Matisse feels; or, if one did, he could not create an equivalent. Because, in addition to this magic power of creation, Matisse has been blest with extraordinary sensibility both of reaction and touch, he is a great artist; because he trusts to it entirely he is not what for a moment apparently he wished to be—*a chef d'école.*

Picasso, on the other hand, who never tried to be anything of the sort, is the paramount influence in modern painting—subject, of course, to the supreme influence of Cézanne. All the world over are students and young painters to whom his mere name is thrilling; to whom Picasso is the liberator. . . .

Picasso is a born *chef d'école.* His is one of the most inventive minds in Europe. Invention is as clearly his supreme gift as sensibility is that of Matisse.

* * *

I do not presume to judge between one method of creation and another; I shall not judge between Matisse and Picasso; but I do say that, as a rule, it is the intellectual artist who becomes, in spite of himself, schoolmaster to the rest. And there is a reason for this. By expressing themselves intellectual artists appeal to us aesthetically; but, in addition, by making, or seeming to make, some statement about the nature of the artistic problem they set us thinking. We feel sure they have something to say about the very stuff of art which we, clumsily enough, can grasp intellectually. With purely aesthetic qualities the intellect can do nothing: but here, it seems, is something the brain can get hold of. Therefore we study them and they become our leaders; which does not make them our greatest artists. Matisse may yet be a better painter than Picasso.

Be that as it may, from Matisse there is little or nothing to be learned, since Matisse relies on his peculiar sensibility to bring him through. If you want to paint like him, feel what he feels, conduct it to the tips of your fingers, thence on to your canvas, and there you are. The counsel is not encouraging. These airy creatures try us too high. Indeed, it sometimes strikes me that even to appreciate them you must have a touch of their sensibility. A critic who is apt to be sensible was complaining the other day that Matisse had only one instrument in his orchestra. There are orchestras in which fifty instruments sound as one. Only it takes a musician to appreciate them.

*   *   *

Amongst the hundred differences between Matisse and Picasso perhaps, after all, there is but one on which a critic can usefully insist. Even about that he can say little that is definite. Only, it does appear to be true that whereas Matisse is a pure artist, Picasso is an artist and something more—an involuntary preacher if you like. Neither, of course, falls into the habit of puffing out his pictures with literary stuff, though Picasso has, on occasions, allowed to filter into his art a, to me, most distasteful dash of sentimentality. That is not the point, however. The point is that whereas both create without commenting on life, Picasso, by some inexplicable quality in his statement, does unmistakably comment on art. That is why he, and not Matisse, is master of the modern movement.

André Gide

NOUVELLE REVUE FRANÇAISE

"Autumn Leaves"

c. 1920

Gide, whom Debussy had characterized as "an old spinster, timid, gracious, and polite in the English manner," had been ambivalent about Matisse's art since he first wrote about it in 1905.

I went to see Matisse in Nice. What a fascinating man! He showed me into a fairly small oblong room as narrow as a wide hallway. This is where he lives and works. The walls are covered with his latest canvases, and he cannot get far enough back to see them, even in the reflection of the wardrobe mirror. He paints until daylight fades, then draws by lamplight. He is not the type who thinks he's working just because he has a pen or brush in hand: he is ever searching, striving. The most exquisite of his paintings are those with which he is least satisfied, for he disdains any effect that he has learned to achieve easily. He urges you to look at other works that are less accomplished but that reveal efforts which his early admirers—and it is for you to judge whether he has any—surely never expected of him, which they may not like and will not understand. He speaks of precision, and of realism; he yearns to be able to draw a hand the right way, "with fingers that don't look like cigar butts," to put an eye in the right place, above the nose and far enough to the side to leave room for the second eye. "It's not enough to draw a hand," he says. "It also has to fit into the whole setting." That "whole setting" is his point of departure, and it is to it that he must return. In his drawings he concentrates on details that strive toward a whole, while in his paintings he strives toward details that will not run counter to the emotional impact of the whole. In other words, at age fifty he is rediscovering those elementary truths that pupils learn in school. Late in life, he is returning anew to the starting point of the great masters, like Mantegna and Michelangelo, reproductions of whose works we later flip through. "Look at this," he cries. "Look how that hand is drawn!" Always hands, the most difficult detail of all. And he quotes Forain's terrible remark: "Now that the Germans have stopped buying our paintings, we young artists are going to have to learn how to draw hands."

Jean-Louis Forain (1852–1931), academic painter, illustrator, and critic.

And it occurred to me that what really mattered most was to unlearn anything that was becoming a merely commonplace achievement, and that all you ever really know is what you toil to learn out of personal need. But then Matisse complained that nothing annoyed him more these days than expressions of admiration for one or another of his paintings, for he views each of them as no more than a step on the road to something else. "What counts for me," he exclaimed, "is not what I've done, but what I want to do. I would like to be judged only on the whole of my work, on the overall curve of my line of development." Hearing this, I could not deny him my sympathy, but I somehow felt that he was asking the impossible, that a painter will always be judged only on his particular works, and that he acts with uncommon rashness when he gives up on making a painting.

The Two Musicians. 1921. Charcoal.
20½ × 12¼" (52.1 × 31.1 cm).
Collection Maurice and Margo Cohen.

Violinist and Young Girl (Divertissement).
1921. Canvas. 20 × 25¾″ (50.8 × 65.4 cm).
The Baltimore Museum of Art: The Cone
Collection, formed by Dr. Claribel Cone
and Miss Etta Cone of Baltimore,
Maryland.

Charles Vildrac

CINQUANTE DESSINS PAR HENRI MATISSE

September 1920

It appears from their works that modern painters have no interest whatever in the human figure; or at least that they fasten onto it to fathom its character, by bringing to it that psychology, that divination, that passionate submission that the portrait demands.

For them, the model is hardly more than an element of composition, a plastic theme, a pretext, like many others, for harmonies and modulations of color; and the painter who looks at it with the most love, that painter, be he the great Renoir himself, more often than not gives us a revelation only of the sensual order, magnificent perhaps, but incomplete.

This is due to the role that contemporary art has assigned itself: In

Charles Vildrac (pseudonym of Charles Messager, 1882–1971), poet, dramatist, and member of Jules Romains' "unanimist" circle. A number of his essays on Matisse in the early 1920s were based partly on his talks with the artist.

Matisse's return to more naturalistic, "analytical" painting in the 1920s was widely noted. Here especially Vildrac seems to draw on talks with Matisse.

an age when so much has been challenged, in an age of probing and reconstitution like ours, we have logically concerned ourselves with the "physical" in painting before giving it a soul. Similarly, an overly exclusive concern for the relationships of lines, volumes, tones, is generally prejudicial to the necessary relationship between art and life.

But the time has come for painters to organize their conquests, to attend to the "moral" in painting—that is, to animate this too often inert body constructed with a great scaffold of reasonings.

This album represents an important testimony. Doesn't Matisse, the creator of a new pictorial expression—and the most acute there is—seem, after advancing toward his own style and the blossoming of that style, to be considering a painter's loftiest subject: the human figure?

Those of his drawings that we already knew were remarkable chiefly for synthesis of form, for arabesque, color, ornament. How greatly Matisse here expands the scope of his investigation! It is no longer only the rhythm and external features of a figure that we see him capture, but the personality, the *moral character*. And now, following the example of the eternal masters, he fervently attunes his own style to the style of the model.

Charles Vildrac
EXPOSITION HENRI-MATISSE
15 October 1920

You arrive one evening at the seaside. It is almost night; it is raining. Everything you encounter on your way, all that you glimpse of the landscape, seems to you blighted forever. How can one conceive that this crushing sky could ever lavish a pure and joyful light?

The next day, you awaken in a half-darkened room, and you immediately think that the weather is as awful as the night before. But you remember that the shutters are closed, and you run to push them open with hope. Sudden astonishment! The weather is beautiful!

You experience at once both the light and the landscape, unable to disassociate them. The impalpable gauze that here and there finishes drying and polishing the sky, the beach, the cliffs, the horizon, the boat resting on the pebbles, the shifting patch of sail, you see all that in a single, absolutely simple image, in which the closest objects seem unreal because of sheer dazzling bareness.

Thus do Matisse's landscapes appear to me; and thus, it seems, did nature appear to him, touched by the miracle of a suddenly rediscovered light.

In reality, the miracle lies in the painter's vision and in the power that he has to reproduce it.

We who are not Matisse, we generally receive fragmentary, successive revelations of an aspect of nature which complement one another, superimpose themselves upon one another, neutralize one another, or even thwart one another, according to whether they are of the same order or not. Our sense perception is uncertain and changes from moment to moment. In a word, we rarely have unity of vision.

Matisse does have unity of vision, in the service of a prodigious "quality of eye," and that, assuredly, is one of the principal reasons for our surprise and delight before his most spontaneous landscapes, as before his most thoughtful studies.

There is also his freedom. But does this not come precisely from the sureness with which the image to be painted jumps out at him?

Matisse never ceases to see the image to be painted—one of a number of images that the same object can offer—exclusively, to hold it single and intact as a musician would hold a single chord among ten heard simultaneously and discern each note in it.

He knows what he can and wants to reveal to us in a painting and, consequently, he takes a stand; that is, he scuttles everything that could interfere with his vision, everything that could distract him and distract us from it.

At the water's edge, he stooped to arrange and examine two soaking wet rays against the pebbles; he handled them so to watch the play of the pink mother-of-pearl of their bellies; then, straightening himself up again, he rediscovered the great space and the great brightness with a slight giddiness.

He portrayed those fish, that space, and that brightness. Do not expect him to curl the waves or carve the cliff. This time that is not his object; the cliff serves him only as decor and boundary. For it is relative to those boundaries that we feel the space.

Do not imagine that such unity of vision can be realized on canvas only through a rapid execution. Matisse has shown us many times, in important works, that neither time, nor reflection, nor difficulty diminish his candor or affect his freshness.

COLORPLATE 73

Otto Grautoff

FRANZÖSISCHE MALEREI SEIT 1914

1921

Otto Grautoff (b. 1876), German art historian.

For some three years now, a new sureness of line and soundness of form is apparent in Henri Matisse's paintings. This gradual transformation of the artist may be traced back to the renewed respect that Ingres, the greatest master of this style, has enjoyed for the past six years or so. While there is something of Nicolas Poussin in Ingres and Delacroix, in the nineteenth century painting split into painterly and linear styles. Although Ingres was never completely forgotten, during the second half of the nineteenth century, the painterly style held sway for fifty years. From Delacroix to Futurism, all the possibilities of the painterly style were savored and exhausted. Even before 1914 there were indications of a revival of Classicism. Some twenty years before, the prophetically gifted Maurice Denis had predicted the return of Classicism. During the catastrophe, French art seemed to realize that its most towering greatness had grown out of a synthesis of the linear and the painterly principles. One consequence of this recognition was that all the artists who for many years had simply been setting off fireworks of color now turned, whether secretly or openly, to Ingres, the champion of line. In this context Ingres represents primarily a catchword. The reference is not always to the master himself, but much more to his style, ideal, and direction. Only in this sense can Matisse's new paintings be considered a turn to Ingres. Perhaps it might be more correct to compare Matisse to Courbet and Degas, a secret "Ingres-ist," rather than to Ingres himself. Except that to omit the name of Ingres would merely cloud the essence of the general transformation in style. It is significant that Matisse now likes to hang his new paintings next to those of Courbet. Courbet is a yardstick for him. This explains why *Villacoublay from an Auto* is so

The terms "painterly" and "linear" represent, according to Heinrich Woelfflin in his Principles of Art History *(1915), opposites that comprise one of five stylistic dynamisms.*

Villacoublay is not far from Issy-les-Moulineaux, as opposed to Nice. Grautoff refers here to The Windshield, *1917.*

illusionistic. It is no longer a question of bringing the canvas to life, but rather of shaping space, of strong clear lines that convey depth. The painting offers all the characteristic hallmarks of the landscape about Nice; a broad, well-tended street, shade trees, the sea, cars. Matisse now spends more time in Nice than in the Paris suburb of Clamart. He does not like the overcast northern sky, but seeks the sun. He has painted a varied series of beach scenes, views of the sea, and sunny interiors penetrated by the blue of the sea. He sometimes closes the windows: a slender girl before a narrow window, framed by narrowly folded curtains and narrow venetian blinds, the whole unity creating a particular rhythm. In the *Woman at the Window* a light, frisky elevation of all shapes vibrates. No heavy darknesses or burdensome masses anywhere. The curves of the light figure become one with the lines.

The most beautiful and mature work of the most recent period is *The Female Nude in an Armchair,* which is reminiscent of Degas. Just as enthusiasm for Ingres shows through in each of Edgar Degas's fluffy dancers, so also is the Courbet enthusiast apparent in this painting by Henri Matisse, along with a revitalization inspired by Ingres. This painting abounds in soft curves; thighs, breasts, arms, the back of the chair, the pattern of the carpet—it all comes together in a soaring musical harmony. It might have been more logical to have made Henri Matisse the center of our examination, for he has become the trailblazer of the new generation. Around 1906 he brought the new youth closer to the late Cézanne. In that year he founded a school on Cézanne's example and provided an underlying solidity of form for the coming generation's color frenzy. He thereby hit upon an unconscious impulse of his time, but remained far too willful in his personal doctrine, which gave rise to discord and rebellion. Although one after another soon defected, almost all of them succumbed to the influence of this energetic and penetrating innovator. Although never very clear about it, Albert Marquet succumbed to Matisse. It is questionable whether Vlaminck would have come to the late Cézanne without Matisse's example. The shift in surface measurement brought about by Marie Laurencin is also primarily attributable to Matisse's model. Much of this influence, of course, is unacknowledged. Nobody wants to follow the path of a contemporary. Everyone emphasizes his own free artistry. Matisse smiles ironically at such emphatic protestations of freedom. He is far too clever not to know that every outsider instantly recognizes his connection with Othon Friesz, Raoul Dufy, Kees van Dongen, and others, and that his leading role remains evident. Is he leading toward simplicity? Matisse knows that radicalism benefits youth alone. He knows that there comes a time in the lives of people and nations when subjective pretensions must be abandoned and the ideology of the race adopted. French art of the post-war period is characterized by the shift from the meaningful to the self-satisfying to the simply beautiful.

Marie Laurencin (1885–1956), French painter.

Kees van Dongen (1877–1968), Dutch-born painter who associated with the Fauves and, in the 1920s, became fashionable for his society portraits.

Elie Faure

L'ART MODERNE

1921

L'Art moderne (1921) was the fourth and final volume of Faure's Histoire de l'art.

Whether [Matisse] paints a portrait, a still life, a landscape, or nude women dancing, the arabesque is always there, dominating in order that it may direct, master, and give shades or subtlety to the harmony, whose rhythm comes from it, and with which it plays, as a bow draws forth from the string, sonorous waves which it swells and contracts. "Nature" is pretty far away. The artist imposes his system with such rigor, such exactitude and logic in the relationships of his sumptuous elements, that he creates a plastic universe of the richest accent.

I think, indeed, that, for this reason, this painter is the one who, least of all since Cézanne, causes one to think of the subject that his works represent. They tend untiringly to organize his universe from the angle of painting alone, absolutely delivered from the attraction of sentiment or of the picturesque in the object. At bottom, they express no object. At all events, the object is, with him, no more than a pretext for the creation of new organisms, which a powerful love for form is alone capable of imagining. And thereby, the recreated object attains a life infinitely more general, in the first place, but also, unexpectedly enough, infinitely more direct, than that which it is supposed to represent. . . . See how, on a red background, the play of the blacks, of the grays, and of the yellows is concentrated, or the play of the grays, of the yellows, and of the reds, on a black background. In the one case, abstract space hovers like a liquid atmosphere; in the other case, we see a mirror in which the light is absorbed. The uniformity of that background which, with a bad painter, would be the most banal of means for masking his indigence, becomes, in the hands of Matisse, the rarest instrument for manifesting the most voluntary and the highest distinction. One would imagine oneself *seeing* music. The most decisive paintings of Matisse make me think of Chinese porcelains, or of hard Japanese lacquers, immobilized, as it were, under some deep water, and in them Goya's power for surprising life seems mysteriously united with the silent and lofty soul of Velázquez. I am thinking of those surfaces, almost black or red, in which some solid apparition—flowers or a face—surges up from the silence, in the ardent solitude of its own reality. It is quite evident that this alone, perhaps—I mean the distant impression which he gives of a chromatic didacticism of the kind used by the Orientals—has not been willed by him. But the forms of sensibility expressed by the art of the Far East have entered so deep into the reason of the Occident that today they determine one of the most splendid aspects of its regenerated symbolism. Were I acquainted with the frontiers of the object and of the subject, curiosity as to the world would be extinguished in me. The grand style lies precisely in their secret meeting, and in our impotence to determine its place. And that, I certainly believe, is what gives to Matisse's painting a decorative majesty which it is practically alone in possessing, at a time when almost all painting tends to decoration. The picturesque and the anecdotal draw away from it. Music rises from it, in absolute silence.

Roger Fry

THE BURLINGTON MAGAZINE
"Henri-Matisse in the Luxembourg"
May 1922

The authorities of the Luxembourg have acquired the picture by Henri-Matisse, which we reproduce on the accompanying plate. The fact that the directors of an institution which has in the past pursued a policy scarcely more enlightened than that of our own Tate Gallery should have accepted an artist of the complexion of Henri-Matisse has caused some sensation. Such a phenomenon may bear two interpretations. It may be a criticism of Henri-Matisse's latest work or it may be the sign of a new era in the state patronage of art in France. There is reason to hope that the latter is the true interpretation. For the fact is that this is not the only

By "plastic" and "plasticity" is generally meant the illusion of three-dimensionality or of a vivid materiality in a painting.

Roger Fry (1866–1934), English painter, critic, and ardent champion of modern French art. Odalisque, the first Matisse painting acquired by a French museum, was a distinctly conservative choice, given the artist's history.

sign that the administration of which M. Benedite has so long been the chief, has adopted a more liberal attitude towards modern art, and is willing at last to go outside the circle of official painting and recognize the importance of the so-called revolutionary school.

The authorities of the Luxembourg are to be congratulated not only on having made the plunge, but on having acquired an admirable and striking example of Henri-Matisse's latest work. *The Odalisque* is more completely realized than many of his pictures, though here as always he maintains an extreme economy of means. However profoundly meditated, however carefully prepared a picture may be, the actual execution has always with this artist the freshness and apparent intuition of a sketch.

The magical qualities of Henri-Matisse's color are universally recognized, and here these qualities are seen at their best. Almost alone Matisse seems able to retain freshness and delicacy while intensifying to the utmost point the resonance and purity of his local colors.

COLORPLATE 76

Charles Vildrac

NICE 1921
Introduction

1922

This essay appeared in a catalogue of the most recent of Matisse's works at the time.

I went to see Matisse once in that room in Nice that overlooks the Promenade and the sea and that he has since left. I knew most of the paintings that he had done the preceding years. I recalled as well the high window and its drapes, the red rug and its patterns, the low armchair in which Matisse has often posed the nude model or which he has positioned, empty, beside the window, enhancing this affable and roly-poly seat with a lace antimacassar. I recognized the decorated porcelain vase and the lacquered dressing table with the oval mirror. Without doubt, I was in the room of Matisse's paintings; and yet. . . .

First, this room was smaller than I had supposed: From certain of his pictures I had formed the impression that, in it, one could walk freely, with long strides, or dance with ease; yet its length was fairly obstructed with furniture, and the window occupied the greater part of its width. At the outset I must state that the painter had lent the place a fresh spirit and had subordinated everything, such as the flowers, to the variations in the sky; had lent it a soul which in reality it did not have. Certainly it was a beautiful hotel room, but with the soul of a hotel room.

Finally, and this struck me above all, these objects that I rediscovered one by one had been oddly eclipsed by the pictorial memory I had formed of them. It seemed to me that they had abdicated a magnificent personality. They were no longer those *solid apparitions,* of which Elie Faure speaks, *arising from the silence in the glowing solitude of their proper reality.*

Vildrac is quoting from "Opinions," Faure's 1920 essay on Matisse.

Did not Matisse paint this window, these drapes saturated with clarity, this red rug, these furnishings, on the same day that some magician created this room with a stroke of his wand, so that each object, taking the only place which suited its form, its volume, and its color, came ingeniously and for the first time to unfold its grace to the light?

You certainly understand that the magician was Matisse himself and that I was able, in looking at his motifs with my nonpainter's eyes, to admire even more the creative power of the painter.

Quality and unity of vision—it is these above all that cause our surprise and enchantment with Henri-Matisse.

Roland Schacht

HENRI MATISSE

1922

Roland Schacht (b. 1888), German art historian and writer.

Because of this approach to color, Matisse, whether consciously or not, made two discoveries that had a major influence on his later creative works. The first was that color need not be distributed simply on the basis of purely formalistic principles. It may seem questionable to make such a claim about an artist who worked so hard to achieve formal perfection. But a comparison of his works with, say, Kandinsky's of the period of his first *Sturm* exhibition proves it correct. (Albeit only relatively correct, like any linguistic statement about a work of art, but nevertheless correct by criteria of average linguistic usage.) Kandinsky detached color from physical objects and distributed it from purely formal standpoints, in accordance with value and countervalue, movement and rest, contrast and gradation. Kandinsky himself also abandoned this style in his later works and reintroduced graphic elements, curves floating in ideal, imaginary space, but also planes and surfaces that provide the arrangement of colors with new structural support. He himself must therefore have decided that this uninhibited effusion of colors—surely not arbitrary, but inevitably based on individual preferences, given the subjective nature of color perception—was untenable in the long run. Matisse has never gone as far as Kandinsky, even his most subjective color creations having a solid objective basis, just as a resistance might be added to an electric current for certain specific purposes. This objective framework is much like the skeleton in a drawing of a nude: though the skeleton is not actually depicted, it is nonetheless assumed to be present; it saves the work from unjustified suspicions of arbitrariness and even enhances the effect of color by allowing it to overcome an obstacle. Perhaps there is no more necessity in these works than in Kandinsky's, but necessity is more clearly visible because of the presence of objects and because the colors must take account of these objects. This prevents the pure color spectrum from degenerating into an apparent arbitrariness.

Matisse's second discovery was that colors must act together and simultaneously, the emphasis being on their "action." It is not a matter of simply playing an instrument's entire range of notes loudly and chaotically; the intent is to achieve a particular formal and emotional effect. The harmony must be created without any empty spaces due to the intervals and the secondary or supporting voices. Older colorists harmonize two or three tones and tend to hold all other parts neutral. Decorators of the Vuillard type sometimes choose even a single tone to which they subordinate the others. Matisse, who sets all colors to work in seeking a new intensity, finds neutral or empty spaces, artificial backgrounds or soffits, intolerable. Whatever is there must resonate and act. A new and more powerful kind of accentuation is needed to prevent chaos on the one hand and excessive abstraction of two, three, or four tones on the other. But the inner necessity of this accentuation is allowed to arise from his objects, which he takes as inevitable and given. It is here that Cézanne's powerful influence sets in. It was Matisse who really raised Cézanne to the status of forerunner to the young generation. However successful his striving for form, Cézanne's real starting point was always nature, which he sought to conquer, to "realize" for humanity through art. But Matisse, unlike many who came after him, was the first to realize that whatever the general validity of his theories, real or apparent, Cézanne was unique—as are all great artists. In the final analysis, the necessities of his art lay within himself, in the special way he organized things. Matisse may well have adopted Cézanne's method, but by modifying its prerequisites he reestablished them himself. It has never occurred to him to look at nature through Cézanne's eyes; he has always aspired to conquer nature on his own. Nor has he ever been satisfied with Cézanne's aphoristic style (which is derived, after all, from Impressionism) but has instead striven to capture nature in a new totality. This explains the endless chain of his fresh attempts to draw nature. It also explains the wide range of his works of discovery, his experiments with position and studies of motion, constantly redone in new ways, with a different starting point every time. Anyone who seeks to lend necessity to accents must grasp the inner nature of things. Besides this study of individual objects, there is also his study of relationships, of harmony. In infinitely laborious studies he tries to capture the natural, immanent structure of a landscape, the canon of the human form. Vallotton helped him with the latter task, teaching him to capture a figure in a single great line. The initial results seem quite academic, until here as well Matisse learns to master his technique and discovers the line that captures form in the simplest, clearest, and most beautiful manner, while fully preserving individual appearance and its expression. But here too, academic arrangements, group formations, and apparently decorative sketches alternate with ever new advances toward ultimate saturation with reality.

Only when accentuation is deliberately distributed does a painting become a painting in the Cézanne sense; only then does it cease to be a copy and embark on a life of its own. For years, during his most exciting experiments, through his ever new studies and discoveries, he concentrated on giving his paintings this life of their own, torn between infusing them with individual liveliness and making them copies of nature. But then he realized something else. Was not this individual life of a static art work really artificial, floating in empty space between the human mind and the material world? Granted, it was related to the artist, but did not the artist strive precisely to minimize this relationship, to render the subjective objective? Granted, too, it was related to nature, but it was precisely nature that was to be transformed into art. Was not art, after all, an abstraction, and like all abstractions arbitrary and unique? Was there not perhaps some other way of establishing the nature of art? Of introducing some new resistance, one that, by placing a new obstacle in its path, would enhance its vitality?

Thus it was that Matisse came to mural painting. There are some indications that he came to murals through portraits. But in any event, this explains psychologically how he took the step toward murals.

*   *   *

The Moroccan paintings came soon after these. It was this series—especially in Germany, after an exhibition at the Gurlitt gallery—that really established Matisse's reputation. Here, under the southern sun, which produces intense colors naturally, Matisse cast off all constraints and seemed to discover himself. Here nature had what he had been looking for: the strong, pure, glowing color that blossoms into a fabulous vision. Now he no longer needed artificial enhancement, for everything was alive as it was. Creation now flowed not from effort but naturally, from nature itself. His dream was fulfilled. Everything turned out well.

Success was a matter of course and largely reassuring. Matisse had the courage to say that his paintings were meant to make people happy, to soothe them, to invite them to rest and relaxation. He thereby decisively abandoned the principle of art for art's sake, jettisoned theory and peculiar foibles, and reestablished his connection with the pulse of universal human life.

But he remained what he was, a seeker, an eternal innovator, a man

The exhibition at the Gurlitt Gallery, Berlin, was in the autumn of 1913. When World War I broke out, Matisse paintings at that gallery were seized as enemy property. The owners, including the Michael Steins, later had difficulty retrieving them.

Moorish Woman (Le Tatouage). 1922.
Canvas. 14 × 9⅝″ (35.6 × 24.4 cm).
National Gallery of Art, Washington,
D.C. Chester Dale Collection.

*Matisse had done a number of etched
portraits in 1914.*

who saw things in a new light every day, a conqueror. He has left many
things in the sketch stage, has occasionally improvised at random, but he
has never been content with mere flourishes or empty formulas. He often
resumes work persistently on things he had apparently abandoned long
before. Conceptions of form lie hidden in what seem to be casual
sketches, their significance becoming evident only through careful study
of his later works. Consider, for example, the concentration with which
the etching of a woman's head was composed, though at first glance it
seems a mere improvisation dashed off quickly. It is not so much a
drawing, nor even a color composition reduced to black and white, but
fundamentally a color study on the white of the paper, its tone differ-
entiated multifariously by the division of the surface into lines and the
highly ingenious but unbelievably simple arrangement of the variously
sized portions of the surface in relation to one another. Matisse achieves
this through differences in the intensity of the black lines and brush
strokes, and the drawing gives an illusion of plasticity that allows the
viewer to divide the whole picture into various grades of light and dark-

ness. The liveliness of the composition is enhanced by shifting the focal point of the greatest formal energy and concentration slightly away from the center, a device similar to the one Giorgione used when drawing his own eyes: the line of sight diverges just a little, almost imperceptibly.

Giorgione (c. 1477–1511), Venetian painter.

* * *

This last style of composition—the greatest possible wealth of plastic or color values embodied in a few great lines—is also seen in Matisse's later landscapes, which seem the great conclusion to an epoch of new experiments. In the meantime, of course, Cubism had arisen, and Matisse showed such interest in it that for a while the cubists entertained hopes of winning him over as their leader. But that hope was never fulfilled. "Picasso," Matisse commented, "has helped us to keep the fundamental forms in mind again. This is a means of simplifying art. But to build an artistic technique into a system is nonsensical. The cubists have a system but no goal. The goal, however, is the essential thing." This last remark (taken from a speech that briefly considered artistic principles), however, sounds somewhat sibylline, and even unjust. The cubists too, of course, had a goal and even achieved it in part. But they labored so heavily on all the individual works along the way that little energy was left to devote to the goal. The essential thing, really, is that Matisse—with his more down-to-earth character, his deliberate efforts to achieve self-discipline and immortality through art, and his strong aversion to any revolutionary view of traditional things, as seen in his attitude to Kandinsky's endeavors—must have been afraid of falling into arbitrariness and chaos, and also was probably too deeply attached to his own skills to turn himself inside out once more. In Cubism, too, as its history proves, the seemingly irrefutable is grounded in purely individually determined laws, whereas Matisse strives for universal validity through the generally determined. Here, too, he is not content to decree how the world should be, but wants rather to lay bare and make visible the essential connection between man and nature in the world as it is.

Hence also his latest manner, in which he distills universal laws from that which seems only contingent or momentary. The broad, agitated surface of the sea is rhythmically partitioned and calmed by the frames of the veranda panes, the perspective and wealth of color of the road to Villacoublay condensed in the heavy, solid frame of the automobile's lines. He sets the contingent against the universal, the near against the far, for the sum of nears and fars, universals and contingents, constitutes human life—or likeness of life—which, contrary to the cubists, does not consist of the lawful alone. It is, however, wholly possible that this manner of using the contingent to illustrate the lawful may ultimately be traceable, whether consciously or not, to a cubist stimulus, such as Braque's celebrated nail and its consequences. These influences are also noticeable in the freer and bolder deploying of accessories, particularly in interiors, now less arbitrary and more abstract, albeit closer to reality.

A witty, paradoxical comment on contradictory pictorial systems is made by an illusionistic rendering of a nail and the shadow it casts at the top of Braque's Violin and Palette, 1909–10.

At the same time, it seems clear how far removed these things are from any sort of Impressionism. They no longer represent the singular subjective moment, but broaden it to represent existence. It is clear that Cézanne stood at the end of Impressionism. Except that what for the giant Cézanne always remained an individual case, however monumentalized, has here been shifted to the more serene terrain of general human existence. The brooding loner has been taken back into the circle of humanity, of "society." Perhaps at the cost of his towering stature, but while gaining a richer and more intimate effect.

It is characteristic that, according to Grautoff, Matisse likes to hang his new works alongside Courbet's, gauging the effect of his own works against his. This confirms the withdrawal from aphorism to affirmation, from the sharpened instant to stable regularity, from mere discovery to quiet enjoyment. "There was a time," he wrote back in 1908, "when I

Schacht refers to Otto Grautoff's Französische Malerei seit 1914 excerpted in this volume.

COLORPLATE 62. *Interior at Nice*. 1917–18. Canvas. 29 × 23⅞″ (73.7 × 60.6 cm).
© 1988, The Philadelphia Museum of Art: The A. E. Gallatin Collection.

COLORPLATE 63. *Reader with Flowers in Her Hair*. 1918–19. Canvas. 31 × 25½″ (78.7 × 64.8 cm).
Stephen Hahn Gallery, New York.

COLORPLATE 64. *Interior with a Violin Case.* 1918/19. Canvas. 28¾ × 23⅝″ (73 × 60 cm).
Collection, The Museum of Modern Art, New York. Lillie P. Bliss Collection.

COLORPLATE 65. *The Artist and His Model*. 1919. Canvas. 23⅝ × 28¾″ (60 × 73 cm).
Collection Mr. and Mrs. Donald B. Marron.

COLORPLATE 66. *White Plumes.* 1919. Canvas. 28¾ × 23¾″ (73 × 60.3 cm). The Minneapolis Institute of Arts.

COLORPLATE 67. *Greek Torso and Bouquet of Flowers*. 1919. Canvas. 45¾ × 35″ (116 × 89 cm).
Museo de Arte, São Paolo/Art Resource.

COLORPLATE 68. *Storm in Nice*. 1919–20. Canvas. 19⅝ × 28¾″ (50 × 73 cm). Musée Matisse, Nice.

COLORPLATE 69. *Woman at the Window, Nice.* 1920. Canvas. 29¼ × 23¼″ (74.2 × 59 cm). © 1988, Sotheby's Inc.

never left my paintings hanging on the wall because they reminded me of moments of over-excitement, and I did not like to see them again when I was calm. Nowadays I try to put serenity into my pictures and re-work them as long as I have not succeeded."

The quotation is from Matisse's "Notes of a Painter."

Matisse's influence on his contemporaries has been very great, though it cannot be measured for individual cases, since it is generally not possible to estimate the extent to which major changes are universal phenomena of the times. Grautoff has outlined his influence in France, describing how it was really he who taught the younger generation how to see the later Cézanne, how he gathered an entire circle around himself—Vlaminck, Marie Laurencin, Dufy, Othon Friesz, Van Dongen, Lévy—providing them with decisive stimulation. But Matisse has had a strong influence in Germany too. Individuals such as Moll and Purrmann have been his direct students, while others such as Pechstein have plainly been decisively impressed by particular paintings, by the 1913 exhibition at Gurlitt's, for example. The war, which impeded the influence of French art, prevented Matisse from taking the place in German exhibitions that his significance properly entitled him to. Had his influence been continuous, it would have helped curtail some curious detours and could have had a soothing and purifying effect on the turbulent development of past years.

André Lhote

NOUVELLE REVUE FRANÇAISE

"Notes"

1923

There are a thousand ways to bring out the mystery concealed in things immobile. Some, like Gauguin, seize it by the scruff of the neck and drag it out like a thief, forcibly trapping it in the world of form and color. Others beckon it gently, seeming never to touch it, even feigning disdain for it, out of a sense of propriety. So it is with Matisse, whose sole concern, one might think at first sight, is the mere delight of painting. In any case, it is with the steadfast intention of condemning this orientation of his that we approach his annual exhibitions at the Bernheim gallery. But Matisse works magic. No sooner do we set eyes on those delicate canvases, seemingly caressed by a rapid, inattentive hand, than the rampart of our objections crumbles. We yield; we are conquered. For color, though it often excites a baser instinct in us, is also capable, if applied with tact and lightened by swift shifts of tone, of moving us to a delectable reverie strongly akin to poetic ecstasy. One of Matisse's landscapes, in which nature is reduced to a few patches of faded green with a hint, in the distance, of flashes of light on a hillside quarry—the entire scene traversed by a shade-swept road in which the outline of a woman adds a faded, rosy touch—unleashes a fresh mystery, reminiscent of Rimbaud and as intoxicating as those imaginatively forceful conjurings wrought in the strangest of climes by Gauguin. Such achievements do much to redeem the trifling with Nature condemned so mercilessly by certain critics who, in the manner of the schools of the stylized Sublime or of bleak Realism, have forgotten the art of smiling.

There remains the question of "content," which many consider inadequate in most of Matisse's paintings. "Déjeuner de soleil" is the term commonly applied to those light scumbles and sweeping glazes of which

This essay was a review of Matisse's April 1923 exhibition at the Bernheim-Jeune Gallery.

this painter is so enamored. Granted, many tones that resemble water-colors more than oils will be dimmed in the light, but in this exhibition several canvases of a heavier than usual impasto attest to a genuine master's aspiration: to express his sensations without falling prey to an excess of perishable technique (overuse of impasto being a danger best avoided in any event).

Yet another concern of a master, so to speak, is to strive to work on more spacious canvases. Indeed, sketches, however delectable, are insufficient to perpetuate properly the memory of a great painter, and if it is true that Matisse sometimes seems descended from Velázquez by way of Manet, all we may ask is that he justify this lineage by bequeathing to us, if he can, his equivalent of *The Lances*, *Las Meninas*, or (at an admittedly less elevated level) *The Balcony* or *Luncheon on the Grass*.

But there is no reason to believe that Matisse does not harbor equally perilous ambitions. Indeed, while walking through the gallery of the rue Richepanse on my way out of the Bernheims, I had the opportunity to see once more, hanging high but losing none of its force, one of those immense paintings of which he was once so fond: some women on chaises longues in the pathways of a park. "An overblown sketch," I heard someone say. It would be more correct to say, "Much more than a sketch, if not quite a painting."

Recalling the many drawings included in this latest exhibit of paintings, and reflecting on the considerable toil required to "master" a painting of large dimensions (especially if the painter wants to preserve the subtlety of the play of color over the vast surface), I could not resist summing up the impression left by my visit in this way: "Here is the most pleasant and appropriate way for a painter to spend the eve of the battle."

Tea. 1919. Canvas. 55³/₁₆ × 83³/₁₆″ (140.1 × 211.3 cm). The Los Angeles County Museum of Art, Bequest of David L. Loew in memory of his father, Marcus Loew.

Julius Meier-Graefe

FAUST

"Matisse, the End of Impressionism"

1923

Julius Meier-Graefe (1867–1935), celebrated German critic and champion of Van Gogh, met Matisse in Berlin in 1908, but had not been particularly impressed by his art then.

After Van Gogh and Gauguin there has come a time, and in Paris too, when the good or ill fortune of individuals is no longer charged with drama, and mere mosaic-work has become the destiny of an epoch. Vagueness has supplanted the determination of the prophet who sacrificed everything for experience. Christ-like people move into the madhouse, and variations on Gauguin multiply endlessly.

In the plethora of variants large and small, two types stand out. One is progressive, the other traditional. "Progress" and "tradition" must not be taken literally but rather like the names of political parties. This is a necessary consequence of the distinction between them. Earlier, everyone sat, safe and obedient, in the shadow of tradition—which is where they belonged when, generally, the word "tradition" meant something. Now that terrain has become bleak and marshy. Weeds proliferate between crumbling banquettes. People stream in all directions on a thousand passable and impassable paths, trampling the fields, destroying the land. Grasshoppers invade the parched countryside, and any topic of interest, however daring, is plucked and devoured as a miraculous flower. Every loyal knight watching over the abandoned sanctuary, dented shield in hand, faces a thousand assailants. But the knights are weary and have lost strength; finely chiseled features, slack thighs; choice shapes, limited power. They fight no more battles. Against whom, and for what, should they fight? Nobility exists for the sake of memory alone, and experience makes do with the fragrance left in emptied goblets. These weary dreamers deserve our sympathy, but not our hopes. It is said that to burden their polite charm with demands would be to misunderstand it.

Matisse is the latest exponent of a taste that, in Paris, has been built into a European standard, the stylistic criterion of a good European, and he is also the highest example of an intellect cultivated with full academic resources. An intelligent taste. It is hard to say whether intellect or sensitivity plays the greater part in it. His rare feeling for comfort enables him to select and combine for a definite, circumscribed goal; moreover, because he selects logically and instinctively, he is able to turn comfort into a thoroughly indispensable concept. Nothing would be more improper than to call Matisse an eclectic. Taste is in an embryonic state when it functions eclectically. One does not possess the values of others in parroting them. Paris has evolved to a higher sensory level. Before Matisse, the derivations yielded coarse products of crude conglomerations. Some toyed with unalloyed fragments of the Spanish and Dutch, producing a kind of garnished soldier's breadloaf whose rough shape had appeal. Or else mixed them together into a dreadful stew. Others refined the ingredients. Simply to make a liquid product of these extractions was considered wonderful. Pampered palates were thrilled. There was always a tangible kernel around which all the stimulation crystallized. The fecundity that flowed from the kernel adhered to the stimuli. Matisse discovered gaseous extractions, and even the magnet that collected them dematerialized. A wisp of memory serves tradition. Delacroix becomes a line, Cézanne a smudge, Bonnard a curl. Contact with nerve endings is the self-sufficiency of this rivulet of precious stones. Touch lightly, and the affected value starts trembling. What trembles is not Delacroix, nor Cézanne, nor Bonnard. Their equivalents are found in the dust on the wings of butterflies. Divested of the residue of their animal quality, they are pinned to a white canvas. Life and work, suffering, love—who needs all that? These only burden color. The meager residue of humanity is condensed into color tones. Cézanne turned modeling into modulating, but with his tones he crafted a squared-stone reality. For Matisse reality is a *faute-de-mieux*. Reality is distilled into an improvised flat surface. In the 1908 *Bonheur de vivre* [sic] motifs not unlike Cézanne's black Baroque were combined kaleidoscopically into a primitive decoration. Cézanne's flower paintings lost volume, were denaturalized. Surface planes lead to tapestry. Where else? But in no way does this conclusion close our discussion. Tapestry is no longer laughed at. Nor is it the romantic renunciation of the newcomers of 1890 who, seeking to turn what had been the avocation of a privileged caste into something of use to the masses, fell into commercial dilettantism, producing cheap substitutes for unmatchable monuments. Nothing is less cheap than Matisse. Tapestry is robbed of its utility. It could not be hung on the wall like the paintings of Maurice Denis and company. The narrow-mindedness of proletarian decorators has no use for the fine-spun delicate fabric. Tapestry becomes a system, a figure of speech, an *idée fixe* of an artist of the Flaubert school. Tapestry is the two-dimensional art to which Manet sacrificed modeling and which helped him to fulfill his claim to contemporaneity; it is the final extraction of modern big-city perception, a form for people who live with nerves alone. It is unthinkable that this whirligig of wallpaper patterns could produce a dramatic effect. The style prohibits heroic gesture. Anything experiential would be awkward. The passions of the soul are no longer required to rise to the heights of art. Art is no exceptional state, but normality. So it must be divested of its soul. But the procedure need not result in loss of intellect—quite the opposite. Even systematic adherence to physiological stimuli of the most select kind operates intellectually. I am here for you to ingest, Matisse's paintings say, but the ingesting must be made an art. With the right organs, you will suck from my tapestry all that others pull from your soul: truth, simplicity, poetry, life—yes, even life.

In a book on Matisse, Léon Werth describes a grand seigneur and devotee of the arts who collects the choicest works of the great masters for his castle in Spain. . . . He owns works by Rembrandt, Vermeer, Tintoretto, Delacroix, Cézanne, and Manet. This grand seigneur lives with the works as though they were human beings. And he relates to them like people. He gets tired of them or cannot see enough of them. Despite all their beauty, he finds a lack of directness of contact in the older paintings, finds them mired in a museum atmosphere. They lack—Werth has wit—the sparkle of a stylish leather bag, a young woman, or a beautiful car. He is therefore leaving the older pictures and buying newer ones: Signac, Bonnard, Roussel, Vuillard, Marquet, de Marval, Vlaminck, Vallotton. And Rousseau, the most beautiful Rousseaus, and of course Picasso, the most extraordinary Picassos. He lives more intimately with them, but intimacy itself brings fresh dangers. In a couple of months he has had enough and gives them away to some little dancer. Then he travels. He is rich, and wealth affords him luxury. Generations of grand seigneurs have handed down to him the sense of luxury as a natural attribute. He savors luxury where run-of-the-mill rich people fail even to perceive it. Rarity, accessible only to rare people at rare moments—that is his delight. He discovers the reasons for the masters' failure. They have all painted for poor wretches. Their motif was life, the thing he scorns the most. Life smells of sweat. Life cannot be seen as a luxury. In Rembrandt the earthy odor is disagreeable, in Tintoretto, the loquacity. Vermeer's imperturbability has too much material bias for an opium smoker.

Faute-de-mieux: *that is, for want of something better.* Le Bonheur de vivre *actually dates from 1905–06.*

Werth had published an amusing parody, written as if by a jaded collector, in Elie Faure, Jules Romains, Charles Vildrac, Léon Werth, Henri-Matisse, *Paris, 1920.*

Ingres is like an irritable notary, Corot is tender, but tenderness is always secondary. There are even greater grievances against more recent painters. Cézanne loses his way in darkness, Renoir paints bonbons. Manet's wholesomeness borders on the bourgeois. And the latest painters are far too close, their purpose too transparent. Instead of going to the theater, he may as well listen to an actor rehearsing his lines. All painting becomes ludicrous. Either they fashion ornaments that scarcely differ from the tattoos with which mere folks decorate the walls of their rented apartments, or they put their heart into their paintings, an even worse blunder. One does not hang one's feelings on the wall. In the end, the grand seigneur returns to Paris, back to his empty rooms, and Matisse becomes the only painter he can bear to have in his home. A single Matisse painting substitutes for all the others. It has the simplicity of ultimate luxury.

Werth's parody, a postscript to the confessions of a Huysmans, exhausts the problem more thoroughly than the interpreter may have realized. Paris would not be Paris had this ultimate luxury gone undiscovered.

J. K. Huysmans (1848–1907) French novelist whose A rebours *(1884) was a celebrated example of the mood of the late nineteenth-century decadents.*

Adolphe Basler
HENRI MATISSE
1924

Adolphe Basler (b. 1878). Excerpted here from the 1924 Leipzig publication in German, this essay appeared in two different languages in very slightly different forms: under Basler's name in Der Cicerone, *January 1921; under the name of Philippe Marcel in* L'art d'aujourd'hui, *summer 1924; and with Charles Kunstler, in* La peinture indépendant en France, *1929, vol. 2.*

Matisse's great merit is to have been the true interpreter of Cézanne's art. He and the Fauves made the greatest contribution to the flowering of the new aesthetic that Cézanne originated. The school that Matisse has led, from which so many German, American, Scandinavian, and Russian painters have emerged, has played a major role in the formation of taste among modern painters. Matisse and his students have, in particular, broadened the influence of Renoir and Cézanne. It is thanks to them that people have learned to understand the sensory and mental power that enabled the master of Aix, with limited means, to sketch a painting extremely true to reality, in which keen perceptiveness is apparent in the smallest fragment, intentions are expressed with great clarity of thought through transformations, foreshortening, and volume, and the essential beauty of the architectural structure—where even the most experienced eye would see no more than inverted geometric figures—becomes indispensable to the realization of rhythm.

As the young painters immersed themselves in the details of Cézanne's art, they followed up his ideas and often generalized their studies. Even before he developed a taste for the exotic, Gauguin grasped the relationship between all types of fine art and had acquired the Fauve generation's predilection for unappreciated or little-known art forms. The fundamentals of the new teaching introduced by the Fauves, and by Matisse most of all, included the awkwardness of the primitives, the monumental figures of the Egyptians and Syrians, the archaism of the Greeks, the naive sincerity of the Romanesque and Gothic masters, the sculptures of Negroes and South Sea islanders. In my view his influence as an educator is equal, if not greater, in importance to his influence as a creative artist. For French painting has changed as a result of that influence.

* * *

The art of Matisse and the Fauves, like the Cubism that followed it, is basically the expression of a Symbolist aesthetic that belatedly appeared in painting long after its first manifestations in French literature. All the works of these painters show signs of this aesthetic, with its

34/50

Seated Nude with Arms Raised. 1924.
Lithograph. 24¼ × 18¹³/₁₆″
(61.6 × 47.8 cm). Collection, The Museum
of Modern Art, New York. Gift of
Abby Aldrich Rockefeller.

reliance on analogy, equivalence, and the intimation of nature. Unfortunately, an unlimited intellectualism, abuse of abstraction, and subjective conception fostered confusion in later painting styles. Easel painting was swamped by a mass of pictures that resembled carpet designs, combinations of garish patches of color. But the sharpness of his eye, his analytical confidence, his strong intellectualism, and most of all his ability to paint in light colors with speed and assurance prevented Matisse—more than Raoul Dufy and many others before him—from slipping into an applied-arts genre.

* * *

The merit of these painters, especially of Matisse and Derain, was that they had really assimilated Cézanne's art. But Matisse, the oldest of the group, showed the greatest maturity. His debut in painting was very difficult. It was at a time when the cultured public was captivated only by the novelty of the art of Bonnard, Vuillard, and Roussel. But these painters were mainly attracted by the superficial richness of the palette of the master of Aix. Similarly, in Gauguin's compositions they took pleasure only in arabesque stylization, Japanese woodcuts, and generalization. Matisse, on the other hand, was already striving for a pictorial design based on highly exact representation on a surface. His paintings had no artificial, conventional background of dull areas, but were composed of very real, indispensable lines that defined the visual field. His design was based on accentuation of the properties of solids, on the decorative, proportional arrangement of surfaces. He strove most systematically for the greatest possible simplicity in the use of color, which gave him the power, the intensity, of chromatic, impressionistic harmonies with an uninterrupted continuity of light. Even his manner of color use is impressionistic. But the substance of his pictures is less material, the structure more subjective; these are no longer merely objects depicted with an impressionist sensibility but things expressed in terms of their function. Every colored plane is a symbol, an evocation, a function that elevates the picture to abstraction, brings it into a single architectural rhythm. This preeminent intellectualist, endowed as he is with a very sensitive eye, has also created quite paradoxical things. And he has sought the stimuli for his creations everywhere. His great wisdom is drawn from everywhere, a wisdom found not only in his superb studies of the proportions of the human body but also in his landscapes, still lifes, and decorative compositions. It can be seen in all his paintings and sculptures, even in the most paradoxical of them, which perhaps betray an immoderate refinement but never lack the great personal ingenuity that characterizes his style. The tenor of his coloring and expressivity of his form are always splendid, purely harmonized, eruptive; he always conceives form abstractly, reduced to its functions.

His analytical confidence, particularly his talent as an exalted and confident master of color, always able to hit the right tone, as well as his predilection for brilliant graphic representations have prevented him from slipping into mannerism. As draftsman and painter, he shows the same freedom. His patches of color are always accompanied by striking brushstrokes; to him pencil and palette go together. His taste enables him to harmonize the most extreme colors extraordinarily, without introducing intermediary shades. He thus creates unique combinations, in which silver and cadmium white, yellow ochre and Venetian red, cinnabar, emerald green, ultramarine, ivory black, and red-brown are brought together wonderfully. One surprising thing about Matisse is the expansive energy he imparts to form. With what truth he draws a line, defines an arabesque! Whether it be a drawing on paper or a compact composition on canvas, the same perfection and vastness of dimensions distinguish him.

Other painters of the Fauve generation returned to easel painting, but Matisse continued to discover new forms and new ways of looking at things, for his power of vision never faded. He takes every liberty in depicting life, using subjective as well as natural transformations. But the natural quality of his talent justifies all his liberties. He has created a type of painting in which the decorator complements the easel painter. His highly logical simplifications aim at a rhythmical composition in which effortlessly modeled forms are effectively bolstered by the beauty of the drawing and the expanded dimensions. Matisse paintings often seem like drawings done with brushstrokes, so delicate and subtle is the execution.

After much groping, Matisse achieved a stylistic perfection that, as long ago as fifteen years, helped to solve various problems facing young painters. Today it is the master's most perfect and suitable instrument, which he alone is able to use. His former students chide him for abandoning the austerity that marked his earlier works. And indeed, since 1916 his paintings have evinced a greater delicacy; they delight through their musical content and seem meant to amuse the eye more than to move the soul. Thus, at the height of his creativity, the artist is striving for greater clarity and simplicity (not to speak of Classicism), a not at all exaggerated expression of his most recent creative period. For Matisse is a Romantic who takes pleasure in order and exuberant rhythms, which the Mediterranean coast, his favorite residence for the past several years, inspires in him. And his felicitous painter's eye finds so much intoxicating joy in life, so much beauty and warmth. No one will say of his odalisques what Théophile Gautier said of Ingres's: that their feet trod only Smyrna carpets and the alabaster stairs of harem baths. But they will be seen as creatures of enchanting grace, with shapes as ideal as they are lovely, creatures that breathe life and spread delight, like his flowers, his interiors with views of the blue Mediterranean, paintings done in some grand hotel in Nice. Such painting as this, with its unerring taste, heralds not greatness and majesty but pleasure and the most refined luxury. Hence its pleasant, comprehensible, and, simultaneously, modern character. It arouses no great excitement, but enchants the eye and grips the soul through its beautiful forms.

Henri Matisse is a great painter, a master, who distills those elements of life that have the greatest reality into fables on the painting's surface, who makes the ordinary and commonplace seem strange and precious. Inventively resourceful, in his more mature years he has been able to sacrifice the austerity of a now-outmoded aesthetic for the sake of seeing naturalistically, which he formerly emphasized in his painting. Art historians will one day accord him an honorable place alongside Renoir, as Lancret and Pater stand alongside Watteau.

Waldemar George HENRI-MATISSE: DESSINS "Drawings of Henri-Matisse"

1925

Waldemar George (pseudonym of Georges Jarocinski, 1893–1970), Polish-born French writer and critic who wrote about a number of modern French artists.

Morphology or ideography? Pure studies of form or representation of ideas by signs that stand for the object? Any drawing may easily be classed in one of these two categories.

With his lines the artist seeks to create a plastic entity or to record a visual emotion. Nicolas Poussin and Matthias Grünewald represent the opposite poles of the art. Poussin's drawing aims above all at composition. Grünewald's concern is dramatic expression. The merit of an arm, a forearm, or hand by the great seventeenth-century Frenchman lies strictly in its proportions. A hand by the German painter, with its painfully clenched fingers, is a harmonious complement to the body. But this hand has the status of a symbol. By analogy, it moves us to certain associations of ideas.

When Matisse was preparing to design his Dominican Chapel at Vence in 1948 he did extensive studies of Grünewald's famed Isenheim Altarpiece.

However varied the manner of expression of artists may be, they may easily be reduced to the two indicated styles, provided we accept that style is not merely a historic but also a psychic notion. This initial distinction, moreover, concerns only the appearance of the works. Their structure, their anatomy seem independent of the artist's creative process. They are, on the contrary, a function of his method. Whether the artist has a pre-existing idea of form and executes it, whether he subjects this idea to the control of the senses, whether his writing constitutes a way to record perceived impressions, his drawing will reflect his system.

Other distinctions could be laid down. A critic doubling as graphologist would probably take delight in studying the "tics" of the handwriting, its distinctive signs and characteristics. Drawing is still a world not well explored. But it would be easy to identify its component parts and codify them. Here we will sketch out a plan for doing this, using Matisse's drawings as our object.

Painter or draftsman? If Picasso is acknowledged as a master of the art of drawing, Matisse is known most of all for his great use of color.

Hasn't he himself contributed, through confession and confidential comment, to the establishment of his entire reputation as a painter for whom lines are mere flexible frames in which color, the sole constructive force of the painting, shifts the elements and alters the proportions? In one of his articles Maurice Denis notes that Cézanne constantly changed the drawing of *The Bathers* as he modified the play of color. Matisse's method is close to that of the master of Aix-en-Provence.

But drawing, contrary to popular belief, is more than beautiful handwriting, or even calligraphy. In his paintings, Matisse draws through color. Though the color may hew to a line, the artist is nonetheless well aware of all its hidden resources, its expressive strengths, its constructive and descriptive qualities. He uses them as he sees fit. When Matisse delimits the zones of his colors, we discover in his polychromatic sweeps, stippled with dark spots that enhance the lighter tones, certain vestiges of writing that offer the eye reference points and make it easier to read the painting.

Matisse's drawings, of course, are a painter's drawings. But most of them do not really represent compositions intended for paintings. Even when the artist did work from them, he later modified them in accordance with the requirements of the rhythm of his color. We are therefore obliged to consider each drawing . . . as an end in itself. Chronology will often guide us. But it cannot form the basis of our study.

Matisse's drawings rarely enlighten us about his development as a painter. At best they help us to a better understanding of the development of form in contemporary art.

The moment he became aware of his mission, Matisse reviewed his technical resources. The men of his generation, I believe, are learning anew, reinventing their craft. They are posing the problem of form, which the impressionists scarcely broached, which Gauguin solved as a decorator, denying the painting any spatial quality, which Degas and those who followed him, Pierre Bonnard and Edouard Vuillard, viewed from the standpoint of Japanese woodcuts. Cézanne is still misunderstood. Only his use of color captures the attention of painters. His drawing, his treatment of space are considered maladroit. No one dreams of making use of them. Matisse must therefore be accorded the title of precursor. Indeed, it is in his drawings that the feeling some call modern anxiety first came to light. This anxiety is not a condition of the soul. It is a state of mind which has caused the young painters of the era to establish new relations between volumes inscribed on the surface and the surface itself, whose quality they seek to respect.

A crouching nude in three-quarter profile shows Matisse coming to grips with volume, whose plastic character he represents by unbalancing the body. A like procedure was familiar to Ingres. Cézanne also used it. It allows for expression of the third dimension without resorting to the techniques of perspective. Matisse is taking a stand. He distorts in the constructive sense. Whereas Gauguin, following Puvis de Chavannes, distorts in the sense of the plan, as befits a decorator, Matisse, without piercing the surface, in his drawings, if not in his paintings, avoids the purely ornamental, two-dimensional arabesque. He distorts—or rather, he makes his themes conform to the new principles of plastic structure. He never stylizes. He alters a body's proportions so as to harmonize them. He uses them freely. He does not lose sight of the objective, living reality. He uses the smallest anatomical details in the interests of composition. This grasp of reality, so exact, will ever be Matisse's compass. It forearms him against certain experiences of a clearly speculative nature. Matisse never loses the sense of nature. The French style, at once truthful and concerned with inner balance, lies between the *maestria* of the Italian artists and the detailed work of the Germans.

Matisse's lines are mobile. Is his dynamism a simple effect of the handwriting? Not at all. His line is not an ideal limit of the form. The form that it contains, or rather that it sums up, sometimes seems as if it could be stretched. The fine line that surrounds it is so supple that it yields, or gives an impression of yielding, under the force of a spontaneous outburst. Matisse knows the art of making empty spaces speak. His lines are often fractured. But so sure is his hand that his empty spaces are themselves eloquent. They indicate the measure of a volume better than any pedantic relief.

*   *   *

Geometric style and naturalistic style have always existed. Aztec bas-reliefs, Mycenaean pottery, pre-Roman belt buckles, African Negro masks, and statuettes of pre-Hellenistic gods attest to the capacity for geometrization and transposition among primitives. Few living artists have taken as much liberty with the human body as the Egyptians, whose bas-reliefs distort the component parts with a constructive aim. The heroic test of Cubism, however, has enabled us to bring many things into focus.

Young Woman in an Armchair. 1923. Canvas. 21⅝ × 15″ (55 × 38 cm). © Succession H. Matisse/1988. Photograph courtesy Archives Matisse, Collection Claude Duthuit.

The prior exclusion of the object, considered as such, ultimately allows us to reintegrate it, provided, however, that it emerges as a plastic element. However paradoxical it may seem, eclecticism is the only appropriate attitude for the contemporary man who wishes to understand all the current forms of artistic expression. In the eyes of this enlightened viewer, Henri-Matisse's recent drawings have the same value as the works of his youth.

Maturity does not mean moderation. Let us admit, though, that Matisse is such a master of form, that from it he creates effects of such plastic import that one cannot long yearn for his past boldness.

I never weary of examining that young girl's turning head, with her almond eyes, her well-chiseled lips, those curls ringing an oval face. That nude woman, stretched out on a soft sofa, standing out against a background of fine lines, like an Oriental brocade. That massive body, although drawn with obvious concern to render the special features faithfully, is posed so unselfconsciously. These two voluptuous adolescents make us think of *Women of Algiers*. Why? Similarity of themes? How could Matisse, the true heir of Eugène Delacroix (and as a colorist, too) have entirely escaped the grip of that great master of drawing, creator of *Crusaders*?

Around the same time and alongside the charcoal drawings, in these painter's drawings *par excellence*, in which merit reigns supreme, he recovers, enriched by experience, his feeling for the sharp and penetrating line. From this period dates a torso which is monumental in all its proportions and a number of lithographs, whose graphic force unifies the figures, accessories and background, forming the groundwork for a single composition, brought forth to the surface.

Landscapes: gardens, houses among the trees. Who would have thought the painter of *Joie de vivre* capable of brooding so lovingly over the tiniest blades of grass? His tree trunks are architectural. His lacy branches unfold through space like the rigging of masts. The topography of the lands he describes is so precise that many an architect could envy him. I think of Renoir, whose Provençal residence Matisse evokes, and who also felt compelled, at one time, to detail with an engraver's insistence leaves, fruit, and female bodies.

Chamber music, some say. I would gladly call Henri-Matisse's works chamber drawings, traced with pen or graphite. They have a limited audience. They are neutral in appearance. They do not seek to produce an effect through outward signs. They are written in a secret language. They constitute a private domain, to which only those able to decipher their meaning can gain access.

Delacroix's Women of Algiers, *1834, and* Entry of the Crusaders into Constantinople, *1840.*

Forbes Watson
THE ARTS
"Henri Matisse"
January 1927

Forbes Watson (1880–1960), American writer and critic whose insistence on the difficult pictorial qualities of Matisse's art is unusual for the period. Watson represents a tendency in Matisse criticism that went largely ignored in subsequent years, as Matisse came increasingly to be thought of as "the good armchair" and the "joy of life" painter.

The art of Henri Matisse can only be appreciated by people experienced in painting because the eliminations are so immense. Matisse takes for granted in his audience an immense familiarity with painting. Today, so great is his fame that those people who tag along in the wake of the famous are included in the great general mass of his admirers. The true lovers of the work of this artist remain limited to those who are versed in the art of painting.

After Matisse closed his school, he was always kind to painters with whose work he sympathized. He received them hospitably and gave them friendly criticisms about their work. One of the points which he used to make at that time, a point which has since been much talked about, although painters only too frequently forget it, was that every inch of the canvas should be as alive as every other inch, that the remotest corner of the canvas is, so to speak, as important as every other part of it.

Remembering this belief of the artist's while looking at his work, the inevitability of his development becomes apparent. It also makes clear why Matisse has added a definite contribution to art. To add something to the art of painting is not necessarily to be greater than any predecessor. In a certain sense it is fair to say that every artist, since the world began, has added something of his own to the art that he practices. Otherwise he would be merely an imitator or a rearranger of what other men before him had already seen. In the case of Matisse, the added contribution that he has given us is of a clear, visible order.

Going back to the time when Matisse first showed the results of the influence on him of Manet, the most important single line of growth in his work seems to be a steady advance toward the employment of pure color in arrangements in which he used stuffs of many patterns, one against the other, in interiors with figures. He selected subjects which, if carried out in values that were unfailingly right, would result in gay, singing and exhilaratingly decorative paintings conceived in purer and more intense color than any of his predecessors attempted.

Those who do not understand or wish to understand the extreme painting knowledge of Matisse himself, and consequently of his art, were wont, before his fame frightened them, to consider his drawing childish and his painting slapdash. No one who has ever painted or who has a civilized attitude toward painting, can fail to realize the astonishing knowledge and the purity of eye necessary to enable the artist to make the various objects and patterns in such a complex and joyous arrangement as Matisse delights in, hold their places in the picture. It is not by an atmospheric graying down of the things in the background that he keeps them from coming forward, for he often reserves the brightest notes of his palette for the remotest corner of the room or the most distant point in a landscape. The answer inevitably lies in the rightness of his color values.

Such rightness cannot be the result of haste. As Matisse once said, "I work as much as I can and as well as I can all day. I give my utmost capacity and all my powers, and afterwards if what I have done is not good, I am no longer responsible for it, for I simply cannot do it any better." The truth of Matisse's statement brings us again to the realization of a predominant characteristic already referred to, namely, his painting knowledge.

In days gone by artists appealed to their audience with ideas which were not so aesthetically skeletonized as are the pictorial ideas of a painter like Matisse. We shall never know, probably, how much the appeal of Giotto to the audience of his own day was religious, how much was purely aesthetic. And coming down through the centuries, no matter what artist is recalled, Michelangelo, Rembrandt, Greco, Rubens, Ingres, Delacroix, Cézanne, there is always an appeal of subject matter which, so to speak, helped the public to swallow the pill of aestheticism.

Though it be true that many of the disparagers of the art of Matisse (all highly successful artists enjoy an inevitable group of antagonists in this bitterly competitive world) claim that Matisse turns out gay and exhilarating paintings of costumed and uncostumed ladies reclining in a sunny room filled with the bright colors of flowers and brightly patterned stuffs and looking out upon a bright blue sea, at a prodigious rate; and though they claim that his later pictures make their appeal through their obvious gaiety and prettiness, the claims seem prejudiced.

Doubtless Matisse, like his old friend Renoir, sees no harm in a picture's being pretty and attractive. Doubtless he, like Renoir, realizes that paintings which make you want to laugh with pleasure can be quite as serious as those which are executed with one hand on the paint brush and the other on the temple. Over-pretty as some of the present-day imitators of Derain's painting, at its brownest, and Segonzac's painting, at its thickest, may consider Matisse's art, its appeal is quintessentially aesthetic. It tells no dramatic story, appeals to no religious instinct and, generally speaking, its subject matter, delightful though it may be, is merely the thinnest possible pretext on which to hang a purely painting idea. That Matisse is not at his best in wholly abstract work, that he needs to establish a human connection, does not contradict the statement that his presentation of an idea is almost exclusively aesthetic.

In this aim, if it is one of his aims, he does not differ from many contemporary painters. One of the outstanding characteristics of contemporary art is its refusal to rely, as did the artists of the past, on the connotations of subject matter. This refusal has, in turn, developed a much more highly investigating audience, or at least an audience more capable of finding its full satisfaction in strictly painting ideas than existed probably in any past period. With such an audience, it is possible for the painter to develop his ideas along lines restricted increasingly within the limits of what he himself wishes to say and how he wishes to say it. He has completely freed himself from the demands of a public uneducated in art; neither the church nor the state commands him; an invisible client is relied upon to support him, and he tells his painting message to this client without ever communicating with him in words.

If, as in the case of Matisse, certain paintings and decorations have been ordered by a client, no such relationship is established between the client and the artist as existed in the much discussed days of the great patrons. The artist, directly or indirectly, convinces the client that he is right, that his viewpoint cannot be questioned or interfered with, and the client in turn either comes to understand this or ceases to be a client.

The situation has come about because the artist represents a small minority and consequently, like all minorities, he is in the position of defending himself against the aggressions of the majority. The process, having gone on now for at least a hundred years, has brought about a situation in which the artist is always at least one step ahead of his own public. He has become accustomed to expect this public to catch up with him in time. He takes it as a foregone conclusion that if he has his own say in his own way, regardless of what anyone may think of his picture at the first moment of its public appearance, it will be received favorably eventually, if he himself is intelligent and original enough to have ideas capable of holding the attention of a sufficient number of people for a sufficient length of time; so that a special public of the artist has developed the habit of thinking that perhaps it is not going ahead fast enough in its appreciation. Consequently unless the artist gives this particular special public something new, in the sense of something not already understood, some unexpected idea to struggle over, it is quite capable of becoming cool toward the artist.

This danger-point in the appreciation of the contemporary artist's highly specialized public furnishes him with the supreme test of his character as a painter. Picasso has not been able to face it calmly; he has watched for the signal which would indicate that his public was saying: "Oh, we know all that!" Imagining that he hears the signal, he jumps this way and that, changing his art again and again until it has lost logical sequence. Matisse, threatened with the same signal, has calmly gone ahead in his own logical manner, intensifying his pattern, painting with purer and purer color, when color was going out of fashion, holding to the thing that he himself wanted to do and doing it steadily better. He has come safely through the period when that hyper-practiced group of appreciators, if we want to call them that, who are avid for something new, stood out against him and disparaged his work.

Going back to the years just after he closed his school, when he would point out on a young aspirant's canvas a spot that was empty and dead, and explain in the simplest terms the necessity for having the whole rectangle completely alive and right in value, and consequently perfectly related, the point of development at which Matisse has arrived, appears to be the logical and inevitable point, which, given his intelligence, painting knowledge and eye, he was bound to reach. The sheer enjoyment which his work gives, the calm pleasure that emanates from his paintings is proof that Matisse has found his natural language. In it he expresses fully his sense of color, his understanding of values, his delight in the brightness of the world.

Florent Fels
HENRI-MATISSE
1929

We know that Matisse teaches us economy and measure: the right tone, the right line.

It would be wonderful if the painter could simply speak painting. But deeds must match purposes. There must be life.

On the face of it, one might say that each of Matisse's works is the product of felicitous meditation. The function of art, some believe, lies in the preposterous. It is usual for a supposed avant-garde—hailed too much by some, fought too much by others—to acquire a large dose of scandalous celebrity. It seems we must, alas, accept the watchword: No enemies on the left.

Matisse resolves the theorem elegantly, like anyone who is good at math, because he is able to skirt the traps that snare oafs and hair-splitters and to choose—above all to choose—among the countless possible ways to transcribe a given theme. Just as he was able to skirt the impressionist misadventure and the cubist catastrophe.

To say what Matisse thinks of painting and of his own painting I had, of course, to question him. I must confess that I expected to find in Matisse a penchant for metaphysics. His illustrious commentators, André Gide and, above all, Elie Faure, had suggested as much.

But Matisse's ideas seem to belong more to the thought processes of life than to pure aesthetics. His painting becomes flesh, like a radiant extension of his life. The spiritual structures he has built for himself, his investigations of the meaning of the *arabesque*, and those *lines of force* intended to express the intensity of sensations and to convey them, those allied powers—he speaks of all this as of living memories.

* * *

One may wonder whether Matisse's work will endure, or whether it can be transmitted, for it is representative of a certain state of contemporary sensibility. Having managed to express it, the artist is qualified to transmit the symbol of it.

The best witness to the development of painting in our time, a rigorous mathematician, formidable aesthetician, and humorist of Cubism, said one day: "You had to have seen Matisse's paintings back around 1900." The ironic tone suggested that they were hardly to his taste.

To our good fortune, it is of no consequence that Matisse constructed the premises of his work with suggested elements. Now that an apologia for the subconscious and the unconscious is recognized as tantamount to aesthetics, it is enough that this man, in his drawings and

Florent Fels (1891–1977), French critic and writer whose numerous interview-essays on Matisse and other School of Paris artists were collected in Propos d'artistes *(1925), the first of three monographs in which the same illustrations were accompanied by different texts in different languages. Roger Fry's* Henri-Matisse *(English), 1930, and Gotthard Jedlicka's* Henri-Matisse *(German), 1930, were the other two.*

"The best witness" apparently refers to André Lhote.

paintings, is conscious and responsible, with complete premeditation in his every line and patch of color, and that his gifts are enhanced by poetry.

The cubists are often hailed for the importance they devote to composition, which they are said to have conquered anew, three centuries after the great Italian and Flemish masters. [In full cubist fashion, one critic has dared to write: "subtle comparisons of false, acid tones, of those colored deliquescences cultivated with such talent by the 'Fauves,' whose master is Matisse." (André Lhote, *La Nouvelle Revue Française*, 1 June 1919.)] But it is easy to see that the elements of color in a Matisse painting are coordinated with premeditated rigor, that nothing in it could be moved without destroying it.

The wonder is that Goethe vaults the railing that rings the city's highest tower and ends his days by affording us a countenance comparable to that of the wise men of ancient Greece. The miracle is that Matisse gave painting a new attitude. Last year I heard Dunoyer de Segonzac say, as he stood before one of Matisse's paintings at the Salon des Tuileries, "He is still the most daring of us all."

Art criticism, which draws its *raison d'être* from aesthetics, is thereby one of the branches of philosophy. In that capacity, it allows the search for absolute values. Taken in itself, each of Matisse's works, whether graphic or sculptural, possesses the power and simplicity of an absolute idea. It may be that some prefer the surprising and the ludicrous to such categorical imperatives. There are impure classical works, made up of subtle admixtures. Some day it will be obvious that a Matisse canvas is like a simple body. It is not an assembly of forms and colors, but a creative act. A Matisse drawing is the geometrical locus of an intelligence and an experience.

Matisse says, "I will go to the islands to look at the night and the light of dawn in the tropics, for they will likely have a different density."

Matisse's entire work seems to be a creative concern based on a spiritual concern, in equal parts. Matisse appears as an ideal point that penetrates the absolute through the abstract reality of will. "Some of my engravings were done after hundreds of drawings, after the testing, knowledge, and definition of the shape—and then I did them with my eyes closed."

That is to attain the supreme reality, that of the mind.

Henri Matisse, Interviewed by André Verdet

ENTRETIENS NOTES ET ECRITS SUR LA PEINTURE

On Odalisques

1978

A.V. Has there been any part of your work that you think has been misunderstood by critics?

H.M. It's useless to recount the time of the early Fauves, when we mostly got the switch. As everyone knows, some of the critics were savage. But there was so much censure even when I did the long *Odalisque* series! Your question gives me the opportunity to offer yet another explanation on this subject, for the charges some people made against me then stuck for a long time, and I was still suffering distant repercussions of

André Dunoyer de Segonzac (1884–1974), French artist known for his landscapes, figure paintings, and engravings.

The "tropics" in this case was Tahiti, which Matisse was already making plans to visit.

Verdet's important interviews with Matisse actually date from c. 1952. Here, Matisse gives a rare evaluation of the role of the odalisque and, by extension, of the subjects and ambience of the so-called Nice period.

them much later. . . . None of us who create is blameless. Did I paint too many *Odalisques*, was I carried away by excessive enthusiasm in the happiness of creating those paintings, a happiness that swept me along like a warm ocean ground swell? I still don't know. . . . What I could not accept was that, in chiding me for a certain profusion of these paintings, people felt entitled to describe them with words like "exoticism" and "Orientalism," used in the pejorative sense, as if my natural bent, my predilection for the arts of the Orient, might have drifted, given the plastic use I was making of some of their elements, might have drifted into mannerism, facile decorativeness, or even a questionable rococo!

Morocco had excited all my senses. . . . The intoxicating sun long held me in its spell. I was coming out of long, wearying years of effort, during which I had given the best of myself to bring those efforts, after many inner conflicts, to the pitch of what I hoped would be an unprecedented creation. Besides that, I had been powerfully attracted by major mural and monumental compositions. After beginning with some exuberance, my painting had evolved toward decantation and simplicity. A synthesis both pictorial and moral, governed always by laws of harmony, held strict dominion over my work. A thirst for rhythmic abstraction was battling with my natural, innate desire for rich, warm, generous colors and forms, in which the arabesque was striving to establish its supremacy. From that duality issued works that crystallized in the union of opposites, overcoming my inner constraints.

A.V. You had to catch your breath after those important years of conquest that weighed so heavily in determining some of the choices the painters of your generation had to make.

H.M. Yes, I had to catch my breath, to relax and forget my worries, far from Paris. The *Odalisques* were the bounty of a happy nostalgia, a lovely, vivid dream, and the almost ecstatic, enchanted days and nights of the Moroccan climate. I felt an irresistible need to express that ecstasy, that divine unconcern, in corresponding colored rhythms, rhythms of sunny and lavish figures and colors.

A.V. The plastic embodiment of an Oriental reverie, in which you let the gods of sensual pleasure command your sated imagination at will, with flourish and ritual. . . . But you kept watch, and your ever-alert creative powers gave us in the paintings of that period, inspired by your stay in Morocco, the feeling of somnolent bodies and consciousness, the feeling of blissful, carefree siestas.

H.M. You alone are responsible for what you are so poetically saying!

A.V. But didn't some critics charge that in the *Odalisques* you were backing down, retreating from your bold, advanced period, more or less from 1908 to 1916 or 1917. . . .

H.M. As I told you before, I am not blameless. The *Odalisques* were a whole, important in number. Undoubtedly, not all the paintings were one hundred percent successful. I would be the first to agree that there may be hesitations or inadequacies in this or that painting. But I deplore the epithet some people unfortunately saw fit to hurl in characterizing this period that was so fruitful for me. You can find flaws in some of the paintings of the *Odalisques* series, but not the flaw that the word "mannerism" means to you and me. In the *Odalisques*, I do not give up what I had recently gained, those plastic advances you mentioned, but I return to a more profound resonance, I again accept a certain kind of model, once more I take possession of a space where air freely circulates again. In them was posed this problem for me: to attune and balance pure colors and half-tones so as to assure the painting's harmony and rhythmic unity against the possible danger of chromatic shrillness.

Matisse had been to Morocco twice in 1912–13.

COLORPLATE 70. *Woman in a Flowered Hat*. 1920. Canvas. 23⅛ × 19½″ (58.9 × 49.9 cm).
Mr. and Mrs. Herbert Klapper, New York.

COLORPLATE 71. *Meditation (Après le bain)*. 1920. Canvas. 28¾ × 21¼″ (73 × 54 cm). Private collection.

COLORPLATE 72. *Interior at Nice*. 1921. Canvas. 52 × 35″ (132.1 × 88.9 cm).
Charles H. and Mary F. S. Worcester Collection. © 1988, The Art Institute of Chicago. All rights reserved.

COLORPLATE 73. *Two Rays, Etretat.* 1920. Canvas. 36 × 28″ (91.4 × 71.1 cm).
Norton Gallery and School of Art, West Palm Beach, Florida.

COLORPLATE 74. *Woman Before an Aquarium*. 1923. Canvas. 31¾ × 39¼″ (80.7 × 100 cm).
Helen Birch Bartlett Memorial Collection. © 1988, The Art Institute of Chicago. All rights reserved.

COLORPLATE 75. *The Moorish Screen*. 1921. Canvas. 36¼ × 29¼″ (92.1 × 74.3 cm).
© 1988, The Philadelphia Museum of Art: Bequest of Lisa Norris Elkins.

COLORPLATE 76. *Odalisque with Red Culotte*. 1921. Canvas. 25½ × 35⅜″ (65 × 90 cm).
Photograph: Musée National d'Art Moderne, Centre Georges Pompidou, Paris.

COLORPLATE 77. *Odalisque with Raised Arms.* 1923. Canvas. 25⅝ × 19¾″ (65.1 × 50.2 cm).
National Gallery of Art, Washington. Chester Dale Collection.

A.V. The *Odalisques*, then, could be considered a challenge to your earlier achievements, rather than a retreat from them.

H.M. Let's say a new round. I was still pursuing my goal, the shining independence of color, but pursuing it by other means. For instance, the components of the paintings compress the empty spaces, the "holes." The tapestry motifs play a role equivalent to the female nude, the central figure that reigns supreme in the interiors. These elements are active, they are not simply dropped there as extras in a supporting, purely decorative, role.

A.V. I took the liberty of bringing along this album with color reproductions of some paintings having the *Odalisques* as their subject. Here they are.

H.M. Very good, that will be easier for us. . . . Look at these *Odalisques* carefully: the sun's brightness reigns in a triumphal blaze, appropriating colors and shapes. Now, the Oriental decors of the interiors, all the hangings and rugs, the lavish costumes, the sensuality of heavy, slumbering flesh, the blissful torpor of faces awaiting pleasure, the whole ceremony of siesta brought to maximum intensity in the arabesque and the color must not deceive us: I have always rejected anecdote for its own sake. In this ambience of languid relaxation, beneath the sun-drenched torpor that bathes things and people, a great tension smolders, a specif-

Odalisque in Striped Pantaloons. 1925.
Lithograph. 21½ × 17⅜"
(54.5 × 44.1 cm). Collection, The Museum of Modern Art, New York. Bequest of Nelson A. Rockefeller.

ically pictorial tension that arises from the interplay and mutual relations of the various elements. I dampened those tensions so that an impression of happy calm could emerge from these paintings, a more or less amiable serenity in the balance of deliberately massed riches.

A.V. Then the period of the *Odalisques* was a kind of pause, might I say an active pause?

H.M. More precisely a tranquil period of transition that marked the beginning of another adventure, in the course of which the painting's rhythmic syntax will be completely changed by the inversion of the relations between forms, figures, and background.

André Levinson

L'ART VIVANT

"Henri Matisse at Sixty"

January 1930

André (Andrei Iakovlevich) Levinson (1887–1933), Russian-born choreographer and dance critic. A strict classicist, he criticized Diaghilev's Ballet Russe for subordinating pure dance to pictorial elements like costume and set design. Here, he reviews Henri-Matisse *(excerpted in this volume) by the* L'Art Vivant *editor, Florent Fels.*

By a happy coincidence, these brief notes on Florent Fels's book, just published by *Chroniques du Jour*, about the painter of *Joie de vivre* will appear just after M. Henri Matisse's sixtieth birthday. M. Fels's study is a mixture of biography and interview in which quotations from the artist are interspersed with aphorisms from the author (fragments of a meandering aesthetic); morals are drawn from all the usual stories, much is made of anecdote, and all the familiar points are made, as the point of departure for poetic digression. We are treated to a leisurely tour of the landscape, with a warmth of conviction and a blend of enthusiasm and irony. The colorful style, part criticism and part literary and documentary information, a kind of modern Vasari taken down by an adept reporter (a style that reflects a manner of being as much as a mode of thought), stimulates contemplation and speeds the circulation of ideas. Like M. Fels's previous efforts, this latest essay is based on the decisive and fundamental notion that the work of art is an emanation of the man who produces it, an embodiment of the *élan vital* of which philosophy speaks, a biological phenomenon. Not that his argument is deliberately antihistorical. "But," he remarks, "it does seem that it is characteristic of modern creators to assert their personalities through the vehicle of their works." Psychology having supplanted ideology, he concentrates on what the works reveal of the individual. There are times when his attitude becomes a provocative and aggressive challenge to "aestheticians of the renunciation of immediate sensation." Let it be noted *pro domo* that I'm afraid I may well be among the heretics thus targeted, one of those who regard sensation (or shock, or "thunderbolt," as the author puts it) as none other than the subject matter, crude but invaluable, of all reasoning about art.

The phrase élan vital *comes from the French philosopher Henri Bergson (1859–1941), whose ideas greatly interested Matisse.*

   In a work published by Marcel Seheur in a series whose very title—*Art and Life*—contains an implicit program, M. Florent Fels summarizes the heartfelt reasons why he likes the paintings of M. Maurice Vlaminck most of all: "Whatever the technique employed, painting such as this will always be superior to painting that views a canvas as an end in itself. It transcends the immediate and the accidental, basing itself, instead, on the absolute constant of human emotion. Art such as this rejects the ridiculous and narrow principle that a painting is a world apart, with its own laws and its own special life. A work of art is no more than an instant of

Fels's Vlaminck *was published in Paris by Marcel Seheur in 1928.*

universal life." It seems clear enough that a profession of faith resistant to systems, a method of penetrating works of art through intuition, of relating to them through emotion, stands violently opposed to the doctrine which, ascribing an immanent existence to forms and seeking out what is general rather than specific in various styles, aspires (in the celebrated words of Heinrich Woelfflin) to replace the history of painters with a history of painting *devoid of the names of artists*. In his brilliant polemic fervor, M. Fels delights in extending the paradox to its extreme, qualifying as "absolute constants" not the forms, categories, and numbers through which we perceive the world, but the amorphous flow and turmoil of emotions. Far be it from us to chide the author for such errors of judgment, for we know only too well that he has a horror of the kind of intellectualism, schematic formalism, and pedantry that withers, parches, and sterilizes the sensual pleasure of enjoying a masterpiece. But how shall this writer set about finding the "open, sesame!" that will afford him access to the work of M. Matisse, who everywhere offers him the dazzling, unadorned, and impermeable surface of a complete art, lucid, fully realized, and detached from its creator, of whom it reveals nothing? A quarter-century ago, more or less, M. Maurice Denis, great critic though he was, expressed irritation at the *abstract* character of M. Matisse's painting, in that it offered no leads for an inquiry into its motives. The least seasoned viewer would recognize one of M. Matisse's paintings at first glance, so glaring is its inimitable originality, but none of its inner being would shine through. We see as little of his person when looking at one of his paintings as we would of the operator of the projector when viewing a motion picture. Everything in a Matisse painting is a function of the form, an aesthetic datum. No drama, no tenderness; nothing emanates. Never has the concept of pure art, detached in the philosophical sense of the word, been practiced with such inconceivable integrity. Each of his paintings is a *spectacle* in the real sense: something to look at, the embodiment of a point of view, a complex of visual sensations that rises, through our eyes, to the brain, producing there a kind of dry intoxication and lucid exaltation in which bombast has no share—nothing murky or soggy. M. Fels speaks of the "spiritual concerns" that lie at the root of this art. Admittedly, in it we find *esprit*, of which the master's slightest sketch is a manifestation. But the *spiritual* appears entirely absent from it, and that is the most disconcerting strangeness, the most characteristic novelty, of this art which is great even though (and this is what is unprecedented about it) it lacks the slightest element of human, moral, heroic, pathetic, or religious grandeur. It is indeed the triumph of "the painting as an end in itself, material organized by the intellect."

It is clear, then, just how firmly the Matisse problem resists psychology and demands formal analysis. It must require all his talent for sympathy for M. Florent Fels to slip through the cracks, and a detective's intuition to catch such a reticent artist in his rare moments of relaxation: this book affords us the most complete exposition of M. Henri Matisse's views since his memorable statements in the *Revue blanche* back in 1908. But quite apart from his patient research, from the facts he has uncovered for the first time and the quotations he has gathered, we are grateful to the author for the accuracy with which he has situated "his personage" and recognized his providential role. "Eliminate Delacroix and Baudelaire," he writes, "and all contemporary aesthetics crumbles. Eliminate Matisse. . . ," he continues—and the mere postulation of the phrase, its rhetoric so felicitous, highlights the capital, *unique* importance of the artist who has shored up and dominated twentieth-century painting both inside and outside France. "In Paris," M. Fels observes, drawing back into order to leap all the higher, "he appears as one painter among others. . . . On a day of lonely misfortune, to pronounce the word 'Matisse' in some lost corner of the world is to summon radiant certain-

Heinrich Woelfflin (1864–1945), Swiss art historian whose Principles of Art History *(1915) emphasized formal over social and biographical interpretation, advocating a formalist approach to painting and a history of art "without names."*

Levinson refers to the Denis review in L'Ermitage *of the 1905 Salon d'Automne, excerpted in this volume.*

Matisse's "Notes of a Painter" appeared in La Grande Revue, *not* La Revue Blanche.

ties." This is not merely an eloquent flourish, but a statement of fact: this French painter commands universal prestige, has incalculable influence. But while the author's commentary gives us the reasons why, the accompanying illustrations shift, twist, and belie the entire question. I am well aware that this is the sore point of the "Matisse case." But I have no qualms about proclaiming aloud: the Matisse whose plates we see in this book *is not* the Matisse of whom M. Florent Fels speaks in his text, the Matisse of "radiant certainties," the leader of those whom M. Louis Vauxcelles, with his glittering wit, christened *fauves*. It is *another* Matisse, perhaps one who harvests, but certainly not one who has planted the seed of modern art.

Let no one believe, however, that I mean to rail against the glorious virtuoso who, with supreme elegance, now plays endless variations on a series of themes designated by popular vote. By no means do I intend to dismiss the art of pleasure. It is just that I am quite certain that the exquisite mannerist of the *Odalisques* would never have been able to turn the art of his age upside down, to enrich and guide it. It just seems to me that there is—in the realm of the possible, in all that depends on conscious volition—a *discontinuity* between the two Matisses. "In the eyes of the enlightened viewer," wrote M. Waldemar George in a recent (1925) work on M. Henri Matisse's drawings, "Henri Matisse's recent drawings have the same qualitative value as the works of his youth." To claim as much, it seems to me, is to put a good face on a bad business and to place procedure on the same level as genius. Despite everything, I could never have contemplated setting one Matisse against the other had I not believed that the second had neglected, evaded, and tacitly disavowed the first, whose discoveries were epoch-making. Books, as well as exhibitions, seem now to have set aside this dangerous revolutionist who not so long ago upheld the supremacy of the French school throughout the world. Such tactics raise serious questions of conscience.

"In 1896," M. Florent Fels explains, "Matisse sent thirteen paintings to the Champs-de-Mars Salon." They immediately aroused controversy. But of the seventy-eight reproductions published in the *Chroniques* book, only four or five predate 1917. In the album that accompanies M. Waldemar George's substantial study, only about ten of the sixty-four drawings are prewar.

But 1906 to 1913 was the decisive period during which the artist's *historic* vocation took root and culminated, and it was then that his influence on his contemporaries reached its apogee. The thirty or forty paintings in the Moscow Museum (from the Shchukin and Morosov collections) constitute the real Matisse museum: they embody a contribution without which certain developments in "contemporary" creativity become incomprehensible. The essence of his art, its substance and key, has thereby been systematically sacrificed to his more recent production. The *Red Room* and the famous panels *Dance* and *Music* are ignored and instead we are favored with the drawing of the Levantine woman (reproduced on page 41 of the Fels book), which dates from 1929 and could well adorn the walls of M. Camille Mauclair's salon, so reminiscent of the late Helleu's drypoint is its precious prettiness.

As if to compound the problem, the verbal offerings of the master (who seems thereby to consign to oblivion the first forty-five years of a dangerous and active existence) reported by our author are not always dated. Some of these are admirable: unadorned, concise, and correct, commensurate with the powerful and simple works that are no longer exhibited, even in reproduction.

"Derain once said to me, 'For you, doing a painting is like risking your life.' "

One shudders at the breath of greatness in that little phrase: everything is open to challenge, everything is at stake in the blank canvas; everything is on the line. But surely this cannot be a reference to the

Most of the illustrations in Fels's book were of paintings done after World War I.

A selection from the 1925 monograph by George on Matisse's drawings is included in this volume.

Matisse exhibited only five, not thirteen, paintings at the 1896 Salon.

These paintings are now divided between the Pushkin Museum, Moscow, and the Hermitage, Leningrad.

COLORPLATE 29
COLORPLATE 35
COLORPLATE 36

Camille Mauclair (pseudonym for Camille Faust, 1882–1945), French Symbolist poet and critic who was intolerant of Post-Impressionism. Paul César Helleu (1859–1927), painter and engraver known for portraits of fashionable women.

Luxembourg *Odalisque*! The man who painted that work was no longer staking his life: he risked nothing, for he always won. But neither did he enrich his own work, nor cause us the slightest new thrill.

What, then, were the unprecedented achievements of that lovely and unruffled maturity of his forties—an epoch on which he firmly brings down the curtain—which so astonished his contemporaries? Defying an unbroken tradition stretching back to the fifteenth century, he endeavored to apply the principles of *decorative* painting to *easel* painting, though without violating the frame. He broke with the *spatial* conception which, through perspective and relief, locates implied volumes in a feigned space. With rigorous intransigence he went beyond Byzantine icons and Persian miniatures, decorating and giving rhythm to the surface of the canvas by inscribing all objects in the same plane, bringing them to the surface and reducing them to two dimensions. In the *Red Room*—to take an example I have already mentioned—the table, the woman at the table, the still life on the table, and the landscape visible through the open window all form a flat and linear composition that adorns, and divides into, a parallelogram. Just a few slanted lines and the tree and house seen in the distance suggest depth, while the coursing, ornamental stencilled wallpaper pattern, gray on a bright red background, is reproduced as on a vertical partition. Thus handled, does the painting itself become a *frieze* that might well extend beyond the frame? Not at all, because it is centered, balanced, contained in a unity, closed and isolated. The same may be said of the "family portrait"—four figures placed against a background (carpet, drapes, dress, chessboard)—illuminated with a variety of recurrent motifs. The group itself, if you will, is a cartoon for a carpet. But isn't the carpet a closed composition circumscribed by the frame of the weaver? We find this oneness of the object that forms a whole, sufficient unto itself, even in some of Matisse's frankly decorative panels: the figures of *Dance* do not exit from the painting; they are not headed anywhere but spin eternally on the axis of the canvas.

With magnificent pride, this art of surfaces (which is, perforce, a "superficial" art devoid of depth in every sense) shuns the major resources of pictorial expression and limits, simplifies, and extravagantly intensifies the techniques employed. Having thrust Paolo Uccello aside, M. Matisse turns away from the example of Da Vinci and Rembrandt. One after the other he renounces the resources of *chiaroscuro*, *execution*, and the gradation of *values*. He refrains from fashioning "his figures by dint of plastic effects" that offer light and shadow. He sweeps away the charms of impasto, superimposed strokes, and tricks of brushwork, of the knife that sculpts the surface and the cuisine of the palette. He eliminates nuance and refuses to shade his tones.

He resorts to pure, unalloyed colors laid down in broad swaths with uniform intensity, their luminosity unaltered. He presses to its ultimate consequences the "return to the playing card" which (according to a phrase of Daumier quoted by M. Fels) was prepared by the technique and vision of Edouard Manet.

In his book *De Delacroix au Néo-Impressionisme*, M. Paul Signac, leader of the now-forsaken school, traces with subtle logic the direct links between two ages of French painting. Except that he mistakes a garage driveway for its terminus. The triumphal road down which he leads us runs from Delacroix to Henri Matisse. But was this splendid chromaticism of the "Fauve" an expression of pictorial painting? M. Matisse is a colorist in the sense of stained-glass windows, not in the Rubens sense. The *line* that delimits the colored areas, ringing them as the frame rings the window, stealing the glance of the viewer, plays a *primordial* role in his painting. The contour, the *arabesque*, becomes the sole armature of flat composition. For M. Matisse the line—indicator of directions, regulator of rhythm—is charged with dynamic energy, as the wire of a con-

COLORPLATE 76

Paolo Uccello (1397–1475), Florentine painter whose studies in perspective contributed to the Renaissance development of pictorial space.

Honoré Daumier (1808–1879), French painter and caricaturist; the "playing card" reference is to the flatness of Manet's paintings.

ductor is charged with electric current. And the primacy of this rhythm in turn dictates a synthetic simplification of the form. Matisse clarifies and reduces his palette. Necessarily, he *summarizes* and *distorts* the personages in his paintings. A panel such as *Music* is content to attain three *monumental* colors: blue, brown, and green. The representation of the human form falls under the same constraint, which guides the style.

Is it aesthetic dogmatism to recall the memory of these great feats as we hail this century's greatest French painter on his birthday? Certainly not. It is rather that his unparalleled personality blossomed and culminated in these works, which represent the acme, the golden age, the unforgettable surprise of his painting. If, today, the celebrated and uncontested master places female figures, drawn with voluptuous foreshortening, in a harshly excavated space, if he respects anatomical proportions and shapes their relief with shadows, if he *superimposes* a delicious color over the composition thus *constructed* (whether with graphite or charcoal) even if it means repeating the painting in a different spectrum, we do not cavil at indulging such a supreme artist, nor do we claim to find no pleasure in his work.

But today more than ever, it is worth remembering where the true greatness of the painter Henri Matisse lay, what assures his place in history, and what brilliant achievements earned him imperishable laurels.

Fritz Neugass

CAHIERS DE BELGIQUE
"Henri Matisse, for His Sixtieth Birthday"
March 1930

The sexagenarian artist today has reached the end of his development. Once the greatest of innovators, the man who opened up new paths for painting twenty years ago, who gathered around himself painters from the whole world, he has become a fashionable artist, like Van Dongen, his companion in the days of struggle. He lives on his large property in Nice and paints odalisques and more odalisques, lying down or seated on silk cushions in front of striped, floral, or checkered rugs and draperies. The abundance of his ornamentation crushes the figures which come to resemble arabesques in the interplay of their delicate outlines. Red vests, blue trousers, black hair, sparkling jewelry on a background and floor of vivid colors, interplaying vertical and horizontal lines all mingle in a clear, transparent, and delicate composition with a perfect rhythm and harmony such as no other artist of our time has been able to execute. But if a painting of this type charms us with its incomparable harmony, a series of such paintings is tiresome. The comprehensive exhibitions of Henri Matisse's works, organized in honor of his sixtieth birthday, confirm this impression.

Moreover, he has himself recognized that he has reached a standstill in his art, for he asks critics to judge him only on the entirety of his works, according to the great curve of his development.

Roger Fry
HENRI-MATISSE
1930

Ever since Caravaggio threw his searchlight on to the face and shoulders of some heavily built Roman model the art of painting has had to face a problem for which it can probably never find a final conclusive solution. It was of course really an older problem posed again with new insistence. It is a problem inherent in the dual nature of painting, where we are forced to recognize, at one and the same moment, a diversely colored surface and a three-dimensional world, analogous to that in which we live and move. It is this equivocal nature of painting that is at once its torment and its inspiration. The artist himself has a double nature and a double allegiance. He longs on the one hand to realize his vision, on the other to be a maker; he longs to tell of his experience and also to create an object, an idol, a precious thing, and almost always the vision and the precious thing—the objet d'art—are at variance. His vision and his craft pull different ways and his orbit is determined by their relative powers and proximities. In the long history of painting we may study many varieties of such dually determined orbits; we can find arts where one or other of these controlling powers has been reduced almost to zero.

But as a rule the maker has tended to share with the seer the artist's preoccupations. Indeed in certain periods and schools this has tended to become the dominant control. In the final periods of Graeco-Roman art the vision carried even to the extent of the trompe l'oeil had no doubt become the chief delight of the vulgar rich clientele who exercised the patronage of the day. But the growth of Christian art and the increasing use of the symbolical expression, together perhaps with some idea of the sanctity of the object itself by transference from the sacred being it represented, brought back the full influence of the "artificial" impulse (if we may be allowed the convenience of using the word artifical in this strict sense). Byzantine art fixes for centuries the compromise between the vision and the objet d'art so strongly on the side of the latter that we may perhaps be allowed to use Byzantine as a term generally expressive of the recovery of the objet d'art from the predominance of the representative side of pictorial art. Most of the arts that sprang from the Byzantine, such as Russian, Bulgarian and Armenian, in spite of their local and national variations, held to the general formula which Byzantium had consecrated. Italian painting almost alone of the Byzantine Family of arts began, from before the end of the thirteenth century, to revert to the representation of an ideated world of three-dimensional space peopled by clearly realized volumes. For the six centuries which lie between the years 1300 and 1900 the history of European art may be described very largely in terms of the increasing power of realizing the ideated space of the picture and the plastic perfection of the volumes it contains. It is the history of a gradual realization of all complexities of interaction of these in virtue of their qualities of form and tone and color and of the influence of the luminous atmosphere with which our actual three-dimensional space is filled.

Before we come to M. Matisse we must analyze a little the painting of the '60s and '70s, the capital era of Impressionism. For indeed many elements of design converge here, and much that is decisive for the twentieth century begins to emerge. And first for Manet. His art is full of paradox. His first and I think his most profound inspiration is that of Caravaggian Spain, of Velázquez, even more perhaps of Ribera, that is to say, form seen immersed in an illusive chiaroscuro. But Manet had a

This important text, first published in English in 1930, was reprinted with different illustrations (1935) and then translated into French (1936). This version combines Fry's own condensation of the essay's first part (for Cahiers d'Art, 5-6, 1931) with the conclusion of the 1930 edition.

Caravaggio (1573-1610), Italian Baroque painter famed for the unidirectional, often side-angle, lighting of his subjects, with sharply contrasting shadows.

deep, perhaps unconscious concern for the picture surface and he soon learnt to swing the source of illumination round till it was behind his own head. In those circumstances the more intense the light the flatter became the modeling of all the lighted planes. For now the shaded planes become reduced almost to a dark contour around the flatly illuminated mask. Thus with scarcely any transition Manet passed from the extreme of illusionist representation to a kind of flattened relief with heavy outline.

And yet another paradox, it was out of Manet's immediate circle of followers that Monet and Pissarro devised that completest destruction of surface organization which alone sufficed to express their vision of atmospheric color and in the end forced Manet altogether out of his natural bent into an imitation of their methods. It was also his ardent admirer and would-be follower, Cézanne, whose work was dominated by acute anxiety about the dual function of the painted surface. On the one hand there is desperate research into the principles of plastic construction of volumes with the theoretic shots at a guiding idea—the famous cone and cylinder—his desire to realize, and on the other his horror of verisimilitude (*il est horriblement ressemblant*) his equal horror of chiaroscuro, his hope of finding some method by which a vigorous plastic construction might be built out of pure values of color without light and shade—in short all that was implied in his ambition to create something durable, something with the quality of an objet d'art.

The total result, for all its intense reality, appears strangely unlike the texture of actual appearance, becomes indeed intensely anti-photographic. Our sense of plasticity is no doubt richly appealed to but it is as it were by implication; it demands the active cooperation of the spectator's imaginative power. And thus once more, though plastic values pervade every part of the design, the surface is not utterly violated.

Literal Representation had weighed so heavily on the art of the nineteenth century that Cézanne's gesture was read mainly as raising the standard of revolt against that enslavement. We are only now beginning to see how one-sided was that reading of Cézanne's heroic pose. That to his immediate followers that was the important thing is made abundantly clear in the art of Gauguin and Van Gogh.

External circumstances aided in imposing on the younger generation this new direction of effort. The discovery of the Japanese print, the new horizons which were clearing and enlarging the taste of the amateur, leading to a tardy recognition of Byzantine and early Oriental art and the overthrow of the age-long tyranny of the standards of Graeco-Roman sculpture, all these influences helped the artist, towards the turn of the century, to a new conception of the importance for painting of the artifical impulse. And color too, with the extended scale which it owed to the plein-air impressionists, was to play a new role and to become of prime importance in pictorial expression, for in Gauguin and Van Gogh already the separate notes of a chord are once more heard in their simple unbroken purity. Here then was the situation as it faced the generation of artists who were growing to maturity in the '90s of last century among whom Henri Matisse was destined to occupy so leading a position.

This apparently irrelevant introduction enables us to put our finger at once on the fundamental quality of Henri Matisse's art, just the quality which distinguishes him from other artists of today and gives him a very singular position in the long sequence of the European tradition of painting. Henri Matisse's style is based on equivoque and ellipsis. So far as I know, in the history of European art no one has ever played so many delightful, unexpected, exhilarating variations upon the theme of the dual nature of painting as he has. His is an art which, in its constant reference to our age-long pictorial tradition, can afford endless reservations and ellipses. An art which dares to rely on the spectator's realizing

Decorative Figure on an Ornamental Background. 1925–26. Canvas. 51⅛ × 38⅝″ (130 × 98 cm). Photograph: Musée National d'Art Moderne, Centre Georges Pompidou.

all that is sub-understood and merely hinted at or implied. Hence perhaps only an artist can fully estimate the miracles of tact, of inventive fertility, of suppressed pictorial science which this allusive-elliptical method implies. And it is only because of Matisse's extraordinary gifts that such a method becomes possible. But it is not only the magnitude of his gifts, it is their peculiarity which is essential. Let us try to enumerate them—first of all we must place an astonishing sense of linear rhythm, a rhythm which is at once extremely continuous and extremely elastic, that is to say it is capable of extraordinary variations from the norm without loss of continuity. The phrase can be held on to through all its changes. Imagine the rhythm rendered the least bit tight and mechanical in its regularity and the whole system of allusion and ellipsis would break down and become ridiculous. Secondly, and this is perhaps Matisse's most obvious gift, an impeccable sense of color harmony. But there, too, we must distinguish clearly. Matisse has in the first place the gift that we note in almost all Mohammedan art, the gift of finding rich new and surprising harmonies of color notes place in apposition upon a flat surface. And like the best of Oriental craftsmen Matisse is never content with a perfect accord of all the colors, there is always with this an element of surprise, there are always appositions which make us say to ourselves, "How the Devil did it ever occur to him that that color

Venus in a Shell, I. 1930. Bronze.
12¼ × 7¼ × 8⅛″
(31.1 × 18.4 × 20.6 cm).
Collection, The Museum of Modern Art,
New York. Gift of Pat and Charles
Simon.

would fit into that scheme? and yet, how perfectly acceptable it is." It is this element of surprise that gives its extraordinary freshness and vitality to his schemes even viewed as pure decoration, viewed as we might view some rare Persian rug.

But Matisse's color has a further quality without which his equivocal method could never have its full effect. He has an almost uncanny gift of situating each color in its place in the scheme viewed as a vision of plastic reality, as a world of volumes in a space. At each point its color holds the plane in its due position. What is peculiarly uncanny about this gift is that Matisse can give the most willful interpretation to natural color. It is in that power that he goes far beyond the pure decorator.

But this dual function of Matisse's color brings us back to his line, for here too the same applies. For his purpose line must not only have its quality of flat melody, it must be able to evoke volumes with incredible power. That power is great just in proportion as the pattern system is strong and demands extreme economy. Matisse cannot afford to lose time, so to speak, upon describing and evoking his volumes because to do so would arrest the sequence of this surface design.

It is, I think, from a perhaps unconscious perception of this necessity that he has developed his deformations of the figure. I would not deny that at times even Matisse may have slipped into a certain willful exaggeration but in the main the purpose is clear. These deformations increase the bare economy of his evocations of volumes. They are epigrammatic, tacit short cuts to the necessary evocation. They render the general movement of the figure more obvious, more easily handled by the spectator's imagination. They increase the clarity and legibility of the design—which indeed serves to remind us of another outstanding characteristic of Matisse's work, namely that, in spite of his methods which seem bound to cause confusion by the violence of his paradoxes, in spite of the brevity of his allusions, of the incessant equivoque, Matisse is nearly always legible at a glance. No one is in doubt as to what anything is or exactly where it is in the picture space even though the design is built on the strangest, most unfamiliar appositions, the oddest turns of nature's kaleidoscope. There are, it is true, examples to which this does not apply. But such conundrums are rare. Matisse never has indulged in the foolish pleasure of mystification. He is far too much in earnest for that. Of that earnestness he has again and again given proof in his evident anxiety not to exploit his own successes. Matisse has shown a great capacity for self-criticism. At any moment he is capable of turning round on his own productions and refusing to follow the path of least resistance. He has again and again put his whole art in question, unbiased by his past achievement. We have already noted some cases of this in his early evolution but Matisse is never satisfied, he can always challenge his own conclusions, and even, in his maturity, has more than once started afresh, giving away the advantage of his momentum along a certain line. So that if any of his admirers feels, as I confess for my part to have felt once or twice, that Matisse is making repeated use of some too charming pictorial syntheses, they may reassure themselves. Matisse himself is sure to scent danger in good time and to throw away a suspiciously convenient tool.

*   *   *

The latest of such proofs of the high quality of Matisse's ambition has occurred in recent years, and is likely enough to put a strain on his popularity. For Matisse's great popularity is based mainly on the work of the years 1920–1925. At this period in the clear light of his atelier at Nice, amid an Oriental *décor* and the spoils of inexhaustible Provençal gardens, he developed richer, more alluring arabesques of gay and sonorous color than ever before. His work had a certain note of elegance. It was exquisitely mundane. A picture of this period seemed as delightfully to summarize the refined social life of today as the 18th-century painters had done that of their contemporaries. Only the Matisse fitted far more nicely into the epicurean simplicity of a modern villa than a Fragonard could and yet had as choice a social emanation. In their delight at such an etherealized expression of their own aspirations, the more cultured rich succumbed at last to his spell. Matisse, indefatigable worker though he is, could never have satisfied the clamorous demand which arose from both sides of the Atlantic. But if the new converts to Matisse's art had forgotten the early Matisse, whom they had wondered at but never liked, M. Matisse himself had not. He had shown himself the creator and consummate exponent of a modern rococo style. But there was another Matisse, a Matisse who responded to quite a different kind of appeal from the visible world. A Matisse who felt the appeal of a stark, structural architecture, who loved above all a bare economy, who would, for the austerer delights of such forms, willingly sacrifice the intricate charm of his dancing arabesque. It would be wrong to suppose that there is anything morose or oppressive about this aspect of Matisse's personality, for he is always serenely joyful, always utterly free from neurotic complications or repressions, always responsive to sensual delights. It is only that this other aspect of his genius aims at a more arduous kind of expression, one in which plastic evocations play a larger part, one in which, though he never loses sight of surface organization, this is effected by the relation of large geometrical units, which attain a more architectural, more monumental unity. In this mood Matisse seeks above all a plasticity of volumes which is at once more complete and more concentrated, held together by more clearly inevitable sequences. To understand the difference between those two directions of Matisse's creative energy the reader may compare Fig. 47 and 46 with such an example of his more recent work as Fig. 1 (Woman with veil). It will be apparent too that to find analogies with the later works we must go back to the years before 1917, in particular to the portrait of Mme. Matisse. It will be seen that the later portrait is at once richer, more vital and more complete in its apprehension of plasticity and also more masterly in its

COLORPLATE 48

Back, IV. 1930. Bronze, Height: 72″ (182.9 cm). The Tate Gallery, London.

synthetic quality. If I may be allowed the expressions of my personal predilections, I would say that to my mind one of the most complete expressions of Matisse's highest powers is to be seen in Fig. 35, where the play of broadly simplified arabesques, light on dark and dark on light, are contrasted with the most surprising felicity and where a familiar scene of everyday life takes on an air of almost monumental grandeur without any sense of rhetorical falsification. The shock of the word rhetorical in relation to Matisse proves, by the by, the fundamental simplicity and sincerity of his attitude to life.

What I look for now with sure confidence is a new series of works in which Matisse will find a scheme capable of expressing his sense of the profounder implications of form in terms of monumental amplitude and yet enriched by all that wealth of pictorial science which he has garnered from the intervening years. For Matisse is of the kindred of the great masters who are capable of continuous growth, whose genius flowers most exuberantly in the years of ripest experience.

René Huyghe

FORMES

"Matisse and Color"

January 1930

René Huyghe (b. 1906), French art historian, critic, and museum administrator. While Waldemar George had dealt with the drawings, Huyghe was the first to give proper attention to Matisse's color.

It remains to study the chromatic vision, properly so called, of Matisse, as it has been constituted in the course of his experiments.

Color, besides, has more than one decorative sense for him: he does not wish merely to arrange the tints of the picture harmoniously. If the reduced limits of an article allow of a schematic presentation—they are constraining—I would say that Matisse sees in color an instrument of truth, of expression and of harmony. For truth, we have already considered it. He wants to give his color all the liberty necessary to tonal invention and yet not to become absolutely arbitrary. For a long time he contented himself with respecting *tone relations*, which left him free with regard to the choice of color itself. Later on, he found a compromise in giving a considerable place in his pictures to objects which, in themselves, already played a decorative role: stuffs, carpets, vases, and which allowed him absolute liberty to invent shades without breaking with "credibility." The first problem, evidently, had the advantage of resolving the difficulty rather than vanquishing it; but what matter!

Expression and harmony remain: an exclusively plastic art, that is to say an art seeking pure harmony of lines and colors, has something inhuman about it. That is the terrible lacuna in Cubism. It is not looking for "literature" to want art to translate an emotion, to be *expressive*, from the moment that the translation of the emotion by pictorial means becomes a matter of necessity to the eyes of him who conceives it. In this, Matisse links up with the tradition of the great painters, he does not harmonize his lines and colors gratuitously; obviously he wishes that their harmony should suffice in itself, but in addition he wants it to express a state of sensibility at the same time.

However, his expressive purpose and his plastic are going to coincide as did his care for plasticity and his anxiety for credibility when he took as subjects from nature those things that already, by themselves, play a decorative role. Here again, the two aims, diverse in appearance, al-

Tiari. 1930. Bronze, with gold chain.
8 × 5⅝ × 7⅝″ (20.3 × 14.3 × 19.4 cm).
The Baltimore Museum of Art: The
Cone Collection, formed by Dr. Claribel
Cone and Miss Etta Cone of Baltimore,
Maryland.

most identify themselves with each other or at least may be realized by
the same means. What does he want to *express*? the joy of living in tranquility, the perfect enjoyment that has intensity without causing fatigue.
Now, whether one wishes it or not, it is precisely that which the sight of
plastic harmony, if it be perfect, procures. This becomes quite evident if
one imagines an essentially decorative art, such as Byzantine: the perfection of the decorative sense there produces that euphorian state of
peaceable pleasure that Matisse wishes to express.

If one wanted to tackle the question on a quite general ground, it
would be curious to place such an art in Art. It would appear as an inventor, as a creator opposed to one who only thinks of fixing and reproducing the effects of the real—like Impressionism. But it would seem
to belong to an order of creation less profound, that of Ingres, for instance, if one opposed it to the art of, if you like, "lyrical" creation, of a
Rembrandt, a Greco, a Delacroix. This is a weighty question and may
only be put forward tentatively here.

The art of Matisse, like that of Ingres, is a middle course between
realist art and the art of pure creation. These painters utilize the linear

and colorful resources of reality, but realize them according to new harmonies of their own, in order to draw more intense and more perfect effects, determined beforehand by their imagination, from them. They arrive at a comprehension of aspects of the world in making them conform to their own tastes, that is to say to a harmony that is their own creation: a harmony of proportions amongst the Greek sculptors, a harmony of linear arabesques with Ingres and a harmony of colors with Matisse. They draw, therefore, from the real, effects that are new because *elaborated* by them, but which were potential.

A Rembrandt, a Delacroix, artists who are, integrally, creators, do more: these never break with the interior reality that is born and dies with them; they employ the lines, the colors, the aspects, of the real in their pictures, but only as a means of transmission, "a bridge built between souls," as Delacroix said. They do not utilize the resources spontaneously offered by nature that an Ingres or a Matisse is contented to bend to a new rhythm; they force the real, of which their pictures seem to reproduce the appearances, to translate, with an imperfect vocabulary, a state of soul, a reality of a different order in its very essence.

But let us get back to Matisse himself: what then are the means he employs to arrive at these results, foreseen and willed by him? It is a delicate question which would seem to allow that the most intimate resources of the artist fall under the axe of analysis. One cannot reach anything more than pseudo-principles in this life and though they may coincide with life their application will not enable us to create a single one of Matisse's harmonies. A reproduction in colors such as we have seen recently respects the tints in principle and yet the harmony of the work itself becomes discordant in it: it is because there is in every harmony, escaping definition, an inequality that is absolutely beyond the grasp of everything except perhaps our sensibility and which reveals the gift. I can only, then, indicate the direction followed by the sensibility of Matisse in order to arrive at its ends. The art of Matisse consists essentially in giving to the enjoyment produced by color its maximum of gaiety while leaving it its maximum of freedom. A color sensation is always agreeable provided it be pure. Isolate even the most glaring color against a black or a white and it pleases.

The difficulty, when a sensation is intense, is to keep its freshness. Prolonged, it becomes tiring, worrying. Matisse's extraordinary success is due to his capacity to play with live color sensations without making the spectator pay the ransom, first of satiety and then of fatigue.

How did he do it? By creating, beside the sensation, a region of rest in which the sensation bathes; a color remains fresh on black or white because the sensation of colored light alternates with one of colorlessness.

More delicate still, the problem remains the same for two color sensations. They must make a diversion from each other. The eye, according to the theory admitted by Young, perceives color through three nervous [fasciculi], the excitation of which creates, respectively, the sensations of violet, green and red (and not of blue, yellow and red which Chevreul believed to be the primary colors). One color will therefore serve as a rest for another if it excites a different nerve; which explains the old theory of complementaries.

If we widen our scope further we recognize that it is a commonplace of psychology that any pleasure only remains fresh if it alternates with a pleasure of an opposed order which relieves it.

This truth does not suffice to explain Matisse, but one of the guarantees of Matisse's art is that it conforms to it. Seen from this point of view, the cleverness (was it spontaneous?) of any of his pictures is extraordinary. . . .

Thus, no color is *impossible* in a picture by Matisse, for his unerring sensibility, which is always on the watch, acts as a necessary *corrective*. And so his harmonies are infinitely variable, and from a certain point of view, it is an advantage that he has over the "lyrical" creators of whom I speak, Rembrandt, Delacroix and, on a lesser plane, Prud'hon, and, in our own day, Vlaminck. As a matter of fact their color harmonies have a permanent principle of identity, a character of *necessity*, opposed to that of irresponsibility (in the Gidian sense) of Matisse, for they are determined by a constant, interior reality, of the soul of which they are, before everything else, a process of translation.

A picture by Matisse is rather a harmonic cycle than a harmony. Take the *Odalisque* of the Luxembourg—or the other of the *White Turban*: on the right, cut-up colors; red, blue, on white; on the left, a dampered tremolo of the same tone of beige, greenish in the band near the body, violet in the outer band, and, in the middle, a harmony of "colorlessness," a white turban, black hair.

The art of this "revolutionary" seems above all to be an art of balance, a balance that is sometimes compromised by the researches of the past, used to ensure the effects of today. There is nothing to be denied in his career: everything happened in its own time as everything in his pictures respects the necessary import and situation. The painter's faculties obey a harmony of a spiritual order, a balance of gifts in which French art recognizes itself: subtle sensibility, attentive to the sensations by which reality enriches itself, and invention—but always lucid, the control of the spirit giving to the emotion not a fugitive quality but a surety, a certainty, analogous to those that a definite method would produce. There is a phrase of Matisse's which echoes Delacroix, who conceived genius as "following a road, necessary and agreed upon by superior laws." Matisse defined the artist as "a man who is sufficiently master of himself to impose a discipline on himself . . . who is capable of *organizing his sensations*."

What, then, are they shouting about, those senile individuals who declare that French art is in danger?

COLORPLATE 76

Henri Matisse, Interviewed by E. Tériade

ART NEWS

"Matisse Speaks"

November 1951

I am too anti-picturesque for traveling to have given me much. I went quickly through Italy. I went to Spain. I even spent a winter in Seville. I went to Moscow at Shchukin's invitation around 1910; it seemed to me like a huge Asian village. I went to Tahiti in 1930.

In Tahiti I could appreciate the light, light as pure matter, and the coral earth. It was both superb and boring. There are no worries in that land, and from our tenderest years we have our worries; they probably help keep us alive. There the weather is beautiful at sunrise and it does not change until night. Such immutable happiness is tiring.

Coming back from Tahiti, I went through America. The first time I saw New York, at seven in the evening, its mass of black and gold was reflected in the water, and I was completely ravished. Near me someone on the boat was saying "it's a spangled dress," and this helped me to arrive at my own image: to me New York seemed like a gold nugget.

In 1930, Matisse went to Tahiti, San Francisco, Baltimore, and New York. He also served on the Carnegie International Prize jury in Pittsburgh and visited the Barnes Foundation in Merion, Pennsylvania.

COLORPLATE 78. *Pianist and Checkers Players (Les Joueurs de dames)*. 1924. Canvas. 29 × 36⅜″ (73.7 × 92.4 cm).
National Gallery of Art, Washington. Collection of Mr. and Mrs. Paul Mellon.

COLORPLATE 79. *Interior with a Phonograph.* 1924. Canvas. 39½ × 31½″ (100.5 × 80 cm). Private collection.

COLORPLATE 80. *Anemones*. 1924. Canvas. 28¾ × 36¼" (73 × 92 cm). Kunstmuseum Bern.

COLORPLATE 81. *Nude with a Tambourine.* 1926. Canvas. 28¾ × 21¼″ (73 × 54 cm).
© Succession H. Matisse/1988. Photograph courtesy Archives Matisse, Collection Claude Duthuit.

COLORPLATE 82. *The Yellow Dress.* 1929–31. Canvas. 39¼ × 31¾″ (99.7 × 80.7 cm).
The Baltimore Museum of Art. The Cone Collection, formed by Dr. Claribel Cone and
Miss Etta Cone of Baltimore, Maryland.

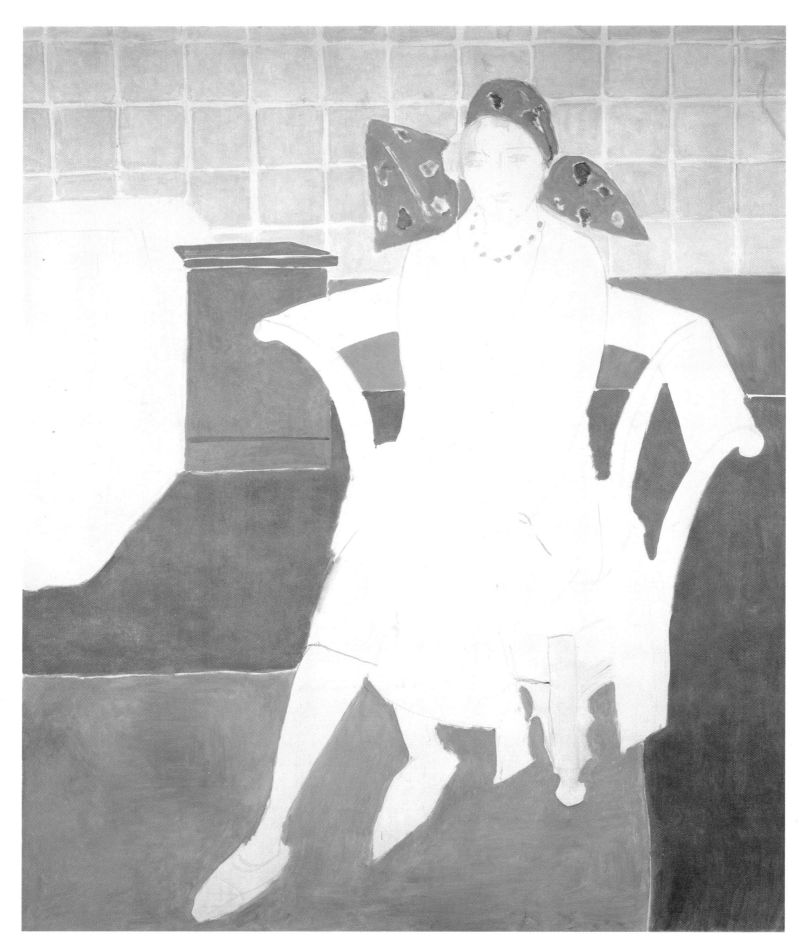

COLORPLATE 83. *Woman with Madras.* 1929–30. Canvas. 70⅞ × 59⅞″ (180 × 152 cm).
© Succession H. Matisse/1988. Photograph courtesy Archives Matisse, Collection Claude Duthuit.

COLORPLATE 84. *Pink Nude.* 1935. Canvas. 26 × 36″ (66 × 92 cm).
The Baltimore Museum of Art. The Cone Collection, formed by Dr. Claribel Cone and
Miss Etta Cone of Baltimore, Maryland. Photograph by Lee Boltin.

COLORPLATE 85. *The Painter and His Model.* 1936. Canvas. 31⅞ × 23⅝″ (81 × 60 cm).
Collection Ira D. Wallach, New York.

George L. K. Morris

LIFE

"A Brief Encounter with Matisse"

28 August 1970

George L. K. Morris (1905–1975), American artist, teacher, critic, and founder of American Abstract Artists, wrote this memoir in his journal soon after meeting Matisse on a train from Cherbourg to Paris in January 1931. Matisse had just returned from Merion, Pennsylvania, where he had studied the site for murals commissioned by the Barnes Foundation.

As we leave the boat at Cherbourg I notice that Matisse is just ahead of us. He looks refreshingly tidy and self-contained; I'm sure it occurs to none of the passengers who are jostling around him that a famous artist is in their midst. Matisse might pass for a good-natured professor out of his element.

Soon after we board the train for Paris, my friend Lanfear Norrie suggests that we investigate the *wagon-restaurant*. We'd just sat down at a table when there are gesticulations from Lanfear who is seated opposite me. Matisse is coming down the aisle followed by William Bullitt (later U.S. ambassador to Russia). Lanfear beckons to them and Matisse approaches smilingly. Bullitt is less enthusiastic; nevertheless he sits down by me. At first the conversation is stilted, but things pick up when Bullitt asks me perfunctorily how long I plan to stay in Europe. I reply that I'm returning to New York in two months. "That's a very good idea," Matisse chimes in. "Artists should stay in their own countries." I had no business, he says, to leave America in the first place—unless I wanted to amuse myself, of course; there's no city like Paris for amusement.

William Christian Bullitt (1891–1967), American diplomat and first U.S. ambassador to the U.S.S.R. (1933–1936).

I catch a twinkle of fun behind his glasses, yet his tone seems to permit no contradiction. As I feel that our brief acquaintance might not weather an argument yet, I make no counter to this unexpected sally. So the conversation returns to trivialities and Matisse begins to sip his coffee. He makes a dreadful face—he can always tell when he's back in France from the taste of the coffee. As he pays his check, a wad of French money protrudes from his wallet. He pulls out a hundred-franc note and holds it up. "That's the demoded art of twenty years ago; today it could only be appropriate as a filling for sardine tins." He then pulls out another, this one from Guadeloupe, and hands it around for our inspection (it depicts female nudes under palm trees, very gay and stylized): "That's a work of art," he says.

As Lanfear and I return to our compartment, we suggest that the others join us. Lanfear and Bullitt embark on a boring conversation about the Lorillard family while I make sketches. . . . Matisse begins to nod and is soon asleep with a lighted cigarette in his hand. I become increasingly alarmed as the burning end gets nearer and nearer to his fingers while ashes scatter over his lap. At last the inevitable contact takes place. Matisse wakes with a jump and puts out the cigarette. After an appropriate interval, I try to get Matisse back to the subject that was so summarily dropped in the dining car.

I begin rather gingerly and ask if he considers it possible for a great and authentic primitive to develop in times such as these. He answers that the Douanier Rousseau was both an authentic primitive and a great painter; he refutes my suggestion that Rousseau was not as naive as he appears and that he'd studied the masters in the Louvre. As soon as Matisse speaks about art his voice becomes gentle and distinct, he talks very slowly.

Emboldened by the relaxed manner, I start a defense of my European trip, declaring that the world is tending to become increasingly united, and perhaps nationalistic bounds will weaken. Besides, our American forebears were Europeans not very long ago. Furthermore,

Poussin had gone to Italy for his studies, as had El Greco, Rubens and others in the past. The gentleness that had characterized Matisse's voice is now gone abruptly. "Poussin and El Greco have been dead 300 years and you consider *them* in your procedure!" He ends up: "The only hope for American art is for the painters there to stay at home; they have a new untried country with beautiful skies and beautiful women—what more do you need?"

Bullitt nods in enthusiastic approval. He asks if the skies in America are as good for painting as the skies of France. Even better, Matisse affirms—they are more crystalline. I am somewhat abashed that a painter whose esthetic approach I have long admired should lay so much emphasis on his subject matter. I try another tack—can't we learn from the museums of Europe? Matisse says that the museums in America are quite adequate. Most important, if an artist stays in his own country he will develop a style and a system of organization that is his own—not one derived from Léger (it had previously slipped into the conversation that I had worked in Léger's studio). I reply that there is little opportunity for a student to establish contact with new developments. Moreover, Americans grow up among surroundings of the lowest quality; and the early years of a student are apt to be misdirected by ignorant teachers or by some elderly relative who does watercolors. Matisse here makes a joke about an elderly relative's watercolors which contains some French words I don't know; the others think it's very funny, however, and jiggle with laughter for quite a while. I pursue my point that the esthetic approach in America seems to result largely in the production of postcards. Matisse rejoins that the artist who has it in his soul to make postcards will always make postcards. There's a silence, as I feel we've run that one into the ground, and Matisse is soon asleep again.

I'm glad to have a few minutes in which to contemplate the curious and powerful character who is dozing opposite me. I've never been in contact with an adversary whose moods can change so suddenly. He will be mild, with manners almost courtly, and a moment later exude a hostility that is truly alarming; his eyes snap behind his glasses while whiskers seem to wave in agitation. I like the sly humor that lurks behind his very positive pronouncements. He is direct and seems to relish an argument; I see no trace of that chichi quality that has disturbed me in much of his recent work. I begin to visualize it as satire.

In the interim Bullitt and I strike up our first conversation. I explain to him how much I feel that the old masters of Spain, Germany and France gained from their sojourns in Italy, just as Van Gogh and Whistler did from working in France. Bullitt (seeing that Matisse is in no condition to overhear) seems favorably impressed. He asks my opinion of several American painters, and tells me how Charles Demuth once compared himself to John Marin: Marin went down to the sea with a bucket; on the return trip he spilled half the water that was in it. Demuth went down with a teaspoon and on the way back never spilled a drop. I tell him how much I admire those spoonfuls which Demuth never spilled. I'm pleased to meet someone who knew Demuth and want to question him further. However, Bullitt is already telling me that he had once rented the house in Paris where my mother now lives and that his daughter was born in the second-floor bedroom.

Matisse has awakened again and the conversation makes another switch. He asks me if I ever knew the American painter Patrick Henry Bruce, who had been among his pupils. I've never met him—I've seen a little of his work and found it rather dry. "That doesn't make any difference," Matisse snaps. I'm uncertain whether it's my expression of an opinion or Bruce's dryness which doesn't make the difference. Matisse adds after a moment that Bruce perhaps hadn't shown much promise and neither had his other pupils. He points out that he's able to talk to me as he does because he once had pupils; and he himself had been a

Fernand Léger (1881–1955), French painter.

Charles Demuth (1883–1935), John Marin (1870–1953), American painters.

pupil too—of Gustave Moreau. I ask him if Moreau had been a good teacher. No—he was too literary. Matisse allows that Moreau had one great virtue—he used to conduct his pupils to the Louvre where they could use their eyes.

I remark that Léger is quite different from Moreau. Matisse finds this very funny—pupils always say that about their teachers. I add that Léger says very little about any pupil's work. "Then he must talk about himself!" Matisse turns to Lanfear and Bullitt for applause. As I dispute this he asks what Léger *does* talk about then. I answer (erroneously and without reflection, alas), "He talks about art." That does it; Matisse fairly explodes: "And what is there to say about art!" He adds emphatically that all artists should have their tongues cut out—then they'd have more time for work. He sticks out a very pink tongue over his beard and snips at it threateningly with his second and third fingers.

As we are recovering our bearings, Matisse discourses on the baneful influences of teachers. With his former twinkle he adds that it's better to study with Léger than with Picasso; if one studied with Picasso, one would imitate not only Picasso but all the people Picasso imitates. Bullitt is convulsed with laughter and I react similarly against my better judgment. I assert, however, that Picasso's recent work I find marvelous. "Yes, it's marvelous," Matisse says with a toss of the head, which implies he finds it the very reverse.

We're now passing Mantes where I always look forward to a glimpse of the Gothic church. Matisse doesn't give it a glance; as though impatient for the journey to end, he puts on his beret and winds his checked muffler round his neck. He then settles back and is soon asleep again. I begin to analyze why it is that Matisse is so different from any artist I've previously met. He doesn't project the conventional image of a painter at all. He is extremely neat—beard immaculately clipped; the elegant gray business suit and sober necktie suggest the Bourse rather than the Left Bank. His eyes don't count for much (owing perhaps to the thickness of his glasses) and his fingers are rather stubby. The hands are muscular, however, and suggest immense capability; in fact, he looks strong all over. In demeanor he seems invulnerable; fame may have helped here, but I suspect he has always been tough. Matisse is above all a man of the world—he wouldn't be ill at ease in any surroundings. One is aware of an undeviating tenacity which comes through in his best work. His face even in repose is imperious, as though he were born to command. His features suggest intense vitality; even when he is dozing, the taut muscles give a look as if he were about to speak, the right hand as if it were about to move.

Matisse awakens while we are traversing a pretty district along the Seine. Bullitt asks what he thinks of the painters in America. Matisse says the trouble with American artists is that as soon as they achieve recognition and make some money, they cut down on their working hours. Annoyed, I assert that I know many American painters (which I don't) and that they are all very hard workers. He asks how many hours they work per day. For a quick answer I say 12 hours per day. Matisse makes a gesture of disgust—"That's ridiculous, no one can paint for 12 hours a day." (Matisse himself was accustomed to working that long, but not steadily in the same medium.)

I try to steer into more interesting topics during the time that remains. I suggest that artists in modern times seem to have lost control of their pictorial structure, except for the few who have revolted against popular trends. He challenges me to name one. In haste I pick on Degas—an unfortunate choice, as he's a painter I admire very much; however I do object to the way he often cuts figures off arbitrarily at the canvas edge. Matisse replies that perhaps Degas *did* have an organization but that today it's not à la mode. He adds under pressure from Bullitt that he no longer enjoys Degas's work particularly. He then depicts the courage that it takes for a painter to strike out into territory that is not à la mode and tells of the starvation among the impressionists. He recounts how he used to sell canvases for 60 francs which dealers now sell for 300,000. Sometimes he wants to buy back an example of his early work and has to meet prices such as that. Bullitt inquires whether any of the artists who are now well known had started out with private means. No—he himself had had no money; Picasso had no money, the impressionists had no money—only Manet had money. Bullitt asks what brand of paint he uses. Matisse answers, "The most expensive." It is essential, he explains, that color relations remain constant. You can often see where the impressionists used cheap colors and in the paintings of Seurat and Van Gogh the reds have already turned yellow.

We pull into the Gare Saint-Lazare with great suddenness and the baggage pandemonium surges quickly around us. After I leave the car and step onto the platform with my suitcase, I look back toward our compartment. Matisse is standing at the window, waving goodbye with one hand and with the other twirling his umbrella like a windmill to attract the attention of a porter. With cordial nods of farewell he suggests I call on him in Nice. At the same moment he is negotiating with the porter. In my final glance I notice again the look of the good-natured professor.

Henry McBride

CAHIERS D'ART

"Matisse in America"

May 1931

Henry McBride (1867–1962), American writer, critic, and illustrator, was an early champion of modernism and of the Photo-Secession Group.

Matisse has been famous in America for twenty years or more. He began by being famous with the young people who saw in him a prophet who might get them out of the impasse into which, in New York, art had been pushed in the early decades of this century. This "impasse" is simply another word for the National Academy of those days. This institution was largely controlled by several individuals whose names are still mentioned whenever bigotry comes under discussion but who are seldom mentioned in any other connection. These official martinets controlled all the politics of the situation. They awarded honors, decided commissions for public work and refused all non-conformists the opportunity to expose. The academy was the sole avenue to success for the American painter. There was not then an Independent Society nor were there dealers who had the courage for experimental painting.

It is difficult to realize in this period of emancipation how restricted and enchained the American painters of 1890–1910 were. One was more or less obliged to be a copyist to live.

Into all this stuffiness the advent of Matisse was, as James Stephens has it, "like a breath of fresh air in a soap factory." The puzzled young artists who had spent years in acquiring manners that might be acceptable to their elders suddenly saw that their elders had nothing to do with the affair and that any manner was all right that gave them a chance to use their own eyes and their own experiences. They probably thought, deep down in their hearts, that Matisse himself was thumbing his nose at officialdom, but— very well—that of all gestures, at the moment, seemed the most superb and the most completely à propos. In the first excitement of worshiping a cult

James Stephens (1882–1950), Irish poet and novelist.

that was to bring them, too, to freedom, the young disciples seized with the greatest glee upon the most daring of Matisse's innovations. The painter was at that time, I suppose, busily engaged in "finding himself" and not all the results of his communions with the muses were of the quality of the paintings assembled in the present exhibition. It was always the painting that was strangest, and most disconcerting to conservatives, that was held up to be the greatest by Matisse's young American admirers. It got to be—during the interval of the greatest excitement—just that: a game of "disconcerting our elders." These unfortunates all rose to the bait. They wrote furious essays in the monthly reviews proving that Matisse was an impostor and a cheat, and the more emphatic they became on this point, the more widely they spread the Matisse fame—for it is almost axiomatic, in modern times, that fame comes to one via the "opposition." It was as pretty a dispute as one could wish for. Not quite so far-reaching in its effects as the celebrated Ruskin–Whistler row in London or the still earlier persecution of Manet in Paris, but fully as intense within its smaller range. And before it had ended the public began to show a sufficient cognizance of Matisse's art, and certain terms descriptive of his colors, such as the famous "Matisse pink," practically "entered into the language." Our brighter writers, at any rate, found the phrase indispensable.

Partly this was because the public had begun to grow up. Partly, too, the major Matisses had begun to come to America; for it must be allowed that the earlier arguers had very little data to go upon. But mainly it was because the public had begun to grow up. In the twenty years, these young people had matured into connoisseurs and collectors. Matisse was more their man than ever. He had not only justified their taste, he had justified the age they lived in. His painting spoke of the period; was the period. It reveled in sheer vision and was untrammeled by the rules. It was disillusioned, perhaps, but it was hearty and robust for all that. The world in spite of civilization and science was a fine old world after all. Young people are always inclined to the feeling that their world is the best of all possible worlds and it is natural for them to seize upon the masters who confirm them in their theories. Their being now "collectors and connoisseurs" made a vast difference in the status of Matisse in America. As young people they had merely admired; as adults, they bought. Previously the championship by the young people had been a thorn in the flesh of the museum directors and other "serious" officials. They little relished the sarcasms at their slowness to recognize genius, etc. Possibly it is not the business of curators to recognize new geniuses, but few of them would concede such a limitation to their powers. But when great collectors finally talk of new geniuses, curators listen more amiably, and the many important American collections in which groups of important Matisses began to have the place of honor produced, in the end, the inevitable effect. Officialdom at last recognized Matisse. This change in the point of view was brought startlingly to the attention of the general public some years ago when Matisse was given the first money prize and a medal of honor at the Pittsburgh International Exposition of Art. This Pittsburgh institution had been markedly conservative and especially so in its attitude toward French art. The new heroes of the day in Paris had been looked on with fear, and shunned. Wherever two or three people were gathered together in America, the talk was of Matisse, Picasso, Braque, Léger, and their associates, but in Pittsburgh one was still confronted with enormous vapidities of the "salon" type. One gathered, unless one happened to know better, that production, along the banks of the Seine, had ceased; and that the creative center in the arts had shifted to Berlin, or possibly, London. The unexpected triumph of Matisse at Pittsburgh corrected the impression; and incidentally confirmed his position with connoisseurs and the great dealers in art. There never has been, in America, a more potent prize-award than this—it almost justifies the system. Since then Matisse himself has been invited to

In 1878 the painter James Abbott McNeill Whistler sued critic John Ruskin for writing that Whistler asked "two hundred guineas for flinging a pot of paint in the public's face." Whistler won the case, but court costs left him bankrupt.

the States to serve on the Pittsburgh jury of awards, and probably was an active agent in choosing his successor for the prize, in the exhibition of last autumn—Picasso.

During his short stay in New York, he appeared to be enchanted with the astonishing architecture of the city, and, in turn, was considerably feted by the citizens. The desire to meet him was so frank, so wholesale, that he must have been convinced, had he had any doubts, of the genuine affection for the man that had been aroused by the paintings.

These paintings, now that the world definitely possesses them, are not sensational in the sense that first they were. Innovations in style, once they are accepted, no longer operate as innovations. It is Matisse's distinction not so much to have defied precedents as to have remained in the great French tradition. "As French as Chardin" is frequently said of him in New York, and so he truly seems to us foreigners. At the same time, we who are living are not so far removed from our original adjustments to the artist's manner as to have forgot the astonishing steps in the progress of his technique. In the period of twenty to thirty years ago, when the impressionists had just about convinced the world that outlines were non-existent in nature, Matisse's occasional insistence upon them, and in heavy black paint, came almost as an insult to the conservatives of that time, although the conservatives of today—so enfranchised are we all—have a special relish for these strong and decorative lines, particularly as used in the great series of pictures devoted to "Gold Fish." There was also an "adjustment"—more easily accomplished this time—when certain interiors with table-covers in striped patterns were shown. The impetuosity of the painting of these striped cloths had a childlike frankness and eagerness to them—the artist not troubling in the least to match the down stripes with the horizontal ones at the edge of the table—but the very term that was first used in reproach of this freedom, was afterward employed to commend it: its naiveté; and it was recalled by those who always insist upon citing authorities for their ideas, that Baudelaire had once defined an artist as a being who united youthful freshness of vision with the adult's power of execution.

Still another staggering problem was presented to inquiring New Yorkers when the large *Seated Odalisque* was shown to them, also some years ago. In this composition there was a vast amount of ornament in the textiles in the background of the figure, all of it handled superbly and in the best Matisse manner. The figure, too, was splendidly indicated, was an almost straight line up the back which was especially entertaining. But the head and neck of this odalisque were—the most devoted students saw it at a glance—in a totally different style of painting from the rest of the picture. Instantly there were queries. Can an artist switch off into a different key, like a musician, in the middle of a composition? The answer, apparently, was that he could; since this powerful work received unstinted admiration and remains to this day one of the best remembered of all odalisques. It was returned to France and is still, I believe, in the artist's possession, but there remains a hope, in America, that it can be obtained for New York's "Musée du Luxembourg" when that institution materializes.

Matisse served on the 1930 jury of the Carnegie International Exhibition, which awarded first prize to Picasso.

268

Christian Zervos
CAHIERS D'ART
"Notes on the Formation and Development of the Art of Henri-Matisse"
1931

Christian Zervos (1889–1970), French critic and publisher. A landmark in the Matisse literature, this special Matisse issue of Cahiers d'Art *assembled a diversity of texts and the most comprehensive set of reproductions up to that time. A friend of Picasso's who began publishing a catalogue of Picasso's work in 1932, Zervos here concludes by comparing Matisse with the cubists.*

We know Matisse much less than we admire him. Undoubtedly, we agree in recognizing that he always shows a rare concern for perfection, that he makes a point of ceaselessly reworking a harmony that dissatisfies him; we recognize that his drawing is accomplished, consonant, and pure. But that is, all things considered, only an external assessment of his work, the importance and value of which is understood only if it is experienced in its entirety. One must follow this work step by step, consider its successive stages and organic evolution, to understand to what extent it is unified in its extreme richness and to grasp its extraordinary freshness, sparkling youth, and constantly renewed audacities. One might say that Matisse has given magnificent examples of most of the daring feats that attract our interest in contemporary painting.

There can be no question of studying Matisse's investigations in detail here. A whole volume would not suffice, so manifold and varied is his effort. We wish only to outline the principal stages of his evolution, to follow the working of his mind, always drawn by the strength of his pictorial instinct toward new undertakings, investigations that leave him always dissatisfied.

We must, first of all, define Matisse's freedom. Freedom in his case does not signify, as it does for too many of his contemporaries, abandoning oneself to every chance impulse, a blind and disorderly submission to all external appeals. Freedom, for Matisse, is not disorder; on the contrary, it is subjected to a rigorous order, it ends in precise, well-defined consequences. It is continuous volition, and it is what gives his audacities their value and their significance, instead of destroying them. It is with a lucid perception, solidly supported by his deepest instincts, accompanied by a sharp sense of the real, that Matisse brings about his innovations. Therein lies the explanation of their richness and fertility, as much for the artist himself as for those who have studied them and adapted them to their methods.

The need to innovate is an obsession for many. The new is desired at all costs. The past is rejected outright, and phantoms of novelty that represent nothing and are nothing are vainly pursued. Matisse has no biases, for either the old or the new. He consults only himself and seeks within himself the eternal actual, the center that exerts a pull on gifts that are at once the most distinct and the most mysterious in man. Any painter who studies and observes himself as meticulously as Matisse does feels capable of the most diverse movements, summoned to the most varied creations. He seizes ideas, flashes of instinct, from the passing moment; he incorporates them into his work, then immediately abandons them, like life itself. The ideal glimpsed, Matisse immediately passes on to the realm of formal and technical transformations. Perfect knowledge of himself and of his art: a rare yet indispensable condition for the growth of a true body of work. Let the young take their inspiration from such an example, let the undeniably gifted learn to exploit freedom in this way, without renouncing any of their personal integrity.

* * *

Since 1917, Matisse has been settled in Nice, where he resides for the greater part of the year and where he stopped painting only during the summer of 1920, which he passed in Etretat. From 1917 to 1929, Matisse did nothing but complete and perfect his art, deepen his feeling for proportion, pinpoint further his sense of form, push further still the internal organization of his painting, seek to give color an even greater breadth and resonance. He took stock: he organized and strengthened all the knowledge that earlier experience afforded him. He appears today more curious than ever about effects and ideas, more impassioned about precision, and he takes his thought even higher than before.

Although he seems to lean more toward abstract reflection, the sense of the plastic never leaves him but, on the contrary, remains within him like the central fiber that supports the whole leaf.

Today, Matisse jealously guards saying what he has to say, in an increasingly precise form, with a more and more formal will toward objectivity, for he has not only been able to elude the accidental; he has also had the rare courage and rare luck to elude his own individuality, to dominate it successfully.

Naturally, the intellectual and moral ideas remain blended into a sensual form. The profound creative force without which there is no enduring oeuvre, no true oeuvre, remains constant and always powerful within him. The form of the work of art, the luminous intensity of the surfaces, the skillful relationships between the volumes, the drawing, the character, have aesthetic value only if they arise from a vibrant sensibility. All artistic media depend necessarily upon sensuality. And if Matisse has been able to master so many media and resources, it is because his sensibility in its richness answered the transcendental demands of his spirit.

Thus, in studying the various stages of Matisse's career, we have followed the progress of a spirit curious about everything the art of painting could hold most secret. The value of the works lies as much in their strength, intensity, and fullness as in their inimitable freshness.

Thanks to his disdain for artificiality, scandal, and that misuse of a facile sensibility that contents too many artists with a few elementary effects, satisfying themselves with nervous jolts; by dint, too, of investigation, of studying the external world, and of introspection, Matisse has managed perfectly to discipline his own nature, his thoughts, and even his visions of the external world. That is how he was able to express his pictorial instinct in a clear and precise oeuvre in which the very audacity ceases to be visible, the effort is not apparent, and the most arduous experience seems a simple and natural gift. At first glance, Matisse's canvases seem to resemble one another; but when one studies them, one notices that they are extremely varied, one encounters in them the most unexpected and diverse correspondences, as well as the most defined purposes. Matisse makes his way toward the denouement of the pictorial drama that guides his most unexpected movements toward an ideal of stability. With every step he takes, it is his practice to obtain the rarest result and to be satisfied with no other. And the slow persistence with which he proceeds successively to all the exclusions and eliminations that he deems necessary leads him to a new, meticulously reasoned form. As I said at the beginning of these notes, Matisse's glory is not only to have created a body of work of rare fullness, but also to have contributed to the liberation of painting, to have reexamined, in order to modify them, so many mistaken appraisals, and to have overturned so many established notions. Matisse continued the revolution undertaken by Cézanne; he pushed the formal and technical investigation of painting to its most extreme as well as most subtle conclusions.

By assimilating certain preoccupations of Cubism and enriching them with his profound knowledge of the realm of sensations and their harmonic resonances, Matisse's work provides the young with a confirmation of certain of their investigations of essentials. Several will probably show surprise that one can speak of exchanges between Matisse and Cubism. Yet nothing is more certain and evident than this exchange. As autonomous as Matisse's spirit may have become, he nonetheless came under the cubist influence. In return, certain of Matisse's investigations exerted an undeniable influence upon Cubism. But Matisse's personality and that of the principal cubists were too powerful not to transform and absorb into their own systems the borrowings amenable to them.

Cubism and Matisse have both contributed to broadening the field and the perspectives of contemporary painting. To Matisse and the cubists is due the glory of making the contemporary Paris school what it is today: the greatest in the world.

Curt Glaser
CAHIERS D'ART
"Henri-Matisse"

1931

Curt Glaser (1879–1943), German art historian who wrote extensively on German graphics and on the Norwegian artist Edvard Munch.

The fundamental significance of Matisse's work, the reason for his position as a constant at a time of intricate and quickly changing trends in style, is that he has exhibited not only a new aesthetic style, but also a new way of seeing: his paintings offer a new view of the world. It would be wrong to think that these two notions always appear in tandem. On the contrary, not a few new trends in style, especially in our time, have been content to establish a new aesthetic style while deliberately ignoring the symbolic connection between the form fashioned in a painting and a given form of perception.

Here we need not quarrel about the validity or worth of this or that kind of art. But we ought not to confuse one with another or seek possibilities in one that are proper only to the preconditions of another. Part of the essence of all mannerism in art is that it rejects any universally binding constraint. The principles of painting are not determined by any given relationship to the law of reality; artists reserve the freedom to arrange and order pictorial elements as they wish.

This complete freedom of imagination, this total detachment from the model of nature claimed by mannerism in earlier periods and by its more recent variations allows the artist to play with pictorial forms and affords an aesthetic appeal that no sensible art lover would want to do without. Bold experiments by inventive innovators have vastly widened the range of artistic possibilities. Our eyes have been treated to exquisite delights of the greatest variety. But only a world of art has been shown, while the beauties of the real world have not been opened up in a new way.

Matisse has tried to do both, and by creating a new way of painting has subjected himself, as well as the viewers of his works, to a new visual constraint. He saw this goal with great clarity from the very beginning of his independent artistic activity and pursued it with such boldness and consistency that his contemporaries in those earlier times found it hard to recognize the important new way of seeing that the relentless transformations of natural phenomena in his paintings seemed to represent.

Today it is no longer difficult to grasp the meaning and beauty of the master's earlier works. Today it is clear that they are the logical sequel of the tradition of his great predecessors. Today we know that Matisse understood the teachings of Cézanne, Renoir, Seurat, and Van Gogh much better than the timid imitators who adopted already established forms without adding any creative ideas of their own. Matisse has taken up the problem of color, which Neo-Impressionism had left only half-solved in a manner not very satisfying in the long run. It is a sign of his extraordinary artistic insight and great courage that he has definitely abandoned the fiction of the objective truth of nature that even Seurat believed in. No longer does he claim that the colors in his paintings ought to combine in the viewer's eye so as to produce the illusion of reality. His colors are combined only by virtue of their interrelationship on the plane of the painting and are intended, like all artistic interpretations of the world, to recreate the world as image, just as a metaphor does. Only when Matisse realized this did he attain the artistic freedom for which two generations of painters before him had struggled. The freedom to which he has laid claim, however, has always been limited by his principles. Others who have regarded such principles as less binding and have sought freedom only through the constant renewal of principle, found it easy to surpass him, at least in appearance. They have done so by entering a different domain of art and breaking from a tradition that an artist like Matisse values as a sacred and eternal principle. Those who recognized the revolutionary power of the master's earlier works have thus come to admire him as the keeper of tradition. Once the way of seeing presented in his works proved its validity, his creations joined the ranks of classical masterpieces, and no one who understands them will wonder that art galleries display them alongside paintings of earlier epochs that basically adhere to the same body of laws, however much the content of the individual statutes has changed.

*　　*　　*

The paintings of Matisse's later years are burdened with fewer problems and are therefore perhaps less interesting to many, but they are more simple, clear, and pure. There is no need to disparage some so as to praise others, for all of this painter's works have abundant merits of their own. In their essential, underlying conception, however, these works remain unchanged. Matisse always builds his paintings on the relationship of colors on the surface. His palette has become no poorer in his later years but is often even richer than in the more strikingly contrasting large compositions of the early years. His paintings have become fuller and more resplendent. Bright walls surround colorfully dressed women to create fantasies of the radiant splendor of the South, whose likeness no painter has ever depicted more convincingly to our eyes, which he himself has trained. Here too the subject is reality itself, for the motif seems so inessential that paintings of dreaming odalisques seem no different from still lifes of flowers and fruits or a view through a window of a sunny landscape. They are all about the reality of light, which this painter has sought where it is most dazzling, and has striven to capture in the imaging of color, just as Monet and Seurat had done. Except that whereas they loved the hazy light of the Ile de France, Matisse sought out—on Mediterranean shores, in Nice and Morocco—the light of the South, the light that scorched Van Gogh, from whose overpowering intensity Cézanne had hidden, and of which Renoir experienced only the sensual magnificence of color that thrives under its rays.

Through the medium of color, Matisse opened up the possibility of experiencing this light in paintings. The content of this art, which seems so arbitrary, is in fact a very definite reality. It is—if we can see it as it really is, in its full and special individuality—just as closely connected to the real world, whose image it is meant to represent, as is the art of Courbet or Renoir, who in a special sense may be called Matisse's forebears. Courbet's dark tones must be understood simply as an image of reality, and the same is true of Renoir's blooming colors and of the power of the pure, unalloyed colors with which Matisse produces his strongest effects. He sometimes likes to carry a still life to such artistic extremes that the objectivity of the subject matter is directly perceptible. By the same token, he can dematerialize a person by releasing the forms of their physical existence and interpreting only the rhythmic relationships of higher or lower positions in the plane through the pure organization of color elements. But the persuasive power of his paintings always rests on their firm consistency and a confident attitude that rejects any direct comparison with the motif as a sin against the spirit of art, which itself takes the place of reality, as the old Chinese, the highest aristocrats among the world's painters, always believed.

They were neither so foolish nor so modest as to hope that their paintings might be taken for objects of nature itself, as is often recounted in old European artistic legends. On the contrary, they were proud enough to believe that their human works would stand on an equal footing with the creations of nature, that a painted landscape was no less real than a landscape in nature. In our day painting has finally come closer to this truly aristocratic belief in the capacities and possibilities of art. Matisse has not created his work against nature, as some have claimed; rather, he deliberately places his paintings alongside reality, as testimony to the human spirit that opens the things of this earth, unfathomable creation of God, to our capacity to understand.

André Lhote

CHRONIQUES DU JOUR
"For or Against Henri-Matisse"
April 1931

For the second in its "For and Against" series (André Derain was the subject of the first), Chroniques du jour *published a Matisse issue in April 1931, just before the June opening of the awaited Matisse retrospective at the Galeries Georges Petit. See also the following two selections.*

I have written so much about Matisse and, in the process, have apparently so displeased him that I have qualms about trying again. Suffice it to say that, so far as I know, there are two painters in this world who know things *about color* unknown to all the others. Those two painters are Matisse and Bonnard. It should be added that Matisse—and this accounts for his special worship of Da Vinci—is among those who have done most to incorporate intelligence into painting again. Cubism owes him much.

Waldemar George

CHRONIQUES DU JOUR
"Psychoanalysis of Matisse:
Letter to Raymond Cogniat"
April 1931

George initially observes that most writing about painters—unlike that about writers—is not really critical but consists of extravagant praise. George had earlier written that way about Matisse, but now announces his more honest approach. His increasingly reactionary views are apparent here. A Polish-born Jew, George was sympathetic to fascist ideas at this time, showing nationalist and racist overtones.

Raymond Cogniat was the editor of the "For and Against" series of Chroniques du jour. *This issue, devoted to Matisse, assembled a diversity of opinion about the artist; see also the preceding and the following selections.*

You ask me, if I am not mistaken, to tell you what I think of Matisse. I think very well of him. I owe Matisse—why deny it?—some exquisite visual impressions. He is a fine colorist. He is the best, as Charles Baudelaire would say, in the present-day decadence of his art. I am certain his exhibition at the Galeries Petit (June 1931) will achieve a well-founded success. What am I saying? It will be a triumph, and a deserved triumph.

Matisse, a columnist for *Art News* wrote recently, made his success in modern painting, and he made modern painting . . . a true success. This wordplay in no way diminishes the proud painter of the *joie de vivre*.

In Matisse, alas, we have a case. Today's public is in this artist's debt for his having wrung the neck of the art of perception. Too bad for the art of perception. God knows, I couldn't care less. But Matisse, this distinguished precursor, is he *a cause* or only *an effect*? When I refer to his early writings, I find that the painter deliberately breaks with Impressionism. First he paints in the local colors; he isolates the colors and makes a clean slate of their radiance and their reactivity. He loses the feeling of cosmic unity. Matisse believes he has achieved a great step forward. He believes that he has liberated painting, hitherto subjugated to nature, enslaved by the laws of optics, the basic principles of vision. I refuse to subscribe to this point of view. Nature *in itself,* nature that gives itself up to the artist, nature liable to imitation and forgery, is a vulgar fable. So-called naturalist art is a purely intellectual acceptance. The act of reacting against Naturalism does not necessarily imply an advance or an emancipation. It is a passage from one state to another. That is all.

Matisse dissociates color from form and distributes his tones beyond the objects, outside the objects. In her book on Dufy, Marcelle Berr de Turique speaks at length about this "dissociation" so widespread in modern painting. The persistence of a tonal sensation is more forceful, more durable, says this sagacious critic, than that of a formal or linear sensation. From a spectacle that streams before him, the artist may therefore retain one dominant color that spans successive forms. Ingenious as it may be, such an explanation seems insufficient to justify the license taken by Matisse, who obeys quite different impulses. Sensation, which Dufy considers the basis, the point of departure, of the artistic task, recedes for Henri-Matisse into the middle ground. The painter conceives his painting as the relationships between tones, independent of reality as it manifests itself to our consciousness and understanding. He proceeds by areas of pure color. When the chromatic disposition of a surface implies a certain quantity of color (read: a color that animates a certain expanse of the canvas), he amplifies "the patch," without the slightest concern for verisimilitude, for credibility. The most typical example of this manner of painting is the *Moroccan Chief.* Matisse extended to the model's face, cleanly split into two distinct parts, the color that belongs to the background. It will be noted, however, that the green that covers one area of the face is neither an echo nor a shade, nor a reflection of the background against which the figure is outlined. This green is arbitrary, justified by nothing save the artist's will for expression. But does the artist have free will? The exceptional success of the dissociation of forms and colors in the twentieth century proves to us that the divorce of man and the world is a *fait accompli*; that for our contemporaries the external world has ceased to be a living, sacred thing; that they look upon it as a stocklist; that they juggle "phenomena."

You will probably tell me, my dear Raymond Cogniat, that the art of painting has nothing to do with Mother Nature. It doesn't matter! Matisse's "absolute painting" inaugurates this reign of the still life that is the attribute of modern French art.

The atheist who sees, who conceives the world from the angle of painting, who believes in nothing (not even sensations), who treats elements, bodies, and faces not as vehicles, as media, or as an alphabet that aids man in saying what he has to say, affirms his primacy, his central position at the heart of the universe, but, with mere pretexts for plastic variations, cannot create, transmit, communicate life. He can only make art based on art. He can please. He can never move. If I were not afraid today of abusing the hospitality that my friend M. di San Lazzaro and

G. di San Lazzaro was the publisher of Chroniques du Jour.

you, my dear Raymond Cogniat, are affording me, I would say that Matisse is a very great artist, but that his work is not a source of enrichment for a European. For Western man, the interior is an intimacy, penetrated by a filtered light (Vermeer, Pieter de Hooch, Chardin, Corot, Degas), not a blueprint or a deserted space swept by the void. The face is an individual, eternally moving testimonial of life, not a mute and unchanging mask. The body signifies the standard of measure, the measure of all things, a dynamic principle, active and acting, not an arabesque. The gaze is a message, a bearer of energy, not a fixed point. I am, you will tell me, a vulgar realist. Not at all, my dear Cogniat. But I consider a painting a sign, a thermometer and a barometer, which indicates exactly the climate and temperature of a man and an age. It is not a question of Realism. I also know that Matisse cannot be held responsible for a condition that dates from Edouard Manet, the first painter to renounce articulation, probably in spite of himself, the first to refuse to externalize physical impressions of density, volume, and weight. I know that he suffers because of it, that he claims to be going against the tide, that he values Courbet very highly, that from time to time he attempts to bring his figures to life, and that more than once he has studied a woman's face, more moving than beautiful. In vain. To Matisse falls not the honor of achieving that difficult passage from still life to living life, to the humanized world where I await the salvation of contemporary art—and also an awakening of the ancient European consciousness.

It is possible, furthermore, that such a revival may be a utopia. It is nevertheless a question in which Europe's destiny is at stake. Art is a microcosm. The white man can only live and fulfill his mission as long as he maintains, in a humanistic world, in a world built in his image, the feeling of his supremacy.

A final word. Matisse's color (chromatic vision) was, for a long time, an enigma to me. How, in an age so much more *musical* than *plastic,* could a painter avoid harmony and orchestration, "sfumato," the charm of chiaroscuro? How does he circumscribe the areas of his colors, how does he cause them to act separately? An eternal recommencement or return, or a deliberate, studied reaction? None of these. Matisse's tendency to delimit and localize colors within their bounds (which are not the conventional boundaries of objects, of forms, to which colors relate) represents the drama of the new man, isolated in time, isolated in space, incapable of understanding the unity of past, present, and future and the continuity of all the dimensions, including the fourth—which is to say, duration.

Paul Fierens

CHRONIQUES DU JOUR

"For or Against Henri-Matisse"

April 1931

Paul Fierens (1895–1957), critic, writer, and museum curator.

Perhaps it is a good thing that some painters today, the youth of several schools, are taking a stance against Matisse. Not against a person, but against a thing. Then at least let that thing be strong, and great. As Matisse's work is. All is thus in order, and the historian *cum* critic states his complete agreement with everyone else.

He, of course—it goes without saying—is for Matisse. He is for good and against bad painting. And to him it seems that Matisse has captured, probed, and disentangled the drama of color, just as Picasso proposed a solution, or a series of solutions, to the drama of form. Matisse has made the harmony of colors say things that had never been said before with such candor, such disregard for convention, such tranquility, such brilliant assurance—just as Picasso did for the balance of foreground and background, of volumes. Matisse has created his music, his counterpoint. Isn't that enough? Shall he be chided, in the name of the absolute, for some lack of humanity, of emotion? We do not ask an apple tree to bear plums.

No one has gone as far as Matisse, continuator of Gauguin, on the road to a pure lyricism based on the particular properties of color and on the melodious arabesque.

Our constructionists, abstractionists, humorists, surrealists, and so on must therefore take a step back—which just may be a step forward. Is this progress? No. Evolution, meandering, history's dotted line, fashionable whims, bursts of conscience.

But how wonderful it is to see how young, how sharp, Matisse remains—not very much less "fauve" in 1931 than he was in 1905 and still, among the masters of the age, the freest and the most true to himself!

Waldemar George

FORMES

"The Duality of Matisse"

June 1931

Matisse, flower of French painting!

Everything in this artist's art is French: his pastel tones, his sinuous but incisive lines, his implacable vision, and his flourish-free, laconic style.

Matisse has long been the rallying point of modern painting. He manifests his magnificent destiny by expressing himself in new ways. After copying Chardin in the Louvre, he pretends to have forgotten the lesson. He challenges all the set standards and elements of old painting. First he uses Seurat's conquests to his advantage. Later, he creates absolute painting, the self-contained color of form, object, air, light, atmosphere, tangible matter. Art, whether hallucination or visual hypnosis, finds its ideal form in Matisse's painted work. That supreme expression of Romanticism, purified, stripped of romantic frills and dross, is the fruit of French intelligence.

Let us attempt to isolate the personality, the inner self, of this painter, whose art presents all the distinctive features of national genius despite its exotic garb. Matisse is particularly disturbing—and edifying—in that he is an artist who has never sought to link himself to the masters of yesteryear, has never tried to look backward, has never spoken of tradition. A happy genius, Matisse has never yearned for past glories. He is connected to the past by obscure, imperceptible bonds. As he matures, Matisse, the painter of tonal arabesques, initiator of Fauvism, scornful of impressionist art, has been moving toward a more complete, more serene form. The influence of Persian art has never altered Matisse's true character. However arbitrary his harmonies, however obvious his intention to sacrifice the physical appearance of bodies and objects to a predetermined mental rhythm, he never loses contact with

In keeping with his increasingly nationalist views, George emphasizes Matisse's Frenchness.

the world, never falls into a decorative style, never abandons the level of painting as a language of images.

Naturally, there is no suggestion in Matisse's attitude or art of any latent tendency to elude the grip of his time. The painter never dreams of reacting. He is not aware of his development. He does not disavow his early efforts or his beginning works. All his gestures, all his deeds, obey an organic law of growth and development.

Matisse has achieved his work of redemption within the borders of the art of our time. Never for a moment has he violated or overstepped them. He has remained within them. His merit is to have subjugated fashion without artificially broadening the principles of painting, of which he is at once the tyrant and the serf. His sphere is narrow. No matter. The Frenchman, whether his name be Matisse or Mallarmé, frequently resorts to rigid poetics. He absorbs them and returns them in the form of a sensitive corpus.

It is typical of Matisse to have the nature of his contribution be forgotten. The significance of this artist is immeasurable. But however strong his influence was, it has been consigned to oblivion. Matisse's reforms, which once caused outrage, now belong to the realm of memory.

Like all French painters, Matisse is great precisely inasmuch as he diverges from the established system and, beyond a style, formulary, and vocabulary, creates an individual body of work.

But Matisse is helpless against his myth. Nothing prevails against his reputation. The entire world still regards him as a hewer of images, a man who reduces a figure, a face, an object, a piece of the landscape, to the status of chromatic pigments.

Matisse is synonymous with the absence of the personal and the utopian dream of painting in itself.

I do not deny that his starting point lends credence to this point of view. But his work as a whole belies such a contention. To the dynamic but too-often sterile principle that governs Pablo Picasso's art, Matisse counterposes the immanent principle of French perfection. He refuses to draw back from any act, discovery, or their inevitable consequences. A painting by Matisse is never a problem stated and solved. Nor a whim translated into plastic figures. Nor a surface covered with colors. What is it then? A complex source of visual delight, a diversion for the senses and the mind, a page that testifies to the presence of French qualities in modern painting, which is not always a French art.

Matisse undoubtedly suffers the misdeeds of the art of our time. He skirts many a difficulty. He simplifies his craft, his technique. He shuns the torments that troubled the masters. He paints passive and motionless, even inanimate, figures. These figures are neither idols, nor symbols, nor allegories. Yet they never act. The density, weight, and volume of their bodies are clever pretenses. They are located neither in time nor in real space. But these unrealistic, fictitious beings somehow live and convey life's sensations. Matisse's merit is to have defeated modern art itself, sublime paradox that it is, on its own ground and with its own arsenal. Only a French artist was capable of such a feat.

An art entirely bare, unadorned, without ingredients, without mendacious ornamentation. An art that tells the truth. Matisse rarely uses impastos. He paints sparely, as befits a distinguished man, chary of words, chary of confidences. He paints clearly, not because he is unaware of the charm, the rare magic of half-shadows, that state so conducive to meditation, but because he likes mystery in broad daylight.

Skin-deep painting! So be it. Painting so candid, so sharp, so transparent in its bareness, in its feigned poverty, that there is nothing to conceal its vices and virtues. Beyond the impressionist masters, whose debilitating influence he fought, yet whose stamp he bears, Matisse joins Manet. But even though the white and pink ghosts of *Olympia* and *Lola de Valence* haunt the modern painter of the odalisques, it is not Manet, enamored of the Spaniards, that his paintings bring to mind. Matisse uses atmospheric pastels in which La Tour's color register persists, green-tinged seascapes, and the sharp, trenchant, excessively exact landscapes that Manet painted very late in life. The lineage is plainly visible if we compare Matisse's figures with the portrait of Mme. Michel Lévy, a typical Edouard Manet pastel. In both cases, the colors are maintained at the same level, the same pitch. In both cases, the intensity of tone never drops, never diminishes. And pastels are surely the most traditional part of Manet's work, the one that entitles us to compare the painter of *Déjeuner sur l'herbe* to Boucher, Lancret, Nattier.

A strange emotional force serves as corrective to the unembellished language in which Matisse takes delight.

People. A woman standing at a window, lightly lifting the corner of a fluid curtain. An atmosphere of gentle intimacy, a filtered, muted, misty light.

A reclining woman. A body whose every limb, every fold has a personal style, a style all its own. A body that resembles no other body. It is a plant, the stem the torso, the arms the branches, the ramifications.

Heads that had mummies' features and now have a human look. Those staring eyes, dead eyes, those mute and inarticulate mouths are laden with expression. Portraits? Not yet. Matisse seems to ignore the face, repository of inner life. In the immense majority of cases, he gives to us humanized masks. And yet I have seen paintings, drawings, and lithographs by Matisse that make obvious the stunning physiognomic genius of this painter, who stands in the tradition of the French portraitists. Matisse, painter of faces and prospector of the life of the mind! There we have a theme capable of puzzling those infallible judges of new painting, whose opinions were fixed long ago and who hold an ironclad belief in the abstract character of contemporary art.

Still lifes . . . fruit, flowers, oysters, shellfish. Here, life is conveyed, expressed by analogies and correspondences. With color alone, the painter communicates, and makes us feel, the sensations of taste and smell.

Landscapes . . . skies, beaches, stone circles, plains. A palette of matte colors, like pearl foam. Here Matisse the painter of space-as-depth, the painter of exact values, of skillfully studied proportions, of perspectives wholly consonant with the laws governing the eye's mechanism, makes us forget the Matisse who interprets space as a vast flat surface and who brings figures and accessories to the fore.

Once one gets accustomed to them, Matisse's visual practice, and his lapses of language, and the liberties he takes, pass unnoticed. The artist's apparent exoticism gradually melts into the whole of his work. His Oriental technique—based on striation, sharp contrasting shades that highlight the motifs of rugs, embroidered fabrics, garish mosaics—is only too similar to the style of Eugène Delacroix, whose Turkish scenes are often pretexts for richly multicolored tonal variations. It has been said that Eugène Delacroix was Matisse's direct teacher. He is not his only teacher. When Matisse paints smoothly, with broad strokes of modulated colors (and it is perhaps then that he paints best), he eludes Delacroix's influence.

Matisse occupies a middle position between Picasso—a painter turned toward a hypothetical future, sacrificing permanent values, invariables, and the laws of harmony to the idea of progress—and Derain, who is discovering, at a cost of countless sacrifices, an art, a melody, whose only end can be delight. Henri Matisse, turned to the present, speaking the vernacular of twentieth-century man, eluded his own generation. At age sixty, the child prodigy of modern painting, has become one of the masters of French painting. The exhibition at the Galeries Georges Petit proves it beyond all doubt.

COLORPLATE 86. *Nymph in the Forest.* 1936–42. 90 × 78″ (228.6 × 198.1 cm). Musée Matisse, Nice.

COLORPLATE 87. *Lady in Blue*. 1937. Canvas. 36½ × 29″ (92.7 × 73.7 cm).
© 1988, The Philadelphia Museum of Art: Gift of Mrs. John Wintersteen.

COLORPLATE 88. *Small Dancer on Red Background.* 1937/38. Painted cut-and-pasted paper.
14⁹/₁₆ × 7¹¹/₁₆″ (37 × 19.5 cm). © Succession H. Matisse/1988.
Photograph courtesy Archives Matisse, Collection Claude Duthuit.

COLORPLATE 89. *The Rumanian Blouse.* 1937. Canvas. 29⅛ × 24″ (74 × 61 cm).
Cincinnati Art Museum, Bequest of Mary E. Johnston.

COLORPLATE 90. *Odalisque in a Striped Coat.* 1937. Canvas. 15 × 18″ (38.1 × 45.7 cm).
Mr. and Mrs. William R. Acquavella, New York.

COLORPLATE 91. *The Conservatory (Le Jardin d'hiver)*. 1938. Canvas. 28¼ × 23½″ (71.8 × 59.7 cm). Private collection.

COLORPLATE 92. *Reader Against a Black Background.* 1939. Canvas.
Photograph: Musée National d'Art Moderne, Centre Georges Pompidou, Paris.

COLORPLATE 93. *The Rumanian Blouse.* 1940. Canvas. 36¼ × 28⅜" (92 × 72 cm).
Photograph: Musée National d'Art Moderne, Centre Georges Pompidou, Paris.

Alfred H. Barr, Jr.
HENRI-MATISSE
"Introduction"
1931

Alfred H. Barr, Jr. (1902–1981), art historian and first director of the Museum of Modern Art, New York. This is an excerpt from his introduction to the catalogue of that museum's 1931 Matisse retrospective, the first major show of a European artist by the recently opened museum.

MATISSE AND THE PUBLIC

Matisse's career so far as public appreciation is concerned reveals certain paradoxes. Ten years before he became the *bête noire* of the official artists one of his own paintings had been purchased by that most conservative of patrons, the French Government, and even after he had been acknowledged a leader among modern artists throughout the world he remained for some time a "prophet in his own country." Even when the Luxembourg acquired its first Matisse in 1921 it followed in the footsteps of several German and Scandinavian Museums (and this one may mention without discourtesy, recalling that American Museums were more backward at that time even than the French).

COLORPLATE 76

It is remarkable also that Matisse who seems so admirably equipped to design murals has found only two patrons with the courage and foresight to commission him to paint large decorations; and one of them was a Russian, the other an American. Really to know Matisse's painting at its greatest one must visit the Museum of Modern Western Art in Moscow, the Rump Collection in the Museum at Copenhagen, and the Museum of the Barnes Foundation at Merion.

That Matisse's work should have become fashionable after many years of neglect on the part of most museums and collectors is perfectly normal. The same sequence has occurred in the fortunes of many great modern artists, unless, of course, like Van Gogh or Seurat, they happened to die young. But that Matisse after having survived becoming fashionable should be in danger of becoming popular while still retaining the esteem of the foremost critics is a most happy innovation, for it suggests that at least one great modern artist has escaped the isolation of his kind. More and more, his lithographs and color reproductions of his paintings are bought by people with no pretensions to advance-guardism, his oils are finding their way into conservative museums and the death of an obscure namesake is announced with headlines in the New York tabloids—a concatenation which may seem flippant but which is really a serious omen.

When his "obscure namesake" the seascape painter Auguste Matisse died in September 1931, it was erroneously reported that Henri Matisse·had died.

CONCLUSION—THE NATURE OF MATISSE'S ART

"Conclusion" in a discussion of Matisse is premature. Estimates of his art vary and will continue to vary as long as his fame lives and critics and historians continue to analyze or evaluate. But one constant remains— the work itself, and while one may join without reluctance the chorus of those who proclaim its "greatness" it may be more profitable to examine its character.

Matisse, as one may discover in the "Notes". . . , had twenty years ago very clear ideas of what painting meant to him, of what he was trying to do. "These fundamental thoughts have not changed but have evolved" is a statement which Matisse has repeated subsequently and would subscribe to at the present time. He believes implicitly in the inner consistency of his work however much its outward forms may have changed— and that they have changed amazingly is evident to the student of the present exhibition. At first glance it is hard to believe that the same man could have painted during his mature years such different versions of similar subject matter as the *Woman on a High Stool* . . . and the *Meditation* . . . or the *Gourds* . . . and the *Pink Tablecloth.* . . .

The catalogue included the first nearly complete English translation of "Notes of a Painter."

COLORPLATE 71

If, however, we survey the whole forty years of Matisse's painting we can see that the contradictory sequences move in recurrent cycles. About 1895 Matisse's work took the form of homage to Chardin and other old masters. During the next five years he began to work in a high-keyed, impressionist palette gradually moving towards an even bolder use of color in pure, strong tones. But by 1901 he was working again in ochres and siennas. Then the cycle is repeated. He leaves behind him two years of sober color to experiment with the sparkling touches of the neo-impressionists. Gradually the spots grow into the broad planes and arabesques of his *fauve* period which in turn moves towards extreme simplification both of color and form in the pure green, red and blue of the Moscow decorations and the flat color of the Moroccan period. By 1913 the cycle begins a third time with a reaction towards gray, black and brown gradually admitting more positive colors in restrained intensities. By 1918 light tones have reasserted themselves as well as small active units of design which carry us back to the impressionist and the neo-impressionist periods. Only a few pictures of 1926 and 1927 indicate by their color the beginning of a new cycle but the more serious mood and the more arbitrary and "unrealistic" forms are symptomatic.

COLORPLATE 35
COLORPLATE 36

A similar pattern appears if one considers the alternation in Matisse's development of a fairly "realistic" style with one so stylized and abbreviated that it approaches the "abstract."

In some such way an observer working from the outside might discover consistency in the sequence of inconsistencies. But Matisse describes the matter more simply: "My destination is always the same, but I work out a different route to get there" and since 1908 there have been many different routes. Yet Matisse has shown no repentance for not having done what was expected of him, explaining in 1929 that "Modes of expression do not have the immense importance attributed to them and I do not feel myself in any way bound by what I have done. Admitting that some richness exists in certain of my canvases, I would not hesitate to give up painting if my ultimate expression could be realized by another means. Thus, to express form, I often turn to sculpture. . . ."

But to return to the "destination": "What I am after, above all, is expression." And expression? He does not define it in so many words but makes it clear that it is nearly equivalent to the art of composition— composition of shapes and colors, the ability to create order out of the accident and confusion of ordinary visual experience. "I think that one can judge of the vitality and power of an artist when, after having received impressions from nature, he is able to organize his sensations." And the result of this expression through composition? It should be a work of art which will "carry in itself its complete significance and impose it on the beholder even before he identifies the subject matter."

Is painting, then, as Matisse said to Purrmann, "nothing but the observation of the relation of colors to one another"? Is it to accomplish nothing more than this? Matisse answers: "What I dream of is an art of balance, of purity and serenity, devoid of troubling or depressing subject matter, an art which might be for every mental worker, be he businessman or writer, like an appeasing influence, . . ."

The painter should not be held strictly accountable for what he says. But in these words of Matisse, removed from their context as they are, may well lie the conscious purpose of his art. He desires, without ever in the least sacrificing his integrity as an artist, to paint pictures which shall refresh the spirit through their perfection of composition, their charm of color, their tranquility. Many times has Matisse fulfilled this gracious intention but we must also be grateful to him for so often transcending his aim by giving us pictures which are by no means a sedative but which stir us by a living power present only in great works of art.

"I myself am fully convinced that the best explanation an artist can give of his aims and ability is afforded by his work."

Meyer Schapiro
ANDROCLES
"Matisse and Impressionism"
February 1932

Meyer Schapiro (b. 1904), American art historian and critic who has written extensively on art, especially of the medieval and modern periods. This is excerpted from his response to the 1931 Matisse retrospective at the Museum of Modern Art. Androcles was a publication of Columbia College.

In hanging the paintings of Matisse in a chronological order, the directors of the Museum of Modern Art have offered us a spectacle of development which is of the greatest interest. We see within the works of a single man the radical transformation of art in the last thirty years, and we see it in the very man who was most effective in it. It has the character of a revolution, in fact, two revolutions—the first in the sudden turn from an impressionistic style to an abstract, decorative manner, which overthrew an almost millenary tradition of European naturalism, the second, towards 1917, in the return to naturalism, which preserved, however, that quality of design, attained in the preceding style by a drastic reduction of nature, by numerous distortions and the complete dissolution of perspective space.

That the changes of his style are not merely the vicissitudes of a restless, unstable sensibility, but have a broad determination and a purposeful end, we can see in the present exhibition, despite regrettable lacunae such as the paintings in Moscow and the Barnes Foundation for Modern Art. His development at first seems purely circular insofar as Matisse returns to the natural objects of his early days after an interval of about fifteen years of abstract painting. But this is to misunderstand the essential contribution of Matisse to modern art. The newer works differ from Impressionism in the closely-knit design and color perceived in objects. This design is arbitrary, yet so interwoven with an apparently faithfully presented reality that the latter maintains its informality, its immediacy and accidental, suddenly emergent visual character. Matisse has thus carried the art of painting from a style primarily naturalistic, without a pervasive or deeply expressive form, to a similar naturalism galvanized and controlled by aesthetic sensibility. He has retained the most modern and for us inevitable, necessary nature without sacrifice of formal completeness and energy of diffused color.

This passage from a formless nature to a nature with an informal coherence and expressiveness could not have been made directly in 1900. It could not be the result of an abrupt transition, since the growing awareness of design toward the end of the 19th century was avowedly antithetic to the impressionists' consciousness of their own end. It required an emphatic expression in its own terms and hence the total rejection of the earlier methods. The evil in Impressionism was attributed to the swift transcription of an outdoor object, faithfully rendered with all its luminous and atmospheric determinants; the new art had therefore to paint from memory, to use broad flat areas instead of minute colored particles, to deform the object in the interest of color and design, to decompose space for the same end.

We can verify this necessity in the very words of Matisse. In an article published in 1908, and translated in the excellent catalogue of the recent exhibition, he has contrasted the formlessness of Impressionism with the rigor of an art which attains form only by sacrificing the "pleasing qualities of painting." Impressionism then stood at the opposite pole of form, or as Matisse would have it, the essentials of nature. Cézanne was the protagonist of the new movement. This is a viewpoint still current in the studios and in aesthetic propaganda, although it is unlikely that we prefer most moderns with their "form" to the "formless" Monet, Sisley, Pissarro, Degas, etc. We understand at once why the doctrine of form, thus propagated as a corrector of Impressionism, should lead to distortion of nature, an increased abstraction in the content of painting, geometrical schematisms in representation, and why for Matisse, the discovery of form should imply a sharp reaction from Impressionism.

This was not a necessary logical conception, but was the only one possible at that moment. The painters could see in the museums numerous admirable works, exemplifying their particular enthusiasm for formal structure in an intricate, magnificent way, yet faithful to a conventional interpretation of nature. But this interpretation involved a concreteness and regularity of objective form, which are inaccessible to modern vision. It was, besides, the appropriated and misunderstood heritage of an unworthy academic art. The conviction of the young painters, grounded in the contrast of an impressionistic style and their own ideals, implied the complete rejection of that style, or at least those aspects which pertained to its formlessness and inadequate expression. The conception of abstract form, as a new discovery, passed through an archaic stage, in which form became the subject-matter of art. The theoretical error was attended in Matisse (and several others) by a great liberation of sensibility, in weaker painters by a truculent parade of quickly standardized distortions and angularities.

If the concept of abstract design was stated in terms of an antithesis to Impressionism, the leap from the apparent impressionistic realism to a theory of abstract design was easy precisely because the subject-matter of Impressionism was already aesthetic. For the first time in the history of Western art aesthetically valued objects had become the exclusive or dominant subject-matter of painting. They were the aspects of nature like sky, water, vistas, light, atmosphere, moving objects, which we enjoy for their own sake. Impressionism is an outdoor art in which the occasional figures are often engaged in the contemplation of nature. Hence it was a simple step to the statement that the art of painting resides in the coherent combination of shapes and colors without respect to their meanings. The meanings were all the less important since Impressionism had destroyed the clarity and integrity of single objects. Already for the impressionists the meaning of a picture pertained to its whole and was primarily aesthetic. Now the expressive quality of Matisse, which we recognize in both the style and content of his pictures, is to some degree present in Impressionism. For he, too, is concerned with an exterior nature, which is independent of human actions, of history, religion or special moods, but is presented as a field for direct and immediate enjoyment as an unweighted, colorful, unsubstantial object. In his more recent pictures, nature is a tranquil, relaxed, semi-tropical, ornamented summer world for convalescents and family vacations; or a harem without men. It contains no animals, few children, mainly women. The latter are purely aesthetic subjects, but their female character is sometimes exposed with uncommented precision in its accidents and animality.

But apart from the subject-matter, even the formal aspects of his abstract manner are inconceivable without Impressionism. If we confront rude definitions of Abstraction and Impressionism, identifying the one with pure design, the other with the rendering of sunlight, they are of course incommensurable or opposed. But if we try to grasp the representational characters of this design and the aesthetic aspects of that imitation of sunlight, the close connection of the two arts will become evident. We will see that the flatness of the field or its decomposition into surface patterns, the inconsistent, indefinite space, the deformed contours, the peculiarly fragmentary piecing of things at the edges of the picture, the diagonal viewpoint, the bright, arbitrary color of objects, unlike their known local color, constitute within the abstract style of Matisse an impressionist matrix.

Riichiro Kawashima
HENRI MATISSE

January 1933

It is my great pleasure to share my memories of the great French painter Henri Matisse, who has deeply inspired me in my work as an artist. On my visits to France I often met Matisse and learned much from him in the course of my conversations with him.

Matisse lived in Paris. But when winter came, he would go to Nice in the south of France. It was in his studio in Nice that he painted many of his impressive and eye-opening paintings. His first exhibition in Nice was held in 1921. He showed many nudes and odalisques and a few landscapes, which could be described as interesting. But by the time he exhibited in Nice in 1922 and 1924, his works showed greater focus and maturity.

Nice has produced such famous personalities as the field marshal André Masséna, Garibaldi, and the artist Carbanrou. Nice is known for its beautiful weather, regarded as among the best in Europe, and for its beautiful scenery. During January and February, as many as 3,000 foreigners visit and live there. The carnival is traditionally known for its extravagance. The racetrack is one of the most beautiful in Europe, and many famous horses from all over the world run there.

The Place Charles-Félix, located at the east end of the town and near the old port, is crowded with market-goers buying flowers, vegetables and fish. At the corner of the square, at number 1, stands a grand old mid-eighteenth-century building, where Matisse lives on the third and fourth floors.

Many of his famous odalisques were painted in the studio on the fourth floor. The studio looks like an ordinary room. Its four doors open to a verandah, where one can look down on one-storied shops with pink, yellow, or light blue walls lining the street that leads to the market. The bright blue sea sparkles invitingly beyond the roofs of the stores. One can watch the people strolling or riding along the palm-tree-lined promenade by the beach. Matisse used this lovely view as a background in his early paintings of women.

On the mantelpiece are Persian porcelains and sculptures of African figures. His unfinished paintings hang all over the wall from floor to ceiling. Strangely, on all the canvases there are white areas apparently scratched by a knife. At first I thought that the artist had prepared the surfaces for repainting. But looking more closely I found parts of a woman's face or half of a body scratched on the surfaces. Some Italian paintings also hang on the walls. Particularly conspicuous is Mantegna's painting of Christ seen from below. The wall on the west side of the room is covered with tiles of Moorish design which might have been brought from Morocco. These are the tiles he painted as fabric designs in the backgrounds of some of his paintings.

In the eighteenth-century building, Matisse lives quietly and comfortably with his old servant, housekeeper, and a domestic.

During my fourth visit to France, I went to see him at his studio in February 1913, in order to ask him to become a member of the National Exhibition of Japan. When I visited him, he was out for a short walk. I waited in a room next to his studio until he came back with his small dog.

He welcomed me. But, unfortunately, on that day he had an appointment with a Russian lady who was his apprentice. Therefore, I talked only briefly about my having taken the dramatist Vildrac around

Japan and about membership in the National Exhibition. Then I left, asking to see him again another day.

On my second visit, I met him mainly to discuss paintings. When it comes to paintings, Matisse becomes very enthusiastic. He will talk passionately about painting with laymen as well as with fellow artists. He did not talk down from the pedestal of a great artist. Nor did he see me as different because I was Japanese. He talked simply as a man sharing his passion for art with another man.

Spreading out his sketches in front of me, he explained to me enthusiastically: "I draw dozens of sketches, sometimes in detail, sometimes in rough outlines. In one instance it took me three hours to draw a sketch in detail. I draw a flower with the root, as if it grew from the ground. I draw the stem of the flower as if it were a person breathing and growing tall. I think that a Japanese artist works the same way."

He continued talking, showing many detailed sketches of the same subject. "There is essentially no difference," he said, "between detailed sketches and rough ones. Art should embody a deep truth, although it may appear simple on the surface. When drawing a building, it is not merely a combination of vertical and horizontal lines. The impression of solidity of the building contains various intangible elements. Unless you find them, you will not be able to express them in your painting. I am studying old paintings. Right now I am attracted to Mantegna. It is essential to pay close attention to the preciseness and faithfulness of old paintings and to understand what the mouth or finger would imply or what kind of characters they would possess when they are drawn. I do not like for a human being to be merely a composition of a mouth or eyes, in other words, just a form, a convention. I devote myself completely to my paintings. I make every effort to turn out good paintings. Then, if any of my works turns out to be not good enough, it would be beyond my control."

While talking, his face became reddish with vigor, and his eyes glared. "Many art students think they can paint fantastic pictures without painstaking effort. Many professional artists view their art merely as work on canvas. This approach eventually results in failure and will not produce truly great art. I think about my paintings and the truth I want to grasp first by sketching. Then, when I finally find my idea, I start to paint. Therefore, once the painting is complete, it cannot be changed. My works appear to be easily drawn. But in fact the opposite is true. Look at these sketches and you will see."

As he talked, he showed me many sketches, one by one. "Artists need to make sketches, always. Whenever there is time, they must sketch. Sketch anything. The subject does not matter. When you sketch, nature will reveal new secrets. If you draw nature as you feel it, the picture will become beautiful, and it will have nature's strength. If it is drawn as you see and feel it, it will provide a vivid new impression that expands the imagination. It will express the painter's personality and individuality. And it will touch the viewer."

Then he referred to music and advised me as follows: "Painting is like music. In short, it has to become a symphony. My painting consists of exact rhythms, which make it beautiful. It is a very strict structure from which you could not remove anything."

Finally he gave me advice about how to use a model: "When using a model, it is essential to make the model feel relaxed and candid. Otherwise, you will lose the true feeling of the model."

Matisse always keeps a pencil in his hand, even while talking to people or smoking a cigarette. Even when he had tea at the Café Casino, he had a pencil and was sketching people around him. Matisse is a person who never stops learning from his surroundings. When he found out that I had a sketchbook, he insisted on taking a look at it. I reluctantly agreed, gave some of my sketches to him and asked for his comments.

He scrutinized them very carefully, almost to my dismay. He kindly commented on each sketch, showing me how to draw lines: "If you accentuate like this, it will look like this. . . ." He finally said, "There are few industrious people. I am very pleased to see your sketches." Matisse is very cold to people, some people say. But he has been very nice to me, and I have a very friendly feeling toward him, which I have not had the privilege to cultivate with great Japanese artists.

Matisse's drawing after 1928 demonstrates the simplification and effective expression of line and color, and rarely shows the naked canvas of his early drawings. He paints original colors very carefully with thick paint. The contrast of respective colors becomes very beautiful and projects the image of dignity and strength. Through his industriousness, he knew Cézanne's technique of contrast—that is, his way of highlighting objects by greatly distorting them. He extended his study to old Greek and Roman paintings and mosaics. He found in them precursors to Cézanne's technique and a way of simplification. Cézanne tried realism. Matisse tried distilling his art down to its essence. Matisse returned again to the classics and studied them in Gustave Moreau's studio. Moreau, at that time, advocated classic art with great enthusiasm. Matisse learned from him the freedom of composition.

In studying the arts of other eras and other lands, Matisse tried hard to understand the emotions and sensibilities of foreign cultures. He found an interesting strangeness and strength of exaggeration, as in the expression of the creative instinct of human beings in the works of Goya in Spain. He observed that in the works of primitive people of early times there was something symmetrical but not rhythmical, and architectural but not real. He learned the characteristics of the Oriental arts. Through Persian art in particular, he realized how much more he would have to work on precision.

Thus, he refined and enriched his art. Matisse was still studying when I met him, and he never intended to stop studying. "I am learning something from the old Italian arts," he said, pointing to a copy of Mantegna's large picture hanging on the wall. Its power and precision are reflected in Matisse's recent works.

Recently I was attracted very much to Matisse's works of 1915, because the works he produced at that time seemed to be filled with a sense of the contemporary. At that time, he maintained a studio at number 19, Quai Saint-Michel, in addition to his residence in Clamart in the suburbs of Paris. It was directly across from Marquet's. He used a room on the third floor as his studio. It commanded a view of the Notre Dame Cathedral across the Seine. In this studio, he painted nudes next to goldfish bowls.

It is surprising to see the effective and bold expression, particularly in these nudes and goldfish bowls. At this time Matisse seemed to be experimenting with different color techniques, such as using the paint to make it look like powder, mixing the paint with varnish to make it shiny, or making the indoor shadows black or cobalt. He seemed to be seeking a way to make the sunlit areas look warm by using a bright color mixed with red, which resulted in contrasting dark and bright areas. The effect is beautiful and natural. In short, Matisse seemed to be trying to find the right way of expressing the inner meaning of what he saw. He also seemed to be trying to focus on what was important to him while omitting the nonessential.

The exhibitions Matisse held during July and August 1931 included several of these older paintings. They look a little rough and unrefined compared with his more mature recent works. But still we are impressed with the touches of boldness, appropriateness, and self-confidence shown in these works.

I went to see these exhibitions more than twenty times and enjoyed all of his works greatly.

Matisse's exhibition at the Galeries Georges Petit ran from 16 June to 25 July 1931.

293

Matisse is always compared to Picasso. It goes without saying that both are great contemporary artists, although they are completely different in personality. While many people tend to show their preference for one or the other, I find a strange common point in their works, in that I am very much impressed with the works of both and like them equally, each for his own individuality, without comparing them.

At one time, I wanted to ask what they thought about each other's work. It was quite a long time ago, when Picasso lived in a fashionable studio overlooking the Montparnasse cemetery. One day I visited him and chatted with him in a room decorated with many black African sculptures. I asked him, "Do you like Matisse?" He widened his big, bright eyes and said, "Well, Matisse paints beautiful and elegant pictures. He is understanding." He would not say more.

When I visited Matisse in Nice four years ago, I asked him, "What do you think about Picasso?" After a moment's silence, he said, "He is capricious and unpredictable. But he understands things."

Their comments on each other sound cynical. But these remarks also reveal their respect and understanding of each other. They know each other's greatness, and both are proud of themselves.

Matisse has developed his works actively and theoretically since his Fauve period. He has put every effort into achieving his present status. On the other hand, Picasso, always capricious and unpredictable, leaped beyond people's expectations and expressed his contemporary talents continually.

In addition to being influenced by various artistic movements, both were well versed in the classical and contemporary arts of the East and West. But their works cannot be explained solely as expressions of any movement. They show individuality, confidence, and much talent. Matisse's remarking, "He understands," and Picasso's saying, "He is understanding," are significant. Men have to grow to the stage where they can be called "understanding."

I would like to finish my reminiscences with a remark that Matisse made frequently: "We—and I myself in particular—use the word 'life' to the point of abuse. But I have to use this word. Life contains something mysterious and strange, similar to God, Nature, or Humanity. Life exists in the midst of objects and in their impressions. Consequently, life expresses not only impressions but also feelings. It also expresses connections to ideas derived from contact with objects and form. The most abstract symbol is more vivid than the most concrete object."

Matisse's works show a light touch and yet express a determined and nonreligious boldness, independence and completeness, and a sense of peace. They are masterpieces that will be admired forever by all people.

Picasso had a studio on the rue Schoelcher, overlooking Montparnasse cemetery, from August 1913 to June or July 1916.

Clive Bell

EUROPA

"Matisse and Picasso"

May–June 1933

Bell had first addressed this subject in a 1920 article bearing the same title, excerpted in this volume.

Let us make no mystery about it, Matisse is interested in what has interested painters always—his vision of things and the problem of expressing that vision. Because he is an artist the expression becomes beauty; because he is original his beauty was at first mistaken for ugliness. Now that he has taught the world to see with him, the enjoyment of his pictures comes as easily as the enjoyment of Renoir's. Matisse looking out of his window at Nice perceives simple, sensuous loveliness and renders his peculiar version of it in his own inimitable way. Picasso, on the beach in Brittany, sees otherwise, sees what is there and a string of implications as well. A vision of that sort is not to be expressed simply and sensuously. It might be expressed coldly and viciously. In fact the rendering is beautiful and precise: precise with the precision of some deadly machine the efficiency of which depends on calculations carried out to the fraction of a millimeter; beautiful because Picasso's task is as impeccable as his manipulation is marvelous. What is rendered, however, is not the joy of seeing and feeling, but, as often as not, something flavored, at times pretty strongly flavored, with disgust, or despair; that is why the whole, in its willful cynicism, is what I call sentimental.

Thus it comes about that Picasso, for all his preoccupation with processes, is not predominantly interested in what absorbs craftsmen. A masterly craftsman he is, and he is interested in craftsmanship; but it is the manifestation in craft of odd scraps of individuality, not necessarily profound, but unexpected, scraps which by hook or crook have escaped industrial regimentation, that catches his eye. The embellishment of a penny match-box, betraying some remnant of artistic feeling, will attract more than a Chippendale chair. Herein he would seem to discover the authentic aestheticism of our age, the last survival of popular art, an overlooked accident, surprising and pathetic. He goes further, and seems to enjoy the very baseness of the contemporary urban mind once he can find an unmistakable expression of it in some queer place where you would last have looked for expression. A lamp-post, a public urinal, the lettering on a suburban grocer's shop, all or any of these may become manifestations of the spirit of the age, and as such for Picasso charged with significance. For it is not merely as curious forms that they interest him, as they might interest any modern painter; they move him as symbols, too, as manifestations. He can be cautiously sentimental about them.

I put it forward as a hypothesis, and as nothing more, that what the journeyman, be he tinker, tailor, toy-maker or house-painter, but be he ever so little individual and an artist, is crudely and unconsciously manifesting, Picasso is trying to express deliberately, in full and perfect consciousness, and with exquisite delicacy. It is the complete consciousness that gives the touch of cynicism. He is trying to express his sense of such idiosyncrasy and oddity as has adhered, parasitewise, to our uniform and machine-ridden civilization. Matisse, meanwhile, is painting rapturously, as a bird sings, in the ageless garden of the French tradition. Probably, because he has founded no school, he will be admired by future generations—and he will be admired as long as painting is enjoyed—as the last of the great impressionists. Picasso may be admired as one of the most original and inventive minds of a peculiarly inventive and harassed age. But Matisse must be: Picasso may.

ART DIGEST

"Challenging Matisse"

15 March 1933

While admiring the thoroughness with which Dr. Albert C. Barnes and Violette de Mazia "performed an autopsy on the art of Henri-Matisse," Thomas Craven, reviewing their volume, *The Art of Henri Matisse*, in the New York *Herald Tribune*, issued a blunt challenge to the subject's standing as "our day's foremost painter." To Craven this painter is "less a pic-

Albert C. Barnes and Violette de Mazia's The Art of Henri Matisse (*1933*), *including extended formal analyses and detailed art-historical comparisons, was the most comprehensive monograph on Matisse to date. Barnes (1872–1951) was a wealthy scientist, manufacturer, and art collector who had commissioned Matisse in 1930 to execute a mural for his private foundation. Thomas Craven (1889–1969) was a writer and critic with a strong anti-modern (and anti-European) bent. This anonymous account of Craven's review of the Barnes and De Mazia book gives a condensed view of one of the battles waged in America over Matisse's art in the 1930s.*

torial artist than a designer for stuffs to be sold by the yard," his art lacking significance as a human document. Writing in the forthright and dogmatic style that made his *Men of Art* such a controversial volume, Craven leads up to the question: "What artistic virtue can atone for poverty of human significance?"

"The Barnes method, known as 'the psychological approach to art,' is, in reality, a clinical process," he said. "It consists in dismembering an object into its technical components, and in describing those components in the terminology invented by the plastic surgeons of art. It is also an academic method; for it considers art as a dead thing. I say this in admiration of the scientific knowledge of the operators, and with due respect for the enormous amount of data which they have managed to bring together. But in a book advertised as 'the definitive work on our day's foremost painter,' we should reasonably expect to find some discussion of the meaning of his art, that is, its significance as a human document. The passages in which Matisse is treated in relation to the life of his time, and the technical components of his art in relation to the living organism, are so brief and scattered as to be practically negligible."

The section of the book devoted to Matisse's debt to Impressionism, Post-Impressionism and the Oriental traditions, stirred Mr. Craven's wrath.

"This tendency," he wrote, "to establish parallels between the old and the new art has led them, at times, into absurdities: as for example the trumped-up comparison between a sharply defined Japanese print and one of Matisse's fluid smudges. . . . We are to conclude that a painter rummages the deposits of his predecessors and rearranges his borrowed forms into a new, or different, pattern which is called a work of art. Thus art becomes a studio process, an academic pastime. We are to believe that all art is measured according to its plasticity. The expressions, plastic form, plastic means, plastic values, which occur with such monotonous regularity in this book, have become as great an obstacle to clear thinking as the old cliches they have superseded—the tactile values of Berenson, and Clive Bell's significant form. Incidentally, the term plastic, as applied to the flat art of Matisse, is a misnomer. One might just as well talk of plastic flowers, plastic light or plastic ribbons."

"The Barnes method . . . is peculiarly adapted to the art of Matisse, which is essentially a studio art. Since the Frenchman is largely concerned with the art of the past; since life has but faintly touched him; his American backers are forced to dwell almost exclusively on the sources he has plundered. But they do not seem to realize that a painter may be a profound student of traditions and yet be a very minor artist. Nor do they realize that an artist's excessive use of traditional practices is an indication of weakness. Matisse has devoted his life to the revamping of old decorative styles. He is a pattern maker in the restricted sense, an interior decorator like Gauguin. There is, of course, a pattern basis to all art, but the recognition of the pattern belongs to the kindergarten of appreciation; and the use of pattern as an end in itself belongs to the pure, or abstract painters, who go to art rather than to life for their materials."

Concerning the authors' statement that Matisse brings to his patterns an eager *joie de vivre,* Craven agreed: "That is true; that little gayety is his own contribution; it absolves him from total eclecticism and distinguishes him from the cold-blooded and complete abstractionists. But is it on the strength of these effects that he is called the foremost painter of our day?

"The higher values of art being almost absent in Matisse, it is almost impossible to discuss him in other than technical language. He is a pattern maker whose motifs lend themselves to endless repetition; he is less a pictorial artist than a designer for stuffs to be sold by the yard. His 'odalisques in hotel bedrooms' are oversized and boring; if reduced in scale and printed on cloth they might serve some legitimate decorative purpose. The larger his canvases, the more vapid he becomes; and when blown to mural dimensions, his work is nothing but leaping silhouettes and empty gestures. The authors of this book have said that his work is 'comparatively poor in human significance.' What artistic virtue can atone for poverty of human significance?"

Henry Miller

TROPIC OF CANCER

1934

Henry Miller (1891–1980), American novelist and essayist, lived in Paris during the 1930s.

In every poem by Matisse there is the history of a particle of human flesh which refused the consummation of death. The whole run of flesh, from hair to nails, expresses the miracle of breathing, as if the inner eye, in its thirst for a greater reality, had converted the pores of the flesh into hungry seeing mouths. By whatever vision one passes there is the odor and the sound of voyage. It is impossible to gaze at even a corner of his dreams without feeling the lift of the wave and the cool of flying spray. He stands at the helm peering with steady blue eyes into the portfolio of time. Into what distant corners has he not thrown his long, slanting gaze? Looking down the vast promontory of his nose he has beheld everything—the Cordilleras falling away into the Pacific, the history of the Diaspora done in vellum, shutters fluting the froufrou of the beach, the piano curving like a conch, corollas giving out diapasons of light, chameleons squirming under the book press, seraglios expiring in oceans of dust, music issuing like fire from the hidden chromosphere of pain, spore and madrepore fructifying the earth, navels vomiting their bright spawn of anguish. . . . He is a bright sage, a dancing seer who, with a sweep of the brush, removes the ugly scaffold to which the body of man is chained by the incontrovertible facts of life. He it is, if any man today possesses the gift, who knows where to dissolve the human figure, who has the courage to sacrifice an harmonious line in order to detect the rhythm and murmur of the blood, who takes the light that has been refracted inside him and lets it flood the keyboard of color. Behind the minutiae, the chaos, the mockery of life, he detects the invisible pattern; he announces his discoveries in the metaphysical pigment of space. No searching for formulae, no crucifixion of ideas, no compulsion other than to create. Even as the world goes to smash there is one man who remains at the core, who becomes more solidly fixed and anchored, more centrifugal as the process of dissolution quickens.

* * *

At the very hub of this wheel which is falling apart, is Matisse. And he will keep on rolling until everything that has gone to make up the wheel has disintegrated. He has already rolled over a goodly portion of the globe, over Persia and India and China, and like a magnet he has attached to himself microscopic particles from Kurd, Baluchistan, Timbuktu, Somaliland, Angkor, Tierra del Fuego. The odalisques he has studded with malachite and jasper, their flesh veiled with a thousand eyes, perfumed eyes dipped in the sperm of whales. Wherever a breeze stirs there are breasts as cool as jelly, white pigeons come to flutter and rut in the ice-blue veins of the Himalayas.

The wallpaper with which the men of science have covered the world of reality is falling to tatters. The grand whorehouse which they have made of life requires no decoration; it is essential only that the drains function adequately. Beauty, that feline beauty which has us by the balls in America, is finished. To fathom the new reality it is first necessary to dismantle the drains, to lay open the gangrened ducts which compose the genito-urinary system that supplies the excreta of art. The odor of the day is permanganate and formaldehyde. The drains are clogged with strangled embryos.

The world of Matisse is still beautiful in an old-fashioned bedroom way. There is not a ball bearing in evidence, nor a boiler plate, nor a piston, nor a monkey wrench. It is the same old world that went gaily to the Bois in the pastoral days of wine and fornication. I find it soothing and refreshing to move amongst these creatures with live, breathing pores whose background is stable and solid as light itself. I feel it poignantly when I walk along the Boulevard de la Madeleine and the whores rustle beside me, when just to glance at them causes me to tremble. Is it because they are exotic or well-nourished? No, it is rare to find a beautiful woman along the Boulevard de la Madeleine. But in Matisse, in the exploration of his brush, there is the trembling glitter of a world which demands only the presence of the female to crystallize the most fugitive aspirations.

Pierre Courthion
HENRI-MATISSE
1934

Pierre Courthion (1902–1988), Swissborn art historian, writer, museologist, and film director, was author of numerous books on modern art.

Everything is lit up when you come into the Boulevard Montparnasse apartment that Matisse uses as a studio and where he has collected canvases and painting materials dating from his earliest efforts. Some furniture, a few knickknacks, nothing too cumbersome, plenty of canvases, the most recent in the first room, then the landscapes from the Fauve period, the charcoal still lifes, and the copies.

Matisse had a studio-apartment at 132, Boulevard Montparnasse.

In these rooms carpeted with Matisse's thoughts, I contemplate this slow, stubborn labor. In short, nothing really extraordinary: unusual tenacity, with talent belittled by his father but encouraged by his mother. "You're going to be a lawyer, son," from the father, and perhaps ridicule from the school principal and the architect in Cateau, both of whom "did some drawing in their youth": "An arm isn't that short, that's not a woman, there's not enough space," and so on.

The struggle, the real struggle, was primarily to resist these remarks, quite damaging to anyone whose character was weak. Why do we always marvel at the early signs of what will later constitute the merit of great men? For most often they triumph through resistance, determination, and the heroism of keeping their faith among doubters, and that is most probably better than a pleasant sketch or a portrait so faithful that it no longer resembles the model.

This first visit to his studio was full of surprises for me. I walked into an apartment with light walls. I was with Matisse's daughter, Madame Duthuit, who was talking to me about her father's beginnings, the difficult years, that whole indecisive, heroic period that preceded the victory, when everything was gestating, when the man was stubbornly and confidently taking a certain road while those around him abandoned him, thinking him foolhardy. But Matisse was not foolhardy. Only his work (especially his older work) was on view in this apartment stripped of all inessentials and ready for work. The walls of each room were alive with joyful colors. Only the earliest studies, way at the back, recalled the time of doubt and frustration, the concentration of an individualist who was able to resist and did not want "to go too fast."

Matisse's daughter Marguerite was married to writer and art historian Georges Duthuit.

The entire visual problem faced by painting since 1895 was there before me, posed and solved by Henri-Matisse: the conquest of the decorative since Gauguin, the search for style through the dab and arabesque, the encounter with the Orient, until the time when it is all reabsorbed and reemerges, *in depth*, as an intimate art, more sober, more subtle, more musical.

In his art, barely tinged with Cubism, Matisse couples abstraction with the simplest subjects borrowed from the world of images. I believe it was less difficult to extract himself from it through a geometry of form than to resurrect life as he did, making it both credible and wonderful. We could inhabit Matisse's planet in that temperate clime where cactuses grow, the balmy fragrance of plants and pines wafts by, and the sea is as steady as a stare. It is a world so balanced, a harmony so subtle, that there is no room for tragedy. Nothing is disturbed; time is there, permanent, ready for our eyes to drink it in.

Matisse plays with complementaries, whose full gamut he knows and to which, like Debussy, he adds his own. He has a consummate sense of color. Never have we seen such sustained muted harmonies (at least without the picture collapsing, becoming emptied of all content, all substance), whether it be the grays of the Etretat landscapes, the pinks of the Moroccan works, or the matte greens of gardens. Matisse is a magician who hurls some luminous powder into his paintings; it is as if he always had a noontime on the Mediterranean before his eyes. Like all great masters of color, he strives for ever greater effects: his mastery of the whole register of yellows, so difficult to handle, is unparalleled. His reds have the depth and brilliance of crushed strawberries, his medleys of color are magical. Sometimes he does his principal figure in faint, vague shades and contrasts it with a background of stunning violence. Henri-Matisse has achieved the boldest color counterpoints in those faint figures surrounded by a whole bedizenment of Arab decoration. His shifting, almost liquid, blues have the sweet resonance, the sapphire brilliance, of Oriental nights.

* * *

For Matisse too, imagination operates only in painting. Is the painter fully aware of this peculiarity? One may well wonder, for why should he have invented the odalisque, an excuse for transferring all the charms of the Orient, the whole gamut of Oriental splendors, to his canvas? To usurp a palette, to rip off the veil and tear a hole in the ceiling of French art? And why these incense-burners, huge shining vessels behind his exotic beauties? Matisse's painting is rich enough in scents and perfumes to forgo these excesses. But this is a mere detail, an incidental observation. Henri-Matisse is never richer than when he lays aside all complex alloys to paint a modern young girl, a bowl of fruit on a green buffet, a lighted room in which a nude woman is secretly concealed as if in a jewel-case, shielded from summer's ravenous rays.

Pure painting, painting-painting—That is what it is; but nothing is more difficult to describe in words.

* * *

From 1914 on, Matisse completely shunned any "*à sujet*" trend in painting, as well as all so-called new methods, though they were actually included in Guillaume Apollinaire's hard-hitting aesthetic of 1913. Matisse had no need to exaggerate. He knew very well how difficult it was to create a form, to paint in depth, so that his work, his effort, his striving for coordination would be limited to the elements he had already been able to extract from himself. Matisse, perhaps alone of all the so-called School of Paris, never let himself be deceived into changing the outward presentation of his painting every season. He knew what he wanted to do, was aware of his limits, and therefore did not waver like Pablo Pi-

Portrait of Marguerite. 1915. Brush and ink. 18½ × 11" (47 × 28 cm). Collection John R. Gaines, Lexington, Kentucky.

casso between concrete and abstract, visual and reflective, archaic and futuristic art. In contrast to Picasso's variegated work, Matisse's is focused on the problem of the two-dimensional painting, his aim being to delve ever more deeply into pictorial expression. Picasso felt the need to speak all languages, separately or simultaneously, and to become the champion of artistic internationalism. Matisse, however, spoke his own language, that of the Mediterranean, and made it a supple tool that he could handle effortlessly.

Compared to Picasso, Matisse is a rest, a melody, the strings as opposed to the brass, and if I were to extend the musical metaphor, I would say that Picasso's orchestration is replete with changes of tempo, with violent and clashing rhythms; Matisse's has continuity, clear lines, and unity. It is from his works—primarily the paintings—that we get an idea of Matisse, whereas it is from Picasso—primarily the wizard—that we get interested in the works of the man from Málaga. That, at bottom, is the main difference between them.

* * *

Matisse is a painter's painter. His work is purely visual, but also intellectual; it is unencumbered by futile efforts, it is unconcerned with ephemeral styles or forms, it is addressed to our visual faculty alone, to the eye, not only as a pleasant image, but also, and above all, *as a spell which, though it enters through the eyes, goes deeper than the eyes and touches our emotions.* This kind of painting resists explanation; it has all the qualities of materially alluring painting, but goes beyond the single work in the subtlety of its resonance, its *melody.*

Thus it is that when we first glance at a Matisse canvas, we can make the mistake of believing that it is quick and facile, that he is no more than an intimist with color skills who somehow manages to bring the most delicate sensations and the most graceful arabesques into play on the canvas. He is like Debussy. But let us look more closely at the work: a simple brushstroke on fabric, a sky barely indicated, everything in its place; a color blazes like a ray of enthusiasm, desire trembles in the light, a line snakes with vine-like elegance—all this does not come by itself. Before making this choice, Matisse studied each detail separately and then eliminated anything that might disturb the unity, his unity, that he had decided to assert.

Matisse is one of those men who will always be controversial, whose vital work will generate numerous commentaries. A fighting artist, a man of battle, whom the pale glories catalogued by the representatives of official art will always shun.

A strong individualist who seems even greater when considered in isolation, a pure painter whose work is devoted only to the expression of permanence, a man determined to paint, come what may, who has heroically assumed, one after the other, all the responsibilities of such a career. Methodical, determined, ardent, never sinking into excesses of logic, a man who believes in the inexplicable, in mystery, in miracle; a *fauve* of explosive color, but above all a Mediterranean, poet of Mediterranean light, messenger of the Orient, friend to the Japanese, by the great shores of his character: a Frenchman of France, member of a family of colorists. Henri-Matisse is a painter *par excellence*, before whose work we receive, without being especially astonished, the sensation of a shade as precious—in Mallarmé's sense—as that of great hothouse flowers, and which exudes a fresh joy, like a piece of paradise torn off and fallen to the earth.

Alexander Romm
HENRI MATISSE
1937

Alexander Georgievich Romm, a Soviet art critic, corresponded with Matisse while writing this text, first published in Russian in 1934 and 1935.

Matisse, as is well known, has also played a considerable role in modern art as a theoretician. He is one of those who write little, but whose comments on art have exerted a powerful and lasting influence. In clear and simple form he has outlined principles that completely correspond to the requirements of certain bourgeois strata in the epoch of imperialism. In his article "Notes of a Painter" (1908) Matisse, already a mature artist with ten years of independent work, enunciated the principles that have determined all of his further creative activity. Discussing the general purpose of art, he resolutely proclaimed the principle of "art for art's sake," of the autonomy of art. He affirmed an art devoid of serious content. Probably no one has formulated the hedonistic view of art so decidedly as has Matisse: "What I dream of is an art that is equilibrated, pure and calm, free of disturbing subject matter, an art that can be for any intellectual worker, for the businessman or the writer, a means of soothing the soul, something like a comfortable armchair in which one can rest from physical fatigue."

This famous definition proclaims, of course, an art "without ideas." "I want my painting to give quiet and rest to the fatigued and over-worked man," says Matisse.

What kind of painting best fulfills this purpose? Painting, obviously, that does not arouse unpleasant associations, that does not necessitate deep thought, that excites no strong emotions. From this it is a logical step not only to Matisse's rejection of all subject matter, but even to his refusal to depict the real life of the machine age. From the days of the first impressionists a considerable place in painting has been devoted to the theme of the great modern city and its industry. In Matisse's pictures one finds neither the city, its traffic, factories or machines, nor, finally, the real man of our day. Everything is invested with an air of unreality, is presented as a part of a fanciful world illumined by a bright and even light, where nothing important ever happens, where time seems to have stood still, where there are no events and no catastrophes, where there is no need of either thought or action.

Consistent in the extreme, Matisse banishes all the unpleasant or "banal" sides of life from his pictures. There is never anything remotely prosaic about his landscapes—there is not one study of a Paris street or a French village. He rejects these "boring" subjects for the sake of exotic luxury, and the more festive states of nature. When living in the North, he seldom pictures bad weather; when working in the South he does not show the sultry oppressiveness of heat. He consistently shuns anything exciting, any excesses: when in Africa, he is not interested in the vastness of the desert; when painting the sea, he shows no feeling of its vast expanses, but likens it to a piece of colored silk.

Matisse has not only shunned "exciting" themes, he has never sought for themes in general; a theme or subject as such does not exist for him. In his own words a picture "must carry its complete significance in itself as such, and must produce an impression on the onlooker even before he elicits its meaning."

He finds motifs for his painting in his own house. He paints his studio, his family, a model, his pupils painting the same model. From year to year he paints the same simple themes, in endless repetition, but every time with new and daring plastic variations: a woman at a piano with a book; a model lying on the divan; children playing at [checkers], learning songs—all these are occasions for experimental painting. Matisse

COLORPLATE 78

loves the four walls of his studio more than open spaces. He has few landscapes and even these are taken in their relation to a room's interior. One of his favorite themes is a room with a glimpse of open country seen through its windows.

He draws from nature in order that later on as occasion demands he can desert her: "I know a study of a garden (painted in Morocco) which Matisse repainted three times, each time more closely approaching to decorativism, to quiet, and abstract beauty. When I saw it the first time, the vivid life put into the trees and grass amazed me; then the earth was covered with a single tone, the grass was transformed into a uniform garland of lianas, the trees became trees of an earthly paradise. Now the picture gives us absolute repose" (M. Sembat).

COLORPLATE 43

The essential significance of Matisse's formula of "tranquillity" lies in this—that the picture should transport the observer out of everyday reality, out of real life, into an abstract self-sufficient world.

The observer must merely contemplate—he must think of nothing, remember nothing, he must be wafted into an abstract world of color and form, extinguishing all senses but the visual. This principle is, in essence, an "escape from reality."

This is the "tranquillity" that Matisse gives in his art. In his fantastic decorative world he calms the soul of the bourgeois, gives him forgetfulness of the social dangers of modern life, whispers to him of eternal well-being.

Matisse has held to his principles unwaveringly and tenaciously. It seems as if all the catastrophic and tragic events of the last few decades have passed him by and left him unchanged. He has remained true to his cult of tranquility. The twenty years that have passed since his first program declaration have been filled with wars and revolutions. They have witnessed the birth of a new socialist world. But all this has not made him review his principles: he has developed them even further. Speaking to F. Fels in 1928 he says: "A picture must hang quietly on a wall. The onlooker should not be perturbed or confused, he should not feel the necessity of contradicting himself, of coming out of himself. A picture should give deep satisfaction, relaxation and pure pleasure to the troubled consciousness."

This Matisse principle of an art without idea, without a subject, is a direct negation of the art of a preceding generation of artists. The 1880s–1890s were exactly the time when the question of overcoming the influence of Impressionism, of creating a more solid and synthetic art, was in the foreground, when the importance of significant themes in art took on new weight.

A leading feature of the new art of this period was its very clearly expressed social subject matter. This had a tradition of many years standing, inherited from the men of 1848 and 1871—Millet, Courbet, Daumier. It had roots springing from Impressionism itself: elements of social satire in Degas's work—the clumsiness of the dancers and scene-shifters of the ballet amid the emphasized brilliance of the stage-settings—and was expressed in an even sharper form in the prostitutes and concert singers of Toulouse-Lautrec. While a central theme in the work of Meunier and several other sculptors, Steinlen and Van Gogh, is the life and labor of the workers and peasants, social themes expressed in his sympathy for the disinherited occupy the attention of the twenty-year-old Picasso.

Constantin Meunier (1831–1905), Belgian painter and sculptor; Théophile-Alexandre Steinlen (1859–1923), Swiss-born lithographer.

This art represents the left wing of Modernism. No less brilliantly represented is the right wing, which inherits the experience of the impressionists, is their direct successor in form, but is reactionary in content. Here on the right we see reactionary attempts to revive religious art, and to attain a mystical communion with nature through color and form, the symbolic mysticism of Odilon Redon and Gustave Moreau, and such Gauguin canvases as *The Last Supper* and *The Nativity*.

COLORPLATE 94. *Interior with Etruscan Vase.* 1940. Canvas. 29 × 39½″ (73.7 × 100.3 cm).
The Cleveland Museum of Art, Gift of Hanna Fund.

COLORPLATE 95. *Still Life with Oysters.* 1940. Canvas. 25½ × 32¼″ (65 × 82 cm). Kunstmuseum Basel.

COLORPLATE 96. *Still Life with a Seashell on Black Marble.* 1940. Canvas. 21½ × 32 (54.6 × 81.3 cm).
The Pushkin Museum, Moscow. Photo APN, Agence de Presse "Novosti."

COLORPLATE 97. *Red Still Life with Magnolia*. 1941. Canvas. 29 × 39″ (74 × 99 cm).
Photograph: Musée National d'Art Moderne, Centre Georges Pompidou, Paris.

COLORPLATE 98. *Idol.* 1942. Canvas. 20 × 24″ (50.8 × 60.9 cm). Private collection.

COLORPLATE 99. *Lemons and Saxifrages.* 1943. Canvas. 21¼ × 31⅞″ (54 × 81 cm). Galerie Rosengart, Lucerne.

COLORPLATE 100. *The Cowboy.* 1943–44. Gouache on cut-and-pasted paper.
16⅝ × 25⅝″ (42.2 × 65.2 cm). Tériade, Paris.

COLORPLATE 101. *Still Life with Pomegranate*. 1947. Canvas. 31½ × 23⅝″ (80 × 60 cm). Musée Matisse, Nice.

COLORPLATE 102. *Composition (Les Velours)*. 1947. Gouache on cut-and-pasted paper.
20¼ × 85⅞″ (51.5 × 218 cm). Kunstmuseum Basel.

COLORPLATE 103. *The Thousand and One Nights.* 1950.
Gouache on cut-and-pasted paper. 54¾ × 147¼" (139.1 × 374 cm). The Carnegie Museum of Art, Pittsburgh.
Acquired through the generosity of the Sarah Mellon Scaife Family, 1971.

COLORPLATE 104. *The Silence Living in Houses (Le Silence habité des maisons).* 1947. Canvas. 24 × 19⅝″ (61 × 50 cm).
© Succession H. Matisse/1988. Photograph courtesy Archives Matisse, Collection Claude Duthuit.

As part of this development there appear the Catholic pictures of Maurice Denis and his followers. In the person of Denis, the right wing has not only a fine decorator, but an outstanding theoretician and a keen critic. Denis attempts to guide the new art into the paths of classicism, preaches a return to the sound traditions of Poussin, without discarding the achievements of the impressionists. Finally, these two tendencies unite in an original way in the extraordinary creations of Van Gogh, which combine social subject matter—labor themes—with cosmic mysticism; misty socialistic ideas, petty-bourgeois humanitarianism and an idealization of the medieval guilds. The development of Van Gogh's art exerted a powerful influence on a whole generation of artists, particularly in Germany. He himself becomes the hero of a myth, a prophet, an object of worship. All this is in the sphere of poetry. But there was also "prose" in the new movement—the art of those followers of Impressionism who somewhat simplified its technique: exponents of an intimate art that depicts everyday bourgeois life, Bonnard and Vuillard introduce an element of genre, a literary element, half ironic, half lyrical.

In the bourgeois art of this time a silent struggle was taking place between the formalists' conception of the functions of art and those who subscribed to an art of ideas. Formalist tendencies were most sharply expressed by the neo-impressionists, with whom at one time Matisse was closely related. Subject matter was far from being the essential basis of their art. Their leaders considered it quite as impossible to express their anarchistic ideals in their painting as Cézanne considered it impossible to paint his conservative and catholic principles. Matisse maintained an even more formalistic stand than this. In order to assert the formal value of his pictures he not only lessened the importance of subject matter but even weakened the element of representation—the connecting link with nature—and for the space of ten years he tended more and more away from realistic representation, toward ever greater abstraction. We can trace specifically how Matisse transforms a theme into a "purely coloristic," almost subjectless, non-representational painting. In 1907–1910, the years during which he experimented in decorative mural painting, he became actively interested in the idea of "Bacchanalia," a theme frequently treated during the Renaissance. In his picture *The Joy of Life* he painted a round dance as a minor detail in the background. Later, this detail grew into an independent picture, *The Dance,* and here it is already treated more abstractly; the formal elements of line and color surface now predominate. Several times Matisse again returns to *The Dance,* often reducing it to a detail of an interior—a corner of the studio, with the figures cut off by the picture frame, and each time the painter transposes the tone of the picture, treating it merely as part of a still life.

COLORPLATE 35

In succeeding years Matisse continues to hold these formalistic principles, and strives never to go beyond the borders of that decorative, joyous garden which he once created.

Hedonism in Matisse's pictures expresses itself in a refined decorativism, in bright, fulsome and harmonious colors, in the selection of pleasant, idyllic subjects and themes, which create an impression of a happy and carefree life, of unchanging well-being and plenty.

Matisse's intimate manner is also characteristic of this hedonism. It is exemplified by that affection for homely interiors that is particularly strongly felt in the so-called Nice Period that begins in 1917. A striking example of this is offered by his *Storm*, showing a smiling woman in a comfortable room, through the window of which is seen a stormy seascape—an obvious contrast of an intimate little personal world and the alien world outside.

Matisse loves luxury: the ordinary objects of everyday use rarely figure in his *nature mortes*. He prefers delicate vases, Oriental rugs, bronzes and chased copper, luxurious costumes and jewelry, bright and gaudy textiles, exotic flowers. A mere list of the things he pictures makes it ob-

The Dance. 1931–32. Canvas.
140½ × c. 564″ (356.9 × c. 1,432.5 cm).
Photograph © Copyright 1988,
The Barnes Foundation.

vious that this is an art for the privileged few. In this respect Matisse breaks sharply with the traditions of the new art which, beginning in the 1850s, takes unpretentious bits of nature, simple themes, and transforms them by the expressive power of color harmony and form, and does not reject subject matter that would, according to the standards of academic painting, be considered vulgar. Such was the fundamentally bourgeois democratic art of Courbet, Manet, Degas, Pissarro, and Van Gogh. In this respect Matisse is a throwback to the refined, festive, and sumptuous romantic art of the time of Delacroix. No less characteristic in this respect is the eroticism that we meet with in Matisse's pictures of the 1920s.

Despite all of these undoubtedly hedonistic tendencies, it is necessary to make certain essential reservations, concerning both the general character of Matisse's work and the social soil out of which it grows. We must note that Matisse is characterized by another tendency besides that of hedonism. In the first place the question arises—does Matisse really achieve that impression of calm which he considers to be his principal aim? It must be admitted that he attains this in only a few of his canvases; the great majority of them are instinct with impetuous movement, particularly noticeable in his more spontaneous creations, his drawings and still lifes. As regards his decorative compositions, particularly of his latest period, it must be said that the observer experiences considerable difficulty in concentrating on them, in immediately deciphering his gleaming designs and patterns of color.

Such typical Matisse productions give one as little feeling of calm as the sight of ocean waves or wind-tossed clouds. As a result of this dynamism, the intelligent perception of Matisse's pictures demands that the observer exert a certain amount of effort, which already precludes the possibility of complete and immediate enjoyment. Besides this, the natural forms of objects are modified and ciphered in this far from realistic style of painting.

In entering this fantastic world, the observer must, in the first place, learn how to approach and decipher these metamorphosed objects. The formalistic principles of the painter demand a certain amount of erudition on the part of the observer, a certain knowledge of the laws of composition, etc. More activity has to be displayed by the observer in appreciating this art than is needed when viewing typically hedonistic art, as, for instance, the delicate and sensual images of women and children in Renoir's work. The dominant trait of many of Matisse's canvases of different periods is not conventional beauty but a certain brevity, conciseness, a merciless distortion of reality. Renoir's painted figures are the same as those that one likes outside the walls of the museum—but the same can certainly not be said of the deformed figures created by Matisse. Matisse wavers between truly hedonistic painting and what might be called "activizing painting." This is particularly so in his later years, when he either approaches closer to the delicacy and lightness of Renoir and the clearness and elegance of Manet, or reveling in formalistic experiments, ruthlessly breaks up his forms.

We see that in practice Matisse often contradicts his own formula. Thus his art is contradictory—reflecting the contradictions of the bourgeois world.

As Matisse has himself said, he caters to the businessman and the intellectual worker. He is supported by well-known patrons of art—the Americans Stein and Barnes, the Russians Shchukin and Morozov, who bought whole series of Matisse's canvases, and gave him orders for murals to adorn their palaces and villas. These men—extremely characteristic representatives of the active and progressive part of the bourgeoisie—were attracted in the first place by his daring experiments. They were not put off even by his "extremism"; the indecipherability of a picture made it even more valuable (that is, for S. Shchukin or Albert Barnes). There is, indeed, a certain special interest in deciphering these pictures just as there is in working out the blueprints of a machine or a chess problem. Thus the intellectual element that Matisse begins by excluding from the content of his picture reasserts itself, nevertheless, in the process of elucidating its form.

In times of social upheavals, when class contradictions are sharpened, some bourgeois circles particularly strive to get away to their own little private world—to the "home museum" in order to forget, for the time being at least, the unpleasantnesses and alarms of real life. In the final analysis the art that most closely conforms to the requirements of some influential progressive groups of the bourgeoisie is that which combines these two elements—hedonism and experimentation, or "formal" activization. The interaction of these two elements defines the character of the art of both Matisse and Picasso: the former, fundamentally a hedonist, introduces the principle of "activization" into his painting, the latter; fundamentally an anti-hedonist, nevertheless in his "rose period" and in his colorful decorative works of the 1920s, approaches the standpoint of hedonism.

Henri Matisse, Interviewed by E. Tériade

MINOTAURE

"The Persistence of Fauvism"

15 October 1936

When the means of expression have become so refined, so attenuated that their power of expression wears thin, it is necessary to return to the essential principles which made human language. They are, after all, the principles which "go back to the source," which relive, which give us life. Pictures which have become refinements, subtle gradations, dissolutions without energy, call for beautiful blues, reds, yellows—matter to stir the sensual depths in men. This is the starting point of Fauvism: the courage to return to the purity of the means.

Our senses have an age of development which does not come from the immediate surroundings, but from a moment in civilization. We are born with the sensibility of a given period of civilization. And that counts far more than all we can learn about a period. The arts have a development which comes not only from the individual, but also from an accumulated strength, the civilization which precedes us. One can't do just

Matisse's statements here reflect his return to a more synthetic art in the mid-1930s.

anything. A talented artist cannot do just as he likes. If he used only his talents, he would not exist. We are not the masters of what we produce. It is imposed on us.

In my latest paintings, I have united the acquisitions of the last twenty years to my essential core, to my very essence.

The reaction of each stage is as important as the subject. For this reaction comes from me and not from the subject. It is from the basis of my interpretation that I continually react until my work comes into harmony with me. Like someone writing a sentence, rewrites it, makes new discoveries . . . At each stage, I reach a balance, a conclusion. At the next sitting, if I find a weakness in the whole, I find my way back into the picture by means of the weakness—I re-enter through the breach—and reconceive the whole. Thus everything becomes fluid again and as each element is only one of the component forces (as in an orchestration), the whole can be changed in appearance but the feeling still remains the same. A black could very well replace a blue, since basically the expression derives from the relationships. One is not bound to a blue, to a green or to a red. You can change the relationships by modifying the quantity of the components without changing their nature. That is, the painting will still be composed of blue, yellow and green, in altered quantities. Or you can retain the relationships which form the expression of a picture, replacing a blue with a black, as in an orchestra a trumpet may be replaced by an oboe.

. . . At the final stage the painter finds himself freed and his emotion exists complete in his work. He himself, in any case, is relieved of it.

Jane Simone Bussy
THE BURLINGTON MAGAZINE
"A Great Man"
February 1986

At this time Matisse often had photographs taken of his works in progress; see the in-progress photos of Large Reclining Nude, *1935, on pages 330–331.*

Jane Simone Bussy (1906–1960), daughter of artist Simon Bussy and author and translator Dorothy Strachey Bussy. This memoir was written to be read to the Bloomsbury "Memoir Club," probably in the autumn of 1947.

I cannot really remember the first time I saw a figure that was later to become so very familiar—a tallish, stoutish, replete-looking figure, with a neatly trimmed pepper and salt beard, large, pale blue short-sighted eyes behind handsome gold-rimmed spectacles, beautifully kept, well shaped hands and much better clothes than those of all our other visitors—a figure that radiated prosperity and was surrounded by an aura of bourgeois respectability—no, I was, I suppose, far too young on that occasion to remember now the first time I set eyes on the great revolutionary painter Henri Matisse.

But, during the course of my childhood this figure, at once rather impressive and not particularly attractive to a child's eye, would appear at rather long and irregular intervals at our house and gradually I became aware that the quiet, distinguished-looking gentleman who paid us these occasional rather stiff and formal calls, and might from his appearance have been a successful stockbroker, was in fact a Great Man—a person who by merely exercising his calling—a quiet and inoffensive enough calling one would have thought—had aroused passionate admiration and no less passionate enmity all over the world and had revolutionized the conceptions of men.

His whole appearance was certainly the antithesis of the vulgar notion of what an artist should look like. He has often been said to resemble a German professor and there is some truth in this comparison, but he looks even more like a French businessman from the north and this

HM 37

Self-Portrait. 1937. Charcoal.
18¹/₁₆ × 15⅜″ (45.9 × 39.1 cm).
The Baltimore Museum of Art: The
Cone Collection, formed by Dr. Claribel
Cone and Miss Etta Cone of
Baltimore, Maryland.

look is not altogether misleading, as art dealers know to their cost, for no one can drive a harder bargain than this exquisite artist. Moreover, this so-called "Mediterranean" painter, this most sensually southern of modern artists, is a native of the cold, muddy, northern village of Bohain in Picardy. (I have often heard him quote in patois and not without approval the Picard proverb: *Chacun son pain, chacun son hareng,* which might be freely translated: "Each man for himself.")

All this, however, dawned upon me very gradually. Matisse was already world-famous when I began to be aware of him, but presently I made out that he had not always been rich and famous—not always even respectable. Always, however, he had possessed extraordinary, unique gifts, as I gradually made out from my father's conversation. My father and he had been co-disciples at Gustave Moreau's famous *atelier* though not indeed at the Ecole des Beaux-Arts itself, whose ultra-stiff academic exams Matisse had never been able to pass. Ever since that time it seemed my father had regarded his gifts with intense admiration and his character with indulgent amusement. He had from their student days predicted great successes for Matisse, discerning in him from the first that rare blend of virtuosity, daring and charm that was to make him famous, but he was never taken in by the extreme seriousness and reverence with which already in those early days Matisse was wont to regard Matisse.

In those days, so Auguste Bréal told me later, my father used to tease

*Auguste Bréal (1875–1938), French
painter and writer on art.*

Matisse unmercifully when he indulged too much in his favorite habit of holding forth in front of his own pictures, proving them by *a* plus *b* to be masterpieces. In front of a still life which Matisse claimed positively "lighted up the room" with its glowing harmony, he had merely expressed a preference for a paraffin lamp and one day, in reply to Matisse's boast that he no longer needed to go to the Louvre, having exhausted the teachings of the old masters, my father's comment: "Yes, but you go to the rue Lafitte" had nearly brought about a breach; for rue Lafitte was where a large collection of Cézannes were then being shown for the first time. The breach, however, was soon healed—Matisse had not so very many friends and seemed hardly to be on the road to fulfilling prophecies of great achievements. He was going through all the traditional agonies of poverty and despair. These agonies would be poured out in immensely long letters, which my father kept for many years but most of which, alas, through a hideous concatenation of circumstances, were finally destroyed.

* * *

It had been going on for nearly twenty years when I first really started to observe him, for it was not, I believe, till the late twenties that he took to coming regularly to tea every Sunday. [To the Bussys' home, La Souco, Roquebrune.] (Although being completely irreligious—he never goes to church—Matisse never works on the Sabbath.) By this time, he had acquired an enormous American motor-car and a chauffeur, which last fact may account for his more frequent visits; for his custom when he drove himself was to draw up by the side of the road every time he saw another car coming towards him, and there to wait till the danger was past. As in those days the Corniche road, where we lived, resembled Piccadilly or Fifth Avenue, his progress was apt to be slow and his range restricted to a very short radius from Nice, where he lived. Be that as it may, in the twenties he suddenly took to coming to tea and appeared to enjoy not our company of course but the monologue he held in our company.

This monologue, for a time at least, was by no means devoid of fascination. Matisse, when he so wishes, can be extremely amusing and even charming. He is far more cultured than most painters, particularly in music, and is curiously well-read. He is one of the best mimics I know, taking people off with an extreme economy of means—a look, an intonation is enough to conjure up a person. One of his star turns was imitating Bouguereau, whose pupil he had been. [Matisse studied under Bouguereau in Paris 1891–92 at the Académie Julian.] My mother once told him jokingly that he had missed his vocation—he should have been an actor. He answered with complete seriousness that he had once earnestly considered that possibility. He is a very good story teller and some of the sagas he used to tell about his lifelong and usually triumphant struggles with dealers or his childhood in Bohain could be fascinating. I particularly remember his description of how a hypnotist once visited Bohain and gave a demonstration in the village hall, where he mesmerized all the school children, suggesting to them that they were out of doors by the side of a stream with flowers growing all round; they would stoop to pick the flowers, they would try to drink the water, so powerful was the hypnotic suggestion. When it came to him, however, just as he was beginning to fall under the spell, something seemed to snap and through the grass and the stream he saw the carpet on the floor. "No", he cried, "I can see the carpet!" And after that the hypnotist could do nothing more to him. That incident became a symbol to him in after life. However far fantasy might lead him, he never lost sight of the carpet.

I shall never forget too his description of New York—the ethereal beauty of the sky-scrapers by day, their black velvety magic, studded with lights, at night, and the extraordinary crystalline quality of the light. I have never heard it so vividly described. Matisse can be witty too on occasion. One day, entering La Coupole restaurant in Montparnasse and seeing a thrill go through the whole place and all the waiters bounding towards him—"*On me prend pour Picasso*," he murmured.

On me prend pour Picasso: *They think I'm Picasso.*

And yet—prodigiously gifted, brilliant, witty as he is, he becomes after a time intensely boring. The reason for this is simple: Matisse is the most complete egoist I have ever come across and that prodigious egoism that lies behind the bland benignity of his manner ends by choking almost everyone off. It is possible that some obscure unrecognized need for friendship and sympathy drove him to our house, for by this time, while gaining millions of fans, he had lost all his old friends except my father. In fact no one except us has been known to stand Matisse for long and I could never quite understand how it was that my father was an exception to this rule, but I finally came to the conclusion that the attitude he took up from the first towards Matisse—that curious mixture of admiration and amusement that I have already mentioned—accounts for it.

"Matisse," Auguste Bréal used to say, "cannot get over the fact that he is Matisse. He can hardly believe his luck." And indeed the egoism of Matisse is something at once so colossal and so childishly simple and natural that one cannot call it vanity. He does not consider himself the greatest painter in the world but, quite simply, the *only* one, for others do not exist in themselves, but only in relation to him. If another artist's work catches his eye, as sometimes happens, it is merely that he has seen in it some reflection of his own problems. For many years now he has ceased to take an interest in the young or in anything new. This is only partly because he is afraid of public opinion and of backing the wrong horse. Fundamentally it is just plain lack of interest. He is quite frank about this. I remember that once we were discussing the possibility of his going to London to see a unique exhibition of Chinese art that was being held there. [At the Royal Academy of Arts, 1936.] But after a few conventional remarks about the wonders of Oriental art he suddenly gave way to sincerity: "After all I don't think I shall go. I don't really want to go. I don't really take an interest in it. I only take an interest in myself. *Je ne m'intéresse qu'à moi!*" And so saying he blushed rosy red and buried his face in his hands. For he is perfectly aware of his own peculiarities and when he is with intimates he will own up to them with a curious and almost disarming mixture of shame and pride.

Je ne m'intéresse qu'à moi! *I only interest myself!*

With all his egoism he is without an atom of affectation and it is this complete naturalness that makes him endurable—at least for a while. Completely absorbed in himself and in his art, Matisse could think and talk of nothing else. Art was a hard taskmaster to him and his apparently effortless creations cost him blood and sweat and agony—none of which were ever spared to his auditors. Hour after hour he would sit pouring out his torments and analyzing the artistic coils he had got himself into. Although a complete unbeliever, his *livre de chevet* at this time was the *Imitation of Christ* and undoubtedly he saw himself as the artistic counterpart of its author. It was not God he cultivated but Art—*his* art. His soul was absorbed in the Imitation of Art—Matisse's art. It was impossible not to admire such single-minded devotion, but sometimes it was difficult not to question the undeviating worship and perhaps the narrowness of the divinity. He once in my presence described a recent meeting with Picasso (his relations with Picasso were roughly those of one crowned head with another) at which they had exchanged reminiscences of the heroic period. 1917! What a tremendous moment that had been in the world of art! What artistic agonies they had gone through! All the old values seemed to be rocking. "You and I," he had told Picasso, "were in the trenches too in those days. . . ." Picasso, I gathered, had heartily agreed. Still, 1917. . . . Had it never occurred to him that not only his own world was rocking then? Were those metaphorical trenches quite as unpleasant as their physical counterparts?

Claude Roger-Marx
HENRI MATISSE
"The Drawings of Henri Matisse"
1938

Claude Roger-Marx (1888–1977), poet, novelist, critic, and son of Roger Marx, author of the catalogue preface (also in this volume) for Matisse's first one-man show (1904). Matisse apparently disagreed strongly with some of Roger-Marx's points; his rebuttal directly follows this selection.

Like his comrades at the Moreau studio, like Rouault, like Marquet especially (to whom his sketches offer many similarities), Matisse will continually hold drawing to be a lifelong pleasure and an indispensable exercise (and I give drawing its vastest meaning, whether it be consigned to blank sheet, copper, or mulled stone). These drawings, for the most part, precede the painter's task. Executed from nature, they are studies for portraits or compositional: variations on dressed, nude, or half-nude models; dancers, odalisques, Spanish women, etc. Many form a series inspired by the same face or the same clothing. More rarely, they are studies from a landscape or a still life. The painter's plastic imagination loves to be aroused by the chamber music that is composed when one or two figures are present (I should say "take their positions") in a room. Though exalted by their nudity, he also loves to ornament them with accessories—scarves, mantillas, strange hairstyles, culottes that match their skin—to adorn them with a certain Oriental luxury. There is, in fact, something Oriental about this northerner. It is as a genuine egoist that he seizes these living beings, conceiving them almost as objects and observing them less for themselves than for the displays and visual pleasures that he wants to derive from them. These young women, adapted to the decor devised to harbor them and decked out in accessories not of their own choosing, are (in the eyes of this observer) nothing but a pretext to assert himself. Even when he takes his inspiration from his dear ones and catches them in a familiar gesture, it is in volumes or in tonal relationships that he is interested, and never in the soul. Hence the rather distant character of this art, which enchants more than stirs the emotions.

Reclining Nude in the Studio. 1935. Ink. 17¾ × 22⅜″ (45.1 × 56.8 cm). Mr. and Mrs. Nathan L. Halpern.

A Lady with a Necklace. 1936. Ink.
21¼ × 17¾″ (54 × 45 cm). Courtesy
The Harvard University Art Museums
(Fogg Art Museum), Bequest: Meta and
Paul J. Sachs.

Consider one of the most deliberate masters of French painting (I mean Ingres); in the presence of his odalisques, does one not feel, in the very distortions, that he is pierced by desire and voluptuousness? When faced with his model, Matisse, so anxious in matters of technique, preserves a sentimental and sensual serenity that is absolute. His figures breathe a somewhat abstract air; charged with decorating the space, adorned with eyes and lips that count for less than the flowers in the wallpaper or the carpet, they are docile instruments upon which he composes a subtle song.

The conviction, the seriousness with which these masterly games are played, the invincible gifts of this sorcerer—who often charms monsters—the tenacity of a tireless arguer, are much more inspiring than a total involvement; an interest that is ceaselessly renewed.

It is perhaps in his pen-and-ink studies and small etchings that Matisse has expressed himself with the most authority. Often the arabesque alone, the contour alone, are enough for him. No cross-hatches, no shading or half-tints. Supreme elegance, in a colorist, is to forbid himself the play of values and modulations. Just as in his paintings he readily disregards modeling and proceeds by flat colors, so too, when he uses only white and black, he is content, as many sculptors are in their drawings (and how could one forget that Matisse has sculpted, when he chose, like Gauguin and Degas?), to imprison volumes in a mobile, quivering contour.

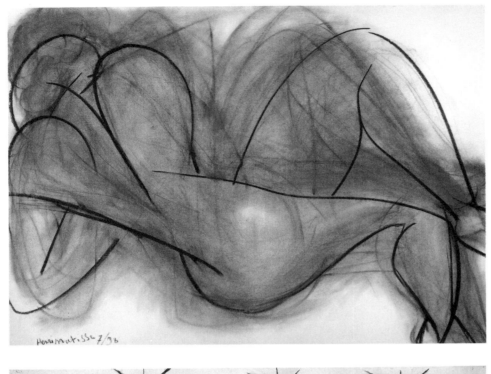

This particular sensitivity and acuity are heightened by their expression with the aid of pointed instruments—pen or hard pencil. The stroke, vivid, manages to suggest color itself, and the feeling is conveyed with a hallucinatory strength. The variations in contour differentiate the planes, the surfaces, accelerate the rhythms, color the whites of the page. Several of these drawings truly constitute masterpieces of plastic intensity and economy. [Matisse has also drawn with brush, stump, charcoal, and soft pencil.]

In contrast to his linear compositions—which are so good because they emphasize only through important omissions—this is a collection of drawings and lithographs of a completely different character. Orchestrated by values, having recourse to the resources of traditional modeling and chiaroscuro, they reveal a respectful concern for translating the most different materials: hair, necklaces, furs, embroideries. The hand lingered over the details. It seems as though the artist wanted to prove to us, and to himself, that nothing would be easier for him than to attain that "finish," of which he is believed incapable. But these demonstrations of ability and these analytical pages remain quite exceptional in an oeuvre that, with a sort of coquetry, puts on its most elliptical face and shuns the pleasures of "craftsmanship." Accustomed as Matisse has made us to more rapid modes of expression, to more categorical affirmations, we would almost reproach him with returning to conventions were we not charmed to discover in these masterly orchestrations—I am alluding especially to certain *Odalisques*—the incomparable subtleties dear to this great painter.

Matisse's best drawings remain equidistant between distillations almost fiercely set down and elaborations lingered over and refined. In such cases, a perfect harmony is realized between instinct and reason, and we forget those inner struggles that have given so many pages the aspect of battlefields covered with wounded forms. There, no more clenchings; the will is forgotten, the theoretician fades away modestly, and we experience delightfully the pleasures devised by a direct, vehement, and marvelously gifted man who knows how to affirm, joyfully and dazzlingly, the intensity of his feelings.

Henri Matisse
LE POINT
"Notes of a Painter on His Drawing"
July 1939

My education taught me an awareness of the different means of expression inherent in color and drawing. My classical education naturally led me to study the old masters, and to assimilate them as much as possible while considering such things as volume, the arabesque, value contrasts and harmony, and to relate my reflections to my work from nature; until the day when I took stock of myself and realized that for me it was necessary to forget the methods of the old masters, or rather to comprehend them in a completely personal manner. Isn't this the rule of all artists of classical training? Next came the recognition and influence of the arts of the Orient.

My line drawing is the purest and most direct translation of my emotion. The simplification of the medium allows that. At the same time, these drawings are more complete than they may appear to some people who confuse them with a sketch. They generate light; seen on a dull day or in direct light they contain, in addition to the quality and sensitivity of line, light and value differences which quite clearly correspond to color. These qualities are also evident to many in full light. They derive from the fact that the drawings are always preceded by studies made in a less rigorous medium than pure line, such as charcoal or stump drawing, which enables me to consider simultaneously the character of the model, the human expression, the quality of surrounding light, atmosphere and all that can only be expressed by drawing. And only when I feel drained by the effort, which may go on for several sessions, can I with a clear mind and without hesitation, give free rein to my pen. Then I feel clearly that my emotion is expressed in plastic writing. Once my emotive line has modeled the light of my white paper without destroying its precious whiteness, I can neither add nor take anything away. The page is written; no correction is possible. If it is not adequate, there is no alternative than to begin again, as if it were an acrobatic feat. It contains, amalgamated according to my possibilities of synthesis, the differ-

Matisse was preoccupied with drawing in the 1930s, and in 1936 Cahiers d'Art had published an album of his drawings. This essay seems prompted by a desire to refute certain aspects of the preceding selection by Roger-Marx (see the notes below), and thus, like "Notes of a Painter," responds to Matisse's critics as it expounds his ideas.

ent points of view that I could more or less assimilate by my preliminary study.

The jewels or the arabesques never overwhelm my drawings from the model, because these jewels and arabesques form part of my orchestration. Well placed, they suggest the form or the value accents necessary to the composition of the drawing. Here I recall a doctor who said to me: "When one looks at your drawings, one is astonished to see how well you know anatomy." For him, my drawings, in which movement was expressed by a logical rhythm of lines, suggested the play of muscles in action.

It is in order to liberate grace and character that I study so intently before making a pen drawing. I never impose violence on myself; to the contrary, I am like the dancer or tightrope walker who begins his day with several hours of different limbering exercises so that every part of his body obeys him, when in front of his public he wants to give expression to his emotions by a succession of slow or fast dance movements, or by an elegant pirouette.

(As regards perspective: my final line drawings always have their own luminous space, and the objects of which they are composed are on different planes; thus, in perspective, *but in a perspective of feeling*, in suggested perspective.)

I have never considered drawing as an exercise of particular dexterity, rather as principally a means of expressing intimate feelings and describing states of mind, but a means deliberately simplified so as to give simplicity and spontaneity to the expression which should speak without clumsiness, directly to the mind of the spectator.

My models, human figures, are never just "extras" in an interior. They are the principal theme in my work. I depend entirely on my model, whom I observe at liberty, and then I decide on the pose which best suits *her nature*. When I take a new model, I intuit the pose that will best suit her from her un-selfconscious attitudes of repose, and then I become the slave of that pose. I often keep those girls several years, until my interest is exhausted. My plastic signs probably express their souls (a word I dislike), which interests me subconsciously, or what else is there? Their forms are not always perfect, but they are always expressive. The emotional interest aroused in me by them does not appear particularly in the representation of their bodies, but often rather in the lines or the special values distributed over the whole canvas or paper, which form its complete orchestration, its architecture. But not everyone perceives this. It is perhaps sublimated sensual pleasure, which may not yet be perceived by everyone.

Someone called me: "This charmer who takes pleasure in charming monsters." I never thought of my creations as charmed or charming monsters. I replied to someone who said I didn't see women as I represented them: "If I met such women in the street, I should run away in terror." Above all, I do not create a woman, *I make a picture*.

In spite of the absence of shadows or half-tones expressed by hatching, I do not renounce the play of values or modulations. I modulate with variations in the weight of line, and above all with the areas it delimits on the white paper. I modify the different parts of the white paper without touching them, but by their relationships. This can be clearly seen in the drawings of Rembrandt, Turner, and of colorists in general.

To sum up, I work *without a theory*. I am conscious only of the forces I use, and I am driven on by an idea which I really only grasp as it grows with the picture. As Chardin used to say, "I add (or I take away, because I scrape out a lot) until it looks right."

Making a picture would seem as logical as building a house, if one worked on sound principles. One should not bother about the *human* side. Either one has it or one hasn't. If one has, it colors the work in spite of everything.

Roger-Marx: "These young women, adapted to the decor devised to harbor them and decked out in accessories not of their own choosing are . . . nothing but a pretext to assert himself. . . . it is in the volumes or in tonal relationships that he is interested, and never in the soul."

Roger-Marx: "the invincible gifts of this sorcerer—who often charms monsters."

Letter from Matisse to Pierre Bonnard
On Drawing and Color
13 January 1940

Your letter this morning finds me feeling depressed, deeply disheartened, and therefore quite unworthy of your praise, however much in harmony with my desires your words may be. For I find myself paralyzed by I don't know what convention that prevents me from expressing myself as I would like in painting. My drawing and my painting are separated.

My drawing suits me well, for it conveys what I distinctively feel. But my painting is bridled by the new conventions of flat color with which I must express myself completely, purely local colors lacking in shading and modeling, which must react with one another to suggest light, spiritual space. That hardly sits well with my spontaneity, which makes me balance a long period of work in an instant, because I reconceive a painting several times during its execution without really knowing where I'm going, relying on my instinct. After much experimentation, I have arrived at a manner of drawing that has the spontaneity that gives full vent to what I feel, but that technique is exclusively my own, as artist and viewer. But a drawing by a colorist is not a painting. It needs to be given an equivalent in color. That is what I cannot seem to manage.

All the same, I thank you for your kind word, which was a great help to me, for it compelled me to rouse myself and strive to deserve it. What a shame that we cannot see each other more often. . . .

Matisse and Bonnard had corresponded with some frequency since the 1920s.

Letter from Matisse to Pierre Bonnard
On His Situation in Occupied France
17 October 1940

I hope that you received the canvas I sent. After your letter, I saw the man who posted it, who found out from Cannes that the package was delivered at a time when both of you were away. They were supposed to come back the next day. I also hope you liked it. I thank you for your offer to help me find something, but I have decided not to leave Nice and the studio where I have put down roots over the past two years. I can't see starting all over somewhere else. I won't leave here unless I am forced to. I recently received an offer to teach painting at an art school in San Francisco where Jules Romains has taught. I declined. For a thousand reasons. In any case, I can hardly see myself leaving France at the moment, even though I have no idea what the future holds. Who has? Your letter confirms that Rosenberg is in America, while Picasso, who was said to be in Mexico, is simply back in Paris after his trip to Royan, where he spent last summer and winter. I don't know when I will go to Cannes. The trip is far from easy, and it is getting chilly. I got a little cold four or five days ago. I had gone down to Nice, and toward evening the wind changed, turned cold, and that has been enough to keep me inside since Friday. I spent two days in bed—no fever, but a head cold that I feared might turn nasty, as has happened to me so often. I do not expect to go out before the end of this week. It would be too risky to go to Cannes before the means of communication improve. I regret that, but in the meantime we can keep in touch by mail. . . .

[P.S.]I found out from Paris that the German painter Paul Klee, a man of rare sensitivity, is dead.

Paul Rosenberg, an art dealer who had been showing Matisse's work since 1937.

Paul Klee (1879–1940), modern painter and printmaker famous for his playful and poetic imagery.

State I, 3 May 1935

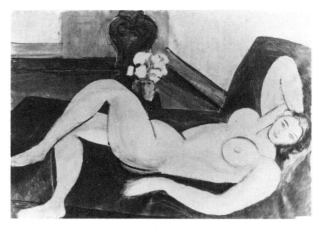

State III, 16 May 1935

State IV, 19 May 1935

State VIII, 28 May 1935

State IX, 29 May 1935

State X, 4 June 1935

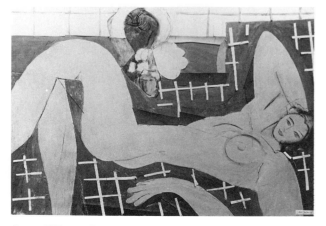

State XI, 20 June 1935

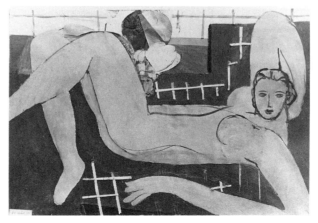

State XII, 20 August 1935

State XIV, 6 September 1935

State XV, 7 September 1935

Sixteen of the twenty-two photographs sent by Matisse to Etta Cone, in letters of 10 September and 16 November 1935, showing states in the development of *Large Reclining Nude*. The Baltimore Museum of Art: Cone Archives.

State XVI, 9 September 1935

State XVII, 14 September 1935

State XVIII, 15 September 1935

State XX, 12 October 1935

State XXI, 16 October 1935

State XXII, 30 October 1935 (definitive)

Letter from Matisse to Pierre Matisse

On Work and Life in Wartime France

1 September 1940

When Nazi Germany occupied France, Matisse considered leaving for America and even procured a visa for Brazil. On 1 September he wrote to his son Pierre, the New York art dealer, explaining why he could not leave France after all.

I am trying hard to settle down to my work. Before arriving here I had intended to paint flowers and fruits—I have set up several arrangements in my studio—but this kind of uncertainty in which we are living here makes it impossible; consequently I am afraid to start working face-to-face with objects which I have to animate myself with my own feelings—Therefore I have arranged with some motion picture agents to send me their prettiest girls—if I don't keep them I give them ten francs. And thus I have three or four young and pretty models whom I have pose separately for drawing, three hours in the morning, three hours in the afternoon. This keeps me in the midst of my flowers and my fruits with which I can get in touch gradually without being aware of it. Sometimes I stop in front of a motif, a corner of my studio which I find expressive, yet quite beyond myself and my strength and I await the thunderbolt which cannot fail to come. This saps all my vitality.

I have seen Bussy very little; he had guests, Gide, etc., literary people, that is, quite a strange crowd to me, so I stay at home. Nevertheless, if I had not written I would have gone to have a cup of tea with them—but I cannot chat and be intimate in their circle in which one does not understand painting. They are absorbed by the war and politics and that tires me and interests me very little.

I shall take a look around Cannes or St. Raphael with a view to moving there in case of need. I am expecting a bird dealer who will, I hope, relieve me of a part [of my collection]. It is not the necessity of doing these things which preoccupies me, but the uncertainty in which we are living and the shame of having undergone a catastrophe for which one is not responsible. As Picasso told me: "It's the Ecole des Beaux-Arts!" If everybody had minded his own business as Picasso and I did ours, this would not have happened.

Matisse in his studio, 1940–41, working on *Nymph in the Forest* (c. 1935–1942/43) with the unfinished *Nymph and Faun with Pipes* (c. 1940–43) in the background. Photograph by Varian Fry.

COLORPLATE 105. *Interior with Egyptian Curtain*. 1948. Canvas. 45¾ × 33⅛″ (116.2 × 84.1 cm).
The Phillips Collection, Washington, D.C.

COLORPLATE 106. *Plum Blossoms, Green Background.* 1948. Canvas. 45⅝ × 35″ (115.9 × 88.9 cm). Private collection.

COLORPLATE 107. *The Pineapple*. 1948. Canvas. 45¾ × 35″ (116.2 × 89 cm).
Alex Hillman Family Foundation, New York.

COLORPLATE 108. *Large Interior in Red.* 1948. Canvas. 57½ × 38¼″ (146.1 × 97. 2 cm).
Photograph: Musée National d'Art Moderne, Centre Georges Pompidou, Paris.

les bêtes de la mer...
H. matisse 50

COLORPLATE 109. *The Beasts of the Sea.* 1950. Paper on canvas (collage).
116⅜ × 60⅝″ (295.5 × 154 cm).
National Gallery of Art, Washington, D.C. Ailsa Mellon Bruce Fund.

COLORPLATE 110. *Chinese Fish*. 1951. Gouache on cut-and-pasted paper.
75^{11}/₁₆ × 35⅞″ (192.2 × 91 cm). Vicci Sperry, Los Angeles.

COLORPLATE 111. *Sorrow of the King.* 1952. Gouache on cut-and-pasted paper. 115 × 155⅞″ (292 × 396 cm).
Photograph: Musée National d'Art Moderne, Centre Georges Pompidou, Paris.

COLORPLATE 112. *Blue Nude, IV.* 1952. Cut-and-pasted paper. 40½ × 29⅛″ (103 × 74 cm). Musée Matisse, Nice.

I hope I shall start painting again soon, but that overwhelms me so—I have to invent and that takes great effort for which I must have something in reserve. Perhaps I would be better off somewhere else, freer, less weighed down. When I was at the other frontier and saw the endless march of those escaping I did not feel the slightest inclination to leave. Yet I had a passport with a visa in my pocket for Brazil. I was to leave on 8 June via Modane and Genoa, to stay a month in Rio de Janeiro. When I saw everything in such a mess I had them reimburse my ticket. It seemed to me as if I would be deserting. If everyone who has any value leaves France, what remains of France? . . .

Letters from Matisse to Charles Camoin
On His Operation and Convalescence
1941

In late 1940, serious intestinal problems halted Matisse's work. Prompted by Camoin, who visited him from Saint-Tropez, he left Nice on 8 January 1941 for surgery in Lyons, expecting only a brief stay; he did not return till 23 May. After surgery for duodenal cancer, he suffered two pulmonary embolisms and a bout with flu. Subsequently, Matisse often worked in a bed or wheelchair, for standing even an hour was made difficult by a prolapsed stomach.

6 JANUARY 1941

I saw the nurse you told me about, and she played a major and happy—very happy—role in my adventure; sometimes one thing leads to another by happy accidents. Your desire to come to see me when you pass through Nice led indirectly to a change in plans. Instead of getting operated on here by some bumbling doctors whom I distrust, I got out of this mess and I leave for Lyons tomorrow night. I'll almost certainly have the operation, which isn't dangerous and will rid me of constant discomfort and of a congenital intestinal malformation which could provoke an occlusion at any moment, possibly at a time when no treatment is available.

So I await your promised visit when you get back to Monaco to thank you for the happy consequences of your influence. Tomorrow evening at 7 o'clock I leave Nice for Lyons, where I arrive at 7 in the morning and go straight to the clinic. I'll keep you up to date about what happens, good or bad. . . .

17 MARCH 1941

Today marks sixty days since my operation. I'm still in bed. Today I put my feet on the floor for ten minutes without lifting my bottom out of bed. All I did was swivel around. You must be surprised. What happened was that although my convalescence was going quite well—I was walking by myself, with my cane, in the clinic hallway, doing 400 meters three times day (what a stag I am!)—a post-operative mishap that had nothing directly to do with the operation (which was and still is perfect) knocked me off my feet forty-six days after the operation and rendered me immobile. It's something to do with circulation, some sort of embolism. I had a lot of pain for a few days, and I had to be patient and just lie in bed. Which is easy enough when you're weak and can't run away anyway. I'm still alive: that's already something. I'll regain a bit of mobility every day, because my lungs—which is where the problem is—have cleared up and I am no longer at risk. Spring is here, and that will help. My daughter, who had left, came back twenty-four hours later, and there you are! Won't you come to Nice this summer to visit your friend? Maybe before the big exhibition? I'll see you because, according to the doctors, I'll be home in three weeks. . . .

16 MAY 1941

I'm still in Lyons!

I've now spent forty days in this hotel, where I checked in for a week in order not to be separated from the surgeon right away. The clinic is crowded, so I had to leave as soon as I was pronounced well, but not yet strong enough for the trip. Since then, I've had a cold—nothing serious, but enough to keep me from leaving; then I got food poisoning from some orange marmalade. Yesterday the doctor finally declared my lung completely clear; it had been rattling. I'm going to take a few days to get some fresh air, but the weather here is so bad—cold, windy, and rainy—that I don't plan on leaving for Nice until next Thursday. . . .

Louis Aragon

HENRI MATISSE, THEMES ET VARIATIONS

"Matisse-in-France"

1943

FROM NATURE

One of the most mysterious things about Matisse, I mean one of those mysteries to which the painter himself draws attention, is that dual attitude towards the model: on the one hand he cannot do without a model, and on the other the model inspires something so detached from itself that, for example, a window opening onto a blue luminous sky produces in the picture a broad black band, or a piece of green and white marble becomes a red network on a black background, and so on. Not to mention the dark girl who becomes, in one particular painting, a mature redhead, and, in one of his drawings, herself in twenty years' time. You will find ten interpretations of the same Arab tapestry hanging here by the window, bearing witness to the painter's faithfulness and unfaithfulness.

And this is surely how he takes us beyond portraiture, in this room

Themes and Variations, Series M: Study of Flowers and Fruit (M1). 1942. Charcoal. 17¾ × 20½" (45 × 52.3 cm). Photograph © Musée des Beaux-Arts.

of his decked out with differing likenesses of the same face, of the same model. Just as I might repeat some hundred times my favorite line:

Amie éclatante et brune

Amie éclatante et brune: *Dazzling and dark friend.*

so Matisse has returned some hundred times to that same face, which is always alike and yet always different. When I tell him humbly what I find disturbing about this apparent contradiction, his need for a model and his detachment from the model, Matisse always insists (I have noticed it repeatedly) on the constant factor in these apparently diverse drawings. In those of this particular model, for instance, the mouth is always the same. Matisse evidently prized the mouth above anything else in this model; it must have been a decisive factor in his choice of her. He points out that it is a perfect mouth, that it corresponds closely to one's idea of a mouth, how wonderfully it is joined to the face with that slight pout of the lower lip, how the two lips not only lie against one another but are pressed against one another, how they curve, how. . . . In short, he is inexhaustible on the subject.

"In my time, you see, we used always to refer to nature, we painted from nature. . . ."

This explanation, which makes education responsible, is of doubtful validity, and Matisse, that free spirit, is well aware of it. He goes on:

"When I draw a mouth it's got to be a real mouth . . . an eye, a real eye. . . . Look, look here . . . and this one, and that one . . . is it an eye, yes or no? It is an eye. . . ."

This is probably just as much a criticism of certain painters whom he has in mind as a defense of what he does himself, or his need for a model. Some painters draw a face: but look at the eye, it's anything you like but not an eye. . . . in the face, it's where the eye should be, and that's all. Nothing of the sort with Matisse. He could put the eye wherever he liked, it would still be an eye. Like this young woman's breast. It is a breast. In the drawing it is not where it is on the young woman. Matisse has drawn it very low. He needed that for the balance of his drawing, one of the series with the veil that I referred to. It's quite true that the breast was needed there. Cover it with your hand and you'll see. It's impossible to leave it out. But it is a breast, not just a line to help out the composition.

THE SIGN-FOR-A-MOUTH

I am almost inclined to see in this contradiction the motive power of Matisse's genius, his fire (to speak like Heraclitus), his war. Perpetually animated by this pair of opposing forces, imitation and invention—when they balance one another a drawing is born and the hand stops. And then Matisse has the twofold feeling that the woman in front of him has dictated the drawing and yet (just as the seaplane forgets its floats) that it has issued from himself and not from her.

This contradiction recurs here in many forms. For instance in the way imitation leads in the end to that which is furthest from portraiture: to a sign. It was in connection with what I said much earlier about signs, and also about the caveman drawings, that Matisse began to speak of his model's mouth and of what he discovered every day about that mouth,

Sketches of "the sign-for-a-mouth," drawn in a letter by Matisse to Aragon, 16 February 1942.

to such an extent that now it always came out the same. So well imitated. So lifelike. Like the mouth, and like his drawings, the other drawings he had made of it. He'd got that mouth at his fingertips . . . d'you see, d'you see? It's always the same mouth. And the result of this knowledge, this skill in reproducing and imitating, is a sign. For he has come to know it so well that now he *writes* it rather than drawing it. The mouth, this particular mouth, has become a hieroglyph. Like the Chinese character that means man, bird, or even mouth. And yet it's still the same mouth we studied so closely, with its slightly pouting lower lip, the lips pressed together in the same way, joined to the face in the same way, the same curve down to the chin. . . . But here we have reached a higher stage of knowledge of this mouth, its sign. . . .

Matisse takes me into the other room to show me something: the drawings for his Ronsard, the mascarons, you know, the same face which is never the same, drawn with a single line. "I hadn't noticed it," he assures me, "somebody pointed it out to me. . . ." And it's true: all the mouths in these faces are drawn in the same way, with no more difference than between different versions of a letter drawn by the same hand, sometimes bigger, sometimes smaller, with certain slight variations which would not mislead a graphologist, a *y* is always a *y*. Here the mouth is somewhat like a 3 on its side, or a sort of complicated S. And it has all the characteristics of the direct drawings, patiently imitated, of the mouth of the model, of one particular model, Mlle. X. . . .

"Well," the painter says triumphantly, "just look . . . isn't this a mouth?"

Exactly in the same tone in which he had said a short while before: "It's an eye!"

* * *

MATISSE CONFESSES

"*To imitate the Chinese* . . ." Matisse says. Here follows the painter's confession, which was not made all at once. I should like to retain the essence of it, I'm afraid of breaking its branches. If he admits that he labored for long years in quest of a theme, or rather of a formula, a sign for each thing, this can be connected with that other admission, the most disturbing one: "I have been working at my craft for a long time, and it's just as if up till now I had only been learning things, elaborating my means of expression."

Once again, what amazing modesty, what scrupulous conscientiousness he shows: that immense lifelong labor, those fifty years of work were merely the preparation of his craft. What is he trying to do? Matisse continues:

"I have shown you, haven't I, the drawings I have been doing lately, learning to represent a tree, or trees? As if I'd never seen or drawn a tree. I can see one from my window. I have to learn, patiently, how the mass of the tree is made, then the tree itself, the trunk, the branches, the leaves. First the symmetrical way the branches are disposed on a single plane. Then the way they turn and cross in front of the trunk. . . . Don't misunderstand me: I don't mean that, seeing the tree through my window, I work at copying it. The tree is also the sum total of its effects upon me. There's no question of my drawing a tree that I see. I have before me an object that affects my mind not only as a tree but also in relation to all sorts of other feelings. . . . I shan't get free of my emotion by copying the tree faithfully, or by drawing its leaves one by one, but only after identifying myself with it. I have to create an object which resembles the tree. The sign for the tree, and not the sign that other artists may have found for the tree: those painters, for instance, who learned to represent foliage by drawing 33, 33, 33, just as a doctor who's sounding you makes you repeat 99. . . . This is only the residuum of the expression of other artists. These others have invented their own sign . . . to reproduce that means reproducing something dead, the last stage of their own emotion."

As he spoke to me I was thinking of Matisse's followers, of all those who imitate him clumsily or too cleverly, but who can see only his superficial gestures: they think they are starting from *his signs,* but they are in fact bound to fail because one can imitate a man's voice but not his emotion.

". . . and the residuum of another's expression can never be related to one's own feeling. For instance: Claude Lorrain and Poussin have ways of their own of drawing the leaves of a tree, they have invented their own way of expressing those leaves. So cleverly that people say they have drawn their trees leaf by leaf. It's just a manner of speaking: in fact they may have represented fifty leaves out of a total two thousand. But the way they place the sign that represents a leaf multiplies the leaves in the spectator's mind so that he sees two thousand of them. . . . They had their personal language. Other people have learned that language since then, so that I have to find signs that are related to the quality of my own invention. These will be new plastic signs which in their turn will be absorbed into the common language, if what I say by their means has any importance for other people. . . ."

And very quickly Matisse adds a truth, his own truth, which sums it all up:

"The importance of an artist is to be measured by the number of new signs he has introduced into the language of art."

Jean Cassou
ART PRESENT
"Matisse's Thought"
1947

Cassou's short book on Matisse, published in 1939, is also excerpted in this volume.

Henri Matisse shares in this orientation. An idealist, intellectualist, whatever term is used, his character and behavior place him among the race of poets born to the mental method. In fact, to define his art we can employ the terms of one of the theoreticians of the idealist doctrine when that doctrine was being expressed in the most absolute, even sterile, form. But we are surprised to find all we need in these terms: "equivalents, metaphors, hyperboles, ellipses, and syncopes."

Matisse has created a language—a rhetoric, if you will—with equivalents, metaphors, hyperboles, ellipses, and syncopes. He has reduced the world of objects to an austere grouping of plastic signs. His master, Gustave Moreau—from whose studio the young brood of Fauves emerged so unexpectedly, not only Matisse and Marquet but also the great Rouault (and that is to the enduring credit of such a generous master)—Moreau had told Matisse: "You will simplify painting." Matisse made the prediction come true. But Impressionism, still burning bright, beckoned its youth to leave painting to its role as interpreter of the full objective and sensual complexity of the visible world. One has only to consider his earliest works, especially *La Desserte* of 1897, to realize that Matisse was as capable as anyone of depicting the fluffy or transparent skin of flavorful objects—fruit, metal, rugs, dishes, everything in the microcosm of a dining room which, bathed in earthly light, excites the senses of taste and touch. Compare these images with the two later versions of *La Desserte* (one in a blue harmony, the other in a red monochrome), with their

This excerpt begins after Cassou's discussion of Matisse in the context of classical idealism, especially in relation to Antoine Quatremère de Quincy's 1837 Essai sur l'Idéal dans ses applications pratiques aux arts du dessin.

COLORPLATE 4

Harmony in Red *had been first painted in a blue harmony.*

COLORPLATE 29

decorative foliage and flat patches of color, and you will see it translated into the language that has become forever Matisse's: Matissian. It is reduced to plastic equivalents, by the will of a lucid and sovereign intelligence.

These equivalents are the arabesque that follows its course, reveals and pursues his intention, and when it must and when it wants, goes all the way to startling hyperbole. The line embodies all the elements that constitute an object's presence. Contour alone has meaning. The various families of artists that make up the history of art refer to one or another element of reality, on the basis of which a kind of hierarchy of values is established. One school will base itself on the primacy of light, which will lead to styles characterized by the play of shadows, either their importance or, conversely, their exclusion. Objects will appear either in marked relief or, conversely, drowned, devoured, and dissolved by shadow or light. Another will start with perspective and combinations of perspective, whether singular or multiple. The family to which Matisse belongs is the one made up of masters who train painters only by bringing them through a door marked *School of Drawing*. The pure line, with no aid from shadow, lays claim to render the greatest possible quantity of reality. And then, after a long period of experimentation, this line, with a marvelous and pleasant modesty, declares itself also ready to bear the burden of those hitherto forbidden properties: volume and expression.

But Matisse's temperament is rich and full. His intellectualism ought not to be taken in the restrictive sense of the word. Matisse uses abstraction, but his is just the opposite of an abstract mind. A draftsman by nature, he nevertheless does more than simply draw. He could never be content to reduce the world's splendor to plane geometry. The world is color, and color, too, must be translated. It demands its own signs and equivalents. And it is here that the most admirable of the revolutions wrought by Matisse bursts forth and here that the most excellent painters of his time have accompanied him, each according to his own genius: Fauvism. Color, through which the succulence of the outside world becomes most visible and enticing, makes its appeal as well (easy prey to avid hunters), but to the intellect. And the intellect responds, for in color it too will find a solution. It will translate color into synthetic signs, simplifying equivalents. So much brilliance and violence will be translated into brilliance and violence, but mentally, ordered by the will, in translation these will also shed their earthly ties, along with everything that the apprehension of them offered of a too haphazard and spontaneous pleasure. Color is sublimated in its pure tone, and in an arbitrary combination of pure tones it recovers its independence and autonomy (just as the line did on the level of drawing) and affords new and prodigious resources which belong to it alone.

Beginning from intellect, Matisse produces an entire painter's oeuvre from which it would seem that the elements have been omitted that tendencies commonly put under the rubric of intellectualism dispense with. But his intellect is satisfied only with totality and is pursuing Poussin's program: neglect nothing. At first we were frivolous enough to place him among the race of draftsmen, even the most abstract of them, and to define him in the terms of the most rigorous professors of the classics, classical to the point of Platonic and academic intellectualism. But in the end we celebrate the colorist in him. For he is a colorist, one of the most subtle, vigorous, and delightful of all time. And his name remains linked to one of the deepest and most joyous revolutions ever effected by color. Matisse's paintings remain the most dazzling miracles of freshness in the realm of color. "Instinct no longer guides. It has lost its way; we search it out." So said the poet Guillaume Apollinaire in his 1907 essay on Matisse. A few lines further on, after discussing the earliest works, he was able to comment, "Instinct has been found again."

Apollinaire's 15 December 1907 article in La Phalange *had been an interview with Matisse and the poet's first study of the artist.*

For indeed these various elements of Matisse's work—which I have split up in the interests of analytical clarity and presented as the subject of a systematic probe conducted, as it were, over time—coexist from the initial affirmation of his own genius. The intellect functions by dividing and distinguishing. But the result appears as a totality. That which is rediscovered and therefore presented as the fruit of analysis is actually present from the outset. Indeed, each particular thing stands in harmony with a whole. It is by study that we unwind each thing over the course of time and at last receive eventually the pleasure of some reward. But that reward was always there, and what we sought was available, to mind and senses alike, as early as 1907.

Having pondered the fate of each element, then, the analyst can become a viewer and delight in the extraordinary novelty of it all, and in what is essentially responsible for the charm and cost of that totality: the range of colors. It is a scale so lively, so sumptuous, so complete that even black has its place, not as an absence but as a color itself, just as much as the other contrasts. Also revealed—revealed through our analytic and didactic fidgeting but actually revealed by the painter in the heat of his

L'Asie. 1946. Canvas. 45¾ × 31⅞″ (116.2 × 81 cm). © Succession H. Matisse 1988. Photograph courtesy Archives Matisse, Collection Claude Duthuit.

effort, as though by the inspiration of his thought—are all the other treasures of the domain of *instinct*, every immediate offering to the senses and the heart without which the findings of the intellect, so purely and strictly intellectual, would be futile, arid, and cold. We attribute the role of mere intervention to external reality. Now let us allow it to intervene fully. It is there, was there, doubtless translated by its signs, though without these signs ever drifting into abstract obscurity. These signs are clearly legible, and from first glance we give them the names dearest to the heart of an inhabitant of our beautiful planet.

Matisse's thought is in no way bitter and never assumes the contorted and distressing airs so often affected by personal intellectual effort. Look at his titles, *La Joie de vivre, Le Luxe,* or those he borrowed from Baudelaire's doctrine in its Elysian aspect: *Luxe, calme et volupté.* The reward implicit in the analysis is truly delightful. And all heartbreak and tragedy must be left aside, even the purely cerebral and imaginary tragedy commonly ascribed to metaphysical quest. Matisse's is a painter's metaphysical quest. His intellectual process, his simplification and schematization, are a painter's. He has discovered the equivalents and signs of objects, but let us refrain from the vulgar assertion that he finds and expresses the essential. The essential! That would be to postulate a *depth* of things that does not exist for painting, which—above all else—concerns itself only with the surface. The whole point is to render an infinity, a luxury, of suggestions with elements which, because simple and chosen, appeared essential to the painter. It is a matter of economy, in Matisse's case of the most knowing and perfect kind. His lines, his intention, even his sometimes excessive affirmation, give all the breadth of form and movement; the colored surface gives all the richness and charm of our universe of sun, women, flowers, and the Mediterranean. These elliptical processes and marvelous crystallizations, through which Matisse's genius matches Mallarmé's, take us to the summit of spiritual dignity. Having reached this peak, keen intelligence breathes with happiness and surveys its conquests, for the eye's pleasure—sovereign pleasure, supreme delight—is here the recompense of the calm and lucid workings of voluptuousness.

COLORPLATE 24
COLORPLATE 13

"Baudelaire's doctrine": The title of Luxe, calme et volupté, *1904–05, had been taken from the refrain of the poet's "Invitation au Voyage."*

Letter from Matisse to Henry Clifford
On the Philadelphia Museum Retrospective
14 February 1948

Henry Clifford (b. 1904), curator of painting at the Philadelphia Museum of Art, organized that Museum's 1948 Matisse retrospective.

I hope that my exhibition may be worthy of all the work it is making for you; your efforts touch me deeply.

However, in view of the great reverberations it may have, seeing how much preparation has gone into it, I wonder whether its scope will not have a more or less unfortunate influence on young painters. How are they going to interpret the impression of apparent facility that they will get from a rapid, even superficial, overall view of my paintings and drawings?

I have always tried to hide my own efforts and wanted my work to have the lightness and joyousness of a springtime which never lets anyone suspect the labors it has cost. So I am afraid that the young, seeing in my work only the apparent facility and negligence in the drawing, will use this as an excuse for dispensing with certain efforts which I believe necessary.

The few exhibitions that I have had the opportunity of seeing during these last years make me fear that young painters may avoid the slow and painful preparation which is necessary for the training of any contemporary painter who claims to construct with color alone. . . .

This slow and painful work is indispensable. Indeed, if gardens were not dug over at the proper time, they would soon be good for nothing. Do we not first have to clear and then to cultivate the soil in season?

The preparatory work of initiation, of renewing, is what I call "cultivating the soil."

When an artist has not known how to prepare for his time of flowering, by work which bears little resemblance to the final result, he has a short future before him; or when an artist who has "arrived" no longer feels the necessity of getting back to the soil from time to time, he ends up going around in circles, repeating himself until, by this very repetition, his curiosity is extinguished.

An artist must possess Nature. He must identify himself with her rhythm, by efforts that prepare for the mastery by which he will later be able to express himself in his own language.

The future painter must be able to foresee what is useful to his development—drawing or even sculpture—everything that will let him become one with Nature, identify himself with her, by penetrating the things—which is what I call Nature—that arouse his feelings. I believe study by means of drawing to be essential. If drawing belongs to the realm of the Spirit and color to that of the Senses, you must draw first to cultivate the Spirit and to be able to lead color through the paths of the Spirit. That is what I want to cry aloud, when I see the work of young people for whom painting is not an adventure, and whose only goal is their impending first exhibition which is to start them on the road to fame.

It is only after years of preparation that the young artist should touch color—not color as description, that is, but as a means of personal expression. Then he can hope that all the images, even the very symbols which he uses, will be the reflection of his love for things, a reflection in which he may have confidence if he has been able to carry out his education with purity, and without lying to himself. Then he will employ color with discernment. He will place it in accordance with a natural, unformulated and completely concealed design that will spring directly from his feelings; this is what allowed Toulouse-Lautrec, at the end of his life, to exclaim, "At last, I no longer know how to draw."

The painter who is just beginning thinks that he is painting from the heart. The artist who has completed his development also thinks that he is painting from the heart. Only the latter is right, because his training and his discipline allow him to accept impulses from within, which he can in part control.

I do not claim to teach; I only want my exhibition not to suggest false interpretations to those who have their own way to make. I should like people to know that they cannot approach color as though it held open house, that one must go through a strict preparation to be worthy of it. But first of all it is clear that one must have a gift for color, as a singer must have a voice. Without this gift one can get nowhere, and not everyone can declare like Correggio, "I too am a painter." A colorist makes his presence known even in a simple charcoal drawing.

My dear Mr. Clifford, here my letter ends. I started it to let you know that I am aware of the trouble you are taking over me at the moment. I see that, obeying an inner necessity, I have made it an expression of what I feel about drawing, color, and the importance of discipline in the education of an artist. If you think that all these reflections of mine can be of any use to anyone, do whatever you think best with this letter. You

The painter Correggio (Antonio Allegri, 1494–1534) is supposed to have uttered "Anch'io son pittore" before Raphael's St. Cecilia in Bologna.

349

may add it, if there is still time, to the explanatory part of your catalogue.

Please accept, Mr. Clifford, the expression of my feelings of deepest gratitude. . . .

Alfred M. Frankfurter
ART NEWS
"Is He the Greatest?"
April 1948

Alfred M. Frankfurter (1906–1965), American art historian and critic.

The number of really great painters alive at any one moment in history—if you balance aesthetic credits and debits as accurately and objectively as entries in a checkbook—is incredibly small. During even so resplendent a flowering as in the middle decades of the fifteenth century, when all Europe blossomed with memorable painting, greatness in the proper sense is attributable to no more than a dozen, if that many, names. Remember, too, that "great" signifies dimension not only in terms of the artist's own time but also in ratio to great artists of other times. Caravaggio is undoubtedly a great painter against the rather barren competition of his own period, but is he still a great painter alongside Titian or Velázquez? What goes for time also goes for nationality: Hogarth is a great painter for all of English history, but is he really great next to Rembrandt or Goya?

Measurement in our own time is, of course, still more difficult. We are not yet quite sure even of relative values *among* the impressionists and post-impressionists (upon whom we can look as on a closed period), less so of their individual masters in relation to the stream of history. Yet we must find the scale of twentieth-century art, precisely because of its multiplicity and complicatedness which make the task so difficult. The very fact that so many widely differing forms of expression today exist side by side with validity for many of them, in direct controversion to the unified stylistic handwriting of all other epochs, imposes a critical obligation to search for the measure out of which alone a standard can evolve.

One such opportunity for evaluation—though, to be hoped, one secondary to the primary purpose of visual pleasure which is its first function—is offered by the unusually complete retrospective exhibition of Henri Matisse which the Philadelphia Museum of Art is offering until 10 May (and which regrettably will not be seen elsewhere in this country). Matisse's own collaboration with his counsel as well as loans of important early works which he has sagely retained for himself, together with other important loans from French and American collections, account for a heretofore unavailable definitive view of an artist who may be called at least one of the most important alive.

Matisse's importance, however, in contradistinction to his inescapable counterpart, the redoubtable Picasso, lies distinctly in his own individuality rather than in his direct influence upon his contemporaries. The present exhibition is significant first of all because we have actually seen so little of Matisse, not only in recent difficult years but over the entire period in which the modern movement, and specifically the School of Paris, may be said to have come of age for itself and in the view of the educated eye. Besides in retrospective and other large exhibitions, Matisse's smaller shows have been outnumbered by Picasso's at least four to one. To Matisse no museum has devoted documentary efforts nor has spent its funds publishing a *catalogue raisonné*, complete with summer addresses and other personalia. The answer can only lie either in quality itself or the talent for what advertising men philosophically call "public relations." Of the latter genius, certainly, Matisse possesses nothing. Those who know him, his serious outer and inner mien, can confirm that he has always meant what he said so long ago, that as a human being he wanted to be only a good husband and father. This does not mean he is not worldly, or witty, or wise in human ways, for he excels in all of these qualities. It does mean, however, that he is not a "clever" man, in the way that Picasso is supremely clever as a man and as an artist.

For that kind of cleverness in life, Matisse substitutes shrewdness and earthiness, which are quite different qualities, defensive instead of offensive, introvert rather than extrovert. They are qualities he shares with Renoir, and though Matisse has none of his predecessor's style or manner, he does also share the idea of pleasure as the objective of art. Of Renoir, the Communist party-line labels in the Moscow Museum say that he lived through the entire period of working-class struggle without ever referring to it in his painting. The same high compliment can be paid to Matisse, and even extended—for he has lived through an age of world struggle, yet he has sought only to bring to that world the poetry and the joy of nature which its battles have trampled beyond most artists' recognition.

This exhibition . . . shows that preoccupation with beauty running as an ineradicable melodic line through all the curious fugue of greater and lesser abstraction, of approach and subject matter, which are evident as recurring, cyclic expressions throughout the fifty-odd years he has been painting. Every now and then, within those years, all these elements seem to resolve themselves into one great chord-like unison. Then, as in a gigantic organ-point of Bach, the whole art of the man can be glimpsed in a single great picture. There is the wonderful year of 1916, with such a masterpiece as *The Studio* from the Phillips Memorial Gallery, or its echo in the marvelous heavy impasto developed in 1926, brilliant in great surfaces like the lode of a rare jewel, as in Mr. W. S. Paley's *Odalisque with Tambourine*. In the between years, now the pattern, now the color, now subject matter, each singly rise to first place and are worked out meticulously, deliberately—or so, at least, as we see them here in the cream of an oeuvre which has always been the most severely and self-critically edited of any living artist's.

The sum proves that comedy, at its best, can be as profound as tragedy. Comedy, that is, in the sense, of *la comédie humaine*, and thus typically and uniquely and wittily French. Thus Matisse is characteristically French, and the question of his stature in the School of Paris may be answered best by a French parable. French painting of the nineteenth century, as Meier-Graefe shows, is characterized by successive pairs of dominant painters. Going backward, there are Gauguin and Van Gogh, Cézanne and Renoir, Manet and Degas, Delacroix and Courbet, David and Ingres. Each, far from resembling or competing on the same ground with the other, complements the other. In that same way, the final answer may be that the logic and vision of French painting still requires dual leadership: Matisse and Picasso. Today's "greatest," then, remains a partnership.

Georges Duthuit
LES FAUVES

1949

Georges Duthuit (1891–1973), art historian, writer, and Matisse's son-in-law.

For me Matisse's work and life were exemplary. He gave me no cause for concern, except by his inability to relax, his killing labor, his absolute incapacity, if only for the space of a tear or a smile, to sit down with his neighbor. "All he lacked, in order to be utterly great, was a little more humanity," said Debussy of Wagner. But on the highest level the painter took part in common life with an extraordinary tension of all his being, with the total participation of his will, with the unsparing conviction and ruinous outpouring of energy required for the accomplishment of the obscure purpose that was to enable him to bring together, in a minimum of gay and lively spots of color, the essence of his character. And in this purpose one could discern fear and torment, because it was possible that help would not come, and one could discern that painful recognition of human limitations, that insatiable, unavowed need of sympathy and succor, which, equally with the need to be reduced to ashes and given broadcast, is a prime condition of love, even among those solitary natures consecrated to creation, who at least are not too proud to accept the consolation of painting or writing. For the paintings of Matisse which then attracted me not only reflected his love for the celestial light, the *gentilissima* which has nothing more for him and for us but smiles and favors. They retained traces of scars, they revealed at the root the existence of the doubt which attaches to the very condition of man and without which, it seems to me, the most radiant stars of happiness shine in the void, with a glacial light. This essential doubt was part and parcel of the possibility of not being utterly confounded in the long passion of things experienced, those things that the painter approached only from very far off, necessarily, since given the slightest degree of lucidity and honesty, we see them totter and crumble to destruction with every passing second. It is perhaps thanks to this struggle with fundamental anguish that Matisse was able to liberate painting from the jumble of grammar and geometry with which it was encumbered. I have admitted that in spite of everything he often loftily affirmed his rigor and his mastery, that in his own sight he possessed his subject like the others, but with this I had no need to concern myself, it is ancient history. The history of Fauvism begins and ends for me only at the moment when the artist radically reverses the direction of his predecessors' quest. Many of these great dramatists, authors of comedies or tragedies in paint or of "characters," real or imaginary, possessed a culture more varied than his, had at their command techniques more versatile and more accomplished and, in some cases, an unequaled creative power. But all of them—and here perhaps I have been guilty of unfairness and excess in my rejection of these "beacons" for the sake of bringing out the difference between them and Matisse—all of them without exception went from themselves to things: the "vibration of the individual" counted less for these vast intelligences than "the object which produces this emotion." With Matisse, the road was reversed, and along his road he encountered the very rare poets who go from the world to themselves: "One renders not matter but human emotion. . . ." And it is in this consciousness that we sometimes succeed in having of ourselves, pygmies in the depths of an abyss of ignorance, that I thought I heard again, beneath the pompous deflagrations of the antagonistic forces harmonized by Fauvism, the groaning source of profound life. It is here that the unique lightning of Baudelaire falls on the one neuralgic point and

Zulma. 1950. Gouache on cut-and-pasted paper. 93¾ × 52⅜" (238 × 133 cm). Statens Museum for Kunst, Copenhagen.

strikes from this fissure of spirit a few limpid and almost unintelligible verses which even a Shakespeare could not have dreamed of. In Matisse's doubt there was an acquiescence in the distress, the anxiety, the suffering of all; there was, and this I never doubted, a true tenderness.

Alfred H. Barr, Jr.

MATISSE, HIS ART AND HIS PUBLIC

"Matisse's Critical Position Since the War"

1951

The big retrospectives of 1948–1949–1950 in Philadelphia, Nice, Lucerne and Paris and a small but important show of his recent canvases at Pierre Matisse's gallery in New York in 1949 gave new opportunities for critical appraisal of Matisse's achievement. Matisse had emerged from the war with a moral position, a prestige, second only to that of Picasso among the artists active in France. And his artistic position among the younger artists of Paris was much stronger than it had been before the war. During the two decades between 1920 and 1940 Matisse had continued to rank as one of the greatest living French painters, but he had not been a leader of the young to nearly the same degree as Picasso, Léger, the abstract painters around Mondrian, the surrealists such as Miro, Arp, Ernst and Dali, or even his own contemporary, Rouault. However sought-after his new paintings were by collectors, the younger artists and critics of the 1930s tended to think of him as an established painter with a great past but little current significance. The *Lady in Blue* . . . is one of Matisse's representative paintings of 1937: it was finished a few days before Picasso began his *Guernica*. No one, of course, thought of comparing them. But even Matisse's major works of the 1930s, such as the Barnes mural and the settings for the *Rouge et Noir*, can scarcely compete with the black and white fury of *Guernica*.

In the art of post-war Paris and its outposts on the Riviera, *Sturm und Drang* had practically disappeared. Picasso, who had drawn his frightful *Charnel-house* in 1945, was within a couple of years engaged in painting lively pastoral frolics on mural-size canvases, or small ones on ceramic plates and vases. Rouault, the stern religious moralist, announced that now, in his advanced years, he was going to paint more like Bonnard and Matisse. Surrealism, too, with its Freudian poetry and prose, had disintegrated along with such lesser but significant groups as the Neo-Romantics and the painters of geometric abstractions in the tradition of Mondrian.

It is significant that in 1946 the Communist Aragon should have defended Matisse under the title *Apologie du Luxe* and that in 1949 Georges Duthuit, in a subtle and beautiful essay called *Matisse and Byzantine Space*, should have pointed out that the "well-meaning intentions" of the socialist realists in their efforts to create a "communal" art "are drastically cancelled by sterile techniques which make their work incomparably more remote from the masses than the exceptional creations painted by Matisse."

Just after the war the most talked-of younger painters were talented

Barr's landmark monograph, excerpted here, provides a good overview of Matisse's critical position in 1951 and is a fine example of Barr's synthetic approach to significant issues.

COLORPLATE 87

Aragon, Apologie du luxe, *Paris, 1946;* Duthuit, "Matisse and Byzantine Space," Transition Forty Nine, *no. 5, 1949.*

eclectics like Tal Coat, Pignon, Bazaine, Gischia, Marchand—men mostly in their forties who depended variously upon their seniors Picasso, Bonnard—and Matisse. They wanted to paint, to use color and line, without program or dogma, and for them the art of Matisse served as a beacon even when the form or color of some other master appeared to be a stronger influence upon the individuals. Edouard Pignon, for instance, finds the color of Matisse "impossible to translate into black and white" and praises his painting as a thing to "meditate upon for its purity of color and admirable economy of means."

As the decade wore on, the work of these painters and their companions grew generally more abstract (except for a few who tried conscientiously to submit to Communist dictation). In fact, abstract painting for the first time became the strongest movement in Paris. It was not, however, the ruled line abstraction of Mondrian, but its opposite, the free arabesque of early Kandinsky mingled with the crystalline iridescence of Villon or the sweeping calligraphy of Magnelli and the younger leader, Hans Hartung. Of the living "old masters," it was Matisse again, especially in his latest work, who perhaps stood closest to the new wave of abstraction.

Jean Bazaine is not the greatest of the younger painters but he is characteristic enough to make his opinion of Matisse significant. In 1949 he stated to Robert Vrinat that without wishing to establish a categorical hierarchy of values he preferred Matisse to all others, and admired him for the power and expressiveness which he gave to line, to the arabesque. He emphasized his astonishing capacity for creation and renewal as demonstrated in his recent works.

Gischia, more conservative, praises Matisse for his "love and use of color for itself and his drawing, always bound essentially to a model, but not to imitate it so much as extract from it all possible artistic riches."

Neither painter refers to the fact that Matisse had himself become an "abstract" artist during the 1940s. Many of his cut-and-pasted-paper designs such as the "lagoons" in *Jazz* are virtually pure abstractions though remotely related to organic or geographical forms.

These remarks about Matisse were made à propos of the comprehensive exhibition of his paintings, drawings and cut-and-pasted-papers of 1947–1948, which had just opened in Paris in June 1949. Some of the best of this exhibition, including the finest paintings of early 1948, had already been shown in New York at Pierre Matisse's early in 1949. There this late flowering of Matisse's art was received with general astonishment and delight. The most enthusiastic review was written by Clement Greenberg. Greenberg is given at times to somewhat reckless exaggeration, but his criticism is significant in part because he is also a painter closely associated with the most conspicuous new American movement of the 1940s called variously Abstract Expressionism or symbolic abstraction or, simply, the "New York School"—though the movement is nationwide and particularly active on the West Coast. Whatever its label, the movement involved some of the most vigorous younger talents in American painting—such men as Pollock, Baziotes, de Kooning, Motherwell, and the late Arshile Gorky. In spite of the abstract appearance of their paintings these artists did not think of themselves as abstract painters. Far more than their work indicated they were striving for an art in which natural forms, including human figures, would once more *emerge* but without any sacrifice of spontaneity or of the direct impact, purity and reality of the painted surface as the primary instrument of their emotions. For these American painters as well as for their French colleagues Matisse began to have a special significance.

The year before, Greenberg had been involved in a controversy with George L. K. Morris, another younger writer, painter and collector who had developed within the cubist tradition during the 1930s. The argument was opinionated, as is fitting in a debate between painter-critics, but

Matisse in Vence, 1942. Photograph by
André Ostier.

throws some light on the conflicting but changing attitudes toward Matisse. Greenberg led off with an article, "The Decline of Cubism," in the *Partisan Review* of March 1948. Cubism, in Greenberg's mind, included all the abstract movements of the previous forty years, a serious historical confusion which does not however becloud his essential question as to "why the cubist generation and its immediate successors have . . . fallen off in middle and old age, and why belated impressionists like Bonnard . . . could maintain a higher consistency of performance during the last fifteen years. . . . And, finally, why Matisse, with his magnificent but transitional style, which does not compare with Cubism for historical importance, is able to rest so securely in his position as the greatest master of the twentieth century, a position Picasso is further than ever from threatening."

In the June 1948 issue of the *Partisan Review* George L. K. Morris calls Greenberg's article "irresponsible" and compares it to a tennis tournament in which "Umpire Greenberg charts the last rounds somewhat as follows: the expected champions (Picasso, Braque, Arp, etc.) have lost their punch, and no new blood is coming along—so to everyone's surprise, a couple of Old Timers (Matisse, Bonnard), who have been relying all these years on poky lobs and drop shots rather than spectacular rushes to the net, were the ones to reach the finals after all. I do not feel that anything as elusive as the ultimate values of contemporary art can be graded as simply as this, certainly not without considerable substantiation. And such a prearranged result might prove highly irritating to a different referee, who thought he saw Matisse pass out of the tournament in love sets around 1917."

To this, in the same issue, Greenberg writes a "Reply." Concerning Morris's opinion that Matisse passed "out of the tournament in love sets around 1917," Greenberg feels that anyone with a real "'instinct for pictorial structure' would have been unable to write that. This is what happens when literal a priori dogmas about the historically necessary are consulted instead of the pleasure and exaltation to be experienced from painting. Historical necessity does operate, but not with the consistency here expected of it."

The Philadelphia exhibition could not include Matisse's paintings of 1948 such as the *Egyptian Curtain* and *Large Interior in Red*. When these were shown in New York in February of the following year, Greenberg wrote in *The Nation*:

COLORPLATE 105
COLORPLATE 108

> The supremacy of Matisse among living painters is a consolation, but it also offers a peculiar problem. Picasso and Braque painted in the decade 1909–1920 what I think are by and large the most important pictures so far of our century. Yet neither appears to be the complete painter by instinct or accomplishment that Matisse is—the brush-wielder and paint-manipulator par excellence, the quiet, deliberate, self-assured master who can no more help painting well than breathing. Matisse may at times execute superficial work, he may do so for years, but he will never lack sensuous certainty. I do not think we can say the same of Picasso or Braque. . . .
>
> However genuine the pleasure received from Matisse's later canvases, it had to be conceded that this pleasure had begun to thin out and that the emotion which had moved us in his masterpieces of the years before 1920 was being replaced by virtuosity. Yet it was always to be expected that some glorious final statement, such as those Titian, Renoir, Beethoven, Milton had issued, would come from him—all the more in so far as his art, pre-cubist in essence if not in inflection, seemed less involved in the crises that had overtaken post-Cubism in the early thirties and better able, precisely because of its greater conservatism, to produce a second flowering.
>
> This expectation has not been disappointed. . . . The present show at Pierre Matisse's (through February) of paintings done in 1947 and 1948 and of drawings and paper cut-outs done since 1945 offers a most effective refutation of those who may still doubt that Matisse is the greatest living painter.

Greenberg's enthusiasm may be balanced by a remark made by another young American painter and writer, Robert Motherwell: "Matisse may be the greatest living painter but I prefer Picasso: he deals with love and death." To which one might reply, on the same level, yes, but Matisse deals with love and life.

Janet Flanner
MEN AND MONUMENTS
"King of the Wild Beasts"
1957

Janet Flanner (1892–1978), American author and journalist. Two "newsletters" for The New Yorker (*under her pseudonym Genêt*), *written from abroad in 1951 and 1954, formed the basis for this selection from her 1957 memoir.*

In 1945, after the Liberation, the Salon d'Automne, which was where Matisse had started from, amid jeers, in 1905, honored him with a large retrospective, afterward repeated in the Victoria and Albert Museum, in London. His pictures were not satisfying to the people of either nation, emotionally depleted by war and by then overflowing with dreams of

COLORPLATE 113. *The Snail*. 1952. Gouache on cut-and-pasted paper. 112⅝ × 113″ (286 × 287 cm).
The Tate Gallery, London.

COLORPLATE 114. *The Sheaf.* 1953. Painted cut-and-pasted paper. 115¾ × 137¾″ (294 × 350 cm).
Wight Art Gallery, University of California, Los Angeles.

COLORPLATE 115. *The Parakeet and the Mermaid.* 1952. Cut-and-pasted paper and charcoal.
$132^{11}/_{16} \times 304^{3}/_{8}''$ (337 × 773 cm). Stedelijk Museum, Amsterdam.

COLORPLATE 116. *Large Decoration with Masks.* 1953.
Painted cut-and-pasted paper, brush and ink.
139¼ × 392½″ (353.7 × 997 cm). National Gallery of Art,
Washington, D.C. Ailsa Mellon Bruce Fund.

COLORPLATE 117. *Apollo.* 1953.
Painted cut-and-pasted paper,
brush and ink.
128¾ × 166½″ (327 × 423 cm.)
Moderna Museet, Stockholm.
Photograph: Statens Konstmuseer.

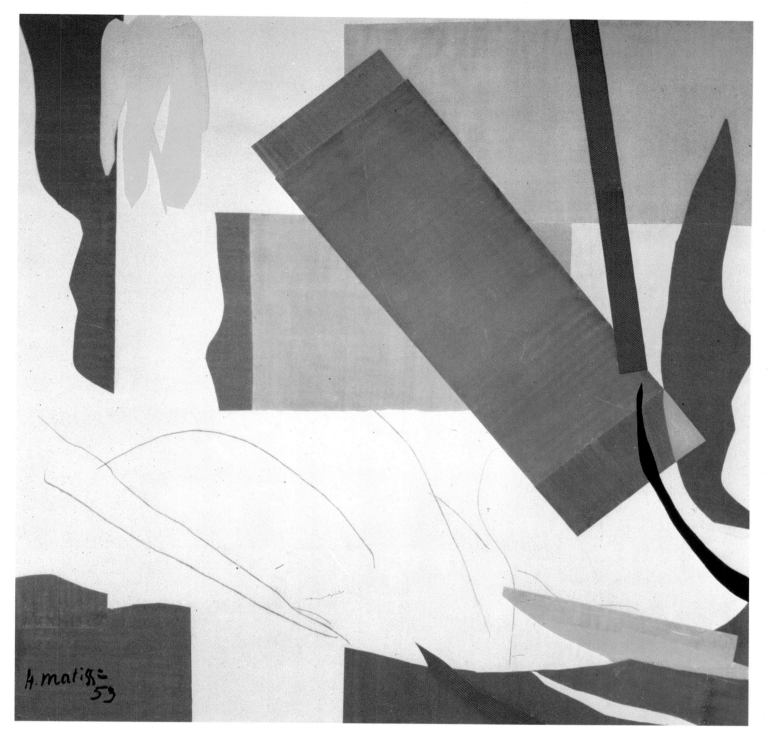

COLORPLATE 118. *Memory of Oceania.* 1953. Gouache and crayon on cut-and-pasted paper over canvas.
112 × 112⅞″ (284.5 × 286.7 cm). Collection, The Museum of Modern Art, New York. Mrs. Simon Guggenheim Fund.

COLORPLATE 119. *The Swimming Pool* (installation view). 1952. Nine-panel mural in two parts (one section shown). Gouache on cut-and-pasted paper mounted on burlap. 90⅝ × 333½″ (230.2 × 847 cm). Collection, The Museum of Modern Art, New York. Mrs. Bernard V. Gimbel Fund.

peace. A Picasso exhibition held simultaneously at the Victoria and Albert provoked a landslide of angry letters in the London newspapers. Matisse's women, as decoratively distant from reality as ever, seemed too far from the physical struggles people had been through, and Picasso's jagged lines too close to what looked like the debris of bombing. In a sharp, brief swing away from the modern times, which had almost extinguished them, bomb-exhausted, ill-fed people, in their survival, on both sides of the Channel, yearned for older, more emotional art, with inspiration in it, and nobility, and faith, and possibly even angels. It was not till 1947 that Matisse's popularity returned, and then it was redoubled. He became—and to his death remained, so museum men and art dealers said—on both sides of the Atlantic the most popular French artist. Their explanation was simple. They said that people who cared about modern art were looking at his and buying it again because they again loved what he painted and had always painted, which gave them notions of beauty, with sensuous, exquisite color, in his own specific palette. He knew success early and late, with little in between, and, at the latest time of all, he was at his zenith. Art dealers often take a one-third commission on pictures, and the facts of life in the painting profession are mercenary indeed. In the early 1950s, a forty-by-fifty-inch Matisse sold for from twelve thousand to twenty thousand dollars—and for even more if it was a canvas particularly characteristic of a special year or period. Matisse had sometimes been short of sales, and of money, in years even when his fame was high. Pictures that were not valued at what he thought they should fetch he kept, as illustrations of stages in his career. Furthermore, he refused to sell certain of his pictures that especially pleased him. As early as 1926, in his Clamart studio when he still badly needed funds, he declined to sell one of his pictures to a rich American lady. Baffled, she asked why. "Because," he answered concisely, "if I sold the painting I would have only the money. And you would have my picture." Matisse is believed to have painted two thousand pictures (as against the twelve thousand pictures that Renoir is believed to have painted in his long lifetime). Because he would not sell himself short, Matisse had a large collection of Matisses. He kept most of them in a bank vault in Nice. As he said of them, *Ce sont des valeurs.* He also owned a small collection of good pictures by other artists who failed at one time or another to sell. He possessed a fine Soutine landscape and several Cézannes and Renoirs. He always regretted a Gauguin he missed when he was poor. He had asked his younger brother, in the family grain business up north, to lend him the cash to buy it. The sum was exactly equal to the price of a good, new bicycle, which his brother bought instead.

Ce sont des valeurs: *They're secure assets.*

In 1951, Matisse began painting pictures again after his four years of work on the Vence chapel. He started by painting his brunette model Paule in a chair, still using a china plate for a palette, as he always had. His only complaint was that he had to fight against the facility that comes with age. Work continued to be the only thing that interested him. "It has never amused me to amuse myself," he often stated. He had the dry speaking voice of the northern French, which, with its special intonation, makes its own scale. In describing what he had aimed at in his painting, he mostly used music as a metaphor—chords, singing colors, and so on. He was an explicit, logical talker, who also, when painting, enjoyed listening to gossip, which he did not repeat. He talked rapidly, and when he became absorbed—especially in talking art with somebody he knew well—almost telegraphically, omitting verbs and reducing his sentences to ellipses of his thoughts; these ellipses were marked by precision and lucidity, and were always perfectly intelligible. With outsiders, he was reserved, punctilious and didactic, for they always asked questions. Not long before his death he succinctly said to a visitor, with the usual curiosities, "Modern is a style. Style is what explains why painters today don't paint in the manner of Titian, for example. They don't see things the way Titian did. The way enough painters—or a dominantly talented painter—see things is what makes for style."

Those who knew Matisse intimately said that only to slight acquaintances did his formal, measured, bourgeois personality seem inappropriate to his sensuous art. They said that the more a student or a critic studied his painting, the more he realized that it represents the fundamental, organized construction that was characteristic of the man. Friends admired him as a heroic, Olympian figure; they were aware that, although he maintained friendships, he made no sacrifices for them, because he preferred making sacrifices only for work. His manner was never intimate. One friend said with admiration that he was *dur comme un tigre,* that his truths were complex, and that he had fought implacably to preserve them even in solitude and during his unpopularity. His maxims about painting were wise, if alarming. To a student who came asking advice, he said, "You want to paint? Start by cutting your tongue out, for you ought to express yourself only with your brushes." "Everything not useful in a composition is harmful to it," he told someone else. His loneliness and philosophy he summed up by saying, "An artist's only enemies are his bad paintings." He rarely talked of his career. He knew his worth early, but his fame came late, and when it arrived, it was as if he had become quite accustomed to its weight in advance. He had an incredible visual memory for his work of the last twenty years, and could recall the multiple stages of any given composition, and where each was painted. When important visitors from the outside world would call, he always asked the news of other famous elderly figures, such as Benedetto Croce, of Naples, or Arturo Toscanini, of New York: How are they holding up? Exactly how do they look now?

During his last years he always received a few local friends and acquaintances in his studios from time to time. He enjoyed the visits of several handsome, privileged young women from among the musicians and writers of Nice and St. Paul, the intellectuals' hill town near Vence. He often saw his art publisher, Tériade, who lived close by on the coast. He saw Mrs. Dorothy Bussy, sister of Lytton Strachey and a translator of André Gide. He used to see Gide, who, he said, was a prisoner of his professional personality, his cape, his big hat and his books. Matisse's bright eyes always sparkled when he was amused by his own malice. With familiars, he had the unvarnished candor of old people and children. He was not witty but Frenchily apropos. His most quoted shaft was directed toward a lady who had asked him where modern art was going. "Can't you ask me a *little* question about art, Madame?" he ventured. He reserved a special, formal manner for his neighbor Picasso, who then was living in the town of Vallauris, not far from Nice. They called back and forth occasionally, and after nearly half a century still saluted each other by their last names.

Hugo Munsterberg
TWENTIETH CENTURY PAINTING
"Henri Matisse"

1951

If there is one painter of the twentieth century who equals Picasso in the greatness of his achievement as well as the influence he has exerted, it is the French artist Henri Matisse. Today at eighty, Matisse is the grand old

Dur comme un tigre: *Tough as a tiger.*

Hugo Munsterberg (b. 1916), American art historian who has written extensively on Oriental art.

man of modern painting just as Frank Lloyd Wright, who was born in the same year, is the dean of modern architects, and such a distinguished critic as Albert C. Barnes, who owns no less than seventy-five pictures by Matisse, has referred to him as the most important living painter. Whatever the judgment of the future, there can be no doubt that Henri Matisse was the first of the twentieth century artists to paint in the modern idiom. Unlike Picasso, who has always reflected the ideas and temper of the period in which he was working, Matisse has been more concerned with purely formal elements and has in many ways remained closer to the great tradition of French painting. Nothing could characterize his attitude better than his own famous saying: "What I dream of is an art of balance, purity and serenity devoid of troubling or depressing subject matter, an art which might be for every mental worker, be he businessman or writer, like an appeasing influence, like a mental soother, something like a good armchair in which to rest from physical fatigue." It is not surprising that the author of these words should have continued painting his beautiful, decorative pictures of nudes and still lifes and landscapes throughout the wars and disturbances of our chaotic age.

Françoise Gilot and Carlton Lake
LIFE WITH PICASSO
1964

Francois Gilot (b. 1921), French painter, author, and illustrator, lived and worked with Picasso 1946–1953. Art critic Carlton Lake had interviewed Picasso several times for the American press before collaborating with Gilot.

Of all the artists Pablo knew and visited during the years I spent with him, no one meant quite as much to him as Matisse. At the time we made our first call on Matisse in February 1946 . . . he was living in a villa called *Le Rêve* in Vence. He had moved there from Cimiez, up in the hills above Nice, where he had gone to convalesce following two very serious operations he had undergone in Lyons in the spring of 1941. The nurse who took care of him in Cimiez had her heart set on becoming a nun. She was young and pretty and it was she who posed for all the drawings he made to illustrate Tériade's edition of *Letters of a Portuguese Nun*. In 1943 Matisse moved to Vence. Across the street from his villa was a Dominican convent. Later on, his former nurse—now Soeur Jacques—came there as a novice, and often visited him. On one of her calls she brought him a design she had made for a stained-glass window to decorate a new oratory the order was planning to build. As a result of their discussions and of others Matisse had with a Dominican novice named Brother Raysséguier [sic] and with Father Couturier, also a Dominican and the leading exponent of modern art in religious circles, Matisse found himself a prime mover in the construction and decoration of the Dominican chapel in Vence.

Matisse was confined to his bed for three-quarters of the day but that didn't dampen his enthusiasm for the project. He had paper fixed to the ceiling over his bed, and at night, since he didn't sleep much, he would draw on it with a piece of charcoal attached to the end of a long bamboo stick, sketching out the portrait of St. Dominic and other elements of the decoration. Later, he would roll around in his wheelchair and transfer his drawings to large ceramic squares covered with a semi-mat enamel on which he could draw in black.

Matisse's idea was that there should be no color inside the chapel, other than what came in with the light shining through the stained-glass windows. He laid out the maquettes for the glass in much the same manner he used for the *papiers découpés* on which he spent a good part

Brother L.B. Rayssiguier, a seminarian with architectural training who helped Matisse launch his chapel project, though unfamiliar with the artist's work when he met him in 1947. Father Pierre-Charles-Marie Couturier (1897–1954), Dominican priest, editor of L'Art Sacré, and painter who helped revive Church-commissioned religious art and was artistic adviser for the decoration of the church of Notre-Dame-de-Toute-Grâce in Assy, for which Matisse did a ceramic panel of St. Dominic.

of his last years. He had Lydia paint large pieces of paper in various tones for background and pin them against the wall in the areas he indicated to her. He then showed her, with his stick, where to place the cut-out pieces in other colors with which he formed his composition. He did three series of maquettes. The first was extremely geometric and very successful on its own terms but he decided not to use it because it did not create just the effect he wanted. The next was very much in the spirit of Tahitian foliage, akin to the one he finally used, but with different proportions. The color range he was working with included ultramarine, a deep yellow, and a green. He wanted each element to have about the same dimensions as the others so that the light entering through them would be uniformly divided. And so he asked for something that had not been done until then: that the glass should be frosted on the outside. He reasoned that if it were not frosted, the blue, for example, would give a great deal less luminosity than the yellow and wouldn't remain on the same plane. With the glass frosted, the luminosity would be uniform throughout. But once the windows were placed in the chapel, they gave a kind of uniform pink-mauve light. And when it reflected on the forty ceramic squares which Matisse had ordered to be semi-mat but which were actually rather shiny, it left a mauve reflection, which wasn't a very pleasing effect; certainly not what he had intended.

Pablo thought it wasn't successful. "If Matisse had realized that the light inside the chapel was going to become this pinkish mauve," he said after one of our visits to the chapel, "he would have been better off to have used some other colors inside the chapel to counteract that effect. If the chapel was supposed to be white and black, there should have been no color except maybe a spot of red or something very clear-cut, but not that pink-mauve. That makes the place look like a bathroom."

*   *   *

On our previous visit Pablo had said to Matisse, "You're crazy to make a chapel for those people. Do you believe in that stuff or not? If not, do

Matisse using a bamboo pole to draw, while bedridden in the Hôtel Régina, Nice, 15 April 1950. To the left: *Studies of Saint Dominic*, 1948–49. To the right: *The Thousand and One Nights*, June 1950, and *The Beasts of the Sea*, also 1950, and the early state of a single-panel cut-out, *The Japanese Mask* (early 1950?), immediately above the bed. Photograph courtesy Arts Council of Great Britain/ photograph by *Paris-Match* (Carone).

Matisse preparing drawings for the
Dominican Chapel at Vence, 1949.
Robert Capa/Magnum Photos, Inc.

you think you ought to do something for an idea that you don't believe
in?" Matisse was telling this to Father Couturier as we arrived that day
and Father Couturier replied, "You can say what you want to about Picasso, but he paints with his blood." Obviously that was designed to please
Pablo, but Pablo wasn't in the mood to be seduced by a phrase, however
flattering it might be, and he began to repeat what he had said to Matisse on our earlier visit. "But why are you doing these things? I'd ap-
prove of your doing them if you believed in what they represent, but if
you don't, I don't think you have any moral right to do them."

"As far as I'm concerned," Matisse said, "this is essentially a work of
art. It's just that I put myself in the state of mind of what I'm working
on. I don't know whether I believe in God or not. I think, really, I'm
some kind of Buddhist. But the essential thing is to put oneself in a
frame of mind which is close to that of prayer."

*　　*　　*

Matisse could afford the luxury of being Pablo's friend. It was more important for him to see Pablo, even with the sarcastic remarks and occasional ill temper that Pablo indulged in than not to see him. He had a
kind of paternal attitude toward Pablo and that, too, helped, because in
friendship it was always Pablo who took and the others who gave. In their
meetings, the active side was Pablo; the passive, Matisse. Pablo always
sought to charm Matisse, like a dancer, but in the end it was Matisse who
conquered Pablo.

"We must talk to each other as much as we can," he told Pablo one
day. "When one of us dies, there will be some things the other will never
to able to talk of with anyone else."

*　　*　　*

One day when we were visiting Matisse, he showed us some catalogs he
had received from his son Pierre, an art dealer in New York. They contained reproductions of paintings by Jackson Pollock and others of that
persuasion.

"I have the impression that I'm incapable of judging painting like that," Matisse said after we had finished looking at the catalogs, "for the simple reason that one is always unable to judge fairly what follows one's own work. One can judge what has happened before and what comes along at the same time. And even among those who follow, when a painter hasn't completely forgotten me I understand him a little bit, even though he goes beyond me. But when he gets to the point where he no longer makes any reference to what for me is painting, I can no longer understand him. I can't judge him either. It's completely over my head.

"When I was young, I was very fond of Renoir's painting. Toward the end of the First World War, I found myself in the Midi. Renoir was still living, but very old. I still admired him and I decided to call on him at *Les Collettes,* his place at Cagnes. He received me in very friendly fashion and so, after a few more visits, I brought him a few of my paintings, to find out what he thought of them. He looked them over with a somewhat disapproving air. Finally he said, 'Well, I must speak the truth. I must say I don't like what you do, for various reasons. I should almost like to say that you're not really a good painter, or even that you're a very bad painter. But there's one thing that prevents me from telling you that. When you put on some black, it stays right there on the canvas. All my life I have been saying that one can't any longer use black without making a hole in the canvas. It's not a color. Now, you speak the language of color. Yet you put on black and you make it stick. So even though I don't like at all what you do, and my inclination would be to tell you you're a bad painter, I suppose you are a painter, after all.'"

Matisse smiled. "You see, it's very difficult to understand and appreciate the generation that follows. Little by little, as one goes through life, one creates not only a language for himself, but an aesthetic doctrine along with it. That is, at the same time one establishes for himself the values that he creates, he establishes them, at least to a degree, in an absolute sense. And so it becomes all the more difficult for one to understand a kind of painting whose point of departure lies beyond one's own point of arrival. It's something that's based on completely different foundations. When we arrive on the scene, the movement of painting for a moment contains us, swallows us up, and we add, perhaps, a little link to the chain. Then the movement continues on past us and we are outside it and we don't understand it any longer."

Matisse was not always so tolerant of abstract painting. See the 1953 account by Marie Raymond, further in this volume.

Bernard Berenson

ESSAYS IN APPRECIATION
"Encounters with Matisse"
May 1955

An Italian version of this essay, "Incontri con Matisse," was published in La Biennale di Venezia, *no. 26, December 1955.*

Just before the first world war I went to the studio of Matisse with Anne, the daughter of J. P. Morgan, the great New York banker and collector. I found the walls of the studio lined with casts of Cambodian sculpture, and as I looked at his paintings I told him that there were in them too many reminders of Cambodian art. He firmly denied it and when I said "but look at what you have on your walls!" he either did not know that the casts were of Cambodian reliefs or—what my experience with artists tells me is more likely—he was unaware of having been influenced by them.

As he was still anything but prosperous I wanted to get something from him and I espied a rather rough painting of a forest clearing and asked what he wanted for it. Five hundred francs (gold francs of course) was all he asked and I gave it gladly and carried away the canvas. . . .

I did not see Matisse again for many years. Instinctively I avoid in every walk of life the individual who is having his day. Matisse had meanwhile been recognized as one of the best artists of his time with no rivals except Picasso. Towards the end he too fell under the spell of the Catalan magician and I deplored this subservience and almost lost interest in him.

In 1950, stopping over at Nice on my way back from Paris, it occurred to me to telephone to the great master who was then living at Cimiez. He remembered me and gave me an appointment. I found him living in one of those huge *pueblos* that had been meant before the first world war to serve as an hotel for a wealthy *clientèle* and had subsequently been divided up into big and small apartments. We rang at the door and a handsome, rather severe young Russian woman let us in, made us wait a few minutes and then led us into the presence. While waiting I looked at the white walls. They were scrawled over with huge, heavily drawn bold sketches for the chapel at Vence. . . .

Matisse was lying, or rather sitting up, in a huge bed, bridged over by a wide table on which there was ample room for his drawing material, pencils, charcoal, yellowish paper in abundance. To right and left two revolving bookshelves within reach of his hands. At his feet several fine Angora cats. His look was majestic and benign, very different from the gaunt, perhaps somewhat undernourished face that I first saw nearly fifty years before. I can never resist giving a sharp look at books within the reach of my eyes and I saw that among all those assembled round him there was not a single one that did not speak of him and of his art. He was kindly condescending, *un très grand seigneur,* spoke of Vence, in his opinion the greatest achievement of his career, mentioned none of the Steins except "Sally," who was still surviving and established in California. He asked me nothing whatever about myself nor did he refer in the slightest to what I had done for him forty years ago. But he did ask about the landscape I had bought from him, wondering whether I still owned it.

Un très grand seigneur: *A very grand lord.*

As we got up I noticed in a corner of his room a cast of the ultra-archaic Dion from Athens and a few casts or perhaps originals of southeast Asiatic and Pacific sculpture. As she led us out the young Russian woman showed me with almost religious fervor other rooms, the walls of which were filled with huge sketches for the chapel of Vence.

My conclusion about Matisse is that in the neck-and-neck race with Picasso for the highest place in the art of the last fifty years he ended by coming in second.

André Verdet

ENTRETIENS NOTES ET ECRITS SUR LA PEINTURE

"The Chapel at Vence"

1978

Verdet's interviews with the aged Matisse, which date from c. 1952, were not published until 1978.

For months and months the completion of the Vence chapel took up a major part of Matisse's creative energy. In so doing, he hoped to fulfill the promise he had made to Sister Jacques, the young nurse from the Lacordaire home, when she was taking care of the painter, who, re-

covering from a serious operation, was staying at the villa *Le Rêve,* on a
hillside near Vence not far from the home. Granted that Sister Jacques
showed a devoted insistence and candid obstinacy, we shouldn't forget
the impassioned and stubborn young Dominican who was there then,
Brother Reyssiguier [sic], who came to take care of himself at the home,
and of whose obscure death I recently learned. The work which led to
the completion was not always without its storms. . . . Reyssiguier was always there, stubborn, sometimes risking an argument, insisting with both
firmness and charm.

After its completion, the chapel remained a major concern for Henri
Matisse, an oft-hidden concern that would reappear depending on circumstances. He spoke about it to his friends, people who came to visit
him, and to newcomers: "Have you seen my chapel, and what do you
think of it?" Many of his interviews of that time dealt with the chapel,
responses to questions as much of an aesthetic as of a spiritual nature.
Did he himself not confide to me, in 1952: "Much has been said and
written. Heaps of rumors were spread in Europe and in America. The
work of art was no longer but a pretext for rumors.

"To begin with, sacred art calls for good moral hygiene. My only religion is that of the love of the work to be created. I did the chapel only
with a feeling for expressing myself in depth. This gave me the opportunity to express myself in the totality of form and color. The job was a
lesson for me. I played the game of equivalencies in it. I balanced material of a crude nature with precious material. A multiplicity of plots
became unity of plot.

"Red could not be introduced into the chapel. Red does exist, how-

*Matisse began work on designs for the
Dominican Chapel at Vence in 1948 and
virtually completed them early in 1950.
The cornerstone was laid on 12 December
1949. Matisse spent most of 1950 and
early 1951 painting the large mural
drawings on tile or supervising other
aspects of the decoration, architecture, and
furnishings. The barely completed chapel
was dedicated on 25 June 1951. In a
message to Bishop Rémond, Matisse called
the chapel "the result of my entire active
life. . . . my masterpiece."*

The Dominican Chapel at Vence, 1952, with the painted enamel drawing of Saint Dominic (right). Photograph courtesy The Museum of Modern Art, New York.

Interior of the Chapel at Vence, 1949–51, looking toward the altar cloth with fish design at left and nuns' stalls at right. Left: *Virgin and Child*. 1949–51. Painted and enameled ceramic. 137 × 252″ (348 × 640 cm). Right: *Stations of the Cross*. 1949–51. Painted and enameled. ceramic. 137 × 208⅝″ (348 × 530 cm). Photograph courtesy The Museum of Modern Art, New York.

ever, and it exists by the contrast of the colors which are there. It exists by reaction in the mind of the person who observes."

Two or three times he alluded to the structure that Perret had conceived for him. From the models, the work seemed to be much easier. In reality, once the concrete structure was completed, it was another story. "I often ask myself and I often ask my work to see if I, the painter and decorator, succeeded in keeping this structure, this mass of cement, entirely under control. Had I thought enough about the exterior?"

But Henri Matisse was especially sensitive to the reproaches some critics had made in opposition to his *Stations of the Cross,* a work to which he was very attached: "I know some of them—good friends even!—reproach it for being too simple, too hasty. But didn't they understand that I treated this in an allusive manner, that it is intentionally an *emblematic* representation? It's like a road sign, a *totality of signs.*"

What few people know is that the artist has taken a large part of his inspiration—for *Stations of the Cross*—from a book published on the admirable frescoes of Mantegna, frescoes that retrace the Stations of the Cross at Calvary and decorate the walls of the Eremitani Church in Padua. These frescoes were destroyed in the last war. The book had been loaned to him by a young painter, Jean Darquet, who was a neighbor and friend from Vence. From these basic spiritual elements, Henri Matisse built his graphic framework. To better immerse himself in this work, which he found to be sublime in its plastic and passionate rhythms, Henri Matisse forced himself to do a large, preparatory iconography. To this effect, like a conscientious student, he had even copied with his own hand many of these scenes of Mantegna's *Calvary*.

Gotthard Jedlicka

DIE MATISSE KAPELLE IN VENCE

"Encounter with Henri Matisse"

1955

Gotthard Jedlicka (1889–1965) published a monograph on Matisse in 1930 and interviewed him again in 1931, during Matisse's Thannhauser Galleries show in Berlin. In 1951 Jedlicka spoke with Matisse about the Chapel at Vence.

"More than ten years ago I underwent a serious operation—so grave that the doctors gave up on me. '*Il est foutu!*' they said to each other. They said it to me, too (of course, not in the same words). 'The only one who can save you is you yourself! We can only give you one more piece of advice: eat; eat!' I never gave up on myself even in the most difficult hours—and so I escaped the worst."

Il est foutu! (politely rendered): He is done for!

He was still as overwhelmed with happiness as he had been at the beginning of his recovery. But his feeling of gratitude was mixed with that of pride; he regarded his recovery largely as a personal achievement.

"I have learned an important lesson from this illness, which took me a long time to recover from, a lesson that has been shaping my life ever since. The doctors gave up on you, I told myself, because they were convinced that you were going to die soon. Therefore, the time that you live from now on is a gift from life itself—each year, each month, each day. So from now on, you will do only what pleases you, without thinking about what others expect and want from you. Everything that I did before this illness, before this operation, gives the feeling of too much effort; before this, I always lived with my belt buckled. Only what I created after the illness constitutes my real self: free, liberated. I have learned this single truth: you have to give yourself entirely, with all your strengths, with all your weaknesses—or in what we see as our weakness: and which is often our strength."

He had never spoken to me like that before. What he said was an insight gained in the past few years. He expressed it with the absolute certainty that had characterized him since his earlier years. And even though, while talking, he may have been convinced of his words, he still would have contradicted those very words, had they come from me.

"In the past, I wanted to understand everything, whatever I painted, drew, modeled; I wanted to understand it so I could explain it, to myself and to others," he continued.

"I was twisted and inhibited by my willpower. I also believed only in whatever I had wrested out of myself through the complete use of my willpower. I thought my work was significant in relation to the degree of effort it had cost me; I equated the degree of my self-fulfillment to the degree of effort it involved. This is a fallacy! It is a great fallacy. Maybe one that every artist has to believe in at first in order for him to make progress."

He picked up one of the red boxes grouped on the small table, placed it on the blue paper, pushed it around slowly and placed it in its original position again. And while he seemed to be thinking once more about what he had just said, he shook his head several times.

"But the time during which an artist fulfills himself only through great effort has to be followed by a time in which he reaches his goal without any such effort; the period of hard preparation has to give way to a period of harvest. Maybe it is good if the young artist overestimates the extent to which his willpower shapes him; but it certainly is good if the aged and mature artist, while working, trusts the power of grace."

He glanced at me every now and then to make sure that I was following his words. I was doing that, but deep down, I felt compelled to contradict him. Didn't the Chapel of the Rosary also prove the contrary of what he had said?

"There is only one thing that counts in the long run: you have to abandon yourself to your work. You have to give yourself over entirely, without thoughts, especially without afterthoughts. Only then does your work contain you totally. You also have to forget completely that the work you have created—whether it has really been seen or experienced or not—will always be judged by others."

Henri Matisse, Interviewed by André Verdet

ENTRETIENS NOTES ET ECRITS SUR LA PEINTURE

"The Paper Cut-outs"

1978

When Verdet interviewed him in 1952, Matisse was deeply involved with his large cut-out compositions. He had begun working in cut paper as a medium around 1943. Earlier he had used cut paper to facilitate revisions in the Barnes murals and for small design projects in the late 1930s.

A.V. Speaking of your colored paper cut-outs and your album *Jazz,* where they first appeared, Picasso says that you achieved a happy combination of the gravity of creation and the pleasure of amusement.

H.M. A good expression. I would agree with what Picasso told you.

A.V. An Apollonian amusement.

H.M. Amusement which is neither facile, nor superficial, nor frivolous. Some, critics or colleagues, will say: "Old Matisse, nearing the end of life, is having fun cutting up paper. He is not wearing his age well, falling into a second childhood." That won't make me happy, of course, but this kind of thing doesn't make me feel angry or bitter either. On the contrary, I try to understand good or bad reactions, to analyze criticisms wherever they come from, to analyze them in relation to what I'm doing.

Well, I had a lot of fun cutting up my paper. But with the utmost seriousness, balancing all the weight of my past experience, the weight of an entire life devoted to incessant effort, with highs and lows, successes and failures, failures that I considered inevitable but intolerable and that I had to counteract as quickly as possible.

What I was trying to do with these paper cut-outs was to rediscover, through unusual technical means, the lovely days of line and color, to wring out of them the resonance and concurrence of a new freshness.

A.V. You had fun doing them, they take you back to your youth, to your fervent but quite secret enthusiasm. Under the impassive mask of the old professional may lie the sincere emotion of the amateur looking at his first painting. Or perhaps Henri Matisse the ex-Fauve is rediscovering himself in the ardor of the first resounding outburst of Fauvism.

H.M. I thank you for the oratory. But at that time, I was unaware of inner light, mental—or, if you prefer, moral—light. Today I see that light every day. Natural light, the light that comes to us from outside, from the sky, merges with it. My light now commands a more concentrated power of crystallization. It is not so much that my sensations have gone through a slight metamorphosis, but that their condensation occurs in a more unusual way, and I try to sublimate as much as possible.

A.V. The fundamental problem of the paper cut-outs was more or less the same as it was for Fauvism: in this case the paper cut-outs are created as a function of the oppositional play of colors.

H.M. But here it is not a brush winding and gliding on canvas, but scissors cutting through stiff paper and color. The procedural conditions are completely different. The shape of the figure springs from the action of the scissors, which give it the motion of organic life. This tool, you see, does not modulate; it does not brush *onto*, but cuts *into*—a point that should be emphasized, for it makes the criteria of observation completely different. The new tool gives the artist who knows how to use it greater authority in dealing with shapes. The product is different. My cut-outs, I would hope, retain the sovereignty of the line that characterizes my drawing. My hand's great experience has had free play in handling the tool. But not all the benefits of this new technique ought to be ascribed to my old drawing habits. My paper cut-outs also owe something to a technical procedure that comes from statuary. Have you read the book *Jazz*? Reread the preface. In it I wrote something like this: that cutting directly in color, drawing with scissors, reminds me of the direct cut of the sculptor.

The mediating line between pure color and myself as its creator is traced in the wake of the tool, in the instantaneousness of the cutting.

A.V. You speak of instantaneousness referring to scissor work?

H.M. Yes. As I just said before, scissors can be as sensitive to line as pencil, pen, or charcoal—maybe even more sensitive. To me, sensitivity often lies in the instantaneousness of the gesture; a freshness always carefully protected from what might elegantly sink into routine.

A.V. Have you thought of taking this new mode of expression even further?

H.M. The cut-outs are not a new departure but a conclusion. They arose as if from a spring, without trial and error. They were a long time in the making, developing in secret. Perhaps they had already beckoned to me. For me the paper cut-outs represent a creation parallel to oil painting. They must not be seen in any way as an indictment of painting.

A.V. Could it be argued that in the paper cut-outs, as in your oil paintings, it is still the background that creates the object?

H.M. Definitely. The object in itself is not so interesting. It is the atmosphere that affords it a kind of individuality.

A.V. So there is no discontinuity between your earlier paintings and your present cut-outs?

H.M. None whatsoever. I create only with concern to draw closer to the absolute, with greater abstraction. I pursue the essential wherever it leads. Previously I presented the object in the complexity of its space.

Matisse cutting painted paper in his studio in the Hôtel Régina, Nice, 1952. Photograph by Hélène Adant/Rapho.

Today all I see in it is the auspicious sign, the bare minimum necessary to its existence in that form and in the context in which I place it.

A.V. *The Sorrow of the King, The Ballerina, The Girl Who Dances on the Tightrope, The Blue Nude*: They are as feasts of music, dance, and poetry, feasts of sign and color in which the brasses and strings are perfectly orchestrated to create a symphonic unity that will pour forth like a pagan hallelujah to the sun. However, behind these rhymes and rhythms, Henri Matisse, do I possibly detect an echo of faint nostalgia?

H.M. Perhaps the lament of Orpheus.

A.V. Nevertheless, living in the heavenly atmosphere of the decoupages around us here, the taste of happiness comes to our lips again.

H.M. Hell, you know, is so close to Heaven, and Heaven so close to Hell. I sometimes try hard to believe that spring and summer, the beautiful seasons that I love so dearly, and the light that floods them, radiate and shine on the imaginary Elysian Fields that I enjoy conjuring up in my dreams, not for reassurance, but for fun. If people knew what Matisse, supposedly the painter of happiness, had gone through, the anguish and tragedy he had to overcome to manage to capture that light which has never left him, if people knew all that, they would also realize that this happiness, this light, this dispassionate wisdom which seems to be mine, are sometimes well-deserved, given the severity of my trials.

COLORPLATE 111
COLORPLATE 112

Marie Raymond

"Matisse vs. the Abstractionists"

1953

Matisse condemns abstract painting with a vehemence that continues to surprise me. I have just had a short—all too short—interview with the great painter, who has rejuvenated the art of painting with the pictorial skill of his striking and subtle harmonies. Without wasting a second, Matisse launched into a turbulent attack against the abstract school:

"Terms such as 'nonobjective' or 'abstract' are nothing more than a screen for concealing a defect. People who have nothing to say take shelter behind a disguise labeled nonobjective or abstract. I'm not in the least bit enthusiastic. Surely you can see that? Just write down exactly what I told you: Matisse is against abstract art. Picasso thinks exactly as I do. Odilon has said, 'People are never objective enough.'"

Matisse refers here to Odilon Redon, one of his favorite artists.

Q. Could you, my dear Master, tell me which period of your work you consider the most important?

A. "The latest—what I'm doing right now."

Q. Exactly as I myself thought, though it's gratifying to hear it directly from you. Nonetheless, it seems to me that the form of your recent work with cut-outs, with their flat surfaces, shows a certain proclivity toward the experimentation of the so-called abstractionists.

A. "Art has always been abstract," was the extremely terse reply I got. (When speaking of abstraction, which has always been the essence of all real painting, isn't it logical to conceive that anything emanating spontaneously has some relation to the intrinsic rhythm of the individual harmonizing with the cosmic whole?)

"Cézanne lamented quite bitterly his inability to set down his own vision; he admired Monet who was indeed capable of reproducing *his* particular vision."

Q. How do you explain Cézanne's difficulty in producing a picture that would represent what he wanted to express?

A. "He was a creator; one might say that he was dominated by his feelings. Didn't the very rhythm to which he wanted to subject those feelings keep him from grasping the fullness of reality, and don't you think it possible that the same creative feelings that shackled Cézanne's self-expression might actually have driven his followers to the very brink of the unknown?"

Q. Somewhere or other you said, "We must return to the essential principles which made human language."

A. "I've kept my eye on Cézanne and Van Gogh; each of them sought desperately to depict his own vision. I wonder now whether I ought to have launched a campaign against abstract art in my younger days."

Q. Don't you think it was precisely the threat to the kind of freedom that you achieved, which gave force to the movement you were denouncing? I find the sincerity and ardent youthfulness of your expression of self-confidence quite sympathetic. . . .

A. "You spoke about 'feelings.' What are feelings? Can an exhalation not unleash anything trivial? Do people not have the right to aspire to purely impetuous perception?"

Matisse's apartment at Hôtel Régina, Nice, 1953, with *The Swimming Pool*. Photograph by Hélène Adant/Rapho.

That was the way we sought, each in his turn, to put our thoughts into words.

Q. In the most recent period of your latest work, I fancied I could perceive an essential difference between your sketches and the design in your paintings.

A. "That's the reason I now work with cut-outs, in order to get a more powerful expression of pure color through the sharpness of the outline."

*   *   *

Q. Regarding the Benedictine [sic] chapel at Vence which you decorated, I would very much like you to hear my opinion: whereas in Gothic and other churches I frequently feel an atmosphere oppressive enough to make me shrink in awe, during my visit to your chapel the impression I experienced was rather one of serene bliss; the iridescent mother-of-pearl tints filtering through the stained-glass windows produced an unforgetable sensation of deliverance.

The Chapel at Vence is Dominican, not Benedictine.

A. "Something quite different," Matisse broke in with a tone of gratification impossible for him to conceal.

Q. You wanted to evoke that state of mind, something different from the impression usually made on people inside a sanctuary.

In the lightest of breaths, his voice barely audible, so soft and moved with emotion that I had to bid him repeat what he had said, so that I could understand his words properly:

Matisse cutting paper at Le Rêve, Vence, 1946–47. Photograph by Camera Photo.

A. "People must live," said he. "And bear their burdens with a light heart."

Q. I did understand that. The emotion you wanted to arouse must overrule the state of oppression. It has to be nurtured positively and led into the state of serenity that must dominate. The sentient being also must direct its thoughts; by no means can they be allowed to become heavy. But should the thirst for bliss and serenity really become an object of quest and expression? Should Cézanne and Van Gogh otherwise have struggled so desperately? Should your own anger be so violent? What should the price of lightheartedness be when the burden was not heavy?

Knowledge compels making a choice. Choice and knowledge constitute the splendor of your work, but, for all that, we cannot rule out another form of art which your human feelings refuse to accept.

John Berger

John Berger (b. 1926), English author and art critic.

THE NEW STATESMAN AND NATION

"Henri Matisse, 1869–1954"

13 November 1954

Matisse's greatness has been recognized but not altogether understood. In an ideological climate of anguish and nostalgia an artist who frankly and supremely celebrated Pleasure, and whose works are an assurance that the best things in life are immediate and free, is likely to be thought not quite serious enough. And indeed, in Matisse's obituaries the word "charming" has appeared too frequently. "I want people who feel worried, exhausted, overworked, to get a feeling of repose when looking at my painting." That was Matisse's intention. And now, looking back over his long life's work, one can see that it represents a steady development towards his declared aim, his works of the last fifteen or twenty years coming nearest to his ideal.

Matisse's achievement rests on his use—or in the context of contemporary Western art one could say his invention—of pure color. The phrase, however, must be defined. Pure color as Matisse understood it had nothing to do with abstract color. He repeatedly declared that color "must serve expression." What he wanted to express was "the nearly religious feeling" he had towards life—towards the blessings of sunlight, flowers, women, fruit, sleep.

When color is incorporated into a regular pattern—as in a Persian rug—it is a subsidiary element: the logic of the pattern must come first. When color is used in painting it usually serves either as a decorative embellishment of the forms—as, say, in Botticelli—or as a force charging them with extra emotion—as in Van Gogh. In Matisse's later works color becomes the entirely dominant factor. His colors seem neither to embellish nor charge the forms, but to uplift and carry them on the very surface of the canvas. His reds, blacks, golds, ceruleans, flow over the canvas with the strength and yet utter placidity of water above a weir, the forms carried along on their current.

Obviously such a process implies some distortion. But the distortion is far more of people's preconceived ideas about art than of nature. The numerous drawings that Matisse always made before he arrived at his final color-solution are evidence of the pains he took to preserve the essential character of his subject whilst at the same time making it "buoyant" enough to sail on the tide of his color scheme. Certainly the effect of these paintings is what he hoped. Their subjects invite, one embarks, and then the flow of their color-areas holds one in such sure equilibrium that one has a sense of Perpetual Motion—a sense of movement with all friction removed.

Nobody who has not painted themselves can fully appreciate what lies behind Matisse's mastery of color. It is comparatively easy to achieve a certain unity in a picture either by allowing one color to dominate or by muting all the colors. Matisse did neither. He clashed his colors together like cymbals and the effect was like a lullaby.

Perhaps the best way of defining Matisse's genius is to compare him with some of his contemporaries who were also concerned with color. Bonnard's colors dissolve, making his subjects unattainable, nostalgic. Matisse's colors could hardly be more present, more blatant, and yet achieve a peace which is without a trace of nostalgia. Braque has cultivated his sensibility until it has become precious; one feels that just to look at his art is almost to violate it. Matisse broadened his sensibility until it was as wide as his color range, and said that he wanted his art to be "something like a good armchair." Dufy shared Matisse's sense of enjoyment and his colors were as gay as the fêtes he painted; but Matisse's colors, no less bright, go beyond gaiety to affirm contentment. The only man who possibly equals Matisse as a colorist is Léger. But their aims are so different that they can hardly be compared. Léger is essentially an epic, civic artist; Matisse essentially a lyrical and personal.

I said that Matisse's paintings and designs of the last fifteen years were his greatest. Obviously he produced fine individual works before he was seventy. Yet not, I think, till then had he the complete control of his art that he needed. It was, as he himself said, a question of "organizing the brain." Like most colorists he was an intuitive painter, but he realized that it was necessary to select rigorously from his many "instincts" to make them objective in order to be able to build upon them rationally. In terms of the picture this control makes the all-important difference between recording a sensation and reconstructing an emotion. The Fauves, whom Matisse led, recorded sensations. Their paintings were (and are) fresh and stimulating, but they depended upon and evoke a forced intoxication. When Matisse painted red flashes against ultramarine and magenta stripes to describe the movement of goldfish in a bowl, he communicated a pleasurable shock; one is brought up short by the climax but no solution follows. It was for this reason, I think, that Matisse finally abandoned Fauvism and returned to a more disciplined form of painting. Between 1914 and 1918 he produced paintings—mostly interiors—which are magnificently resonant in color, but in which the colors seem *assembled* rather than dynamic—like the furnishings in a room. Then for the next ten years he painted his famous Odalisques. In these the color is freer and more pervasive, but, being based on a heightening of the actual locale of each object, it has a slightly exotic effect. This period, however, led him to his final great phase: the phase in which he was able to combine the energy of his early Fauve days with a quite objective visual wisdom.

A word about the political and social implications of Matisse's art. Because he painted subjects with associations of Leisure it is as absurd on the one hand to accuse him of working for the leisured classes, as it is on the other to deny the significance of his membership of the French Communist Party. He wished to paint what one has a right to as a welcome and a reward after a hard day's work. Let it stand at that. Historically it may eventually be seen that Matisse simplified and sacrificed too much for the sake of the peace of his art. But he lived through a far from peaceful age. He may have chosen the unnaturally smooth, placid water above the weir, but the weir was there. To temper our gratitude now in view of a possible future perspective would be the worst form of academic cowardice.

Matisse was in fact not a member of the Communist party.

Madame Ulrich

PARIS-MATCH

An Encounter with Matisse

4 December 1954

The death of the painter, Henri Matisse, has profoundly moved me, and I pay a last tribute to the whole work of one of the greatest representatives of contemporary painting. Having lived for many years in Nice, at one time close to the immense Regina palace which dominates the town from the hill of Cimiez, I was twice able to visit important exhibitions of the master.

At the time of the first visit, I was thirteen and in the fourth class at school. One of our teachers took us in a group to a gallery which was showing some of Matisse's finest pictures. At one moment we all stopped dead in front of a picture we couldn't understand, judging it with one of those terrible spontaneous criticisms of childhood, "that's good" or "I don't like that." And to our eyes, conditioned to perfect classical art, that work appeared as just "bad." Judgment I considered irrefutable at the time.

Matisse, who was walking incognito among the visitors, passed behind our little group at that moment, and we recognized him because we

Matisse at the Hôtel Régina, Nice, 1952.
Photograph by *Paris-Match* (Carone).

had seen his photograph in the papers the day before. One of us asked him, very politely too, if he were not "Monsieur Matisse"?

The old man he was even then, retired behind his white beard and spectacles and said he had nothing to do with the painter. Excuses, regrets, doubts.

As we were preparing to leave the gallery, the same old gentleman discreetly took our teacher aside: "Madame, I am indeed the painter Henri Matisse, but I should never have dared admit it to children who judged my painting so severely. The ruthless criticism of children, although without thought, has the power to intimidate me so much that I believe they are the only ones who see rightly, and for the moment I hate that picture in my heart for having shocked the eyes of a child, even if the critics should later call it a masterpiece. Forgive me my fib, Madame."

And the old man disappeared in the crowd.

INDEX

*Page numbers in italics
refer to illustrations.*